TURKEY

BUSINESS AND INVESTMENT OPPORTUNTIES YEARBOOK

VOLUME 2

LEADING EXPORT-IMPORT, BUSINESS, INVESTMENT OPPORTUNITIES AND PROJECTS

International Business Publications, USA
Washington DC, USA - Turkey

TURKEY

BUSINESS AND INVESTMENT OPPORTUNTIES YEARBOOK

VOLUME 2 LEADING EXPORT-IMPORT, BUSINESS, INVESTMENT OPPORTUNITIES AND PROJECTS

UPDATED ANNUALLY

We express our sincere appreciation to all government agencies and international organizations which provided information and other materials for this yearbook

Cover Design: International Business Publications, USA

2014 Edition Updated Reprint International Business Publications, USA
ISBN 1-5775-1965-5

For customer service and information, please contact:

in the USA: **International Business Publications, USA**
P.O.Box 15343, Washington, DC 20003
Phone: (202) 546-2103, Fax: (202) 546-3275.
E-mail: rusric@erols.com

Printed in the USA

TURKEY

BUSINESS AND INVESTMENT OPPORTUNTIES YEARBOOK

VOLUME 2

LEADING EXPORT-IMPORT, BUSINESS, INVESTMENT OPPORTUNITIES AND PROJECTS

TABLE OF CONTENTS

STRATEGIC AND DEVELOPMENT PROFILES

STRATEGIC PROFILE

Capital	Ankara 39°55′N 32°50′E39.917°N 32.833°E
Largest city	Istanbul 41°1′N 28°57′E41.017°N 28.950°E
Official languages	Turkish
Ethnic groups	70–75% Turks 18% Kurds 7–12% others
Demonym	Turkish
Government	Unitary parliamentary constitutional republic
- President	Recep Tayyip Erdoğan
- Prime Minister	Ahmet Davutoğlu
- Speaker of the Parliament	Cemil Çiçek
- President of the Constitutional Court	Haşim Kılıç
Legislature	Grand National Assembly
Succession to the Ottoman Empire	
- Government of the Grand National Assembly	23 April 1920
- Treaty of Lausanne	24 July 1923
- Declaration of Republic	29 October 1923
- Current constitution	7 November 1982
Area	
- Total	783,562 km^2 (37th) 302,535 sq mi
- Water (%)	1.3
Population	
- 2013 census	76,667,864 (18th)
- Density	100/km^2 (108th) 259/sq mi
GDP (PPP)	2014 estimate
- Total	$1.512 trillion (17th)
- Per capita	$19,556 (61st)
GDP (nominal)	2014 estimate
- Total	$813.316 billion (18th)
- Per capita	$10,518 (67th)
Gini (2010)	▲40.2 medium · 56th
HDI (2013)	▬0.759 high · 69th
Currency	Turkish lira (₺) (TRY)
Time zone	EET (UTC+2)
- Summer (DST)	EEST (UTC+3)
Date format	dd/mm/yyyy (AD)

Drives on the	right
Calling code	+90
ISO 3166 code	TR
Internet TLD	.tr

BASIC PROFILE

Turkey officially the **Republic of Turkey** is a contiguous transcontinental country, located mostly on Anatolia in Western Asia and on East Thrace in Southeastern Europe. Turkey is bordered by eight countries: Bulgaria to the northwest; Greece to the west; Georgia to the northeast; Armenia, Iran and the Azerbaijani exclave of Nakhchivan to the east; and Iraq and Syria to the southeast. The Mediterranean Sea is to the south; the Aegean Sea is to the west; and the Black Sea is to the north. The Sea of Marmara, the Bosphorus and the Dardanelles (which together form the Turkish Straits) demarcate the boundary between Thrace and Anatolia; they also separate Europe and Asia. Turkey's location at the crossroads of Europe and Asia makes it a country of significant geostrategic importance. The area now called Turkey has been inhabited since the Paleolithic, including various Ancient Anatolian civilizations and Thracian peoples. After Alexander the Great's conquest, the area was Hellenized, which continued with the Roman rule and the transition into the Byzantine Empire. The Seljuk Turks began migrating into the area in the 11th century, starting the process of Turkification, which was greatly accelerated by the Seljuk victory over the Byzantines at the Battle of Manzikert in 1071.

The Seljuk Sultanate of Rûm ruled Anatolia until the Mongol invasion in 1243, upon which it disintegrated into several small Turkish beyliks. Starting from the late 13th century, the Ottoman beylik united Anatolia and created an empire encompassing much of Southeastern Europe, Western Asia and North Africa. After the Ottoman Empire collapsed following its defeat in World War I, parts of it were occupied by the victorious Allies. The Turkish War of Independence, initiated by Mustafa Kemal Atatürk and his colleagues, resulted in the establishment of the modern Republic of Turkey in 1923, with Atatürk as its first president.

Turkey is a democratic, secular, unitary, constitutional republic with a diverse cultural heritage. The country's official language is Turkish, a Turkic language, which is spoken by approximately 85% of the population as mother tongue. Turks constitute 70% to 75% of the population. Minorities include Kurds (18%) and others (7–12%).The vast majority of the population is Muslim. Turkey is a member of the Council of Europe, NATO, OECD, OSCE and the G-20 major economies. Turkey began full membership negotiations with the European Union in 2005, having been an associate member of the European Economic Community since 1963 and having joined the EU Customs Union in 1995. Turkey is also a member of the Turkic Council, Joint Administration of Turkic Arts and Culture, Organisation of Islamic Cooperation and the Economic Cooperation Organisation. Turkey's growing economy and diplomatic initiatives have led to its recognition as a regional power

Background:	Turkey was created in 1923 from the Turkish remnants of the Ottoman Empire. Soon thereafter the country instituted secular laws to replace traditional religious fiats. In 1945 Turkey joined the UN and in 1952 it became a member of NATO. Turkey occupied the northern portion of Cyprus in 1974 to prevent a Greek takeover of the island; relations between the two countries remain strained. Periodic military offensives against Kurdish separatists have dislocated part of the population in southeast Turkey and have drawn international condemnation.

GEOGRAPHY

Location:	southeastern Europe and southwestern Asia (that portion of Turkey west of the Bosporus is geographically part of Europe), bordering the Black Sea, between Bulgaria and Georgia, and bordering the Aegean Sea and the Mediterranean Sea, between Greece and Syria
Geographic coordinates:	39 00 N, 35 00 E
Map references:	Middle East
Area:	total: 780,580 sq km land: 770,760 sq km water: 9,820 sq km
Area - comparative:	slightly larger than Texas
Land boundaries:	total: 2,627 km border countries: Armenia 268 km, Azerbaijan 9 km, Bulgaria 240 km, Georgia 252 km, Greece 206 km, Iran 499 km, Iraq 331 km, Syria 822 km
Coastline:	7,200 km
Maritime claims:	exclusive economic zone: in Black Sea only: to the maritime boundary agreed upon with the former USSR territorial sea: 6 NM in the Aegean Sea; 12 NM in Black Sea and in Mediterranean Sea
Climate:	temperate; hot, dry summers with mild, wet winters; harsher in interior
Terrain:	mostly mountains; narrow coastal plain; high central plateau (Anatolia)
Elevation extremes:	lowest point: Mediterranean Sea 0 m highest point: Mount Ararat 5,166 m
Natural resources:	antimony, coal, chromium, mercury, copper, borate, sulfur, iron ore, arable land, hydropower
Land use:	arable land: 32% permanent crops: 4% permanent pastures: 16% forests and woodland: 26% other: 22%
Irrigated land:	36,740 sq km
Natural hazards:	very severe earthquakes, especially in northern Turkey, along an arc extending from the Sea of Marmara to Lake Van
Environment - current issues:	water pollution from dumping of chemicals and detergents; air pollution, particularly in urban areas; deforestation; concern for oil spills from increasing Bosporus ship traffic

Environment - international agreements:	party to: Air Pollution, Antarctic Treaty, Biodiversity, Desertification, Endangered Species, Hazardous Wastes, Nuclear Test Ban, Ozone Layer Protection, Ship Pollution, Wetlands

	signed, but not ratified: Antarctic-Environmental Protocol, Environmental Modification
Geography - note:	strategic location controlling the Turkish Straits (Bosporus, Sea of Marmara, Dardanelles) that link Black and Aegean Seas; Mount Ararat, the legendary landing place of Noah's Ark, is in the far eastern portion of the country

PEOPLE

Population:	66,493,970
Age structure:	0-14 years: 28.42% (male 9,620,291; female 9,276,347) 15-64 years: 65.45% (male 22,116,599; female 21,401,165) 65 years and over: 6.13% (male 1,878,571; female 2,200,997)
Population growth rate:	1.24%
Birth rate:	18.31 births/1,000 population
Death rate:	5.95 deaths/1,000 population
Net migration rate:	0 migrant(s)/1,000 population
Sex ratio:	at birth: 1.05 male(s)/female under 15 years: 1.04 male(s)/female 15-64 years: 1.03 male(s)/female 65 years and over: 0.85 male(s)/female total population: 1.02 male(s)/female
Infant mortality rate:	47.34 deaths/1,000 live births
Life expectancy at birth:	total population: 71.24 years male: 68.89 years female: 73.71 years
Total fertility rate:	2.12 children born/woman
HIV/AIDS - adult prevalence rate:	0.01%
HIV/AIDS - people living with HIV/AIDS:	NA
HIV/AIDS - deaths:	NA
Nationality:	noun: Turk(s) adjective: Turkish
Ethnic groups:	Turkish 80%, Kurdish 20%
Religions:	Muslim 99.8% (mostly Sunni), other 0.2% (Christian and Jews)
Languages:	Turkish (official), Kurdish, Arabic, Armenian, Greek
Literacy:	definition: age 15 and over can read and write total population: 85% male: 94%

	female: 77%

LARGEST CITIES OF TURKEY BY POPULATION

Rank	Core City	Province	Pop.	Rank	Core City	Province	Pop.
1	**Istanbul**	Istanbul	12,573,836	11	Diyarbakır	Diyarbakır	1,460,714
2	**Ankara**	Ankara	4,466,756	12	Izmit	Kocaeli	1,437,926
3	**Izmir**	Izmir	3,739,353	13	Antakya	Hatay	1,386,224
4	**Bursa**	Bursa	2,439,876	14	Manisa	Manisa	1,319,920
5	**Adana**	Adana	2,006,650	15	Samsun	Samsun	1,228,959
6	**Konya**	Konya	1,959,082	16	Kayseri	Kayseri	1,165,088
7	**Antalya**	Antalya	1,789,295	17	Balıkesir	Balıkesir	1,118,313
8	**Mersin**	Mersin	1,595,938	18	Kahramanmaraş	Kahramanmaraş	1,004,414
9	**Gaziantep**	Gaziantep	1,560,023	19	Van	Van	979,671
10	**Şanlıurfa**	Şanlıurfa	1,523,099	20	Aydın	Aydın	946,971

GOVERNMENT

Country name:	conventional long form: Republic of Turkey conventional short form: Turkey local long form: Turkiye Cumhuriyeti local short form: Turkiye
Government type:	republican parliamentary democracy
Capital:	Ankara
Administrative divisions:	80 provinces (iller, singular - il); Adana, Adiyaman, Afyon, Agri, Aksaray, Amasya, Ankara, Antalya, Ardahan, Artvin, Aydin, Balikesir, Bartin, Batman, Bayburt, Bilecik, Bingol, Bitlis, Bolu, Burdur, Bursa, Canakkale, Cankiri, Corum, Denizli, Diyarbakir, Edirne, Elazig, Erzincan, Erzurum, Eskisehir, Gaziantep, Giresun, Gumushane, Hakkari, Hatay, Icel, Igdir, Isparta, Istanbul, Izmir, Kahramanmaras, Karabuk, Karaman, Kars, Kastamonu, Kayseri, Kilis, Kirikkale, Kirklareli, Kirsehir, Kocaeli, Konya, Kutahya, Malatya, Manisa, Mardin, Mugla, Mus, Nevsehir, Nigde, Ordu, Osmaniye, Rize, Sakarya, Samsun, Sanliurfa, Siirt, Sinop, Sirnak, Sivas, Tekirdag, Tokat, Trabzon, Tunceli, Usak, Van, Yalova, Yozgat,

	Zonguldak; note - there may be another province called Duzce
Independence:	29 October 1923 (successor state to the Ottoman Empire)
National holiday:	Independence Day, 29 October (1923)
Constitution:	7 November 1982
Legal system:	derived from various European continental legal systems; accepts compulsory ICJ jurisdiction, with reservations
Suffrage:	18 years of age; universal

Executive branch:

PRESIDENT - Recep Tayyip Erdoğan - from 2014

Functions		Holder	Inauguration
English title	Turkish title		
Deputy Prime Minister I	Başbakan Yardımcısı	Bülent Arınç	1 May 2009
Deputy Prime Minister II	Başbakan Yardımcısı	Ali Babacan	1 May 2009
Deputy Prime Minister III	Başbakan Yardımcısı	Yalçın Akdoğan	29 August 2014
Deputy Prime Minister IV	Başbakan Yardımcısı	Numan Kurtulmuş	29 August 2014
Minister of Culture and Tourism	Kültür ve Turizm Bakanı	Ömer Çelik	24 January 2013
Minister of Customs and Trade	Gümrük ve Ticaret Bakanı	Nurettin Canikli	29 August 2014
Minister of Development	Kalkınma Bakanı	Cevdet Yılmaz	6 July 2011
Minister of Economy	Ekonomi Bakanı	Nihat Zeybekci	25 December 2013
Minister of Energy and Natural Resources	Enerji ve Tabii Kaynaklar Bakanı	Taner Yıldız	1 May 2009
Minister of Environment and Urban Planning	Çevre ve Şehircilik Bakanı	İdris Güllüce	25 December 2013
Minister of European Union Affairs and Chief Negotiator	Avrupa Birliği Bakanı ve Baş Müzakereci	Volkan Bozkır	29 August 2014
Minister of Family and Social Policy	Aile ve Sosyal Politikalar Bakanı	Ayşenur İslam	25 December 2013
Minister of Finance	Maliye Bakanı	Mehmet Şimşek	1 May 2009
Minister of Food, Agriculture and Animal Breeding	Gıda, Tarım ve Hayvancılık Bakanı	Mehmet Mehdi Eker	2 June 2005
Minister of Foreign Affairs	Dışişleri Bakanı	Mevlüt Çavuşoğlu	29 August 2014
Minister of Forestry and Water Works	Orman ve Su İşleri Bakanı	Veysel Eroğlu	29 August 2007
Minister of Health	Sağlık Bakanı	Mehmet Müezzinoğlu	25 December 2013
Minister of Justice	Adalet Bakanı	Bekir Bozdağ	25 December 2013
Minister of Labour and Social Security	Çalışma ve Sosyal Güvenlik Bakanı	Faruk Çelik	6 July 2011

Functions		Holder	Inauguration
English title	Turkish title		
Minister of National Defense	Millî Savunma Bakanı	İsmet Yılmaz	6 July 2011
Minister of National Education	Millî Eğitim Bakanı	Nabi Avcı	24 January 2013
Minister of Science, Industry and Technology	Bilim, Sanayi ve Teknoloji Bakanı	Fikri Işık	25 December 2013
Minister of the Interior	İçişleri Bakanı	Efkan Ala	25 December 2013
Minister of Transport, Maritime Affairs and Communication	Ulaştırma, Denizcilik ve Haberleşme Bakanı	Lütfi Elvan	25 December 2013
Minister of Youth and Sports	Gençlik ve Spor Bakanı	Akif Çağatay Kılıç	25 December 2013
Prime Minister	Başbakan	Ahmet Davutoğlu	29 August 2014

Executive branch:	*chief of state:* *head of government:* Deputy Prime Minister Cemil CICEK; Deputy Prime Minister Hayati YAZICI (since 29 August 2007); Deputy Prime Minister Nazim EKREN (since 29 August 2007) *cabinet:* Council of Ministers appointed by the president on the nomination of the prime minister *elections:* president elected directly for a five-year term (eligible for a second term); prime minister appointed by the president from among members of parliament *election results:* on 28 August 2007 National Assembly elected Abdullah GUL president on the third ballot; National Assembly vote - 339 *note:* in October 2007 Turkish voters approved a referendum package of constitutional amendments including a provision for direct presidential elections

Legislative branch:	unicameral Grand National Assembly of Turkey or Turkiye Buyuk Millet Meclisi (550 seats; members elected by popular vote to serve four-year terms) elections: last held on 12 June 2011 (next to be held by June 2015) election results: percent of vote by party - AKP 49.8%, CHP 25.9%, MHP 13%, independents 6.6%, other 4.7%; seats by party - AKP 326, CHP 135, MHP 53, independents 36; note - only parties surpassing the 10% threshold are entitled to parliamentary seats
Judicial branch:	Constitutional Court (judges are appointed by the president); Court of Appeals (judges are elected by the Supreme Council of Judges and Prosecutors)
Political parties and leaders:	Anavatan Partisi (Motherland Party) or Anavatan [Salih UZUN]; Democratic Left Party or DSP [Ahmet TURK]; Democratic Society Party or DTP [Nurettin DEMIRTAS]; Felicity Party or SP [Numan KURTULMUS] (sometimes translated as Contentment Party); Justice

	and Development Party or AKP [Recep Tayyip ERDOGAN]; Nationalist Movement Party or MHP [Devlet BAHCELI] (sometimes translated as Nationalist Action Party); People's Rise Party (Halkin Yukselisi Partisi) or HYP [Yasar Nuri OZTURK]; Republican People's Party or CHP [Deniz BAYKAL]; Social Democratic People's Party or SHP [Murat KARAYALCIN]; True Path Party or DYP [Suleyman SOYLU] (sometimes translated as Correct Way Party); Young Party or GP [Cem Cengiz UZAN] *note:* the parties listed above are some of the more significant of the 49 parties that Turkey had on 1 December 2004
Political pressure groups and leaders:	Confederation of Revolutionary Workers Unions or DISK [Ridvan BUDAK]; Independent Industrialists and Businessmen's Association or MUSIAD [Erol YARAR]; Moral Rights Workers Union or Hak-Is [Salim USLU]; Turkish Industrialists' and Businessmen's Association or TUSIAD [Muharrem KAYHAN]; Turkish Confederation of Employers' Unions or TISK [Refik BAYDUR]; Turkish Confederation of Labor or Turk-Is [Bayram MERAL]; Turkish Union of Chambers of Commerce and Commodity Exchanges or TOBB [Fuat MIRAS]
International organization participation:	AsDB, Australia Group, BIS, BSEC, CCC, CE, CERN (observer), EAPC, EBRD, ECE, ECO, ESCAP, EU (applicant), FAO, IAEA, IBRD, ICAO, ICC, ICFTU, ICRM, IDA, IDB, IEA, IFAD, IFC, IFRCS, IHO, ILO, IMF, IMO, Inmarsat, Intelsat, Interpol, IOC, IOM (observer), ISO, ITU, NATO, NEA, NSG, OAS (observer), OECD, OIC, OPCW, OSCE, PCA, UN, UNCTAD, UNESCO, UNHCR, UNIDO, UNIKOM, UNMIBH, UNMIK, UNOMIG, UNRWA, UNTAET, UPU, WEU (associate), WFTU, WHO, WIPO, WMO, WToO, WTrO
Diplomatic representation in the US:	chief of mission: Ambassador Baki ILKIN chancery: 2525 Massachusetts Avenue NW, Washington, DC 20008 telephone: Turkey (202) 612-6700 FAX: Turkey (202) 612-6744 consulate(s) general: Chicago, Houston, Los Angeles, and New York
Diplomatic representation from the US:	chief of mission: Ambassador Robert W. PEARSON embassy: Ataturk Bulvarii 110, Ankara mailing address: PSC 93, Box 5000, APO AE 09823 telephone: [90] (312) 468-6110 FAX: [90] (312) 467-0019 consulate(s) general: Istanbul (closed as of December 2000 for security review) consulate(s): Adana (closed as of December 2000 for security review)
Flag description:	red with a vertical white crescent (the closed portion is toward the hoist side) and white five-pointed star centered just outside the crescent opening

ECONOMY

Turkey's largely free-market economy is increasingly driven by its industry and service sectors, although its traditional agriculture sector still accounts for about 25% of employment. An aggressive privatization program has reduced state involvement in basic industry, banking, transport, and communication, and an emerging cadre of middle-class entrepreneurs is adding dynamism to the economy and expanding production beyond the traditional textiles and clothing sectors. The automotive, construction, and electronics industries, are rising in importance and have surpassed textiles within Turkey's export mix. Oil began to flow through the Baku-Tbilisi-Ceyhan pipeline in May 2006, marking a major milestone that will bring up to 1 million barrels per day from the Caspian to market. Several gas pipelines projects also are moving forward to help transport Central Asian gas to Europe through Turkey, which over the long term will help address Turkey's dependence on imported oil and gas to meet 97% of its energy needs. After Turkey experienced a severe financial crisis in 2001, Ankara adopted financial and fiscal reforms as part of an IMF program. The reforms strengthened the country's economic fundamentals and ushered in an era of strong growth - averaging more than 6% annually until 2008. Global economic conditions and tighter fiscal policy caused GDP to contract in 2009, but Turkey's well-regulated financial markets and banking system helped the country weather the global financial crisis and GDP rebounded strongly to 9.2% in 2010, as exports returned to normal levels following the recession. Growth dropped to approximately 3% in 2012. Turkey's public sector debt to GDP ratio has fallen to about 40%, and at least one rating agency upgraded Turkey's debt to investment grade in 2012. Turkey remains dependent on often volatile, short-term investment to finance its large trade deficit. The stock value of FDI stood at $117 billion at year-end 2012. Inflows have slowed because of continuing economic turmoil in Europe, the source of much of Turkey's FDI. Turkey's relatively high current account deficit, uncertainty related to monetary policy-making, and political turmoil within Turkey's neighborhood leave the economy vulnerable to destabilizing shifts in investor confidence.

GDP (purchasing power parity):
$1.142 trillion (2012 est.)
country comparison to the world: 17
$1.113 trillion (est.)
$1.026 trillion (est.)
note: data are in 2012 US dollars

GDP (official exchange rate):
$794.5 billion (2012 est.)

GDP - real growth rate:
2.6% (2012 est.)
country comparison to the world: 117
8.5% (est.)
9.2% (est.)

GDP - per capita (PPP):
$15,200 (2012 est.)
country comparison to the world: 90
$15,000 (est.)
$14,000 (est.)
note: data are in 2012 US dollars

Gross national saving:
20.4% of GDP (2012 est.)
country comparison to the world: 72
23.6% of GDP (est.)
19.6% of GDP (est.)

GDP - composition, by end use:
household consumption: 70%
government consumption: 14.7%
investment in fixed capital: 20.3%
investment in inventories: 0.1%
exports of goods and services: 26.4%
imports of goods and services: -31.6%
(2012 est.)

GDP - composition, by sector of origin:
agriculture: 9.1%
industry: 27%
services: 63.9% (2012 est.)

Agriculture - products:
tobacco, cotton, grain, olives, sugar beets, hazelnuts, pulses, citrus; livestock

Industries:
textiles, food processing, autos, electronics, mining (coal, chromate, copper, boron), steel, petroleum, construction, lumber, paper

Industrial production growth rate:
1.7% (2012 est.)
country comparison to the world: 106

Labor force:
27.34 million
country comparison to the world: 22
note: about 1.2 million Turks work abroad (2012 est.)

Labor force - by occupation:
agriculture: 25.5%
industry: 26.2%
services: 48.4%

Unemployment rate:
9.2% (2012 est.)
country comparison to the world: 104
9.8% (est.)
note: underemployment amounted to 4% in 2008

Population below poverty line:
16.9%

Household income or consumption by percentage share:
lowest 10%: 2.1%
highest 10%: 30.3%

Distribution of family income - Gini index:
40.2

country comparison to the world: 58
43.6 (2003)

Budget:
revenues: $184.7 billion
expenditures: $200.7 billion (2012 est.)

Taxes and other revenues:
23.2% of GDP (2012 est.)
country comparison to the world: 138

Budget surplus (+) or deficit (-):
-2% of GDP (2012 est.)
country comparison to the world: 84

Public debt:
36.1% of GDP (2012 est.)
country comparison to the world: 99
40% of GDP (est.)
note: data cover central government debt, and excludes debt instruments issued (or owned) by government entities other than the treasury; the data include treasury debt held by foreign entities; the data exclude debt issued by subnational entities, as well as intra-governmental debt; intra-governmental debt consists of treasury borrowings from surpluses in the social funds, such as for retirement, medical care, and unemployment; debt instruments for the social funds are sold at public auctions

Fiscal year:
calendar year

Inflation rate (consumer prices):
8.9% (2012 est.)
country comparison to the world: 188
6.5% (est.)

Central bank discount rate:
5.25% (31 December 2011)
country comparison to the world: 10
15% (22 December 2009)

Commercial bank prime lending rate:
19% (31 December 2012 est.)
country comparison to the world: 30
17% (31 December 2011 est.)

Stock of narrow money:
$85.23 billion (31 December 2012 est.)
country comparison to the world: 40
$71.95 billion (31 December 2011 est.)

Stock of broad money:

$386.5 billion (31 December 2012 est.)
country comparison to the world: 27
$346.2 billion (31 December 2011 est.)

Stock of domestic credit:
$552.3 billion (31 December 2012 est.)
country comparison to the world: 24
$456.4 billion (31 December 2011 est.)

Market value of publicly traded shares:
$201.8 billion (31 December 2011)
country comparison to the world: 28
$306.7 billion (31 December 2010)
$225.7 billion (31 December 2009)

Current account balance:
-$59.74 billion (2012 est.)
country comparison to the world: 189
-$77.24 billion (est.)

Exports:
$163.4 billion (2012 est.)
country comparison to the world: 30
$143.5 billion (est.)

Exports - commodities:
apparel, foodstuffs, textiles, metal manufactures, transport equipment

Exports - partners:
Germany 8.6%, Iraq 7.1%, Iran 6.5%, UK 5.7%, UAE 5.4%, Russia 4.4%, Italy 4.2%, France 4.1% (2012)

Imports:
$228.9 billion (2012 est.)
country comparison to the world: 22
$232.5 billion (est.)

Imports - commodities:
machinery, chemicals, semi-finished goods, fuels, transport equipment

Imports - partners:
Russia 11.3%, Germany 9%, China 9%, US 6%, Italy 5.6%, Iran 5.1% (2012)

Reserves of foreign exchange and gold:
$119.2 billion (31 December 2012 est.)
country comparison to the world: 21
$88.21 billion (31 December 2011 est.)

Debt - external:
$336.9 billion (31 December 2012 est.)

country comparison to the world: 32
$307 billion (31 December 2011 est.)

Stock of direct foreign investment - at home:
$152.9 billion (31 December 2012 est.)
country comparison to the world: 29
$140.5 billion (31 December 2011 est.)

Stock of direct foreign investment - abroad:
$30.95 billion (31 December 2012 est.)
country comparison to the world: 41
$26.86 billion (31 December 2011 est.)

Exchange rates:
Turkish liras (TRY) per US dollar -
1.796 (2012 est.)
1.675 (est.)
1.5028 (est.)
1.55
1.3179

ENERGY

Electricity - from other renewable sources:
2.2% of total installed capacity (est.)
country comparison to the world: 55

Crude oil - production:
45,740 bbl/day (est.)
country comparison to the world: 60

Crude oil - exports:
0 bbl/day (est.)
country comparison to the world: 193

Crude oil - imports:
284,400 bbl/day (est.)
country comparison to the world: 25

Crude oil - proved reserves:
270.4 million bbl (1 January 2012 est.)
country comparison to the world: 57

Refined petroleum products - production:
343,400 bbl/day (est.)
country comparison to the world: 39

Refined petroleum products - consumption:
706,100 bbl/day (est.)
country comparison to the world: 26

Refined petroleum products - exports:
68,450 bbl/day (est.)
country comparison to the world: 50

Refined petroleum products - imports:
297,400 bbl/day (est.)
country comparison to the world: 22

Natural gas - production:
761 million cu m (est.)
country comparison to the world: 67

Natural gas - consumption:
44.71 billion cu m (est.)
country comparison to the world: 21

Natural gas - exports:
713 million cu m (est.)
country comparison to the world: 41

Natural gas - imports:
43.9 billion cu m (est.)
country comparison to the world: 9

Natural gas - proved reserves:
6.173 billion cu m (1 January 2012 est.)
country comparison to the world: 84

Carbon dioxide emissions from consumption of energy:
263.5 million Mt (est.)
country comparison to the world: 23

COMMUNICATIONS

Telephones - main lines in use:
15.211 million (2011)
country comparison to the world: 18

Telephones - mobile cellular:
65.322 million (2011)
country comparison to the world: 20

Telephone system:
general assessment: comprehensive telecommunications network undergoing rapid modernization and expansion, especially in mobile-cellular services
domestic: additional digital exchanges are permitting a rapid increase in subscribers; the construction of a network of technologically advanced intercity trunk lines, using both fiber-optic cable and digital microwave radio relay, is facilitating communication between urban centers; remote areas are reached by a domestic satellite system;

combined fixed-line and mobile-cellular teledensity is roughly 100 telephones per 100 persons
international: country code - 90; international service is provided by the SEA-ME-WE-3 submarine cable and by submarine fiber-optic cables in the Mediterranean and Black Seas that link Turkey with Italy, Greece, Israel, Bulgaria, Romania, and Russia; satellite earth stations - 12 Intelsat; mobile satellite terminals - 328 in the Inmarsat and Eutelsat systems

Broadcast media:
Turkish Radio and Television Corporation (TRT) operates multiple TV and radio networks and stations; multiple privately owned national television stations and up to 300 private regional and local television stations; multi-channel cable TV subscriptions available; more than 1,000 private radio broadcast stations

Internet country code:
.tr

Internet hosts:
7.093 million (2012)
country comparison to the world: 16

Internet users:
27.233 million
country comparison to the world: 15

TRANSPORTATION

Railways:	total: 8,607 km standard gauge: 8,607 km 1.435-m gauge (2,131 km electrified)
Highways:	total: 382,059 km paved: 106,976 km (including 1,726 km of expressways) unpaved: 275,083 km
Waterways:	1,200 km (approximately)
Pipelines:	crude oil 1,738 km; petroleum products 2,321 km; natural gas 708 km
Ports and harbors:	Gemlik, Hopa, Iskenderun, Istanbul, Izmir, Kocaeli (Izmit), Icel (Mersin), Samsun, Trabzon
Merchant marine:	total: 548 ships (1,000 GRT or over) totaling 5,617,302 GRT/9,088,451 DWT ships by type: bulk 140, cargo 242, chemical tanker 41, combination bulk 5, combination ore/oil 6, container 21, liquefied gas 6, passenger/cargo 1, petroleum tanker 43, refrigerated cargo 3, roll on/roll off 25, short-sea passenger 10, specialized tanker 5
Airports:	121
Airports - with paved runways:	total: 86 over 3,047 m: 16

	2,438 to 3,047 m: 29 1,524 to 2,437 m: 19 914 to 1,523 m: 16 under 914 m: 6
Airports - with unpaved runways:	total: 35 1,524 to 2,437 m: 1 914 to 1,523 m: 8 under 914 m: 26
Heliports:	2

MILITARY

Military branches:	Land Force, Navy (includes Naval Air and Naval Infantry), Air Force, Coast Guard, Gendarmerie
Military manpower - military age:	20 years of age
Military manpower - availability:	males age 15-49: 18,882,272
Military manpower - fit for military service:	males age 15-49: 11,432,438
Military manpower - reaching military age annually:	males: 674,805
Military expenditures - dollar figure:	$10.6 billion
Military expenditures - percent of GDP:	5.6%

TRANSNATIONAL ISSUES

Disputes - international:	complex maritime, air, and territorial disputes with Greece in Aegean Sea; Cyprus question with Greece; dispute with downstream riparian states (Syria and Iraq) over water development plans for the Tigris and Euphrates rivers; traditional demands regarding former Armenian lands in Turkey have subsided
Illicit drugs:	key transit route for Southwest Asian heroin to Western Europe and - to a far lesser extent the US - via air, land, and sea routes; major Turkish, Iranian, and other international trafficking organizations operate out of Istanbul; laboratories to convert imported morphine base into heroin are in remote regions of Turkey as well as near Istanbul; government maintains strict controls over areas of legal opium poppy cultivation and output of poppy straw concentrate

IMPORTANT INFORMATION FOR UNDERSTANDING TURKEY

Official Name: Republic of Turkey

PROFILE

Geography
Area: 780,580 sq. km.
Cities: *Capital*--Ankara (pop. 4.77 million). *Other cities*--Istanbul (13.256 million), Izmir (3.949 million), Bursa (2.605 million), Adana (2.085 million), Gaziantep (1.701 million).
Terrain: Narrow coastal plain surrounds Anatolia, an inland plateau becomes increasingly rugged as it progresses eastward. Turkey includes one of the more earthquake-prone areas of the world.
Climate: Moderate in coastal areas, harsher temperatures inland.

People
Nationality: *Noun*--Turk(s). *Adjective*--Turkish.
Population (December 2010 estimate): 73.7 million.
Annual population growth rate (2010 estimate): 1.312%.
Ethnic groups: Turkish, Kurdish, other.
Religions: Muslim 99% (majority Sunni), Christian, Bahai, and Jewish.
Languages: Turkish (official), Kurdish, Arabic, Armenian, Greek.
Education: *Years compulsory*--8. *Attendance*--97.6%. *Literacy*--87.4%.
Health: *Infant mortality rate*--23.94/1,000. *Life expectancy*--72.5 yrs.
Work force (27.43 million): *By occupation*--services 47.1%; agriculture 26.5%; industry 18.9%; and construction 7.5%.

Government
Type: Republic.
Independence: October 29, 1923.
Constitution: November 7, 1982. Amended in 1987, 1995, 2001, 2007, and 2010.
Branches: *Executive*--president (chief of state), prime minister (head of government), Council of Ministers (cabinet--appointed by the president on the nomination of the prime minister). *Legislative*--Grand National Assembly (550 members) chosen by national elections at least every 4 years. *Judicial*--Constitutional Court, Court of Cassation, Council of State, and other courts.
Political parties with representatives in Parliament: Justice and Development Party (AKP) (327 seats), Republican People's Party (CHP) (135 seats), Nationalist Action Party (MHP) (52 seats), Peace and Democracy Party (BDP) (29 seats), and seven independents.
Suffrage: Universal, 18 and older.
National holiday: Republic Day, October 28-29.

Economy
GDP (nominal): $481.5 billion; $526.4 billion; $658.8 billion; $680 billion; $618 billion; (2010 estimated) $741.9 billion; (2011 forecast) 797.6 billion.
Annual real GDP growth rate: 8.4%; 6.9%; 4.5%; 1.1%; -4.7%; (2010 estimated) 8.2%; (2011 forecast) 4.6%.
GDP (nominal) per capita: $7,108; $7,766; $9,422; $10,484; $8,711; (2010 estimate) $10,398; (2011 forecast) $11,054.
Annual inflation rate/CPI: 7.7%; 9.7%; 8.4%; 10.1%; 6.5%; 6.4%; (2011 forecast) 7.0%.
Natural resources: Coal, chromium, mercury, copper, boron, oil, gold.
Agriculture (9.3% of GDP): *Major products* (CIA World Factbook)--tobacco, cotton, grain, olives, sugar beets, hazelnuts, pulse, citrus; livestock. Provides about 26.5% of jobs (2011) and 3.5% of exports (Jan.-July 2011).
Industry (25.6% of GDP): *Major growth sector, types*--automotive, electronics, food processing, textiles, basic metals, chemicals, and petrochemicals. Provides about 18.9% of jobs and 93.8% of exports.
Trade: *Exports* (merchandise)-- $73.5 billion; $85.5 billion; $107.2 billion; $132 billion; $102.1 billion; $113.9 billion. *Export types* (Turkish Statistical Institute, 2011)--textiles and apparel, industrial machinery, iron and steel, electronics, petroleum products, and motor vehicles. *Imports*

(merchandise)-- $116.8 billion; $139.6 billion; $170.1 billion; $201.8 billion; $140.4 billion; $185.9 billion. *Import types*--chemicals, petroleum, machinery, motor vehicles, electronics, iron, steel, plastics, precious metals. *Major partners*--Germany, U.S., Italy, France, Russia, Japan, China, Iran, Iraq, U.K.

PEOPLE

Modern Turkey encompasses bustling cosmopolitan centers, pastoral farming villages, barren wastelands, peaceful Aegean coastlines, and steep mountain regions. More than 70% of Turkey's population lives in urban areas that juxtapose Western lifestyles with more traditional ways of life.

The Turkish state has been officially secular since 1924. Approximately 99% of the population is Muslim. Most Turkish Muslims follow the Sunni traditions of Islam, although a significant number follow Alevi and Shiite traditions. Questions regarding the role of religion in society and government, the role of linguistic and ethnic identity, and the public's expectation to live in security dominate public discourse. There are at least 12 million Turkish citizens who assert a Kurdish identity, making them the largest ethnic minority in Turkey.

HISTORY

Mustafa Kemal, celebrated by the Turkish State as a Turkish World War I hero and later known as "Ataturk" or "father of the Turks," led the founding of the Republic of Turkey in 1923 after the collapse of the 600-year-old Ottoman Empire and a 3-year war of independence. The empire, which at its peak controlled vast stretches of northern Africa, southeastern Europe, and western Asia, had failed to keep pace with European social and technological developments. The rise of national consciousness impelled several national groups within the Empire to seek independence as nation-states, leading to the empire's fragmentation. This process culminated in the disastrous Ottoman participation in World War I as a German ally. Defeated, shorn of much of its former territory, and partly occupied by forces of the victorious European states, the Ottoman structure was repudiated by Turkish nationalists brought together under the leadership of Mustafa Kemal. The nationalists expelled invading Greek, Russian, French and Italian forces from Anatolia in a bitter war. After the proclamation of the Republic of Turkey the sultanate and caliphate were abolished.

The leaders of the new republic concentrated on consolidating their power and modernizing and Westernizing what had been the empire's core--Asian Anatolia and a part of European Thrace. Social, political, linguistic, and economic reforms and attitudes decreed by Ataturk from 1924-1934 continue to be referred to as the ideological base of modern Turkey. In the post-Ataturk era, and especially after the military coup of 1960, this ideology came to be known as "Kemalism" and his reforms began to be referred to as "revolutions." The core elements of Kemalism are secularism, nationalism, statism, and identification with Europe. All of these concepts are the subject of lively debate in today's Turkey, and the ruling Justice and Development Party (AKP) comes from a tradition that challenges many of the Kemalist precepts.

Turkey entered World War II on the Allied side shortly before the war ended, becoming a charter member of the United Nations. Difficulties faced by Greece after World War II in quelling a communist rebellion and demands by the Soviet Union for military bases in the Turkish Straits prompted the United States to declare the Truman Doctrine in 1947. The doctrine enunciated American intentions to guarantee the security of Turkey and Greece and resulted in large scale U.S. military and economic aid under the Marshall Plan. After participating with United Nations forces in the Korean conflict, Turkey in 1952 joined the North Atlantic Treaty Organization (NATO). Turkey is currently a European Union candidate.

GOVERNMENT AND POLITICAL CONDITIONS

The 1982 Constitution, drafted by the military in the wake of a 1980 military coup, proclaims Turkey's system of government as democratic, secular, and parliamentary. The prime minister serves as head of government, and the president serves as head of state. The current president, Abdullah Gul, was elected by Parliament in August 2007 for a 7-year term. Pursuant to a constitutional amendment package approved by voters in an October 2007 referendum, the president is directly elected by the voters for a term of 5 years and can serve for a maximum of two terms.

The 550-member Parliament carries out legislative functions. Pursuant to the October 2007 constitutional amendment package, members of Parliament are directly elected by the voters for a term of 4 years, although general elections may be called at any time. Seat distribution is by the D'Hondt system of party-list proportional representation in combination with a 10% popular vote threshold. To participate in the distribution of seats, a party must obtain at least 10% of the votes cast at the national level. The president enacts laws passed by Parliament within 15 days. With the exception of budgetary laws, the president may return a law to the Parliament for reconsideration. If Parliament reenacts the law, it is binding, although the president may then apply to the Constitutional Court for a reversal of the law. Constitutional amendments pass with a 60% vote, but require an additional popular referendum unless passed with a two-thirds majority. The president may also submit amendments passed with a two-thirds majority to a popular referendum.

Nationwide local elections for provincial general assemblies, municipal assemblies, and mayoral positions were held March 29, 2009. The AKP received 38.39% of the votes in provincial general assemblies and a similar percentage in municipal assemblies. The Republican People's Party (CHP) and the Nationalist Action Party (MHP) won, respectively, 23% and 15% of the votes. AKP won 10 of 16 metropolitan municipality mayoralties. The next local elections are scheduled for March 2013.

In the June 2011 parliamentary election for Turkey's 61st government, the AKP captured 49.9% of the total votes, and Recep Tayyip Erdogan became the Prime Minister of a single-party government for a third consecutive term. The CHP, led by Kemal Kilicdaroglu, won 25.9% of the vote. The MHP, led by Devlet Bahceli, garnered 12.9% of the vote. Candidates running as independents but affiliated with a voting bloc supported by the Peace and Democracy Party (BDP) earned 6.8% of the popular vote, to encumber 29 seats in Parliament. The next general elections will occur in or before June 2015.

The Judiciary. The judiciary is declared to be independent, but the need for judicial reform and confirmation of its independence are subjects of open debate. Internationally recognized human rights, including freedom of thought, expression, assembly, and travel, are officially enshrined in the Constitution but have at times been narrowly interpreted, can be limited in times of emergency, and cannot be used to violate what the Constitution and the courts consider the integrity of the state or to impose a system of government based on religion, ethnicity, or the domination of one social class. The Constitution prohibits torture or ill treatment; the current government has focused on ensuring that practice matches principle. The law provides most but not all workers with the right to associate and form unions, subject to diverse restrictions.

The high court system includes a Constitutional Court responsible for judicial review of legislation, a Court of Cassation (or Supreme Court of Appeals), a Council of State serving as the high administrative and appeals court, a Court of Accounts, and a Military Court of Appeals. The High Council of Judges and Prosecutors, appointed by the president, supervises the judiciary.

PRESIDENTIAL ELECTIONS 2014

Erdoğan took the oath of office on 28 August 2014 and became the 12th president of Turkey. He administered the new Prime Minister Ahmet Davutoğlu's oath on 29 August.

Assuming the role of President, Erdoğan was criticized for openly stating that he would not maintain presidential neutrality. Erdoğan has also claimed that he intends to pursue a more active role as President, such as utilising the President's rarely used cabinet-calling powers. The political opposition has claimed that Erdoğan will continue to pursue his own political agenda, controlling the government, while his new Prime Minister Ahmet Davutoğlu would take a docile and submissive approach. One reason for this allegation was the fact that Erdoğan himself chose Davutoğlu to succeed him as Prime Minister, meaning that Davutoğlu was unanimously elected leader unopposed. Furthermore, the domination of loyal Erdoğan supporters in Davutoğlu's cabinet has also fuelled speculation that Erdoğan intends to exercise substantial control over the running of the government

Presidential elections were held in Turkey on 10 August 2014 in order to elect the 12th President of Turkey.[2] The result was a victory for the incumbent Prime Minister Recep Tayyip Erdoğan, who was elected outright by a simple majority of the vote in the first round. If no candidate had received more than 50% of the vote in the first round, a run-off election would have been held on 24 August between the two highest polling candidates. Three candidates ran for election.

As a result of the 2007 constitutional referendum, the election is the first presidential election in Turkey to be held nationally rather than by MPs within parliament. Over 55 million citizens were eligible to vote, both within Turkey and abroad. Recep Tayyip Erdoğan, the leader of the AKP who was elected Prime Minister in 2002, won the election with 51.79% of the vote and thus obviated the need for a run-off. Former Organisation of Islamic Cooperation General Secretary Ekmeleddin İhsanoğlu, who ran as the joint candidate of 13 opposition parties including the Republican People's Party (CHP) and Nationalist Movement Party (MHP), came second with 38.44% of the vote. The co-leader of the Peoples' Democratic Party (HDP) Selahattin Demirtaş, who received the backing of 8 other left-wing parties, came third with 9.76% of the vote.[3] Recep Tayyip Erdoğan took over over as President from Abdullah Gül on 28 August, while Ahmet Davutoğlu, who was elected leader of the AKP, succeeded Erdoğan as Prime Minister on the same date. It has been speculated that Erdoğan will continue to pursue his political agenda as president while Davutoğlu takes a docile approach as Prime Minister, breaking away from the ceremonial and neutral functions of the Presidency.[4][5][6]

The election was criticised by both the political opposition and international observers for alleged media bias in favour of Recep Tayyip Erdoğan, corruption allegations, the inaccuracy of opinion polls and the misuse of official public resources during Erdoğan's campaign.[7][8][9][10] While praising the authorities for safeguarding the right to assembly as well as the peaceful electoral conduct, the Organization for Security and Co-operation in Europe (OSCE) voiced concerns over the unequal distribution of campaign resources and media intimidation.[11][12] The historic 12-year low turnout of 74.13%, attributed to the fact that the election was held in summer while many citizens were on holiday, was seen by many politicians such as MHP leader Devlet Bahçeli as a significant factor in affecting the outcome. The election loss for the opposition CHP resulted in its leader Kemal Kılıçdaroğlu taking the decision to hold a party convention with a leadership election in response to growing dissatisfaction against his electoral performance

RESULST

Candidate	Nationwide	%	Overseas	%	Customs	%	Total votes	%

	votes		votes		votes			
Recep Tayyip Erdoğan	20,670,826	51.65	143,873	62.30	185,444	62.73	21,000,143	51.79
Ekmeleddin Mehmet İhsanoğlu	15,434,167	38.57	64,483	27.92	89,070	30.13	15,587,720	38.44
Selahattin Demirtaş	3,914,359	9.78	22,582	9.78	21,107	7.14	3,958,048	9.76
Invalid/blank votes	734,140	-	1,857	-	1,719	-	737,716	–
Total	40,019,352	100	230,938	100	297,340	100	41,283,627	100
Registered voters/turnout	52,894,115	77.05	2,798,726	8.32	-	-	55,692,841	74.13

Principal Government Officials

PRESIDENT - Recep Tayyip Erdoğan - from 2014

Functions		Holder	Inauguration
English title	Turkish title		
Deputy Prime Minister I	Başbakan Yardımcısı	Bülent Arınç	1 May 2009
Deputy Prime Minister II	Başbakan Yardımcısı	Ali Babacan	1 May 2009
Deputy Prime Minister III	Başbakan Yardımcısı	Yalçın Akdoğan	29 August 2014
Deputy Prime Minister IV	Başbakan Yardımcısı	Numan Kurtulmuş	29 August 2014
Minister of Culture and Tourism	Kültür ve Turizm Bakanı	Ömer Çelik	24 January 2013
Minister of Customs and Trade	Gümrük ve Ticaret Bakanı	Nurettin Canikli	29 August 2014
Minister of Development	Kalkınma Bakanı	Cevdet Yılmaz	6 July 2011
Minister of Economy	Ekonomi Bakanı	Nihat Zeybekci	25 December 2013
Minister of Energy and Natural Resources	Enerji ve Tabii Kaynaklar Bakanı	Taner Yıldız	1 May 2009
Minister of Environment and Urban Planning	Çevre ve Şehircilik Bakanı	İdris Güllüce	25 December 2013
Minister of European Union Affairs and Chief Negotiator	Avrupa Birliği Bakanı ve Baş Müzakereci	Volkan Bozkır	29 August 2014
Minister of Family and Social Policy	Aile ve Sosyal Politikalar Bakanı	Ayşenur İslam	25 December 2013
Minister of Finance	Maliye Bakanı	Mehmet Şimşek	1 May 2009
Minister of Food, Agriculture and Animal Breeding	Gıda, Tarım ve Hayvancılık Bakanı	Mehmet Mehdi Eker	2 June 2005
Minister of Foreign Affairs	Dışişleri Bakanı	Mevlüt Çavuşoğlu	29 August 2014
Minister of Forestry and Water Works	Orman ve Su İşleri Bakanı	Veysel Eroğlu	29 August 2007
Minister of Health	Sağlık Bakanı	Mehmet Müezzinoğlu	25 December 2013
Minister of Justice	Adalet Bakanı	Bekir Bozdağ	25 December 2013

Functions		Holder	Inauguration
English title	Turkish title		
Minister of Labour and Social Security	Çalışma ve Sosyal Güvenlik Bakanı	Faruk Çelik	6 July 2011
Minister of National Defense	Millî Savunma Bakanı	İsmet Yılmaz	6 July 2011
Minister of National Education	Millî Eğitim Bakanı	Nabi Avcı	24 January 2013
Minister of Science, Industry and Technology	Bilim, Sanayi ve Teknoloji Bakanı	Fikri Işık	25 December 2013
Minister of the Interior	İçişleri Bakanı	Efkan Ala	25 December 2013
Minister of Transport, Maritime Affairs and Communication	Ulaştırma, Denizcilik ve Haberleşme Bakanı	Lütfi Elvan	25 December 2013
Minister of Youth and Sports	Gençlik ve Spor Bakanı	Akif Çağatay Kılıç	25 December 2013
Prime Minister	Başbakan	Ahmet Davutoğlu	29 August 2014

Ambassador to the US	Namik TAN
Permanent Representative to the UN, New York	Yasar Halit CEVIK

Turkey maintains an **embassy** in the United States at 2525 Massachusetts Avenue NW, Washington, DC 20008, tel. (202) 612-6700. Consulates general in Chicago (360 N. Michigan Ave., Suite 1405, Chicago, IL 60601, tel: 312-263-0644, ext. 28); Los Angeles (4801 Wilshire Blvd., Suite 310, Los Angeles, CA 90010, tel: 323-937-0118); New York (821 United Nations Plaza, New York, NY 10017, tel: 212-949-0160); and Houston (1990 Post Oak Blvd., Suite 1300, Houston, TX 77056, tel: 713-622-5849). The Permanent Representative of Turkey to the **United Nations** is located on 821 United Nations Plaza, 10th floor, New York, NY 10017, tel: 212-949-0150.

ECONOMY

Rank	17th (nominal) / 15th (PPP)
Currency	Turkish lira (TRY)
Fiscal year	calendar year
Trade organisations	G-20 major economies, OECD, EU Customs Union, WTO, ECO, BSEC
	Statistics
GDP	$1.358 trillion (PPP, 2012) $789.257 billion (Nominal, 2012)
GDP growth	▲4.4% (Q2 2013) ▲5.2% (2002-2011 average) ▲6.7% (2011-2017 avg. Forecast in OECD)
GDP per capita	$18,348 (PPP, 2012) $10,666 (Nominal, 2012)
GDP by sector	agriculture: 8.9%; industry: 28.1%; services: 63.0% (2012 est.)
Inflation (CPI)	6.1% (April 2013) 5.3% (2013 target) 5.0% (2014 target)
Population	16.9% (2010)

below poverty line	
Gini coefficient	40.2 (2010)
Labour force	27.34 million (2012 est.) note: about 1.2 million Turks work abroad
Labour force by occupation	agriculture: 25.5%, industry: 26.2%, services: 48.4% (2010)
Unemployment	8.8% (June 2013) 8.9% (2013 In Medium Term Programme) 8.8% (2014 In Medium Term Programme)
Main industries	textiles, food processing, autos, electronics, tourism, mining (coal, chromate, copper, boron), steel, petroleum, construction, lumber, paper
Ease of Doing Business Rank	71st
	External
Exports	▲$163.40 billion (29th) (2012)
Export goods	apparel, foodstuffs, textiles, metal manufactures, transport equipment
Main export partners	Germany 8.6% Iraq 7.1% Iran 6.5% United Kingdom 5.7% United Arab Emirates 5.4% Russia 4.4% Italy 4.2% France 4.1% (2012 est.)[19]
Imports	$228.90 billion (22nd) (2012)[20]
Import goods	machinery, chemicals, semi-finished goods, fuels, transport equipment[21]
Main import partners	Russia 11.3% Germany 9.0% China 9.0% United States 6.0% Italy 5.6% Iran 5.1% (2012 est.)
FDI stock	$152.90 billion (29th) (31 December 2012)
Gross external debt	$336.90 billion (30th) (31 December 2012)
	Public finances
Public debt	35.5% of GDP (2013)
Revenues	$209 billion (2013)
Expenses	$228.3 billion (2013)
Economic aid	donor: $1.03 billion, 0.13% of GDP. Also, Turkey is ranked 4th on the ODA in 2012 report.
Credit rating	Standard & Poor's: BBB (Domestic) BB+ (Foreign) BBB(T&C Assessment) Outlook: Stable Moody's: Rating: Baa3 Outlook: Stable Fitch: Rating: BBB- Outlook: Stable
Foreign reserves	$134.269 billion (October 2013)

Turkey is a large, middle-income country with relatively few natural resources. Its economy is currently in transition from a high degree of reliance on agriculture and heavy industry to a more diversified economy with an increasingly large and globalized services sector. Coming out of a tradition of a state-directed economy that was relatively closed to the outside world, Prime Minister and then President Turgut Ozal began to open up the economy in the 1980s, leading to the signing of a customs union with the European Union in 1995. In the 1990s, Turkey's economy suffered from a series of coalition governments with weak economic policies, leading to high-inflation boom-and-bust cycles that culminated in a severe banking and economic crisis in 2001, a deep economic downturn (GNP fell 9.5% in 2001), and an increase in unemployment. Turkey's economy recovered strongly from the 2001 recession thanks to good monetary and fiscal policies and structural economic reforms made with the support of the International Monetary Fund and the World Bank.

The **economy of Turkey** is defined as an emerging market economy by the IMF and is largely developed, making Turkey one of the world's newly industrialized countries. The country is among the world's leading producers of agricultural products; textiles; motor vehicles, ships and other transportation equipment; construction materials; consumer electronics and home appliances. In recent years, Turkey had a rapidly growing private sector, yet the state still plays a major role in industry, banking, transport, and communications

Turkey's economy grew an average of 6.0% per year from 2002 through 2007--one of the highest sustained rates of growth in the world. During this period, inflation and interest rates fell significantly, the currency stabilized, and government debt declined to more supportable levels (39.5% of GDP in 2008). However, booming economic growth contributed to a growing current account deficit (5.6% of GDP or $41.6 billion in 2008). Growth fell to 1.1% in 2008, and the economy contracted by 4.7% in 2009 due to the global economic slowdown and reduced exports. Growth picked up to 8.2% in 2010. Continued implementation of reforms, including tight fiscal policy, and securing independent Central Bank monetary policies is essential to sustain growth and stability.

After years of low levels of foreign direct investment (FDI), Turkey succeeded in attracting $18.3 billion in net FDI in 2008. Global market conditions reduced foreign capital inflows in 2009, and Turkey attracted $7.7 billion in net FDI in 2009. This amount was expected to fall to around $5 billion in 2010. A series of large privatizations, the stability fostered by the start of Turkey's EU accession negotiations, strong and stable growth, and structural changes in the banking, retail, and telecommunications sectors contributed to the 2008 rise in foreign investment. Turkey has taken steps to improve its investment climate through administrative streamlining, an end to foreign investment screening, and strengthened intellectual property legislation. However, a number of disputes involving foreign investors in Turkey and certain policies, such as high taxation and continuing gaps in the intellectual property regime, inhibit investment. Turkey has a number of bilateral investment and tax treaties, including with the United States, which guarantee free repatriation of capital in convertible currencies and eliminate double taxation.

While Turkey's long-term economic prospects are bright, the government is working to limit growth of its current account deficit, which almost doubled in 2010, reaching an alarming 9% of GDP.

EU Accession. Turkey adopted the EU's Common External Tariff regime in 1963, effectively lowering Turkey's tariffs for third countries, including the United States. Turkey and the then-European Economic Community (EEC) entered into an Association Agreement in December 1964. Turkey and the EU also formed a customs union beginning January 1, 1996. The agreement covers industrial and processed agricultural goods and has prompted Turkey to harmonize its laws and regulations with EU standards. In 1999 the European Council granted the status of candidate country to Turkey, and accession negotiations with Turkey were opened in

October 2005.

Accession talks include a process of adopting the body of EU law called the *acquis communautaire.* The *acquis* is divided into 33 chapters regulating areas ranging from the free movement of goods to agriculture to competition policy.

As of late November 2010, Turkey had met the benchmarks to open 13 chapters, including the provisionally closed chapter on Science and Research. Most recently, in June 2010, the chapter on Food Safety, Veterinary & Phytosanitary Policy was opened. Eighteen chapters are blocked. Three chapters remain unblocked and have yet to be opened. One of the key stumbling blocks to opening new chapters is that Turkey has yet to fully implement the Ankara Protocol, which requires normalizing bilateral relations with EU member Cyprus, which Turkey has said it will not do until the Greek and Turkish Cypriot communities on the island are reunited.

Energy. In 2010, total electricity supply in Turkey reached 194 terawatt-hours (TWh), up by 51% from 2000. Natural gas fueled 49% of power generation, while coal provided 28%, hydropower 19%, oil 3%, and other sources 1%. Electricity demand in Turkey continues at an annual growth rate of between 6.5% and 8% per year, which is higher than the average rate of GNP growth over the last few years. This, combined with the lack of investment in the sector, mainly due to the Government of Turkey's (GOT) control over prices and slow progress in market liberalization, increased concerns regarding electricity shortages. Official data indicated that Turkey would face electricity shortages as of 2009; however, the GOT revised its projections after experiencing reductions in demand in late 2008, and, due to the global economic crisis and relatively mild weather, Turkey was able to meet its demand. The Ministry of Energy declared a 4.5% annual growth in electricity demand in 2009, half the amount of demand growth in previous years. In 2008, the GOT passed new legislation to encourage investment in the sector, which introduces incentives for companies bringing their facilities online by 2012. Turkey is currently undertaking privatization of its electricity distribution. The private sector has responded, adding 6,644 megawatts (MW) of electricity generation capacity since 2009.

In 2009, fossil fuels accounted for 89% of total primary energy supply (TPES) in Turkey. Coal and natural gas each provided 31% of the total, and oil provided 27%, while renewable energy sources provided the remaining 11%. In 2011, on an energy basis, coal and lignite provided 31% of total final consumption, natural gas 31%, oil 27%, and renewable (biomass, hydro, and geothermal) 11%. Coal is the only energy source with significant domestic availability; over 90% of both oil and natural gas is imported. Domestic oil and gas production is mostly from small fields in the southeast, although major exploration projects are active in the Black Sea. TUPRAS, the largest refiner in Turkey, was privatized in 2005. Turkey has a refining capacity of 714,275 barrels per day (b/d).

Turkey acts as an important link in the East-West Southern Energy Corridor bringing Caspian, Central Asian, and Middle Eastern energy to Europe and world markets. The Baku-Tbilisi-Ceyhan pipeline, which came online in July 2006, delivers up to 1 million barrels/day of petroleum, and in 2007, the South Caucasus Pipeline (from Shah Deniz) started bringing natural gas from Azerbaijan to Turkey. Turkey's interconnector pipeline to Greece, an important step in bringing Caspian natural gas to Europe via Turkey, came online in November 2007. In July 2009, Turkey signed the Nabucco Intergovernmental Agreement, along with Austria, Bulgaria, Romania, and Hungary, which includes plans for a 2,000-mile natural gas pipeline running from Erzurum, Turkey to Baumgarten, Austria with a 31 billion cubic meter capacity. Alternative proposals to Nabucco include the Trans-Adriatic Pipeline (TAP) and the Italy-Turkey-Greece Interconnector.

Telecommunications. Parliament enacted legislation separating telecommunications policy and regulatory functions in January 2000, by establishing an independent regulatory body, the Telecommunication Authority. The authority is responsible for issuing licenses, supervising operators, and taking necessary technical measures against violations of the rules. Most regulatory functions of the Transport Ministry were transferred to the authority, and the regulator is slowly gaining competence and independence. The Electronic Communication Law passed in 2008 gave greater autonomy to the Telecommunication Authority. The authority realized some important projects in 2008. Introduction of number portability was a big step forward, encouraging more competition among the GSM mobile phone operators. The authority also held a 3G license tender in 2008, where all the GSM operators participated and started implementing this new technology in Turkey.

The long-expected privatization of the state-owned fixed-line telecommunications company was accomplished by the sale of 55% of Turk Telekom to the Saudi-owned Oger Group in November 2005. The company remains as a monopoly in fixed lines, but the GSM operators' competition against Turk Telekom has been increasing. With liberalization and growth in the economy, there is growing competition for Internet provision, but Turk Telekom remains the sole provider of ADSL wide band Internet.

Environment. With the establishment of the Environment Ministry in 1991, Turkey began to make significant progress addressing its most pressing environmental problems. The most dramatic improvements were significant reductions of air pollution in Istanbul and Ankara. However, progress has been slow on the remaining--and serious--environmental challenges facing Turkey.

In 2011 the Ministry of Environment and Forestry was split into the Ministry of Environment and Urbanization and the Ministry of Forest and Water Affairs. With its goal to join the EU, Turkey has made commendable progress in updating and modernizing its environmental legislation. However, environmental concerns are not fully integrated into public decision-making and enforcement can be weak. Turkey faces a backlog of environmental problems, requiring enormous outlays for infrastructure. The most pressing needs are for water treatment plants, wastewater treatment facilities, solid waste management, and conservation of biodiversity. The discovery of a number of chemical waste sites in 2006 has highlighted weakness in environmental law and oversight.

After long years of silence, Turkey signed the Kyoto Protocol in 2008 and ratified it in 2009. Turkey will not be obligated to reduce its greenhouse emissions until 2012, when the agreement's second commitment period may go into force.

Transport. The Turkish Government gives special priority to major infrastructure projects, especially in the transport sector. The government is in the process of building new airports and highways, thanks to an increased public investment budget. The government will realize many of these projects by utilizing the build-operate-transfer (BOT) model.

Turkey has the world's 17th largest nominal GDP, and 15th largest GDP by PPP. The country is a founding member of the OECD (1961) and the G-20 major economies (1999). Since December 31, 1995, Turkey is also a part of the EU Customs Union.

While many economies have been unable to recover from the recent global financial recession, the Turkish economy expanded by 9.2% in 2010, and 8.5 percent in 2011, thus standing out as the fastest growing economy in Europe, and one of the fastest growing economies in the world. Hence, Turkey has been meeting the "60 percent EU Maastricht criteria" for public debt stock since 2004. Similarly, from 2002 to 2011, the budget deficit decreased from more than 10 percent to less than 3 percent, which is one of the EU Maastricht criteria for the budget balance.

The CIA classifies Turkey as a developed country. Turkey is often classified as a newly industrialized country by economists and political scientists; while Merrill Lynch, the World Bank, and *The Economist* describe Turkey as an emerging market economy.

The World Bank classifies Turkey as an upper-middle income country in terms of the country's per capita GDP in 2007. Mean graduate pay was $10.02 per manhour in 2010.

According to a survey by *Forbes*, Istanbul, Turkey's financial capital, had a total of 28 billionaires as of March 2010 (down from 34 in 2008) ranking 4th in the world behind New York City (60 billionaires), Moscow (50 billionaires), and London (32 billionaires).

In 2009 the Turkish government introduced various economic stimulus measures to reduce the impact of the 2007–2012 global financial crisis such as temporary tax cuts on automobiles, home appliances, and housing. As a result, the production of durable consumer goods increased by 7.2%, despite a decrease in automotive production.

The Turkish Stock Market and credit rating agencies have responded positively. According to *The Economist*, share prices in Turkey nearly doubled over the course of 2009. On 8 January 2010, International credit rating agency Moody's upgraded Turkey's rating one notch. In 2012, Fitch upgraded Turkey's credit rating to investment grade (long-term foreign currency Issuer Default Rating (IDR) was upgraded to BBB- (from BB+) and long-term local currency IDR was upgraded to BBB (from BB+)) after an 18-year gap; this was followed by a ratings upgrade by Moody's in May 2013, as the service lifted Turkey's government bond ratings to the lowest investment grade Baa3. The decision is Moody's first investment-grade rating for Turkey in two decades and the service stated in its official statement that the nation's "recent and expected future improvements in key economic and public finance metrics" was the basis for the ratings boost.

Turkish President Abdullah Gul said that Turkey was one of the rare countries whose financial institutions made profits in the last three years at a time of global economic crisis. Turkey is the world's 15th and Europe's 6th largest economy and the Turkish economy grew 11% in the first six months of 2010. Turkey is the country in OECD with the biggest growth of economy. According to the International Monetary Fund (IMF) Turkey will exceed China, United States, Brazil, and Japan in the rise of national income.

According to the *Financial Times* Special Report on Turkey, Turkish business executives and government officials believe the quickest route to achieving export growth lies outside of traditional western markets. According to Daniel Dombey of the *Financial Times*, a bit over five years ago, the "European Union accounted for much more than half of all Turkey's exports. Now the figure is heading down toward not much more than a third". Erdem Başçı, Turkey's central bank governor, predicts that Iraq will eventually become Turkey's largest export market.

The Turkish government is intricately involved in helping to facilitate private sector expansion in emerging markets. "The government has a strategic vision, saying: 'We will open up more embassies in growth regions and emerging markets such as Africa, Turkish Airlines will fly there, so Turkish businessmen can go there to do business there,'" says Hüsnü Özyeğin, one of Turkey's most prominent businessmen and bankers. Similarly, Ahmet Davutoğlu, Turkey's foreign minister, is focusing his attentions on the Middle East and striking a series of visa-free travel deals, while eyeing to establish free trade zones with the countries in the region. The AKP government is also seeking to improve economic and political relations with the autonomous Kurdish Regional Government (KRG) in northern Iraq. In 2013 Turkey had a "huge current account deficit and high external financing need."

FOREIGN RELATIONS

Turkey is a member of NATO and candidate for the EU, and its primary political, economic, and security ties are with the West. However, the AKP government has also sought to strengthen relations with its Middle Eastern neighbors, and with Central Asian, African, and Latin American countries.

Turkey entered NATO in 1952 and serves as the organization's vital eastern anchor, as it controls the straits leading from the Black Sea to the Aegean and shares a border with Syria, Iraq, and Iran. NATO's Air Component Command Headquarters is located in Izmir and NATO's Rapid Deployable Corps-Turkey is headquartered in Istanbul. As part of NATO command structure reforms, the headquarters in Izmir will transform into the new NATO Land Forces Command headquarters in 2012. Turkey has made important contributions to the International Security Assistance Force (ISAF) in Afghanistan, commanding ISAF four times (2002, 2005, 2009-2010, and 2010-2011). Turkey currently commands Regional Command Capital and has set up two Provincial Reconstruction Teams, in Wardak and Jowzjan Provinces, with approximately 1,700 troops stationed in Afghanistan. Turkey also provides approximately 400 troops to the NATO mission in Kosovo. In Libya, Turkey played an active role in NATO's Operation Unified Protector to protect civilians in 2011. Turkey agreed in 2011 to host a radar as part of NATO's missile defense architecture.

Turkey and the EU formed a customs union beginning January 1, 1996. In December 1999, Turkey became a candidate for EU membership. On December 17, 2004, the EU decided to begin formal accession negotiations with Turkey in October 2005. Besides its relationships with NATO and the EU, Turkey is a member of the Organization for Economic Cooperation and Development (OECD), the Council of Europe, and the Organization for Security and Cooperation in Europe (OSCE).

Turkey is a member of the World Trade Organization (WTO). It has signed free trade agreements with the European Free Trade Association (EFTA), Israel, and many other countries. In 1992, Turkey and 10 other regional nations formed the Black Sea Economic Cooperation (BSEC) Council to expand regional trade and economic cooperation. Turkey chaired BSEC in 2007 and hosted the 15th BSEC Summit in Istanbul in June 2007 and the 17th BSEC Council of Foreign Ministers in Ankara in October 2007. It also belongs to the Organization of Islamic Cooperation (OIC).

Turkey is a UN member and held a non-permanent seat on the Security Council from January 1, 2009 to December 31, 2010. It held the rotating presidency in June 2009 and September 2010. In May 2011 Turkey announced its candidacy for a non-permanent seat for 2015-2016.

U.S.-TURKEY RELATIONS

U.S.-Turkish friendship dates to the late 18th century and was officially sealed by a treaty in 1830. The present close relationship began with the agreement of July 12, 1947, which implemented the Truman Doctrine. As part of the cooperative effort to further Turkish economic and military self-reliance, the United States has loaned and granted Turkey more than $7 billion in economic aid and more than $14 billion in military assistance over several years.

U.S.-Turkish relations focus on areas such as strategic energy cooperation, trade and investment, security ties, regional stability, counterterrorism, and human rights progress. Relations were strained when Turkey refused in March 2003 to allow U.S. troops to deploy through its territory to Iraq in Operation Iraqi Freedom, but regained momentum steadily thereafter, and mutual interests remain strong across a wide spectrum of issues. Turkey currently allows the use of Incirlik Air Base for the transport of non-lethal cargo in support of Operation Enduring Freedom and Operation Iraqi Freedom. On July 5, 2006, Secretary of State Condoleezza Rice and Foreign Minister Abdullah Gul signed a Shared Vision Statement to highlight the common values and goals between the two countries and to lay out a framework for increased strategic dialogue. During a November 5, 2007 meeting in Washington with Prime Minister Erdogan, President George W. Bush committed to provide greater assistance to Turkey in its fight against terrorism from the Kurdistan Workers' Party (PKK or Kongra Gel), which he characterized as a "common enemy" of Turkey, Iraq, and the United States. He reiterated this commitment during President Gul's January 8, 2008, White House visit.

President Barack Obama paid a historic visit to Turkey April 5-7, 2009, the first bilateral visit of his presidency. During the visit, he spoke before the Turkish Parliament and outlined his vision of a model U.S.-Turkish partnership based on mutual interests and mutual respect. Secretary of State Hillary Clinton has also prioritized the U.S.-Turkey relationship, and visited Turkey in March 2009 and July 2011. On December 7, 2009, Prime Minister Erdogan and President Obama launched the Framework for Strategic Economic and Commercial Cooperation (FSECC), a new cabinet-level initiative focused on boosting trade and investment ties. The inaugural FSECC meeting was held in Washington in October 2010. In addition to the new framework, the U.S. and Turkey hold meetings of the Trade and Investment Framework Agreement (TIFA) Council and Economic Partnership Commission (EPC). As of June 2011, bilateral trade had increased by 50% since 2010 from $6.9 billion to $10.4 billion, with U.S. exports to Turkey up 58% from $4.9 billion to $7.8 billion and Turkish exports to the United States up 32% from $2.0 billion to $2.6 billion. This puts Turkey very close to its all-time record of exports to the U.S., and its export growth to the U.S. is outpacing export growth to the rest of the world (32% vice 23%).

Principal U.S. Officials
Ambassador John Bass
Deputy Chief of Mission--Jess L. Baily

Counselors
Political Affairs--Yuri Kim
Political-Military Affairs--Edward G. Stafford
Economic Affairs--Laird Treiber
Regional Affairs--Thomas Sylvester
Consular Affairs--Laurence Tobey
Management Affairs--Richard Jaworski
Public Affairs--Mark Wentworth
Agricultural Affairs--Clay Hamilton
Commercial Affairs--Michael Lally

Senior Defense Official--Brig. Gen. James “Ed” Daniel

The **U.S. Embassy** is located at 110 Ataturk Boulevard, Kavaklidere, Ankara 06100, tel: (90) (312) 455-5555.

TRAVEL AND BUSINESS INFORMATION

Travel Alerts, Travel Warnings, Trip Registration
The U.S. Department of State's Consular Information Program advises Americans traveling and residing abroad through Country Specific Information, Travel Alerts, and Travel Warnings. **Country Specific Information** exists for all countries and includes information on entry and exit requirements, currency regulations, health conditions, safety and security, crime, political disturbances, and the addresses of the U.S. embassies and consulates abroad. **Travel Alerts** are issued to disseminate information quickly about terrorist threats and other relatively short-

term conditions overseas that pose significant risks to the security of American travelers. **Travel Warnings** are issued when the State Department recommends that Americans avoid travel to a certain country because the situation is dangerous or unstable.

For the latest security information, Americans living and traveling abroad should regularly monitor the Department's Bureau of Consular Affairs Internet web site at http://travel.state.gov, where current Worldwide Caution, Travel Alerts, and Travel Warnings can be found. The travel.state.gov website also includes information about passports, tips for planning a safe trip abroad and more. More travel-related information also is available at http://www.usa.gov/Citizen/Topics/Travel/International.shtml.

The Department's Smart Traveler app for U.S. travelers going abroad provides easy access to the frequently updated official country information, travel alerts, travel warnings, maps, U.S. embassy locations, and more that appear on the travel.state.gov site. Travelers can also set up e-tineraries to keep track of arrival and departure dates and make notes about upcoming trips. The app is compatible with iPhone, iPod touch, and iPad (requires iOS 4.0 or later).

The Department of State encourages all U.S. citizens traveling or residing abroad to enroll in the State Department's Smart Traveler Enrollment Program (STEP). A link to the registration page is also available through the Department's Smart Traveler app. U.S. citizens without internet access can enroll directly at the nearest U.S. embassy or consulate. By enrolling, you make your presence and whereabouts known in case it is necessary to contact you in an emergency and so you can receive up-to-date information on security conditions. Emergency information concerning Americans traveling abroad may be obtained by calling 1-888-407-4747 toll free in the U.S. and Canada or the regular toll line 1-202-501-4444 for callers outside the U.S. and Canada.

Passports

The National Passport Information Center (NPIC) is the U.S. Department of State's single, centralized public contact center for U.S. passport information. Telephone: 1-877-4-USA-PPT (1-877-487-2778); TDD/TTY: 1-888-874-7793. Passport information is available 24 hours, 7 days a week. You may speak with a representative Monday-Friday, 8 a.m. to 10 p.m., Eastern Time, excluding federal holidays.

SECTORAL DEVELOPMENT AND BUSINESS OPPORTUNTIES[1]

Turkey is implementing a wide-ranging programme to restructure its agriculture, so as to reduce the burden of support on its economy and move its policies closer to those of the EC's. Some of the potentially most production-distorting measures in the sector (e.g. administered output prices) are being phased out and replaced by a less distortionary direct support system. Nonetheless, the simple average applied MFN tariff in agriculture (Major Division 1 of ISIC Revision 2) is 28.3%, up from 25% in 2003. This relatively high tariff protection and the limited coverage of agricultural products in Turkey's preferential trade arrangements, with products generally subject to preferential tariff quotas, impede the exposure of the sector to greater competition.

In mining and quarrying, customs tariffs average 0.3% (0.2% in 2003); imports of electricity are duty free. Several new energy-related laws have been enacted over the last few years aiming to further liberalize the subsector. The lack of adequate investment, together with high energy wastage, still causes power shortages in some areas. Increasing the country's electricity generation capacity continues to be a top priority for the Government, which has open all segments of the electricity subsector (except transmission) to private participation.

Manufacturing is the major beneficiary of state aid. It is also the main beneficiary of various incentive schemes (duty and tax concessions in particular), as well as export credits and guarantees. MFN customs tariffs on manufactured goods average 10.9% (down from 11.1% in 2003); relatively high rates (to 225%) continue to apply to some processed food products. The tariff structure does not encourage investment in certain manufacturing activities, for example, chemical and plastic industries, where the tariff displays negative escalation. Furthermore, high effective protection of industries such as textiles and apparel, beverages, and tobacco products hampers their competitiveness.

Since its previous TPR, Turkey has taken measures to tackle structural problems in some services subsectors, notably the monopoly of Turk Telekom over fixed line, domestic long-distance and international telephony services ended in on 31 December 2003. Nevertheless, some state-owned enterprises (SOEs) continue to dominate services activities, for example, postal services, and air, rail, and maritime transport. Under the GATS, Turkey scheduled commitments in several categories (AIV.2), and maintains some MFN exemptions (Table AIV.3). It has also tabled its initial and revised conditional offers in the ongoing services negotiations.

AGRICULTURE AND RELATED ACTIVITIES

MAIN FEATURES

Agriculture remains a key sector in the Turkish economy (Chapter I(1)). The average farm has around 6 ha, and arable land in each farm is generally divided into a large number of parcels. Despite the recent emergence of more commercial farms, the bulk of farming has remained small

[1] Government of Turkey and WTO materials

and family-owned, highly fragmented, and capital-low; it continues to use only elementary technologies. The majority of the sector is informal.[2]

Turkey is self-sufficient in food, and has increased its exports of some agricultural products. It is a key player in its traditional specialities (hazelnuts, oriental tobacco, dried fruit), and in some new areas (tomatoes, potatoes, watermelons). Nonetheless, its share in world agricultural markets is only about 1%, well below potential, given that it has more arable land than any West European country and a temperate climate. Crops contribute about 65% of total agricultural production; the main crops are cereals (wheat, barley, and maize); cash crops (sugar beet, cotton); and fruit and vegetables (grapes, citrus fruit, apples, watermelon, tomatoes, potatoes, dry onion). Agriculture has the lowest productivity among Turkey's economic sectors.[3]

The livestock sub-sector, consisting mainly of cattle, buffalo, sheep, and goats, includes traditional and commercial activities. Turkey is implementing an animal identification system; 10 million bovines have been registered. The main objective is to increase livestock production in order to provide adequate and balanced nutrition for the population. Total meat production averaged some 430,000 tonnes during 2000-06[4], while milk production remained constant at around 10 million tonnes.

Despite the great potential of fishing activities in Turkey, their contribution to the economy is low mainly because of lack of modern vessels, and inefficient catching and processing methods. Fisheries production, including aquaculture[5], averaged 640,000 tonnes over 2000-06; it is composed largely of marine fish (about 70% of the total in 2006), aquaculture (15%), freshwater fish (8%), and other sea products (7%). Some of the main species caught are anchovy, mackarel mullet, hake, sardine, crustaceans, grey mullet, pilchard, and common carp. The Black Sea is the main production area, followed by the Mediterranean Sea. High-seas fishing has diminished considerably due to pollution, ecological changes, and unsustainable use of resources.

Forests cover 20.7 million hectares or 26.9% of the total area of Turkey. Timber is the main forest product. Coniferous trees represent 54.4% of the forests, the remainder being broad-leaved trees. Forests in Turkey are classified in terms of quality and purpose: protection forests, national parks, and production forests. Biological diversity is high with 9,000 plant species, 3,000 of which are endemic. About 99.9% of forest lands and resources belong to the State; the area of private forests is only about 20,000 ha. Some 9% of the afforested areas were destroyed by fires during 2001-05. The main problems in the subsector include incomplete cadastral works, deficiency in specialized technical staff and workers, limited number of national parks and similar protected areas, low levels of annual reaforestation to avoid erosion and ensure long-term balance in wood supply and demand, uncertainties in management targets, delays in regeneration works, and inadequate financing.[6]

POLICY DEVELOPMENTS

The Ministry of Agriculture and Rural Affairs (MARA) is responsible for the overall running of the sector, including coordinating and carrying out research and extension services, assisting

[2] Although participation in the self-employed social security scheme is mandatory, 91% of farmers do not participate, and only a small minority pay income taxes (OECD, 2006b).

[3] Labour productivity in agriculture is about one third of the average for the whole economy (OECD, 2003).

[4] This figure excludes the meat consumed in rural areas.

[5] Rainbow trout, sea bass, sea bream, and bluefin tune are the main species cultured. Small numbers of carp, mussels and shrimp are also farmed.

[6] State Planning Organization (2006).

agricultural cooperatives, and providing infrastructure. Turkey's key policy objectives for agriculture are, *inter alia*: increasing producers' welfare; promoting rural development; ensuring food security and safety; and improving efficiency, productivity, quality, and competitiveness. Some of Turkey's main targets for improving efficiency in agriculture under its Ninth Development Plan 2007-13 are shown in Table IV.1.

Table IV.1
Agricultural structure, 2006 and 2013

	2006	2013
	Per cent	
The share of animal production in total agricultural production	28.0	37.0
Percentage of certified cereal (wheat-barley) seed usage	30.0	50.0
Proportion of cultured and cross bred to total cattle stock	67.0	77.0
Proportion of organic agricultural to total agricultural land	1.0	3.0
	Million hectares	
Irrigation area (net cumulative)	2.55	3.00
Land consolidation activities (cumulative)	0.60	1.27
Industrial and soil protection plantation (cumulative)	2.60	3.30

Source: State Planning Organization (2006), *Ninth Development Plan 2007-13,* Ankara.

The main policy developments since the last TPR have been the extension of the 2001-05 Agricultural Reform Implementation Project (ARIP) to the end of 2008, with the addition of the Rural Development Investment Supporting Programme and Village-based Participatory Investment Programme[7], Land Consolidation, Conservation Reserve Payment (CATAK), the launching of the Agricultural Strategy Paper 2006-10 (ASP), and the adoption, in 2006, of a new Agricultural Law (No. 5488) to implement the ASP and move Turkey's agricultural policies closer to those of the EC.

Under the ARIP, measures are being taken in four main areas[8]: (i) phasing out price support and credit subsidies, and replacing them with a less distortionary direct income support (DIS) system to farmers, based on a uniform per-hectare payment (about US$90/ha) rather than on inputs or output, and on the National Farmer Registration System (NFRS) initiated in 2001[9]; (ii)

[7] Under the Rural Development Investment Supporting Programme and Village-based Participatory Investments Programme, producers are supported for certain investment projects (e.g. irrigation and infrastructure facilities). The Rural Development Investment Supporting Programme is financed through the general budget and is implemented in 65 provinces, while the Village-based Participatory Investments Programme is supported by the World Bank and implemented in 16 provinces.

[8] These measures were introduced in 2002 and accelerated in 2003, the first year of full implementation of ARIP. For a full description of ARIP, see WTO (2003), *Trade Policy Review of Turkey*, Geneva.

[9] More than 2.75 million farmers (89% of the total), and 17 million hectares (80% of total agricultural land) have been registered by the NFRS for receiving DIS payments. About 10 million people benefit from NFRS. DIS has become the major support instrument in Turkey's agriculture, accounting for about 80% of the total support provided to agricultural producers in monetary terms (OECD, 2006a).

withdrawing the State from direct involvement in crops production, processing, and marketing; (iii) reducing output intervention purchases financed from the budget leading to price cuts[10]; and (iv) one-time grants made available to farmers switching out of crops suffering excess supply, such as hazelnuts and tobacco, to help cover their transitional costs, and facilitate the transition to efficient production patterns.[11]

With CATAK, Turkey aims, *inter alia*, to ensure proper agricultural policies in vulnerable areas (i.e. areas subject to toxic residuals and/or erosion, and with water and environmental pollution); and increase farmers' income levels. The total cost of CATAK is US$9 million (fully financed by World Bank funds) for 2005-08; this is being used in four different regions with a total land area of 5,000 ha.[12] In 2004, Turkey adopted its ASP, which fixed the budgetary funds available for the sector to around 1% of GNP, and targeted the allocation of these funds in 2010 as follows: 45% for DIS payments; 13% for deficiency payments; 12% for livestock support; 10% for rural development support; 5% for compensatory payments; 5% for ÇATAK; 5% for crop insurance support; and 5% for other supports.[13]

Agricultural Law No. 5488 puts emphasis on increasing productivity and ensuring food supply, and makes the competitiveness and modernization of the sector a priority. It also creates the legal basis for certain management systems (Integrated Administrative Control System, Farm Accountancy Data Network) necessary for implementation of the *acquis communautaire*; nonetheless, the Law moves Turkey further away from the principles of the EC's reformed Common Agricultural Policy (CAP) by defining support linked to production as a key instrument of agricultural policy.[14] For a more market-based agricultural sector in Turkey, particular attention is needed in technology transfer, irrigation, land consolidation, competition, financing, and easing the social costs of adjustment.[15]

In 2004, the Agricultural Producer Unions Law (No. 5200) came into effect with the objective of improving farmers organizations. The Agricultural Insurances Law (No. 5363) was enacted, in 2005, to protect farmers and their production levels against risks. The closing of the General Directorate of Rural Services, in 2005, brought about the need for additional measures to, *inter alia*, implement land consolidation, drainage, soil protection, and ground water irrigation investment.[16]

The largest purchasing agencies, e.g. the Turkish Grain Board (TMO), the Turkish Sugar Factories Corporation (TSFAS), the Directorate-General for Tea Enterprises (CAYKUR), and the tobacco company TEKEL, are still state-owned. TEKEL is in the privatization portfolio (Chapter III(4)(ii)). In 2002, most administered prices were abolished. However, these agencies

[10] Targeted price cuts were as large as 20-30% for most products. Intervention prices were to be reduced by 45% for wheat, the main commodity, within two years (WTO, 2003).

[11] The cultivated areas for hazelnuts and tobacco are to decrease by about 16,000 ha and 9,000 ha, respectively. The hazelnut and tobacco programmes are to be discontinued by the end of 2007. Funding for transition payments to help farmers switch from some commodities was fixed at YTL 298 million for 2001-05 (OECD, 2005a).

[12] The regions are: Seyfe Lake; Kovada Lake Canal Area; Sultan Marshes; and Eregli Marshes. CATAK started in 2006 as a pilot study. As of December 2006, about US$540,000 had been disbursed on CATAK of ARIP loan funds.

[13] MARA Agriculture Strategy Paper 2006-10 (No. 2004/92 of 2004).

[14] European Commission (2006).

[15] OECD (2006b), p. 189.

[16] State Planning Organization (2006).

continue to set prices before the purchasing campaign[17]; during 2003-04, purchase prices increased by around 23% for white barley, and 14% for wheat (white and red Anatolian), well above the inflation rate. According to the authorities, in the following years the purchase prices increased in line with the inflation rate.

Farmers still benefit from loans extended at concessional rates. A credit arrangement in the form of a revolving fund at an interest rate of 13.125% can be used by the Agricultural Sales Co-operatives (ASC) and their Unions (ASCU) to purchase selected crops and cereals from producers. The overall amount of the fund is around YTL 640 million (including the extended credits). The loans are channelled through the state-owned Ziraat Bank (for hazelnuts, cotton, sunflower seeds, figs, raisins, olives, and olive oil, etc.). In addition, Ziraat Bank extends credit facilities for fisheries and forestry activities.

In 2004, 26,168 ha of the area covered by irrigation schemes operated by the State Hydraulic Works (DSI) was transferred to farmers' cooperatives and water users' associations, which now manage over 40% of the total irrigated area.[18] Farmers on the DIS payment register also receive a "diesel payment" per ha (to a maximum of 50 ha) to cover 35% of the country average farmers' consumption of fuel (80 litres/ha).[19] Farmers also receive an area-based payment for fertilizer. Electrical power used in agriculture (including by poultry producers and for aquaculture) is no longer subsidized. Overall, input subsidies fell from 30% of total agricultural subsidies in 1986-88 to less than 2% in 2003-05.[20]

Pruning and premium payments (per kg) to tea growers were introduced in 2005.[21] The a tea leaf price premium is paid to tea producers whose fields are licensed; the pruning payment based on the average yield, is to compensate for 70% of the loss of farmers' income due to to trimming (pruning) of tea fields. In 2006, pruning and premium payments amounted to YTL 39 million and YTL 82 million, respectively. In 2004, a total of YTL 4 million of compensatory payments were granted for the first time to sugar beet growers for losses associated with the production quota, which has been at 2.2 million tonnes since 2002.[22] A price premium for meat producers was granted for the first time in 2004.

Livestock incentive payments, such as the artificial insemination premium and milk incentive premium, are paid to farmers to, *inter alia*, support livestock production, raise product quality, upgrade technology, improve food safety conditions, and offer consumers better quality products. On artificial insemination, YTL 15.8 million in 2005 and YTL 25.4 million in 2006 were paid. The milk incentive premium reached YTL 115.7 million in 2005 and YTL 161.7 million in 2006.

---

[17] TMO, for example, is responsible for intervention purchases, and sets minimum purchase prices for cereals.

[18] Users pay an annual lump sum (negligible fee) for the operation and maintenance of irrigation schemes by the DSI.

[19] During 2003-05, farmers received YTL 39/ha as diesel payment. In 2006, no diesel payment was made, while in 2007 payments varied according to products. YTL 54/ha was paid for oily and seedy plants; YTL 28.8/ha for cereals, feeding plants, leguminous and lumpy plants; and YTL 18/ha for vegetables, fruits, special forests, fields, and meadows.

[20] OECD (2006b).

[21] Pruning payments are made under Decision of the Council of Ministers No. 5096, published in the *Official Gazette* of 27 December 1993, amended by Decree Law No. 7758 of 23 August 2004. According to Articles 2 and 3 of the Decree Law, licensed tea gardens are subject to pruning for 7 years (in ratio of 1/7 of the tea garden each year), to produce qualified tea leaves in compliance with maintenance and leaf production techniques. The premium payment is decided each year through decisions of the Council of Ministers.

[22] To receive this payment, sugar beet growers must grow certain crops (OECD, 2005a).

Deficiency payments (i.e. a price support) are granted for several agricultural products, for example, olive oil, cotton, oilseeds, wheat, and canola.[23] In addition, direct payments are given to producers of, *inter alia*, silk cocoon and mohair.

Turkey's WTO commitments on export subsidies include 44 agricultural product groups.[24] Export subsidies are set at 10% to 20% of the export values, on 14% and 100% of exports of eligible products (Table IV.2). Since Turkey's last TPR, export subsidies have been eliminated for potatoes and onions (dried), and introduced for honey and edible offal of poultry (Chapter III(3)(iv)). According to the authorities, the main policy objective regarding export subsidies is to develop Turkey's export potential in processed agricultural products.

Table IV.2
Export subsidies by agricultural product, 2007

Product	Rate (US$/tonne)	Share of exported quantity eligible for the subsidy (%)
Cut flowers (fresh)	205	37
Vegetables, frozen (exc. potatoes)	79	27
Vegetables (dehydrated)	370	20
Fruits (frozen)	78	41
Preserves, pastes	75	51
Honey	65	32
Homogenized fruit preparations	63	35
Fruit juices (concentrated)	150	15
Olive oil	125	100
Prepared or preserved fish	200	100
Meat of poultry (excl. edible offals)	186	14
Preserved poultry meat products	250	40
Eggs	US$15/1,000 pieces	78
Chocolate and other food preparations containing chocolate	119	48
Biscuits, waffles	119	18
Macaroni vermicelli	66	32

Source: WTO document G/SCM/N/123/TUR/Add.1, 26 January 2006, and Decree No. 1/2007.

Exporters must present relevant documents to the Exporters Associations authorized by the Undersecretariat of Foreign Trade (UFT) for refund application (e.g. customs declaration, invoice). Products must leave the customs territory of Turkey within the implementation period of the Decree, which is published annually or for a specific time period. Products must be of Turkish

[23] Deficiency payments are the difference between production costs and market price.

[24] **Due to budgetary restraints, Turkey generally gives export refunds only to 16 products/ product groups: cut flowers, frozen vegetables, dehydrated vegetables, frozen fruit, preserved vegetables and fruit, tomato paste, honey, homogenized fruit preparations, fruit juice, olives and olive oil, prepared or preserved fish, poultry meat, eggs, preserved poultry meat products, chocolate and other food preparations containing chocolate, biscuits, waffles, pasta.**

origin. Export refunds are not differentiated on the basis of destinations. The products must have sound and marketable quality to be eligible for the export refund: if the exported products are returned to Turkey or rejected by importing countries for any reason the refunds are taken back.[25]

According to the OECD, producer subsidy equivalents (PSEs), which capture the annual value of transfers under agricultural policies, as percentages of total value of production, rose from 16% in 1986-88 to 26% in 2003-05; the implicit tax on consumers, as measured by consumer subsidy equivalents (CSEs), which indicate the annual value of transfers to consumers under agricultural policies, also increased (in absolute value), from -16% in 1986-88 to -23% in 2003-05; while the general services subsidy equivalent (GSE), which estimates the annual monetary value of gross transfers to general services provided to agriculture (e.g. research, infrastructure, inspection, and marketing and promotion), decreased to 9% in 2003-05 from 10% in 1986-88.[26] The total support to agriculture (TSE), as a percentage of GDP, increased from 4% during 1986-88 to 4.2% in 2003-05; after peaking at 5.1% in 2003, it decreased to 3.8% in 2005 (Table IV.3).[27]

Table IV.3
Transfers associated with agricultural policies, 1986-88, and 2003-05

		1986-88	2003-05	2003	2004	2005[a]
PSE	€ million US$ million (%)[b]	2,873 3,169 16	9,593 11,550 26	9,862 11,142 28	9,055 11,250 25	9,862 12,257 25
CSE	€ million US$ million (%)[c]	-2,224 -2,446 -16	-7,152 -8,593 -23	-7,825 -8,840 -26	-6,395 -7,946 -21	-7,237 -8,994 -21
GSE	€ million US$ million (%)[d]	277 309 10	916 1,105 9	871 984 8	534 664 6	1,341 1,667 12
Total transfers [e]	€ million US$ million (% of GDP)	3,149 3,478 4.0	10,509 12,655 4.2	10,734 12,126 5.1	9,589 11,914 3.9	11,203 13,924 3.8

[25] Decree No. 2007/1 (Export Subsidy Programme for Agricultural Products), published in the *Official Gazette* of 22 March 2007, applies throughout 2007.

[26] The PSE estimate includes both transfers from consumers of agricultural products (through domestic market price support) and transfers from taxpayers (through budgetary or tax expenditures). The CSE, when negative, measures the implicit tax imposed on consumers by agricultural policy. The major component is market transfers due to market price support to production; it also includes other transfers such as subsidies to consumers from government budgets. Unlike the PSE and CSE, the GSE transfers are not received by producers or consumers individually, and do not directly affect farm receipts (revenue) or consumption expenditure, although they affect the production and consumption of agricultural products (OECD, undated).

[27] TSE is an indicator of the monetary value of all gross transfers from taxpayers and consumers arising from policy measures that support agriculture, net of the associated budgetary receipts. When expressed as a percentage of GDP, it gives an indication of the burden this overall support represents for the economy.

Memo item: Total transfers for all OECD countries	€ million US$ million (% of GDP)	276,039 303,771 2.3	308,139 371,243 1.1	309,969 350,183 1.1	304,464 378,281 1.1	309,983 385,264 1.1

a Provisional.
b PSE as a percentage of total value of production (valued at domestic producer prices), adjusted to include direct payments and to exclude levies on production.
c CSE as a percentage of total value of consumption (valued at domestic producer prices).
d GSE as a percentage of total transfers (valued at domestic producer prices).
e Total transfers are not the sum of PSE, CSE, and GSE; they cover the total value of production and include not only transfers to agriculture, as measured by the PSE, CSE, and GSE, but also other transfers associated with agricultural policies.

Source: OECD (2006), *Agricultural Policies in OECD Countries: At a Glance,* Paris.

Almost 100% of Turkey's producer support up to 2000 was aid that potentially has the most production distorting effects (market price support, payments based on output, and input subsidies), benefited mainly larger farms, and increased the pressure on the use of natural resources (such as water). This share fell to 83% in 2003-05 thus increasing the exposure of farmers to world market signals.[28]

All farmers are subject to the withholding tax at 2% on the sale value of livestock products, and 4% on the sale value of other agricultural products. When the agricultural product is sold through trading stocks, the withholding rates are halved. Export taxes still apply at the rate of US$0.04 per kg on unshelled hazelnuts and US$0.08 per kg on shelled hazelnuts.

Tariff protection for agriculture remains relatively high. The simple average MFN tariff in agriculture (Major Division 1 of ISIC Revision 2) is 28.3% (up from 25% in 2003, partly due to the increase in the tariffs on grains and vegetable oils). Imports of agricultural products, such as live animals for breeding purposes are duty free. Tariff rates on some processed meat products range up to 225%, while some dairy products (e.g. buttermilk, and cream) carry duties up to 170% (Table AIV.1). Moreover, the specific, compound, and variable duties apply mainly to agricultural products (Chapter III(2)(iii)(b)).

In the Uruguay Round, Turkey undertook to reduce its budgetary outlays for export subsidies for 44 products (at the HS four-digit level) by 24%, and the volume of subsidized exports by 14% in equal instalments over a ten-year period starting in 1995. Turkey did not make any commitments to cut financial support to agricultural producers because the authorities estimated that support – as measured by the Aggregate Measurement of Support (AMS) - was below the de minimis level of 10%, for which no reduction commitments were required.[29]

[28] Prices received by farmers in 2003-05 were about 32% higher than those in the world market (OECD, 2006a).

[29] The main difference between the AMS and the PSE is that price differences in the AMS calculations are estimated by reference to domestic administered prices and not actual producer prices. Moreover, the AMS fixes the external reference prices at the average levels of the 1986-88 base period, and certain budgetary transfers are included in the PSE but not in the AMS.

Some Members have raised concerns in the WTO Committee on Agriculture about Turkey's new import regime for rice[30]; and issues related to the 2005 and 2006 tariff rate schedules published in the Turkish *Official Gazette*.[31] Turkey has been increasingly challenged on animal disease control measures over the last few years (Chapter III(2)(vi)(d)).

At the regional level, in addition to non-agricultural products, Turkey and the EC have agreed to work towards bilateral free-trade in agricultural goods (Chapter II(3)(ii)(a)). In line with the CUD, processed agricultural products imported into Turkey from the EC are subject to customs duties comprising an industrial and an agricultural component: all industrial components enjoy duty-free treatment and customs duties applicable to agricultural components are below MFN rates[32]; a group of processed agricultural products are subject to zero duty but under quota. The limited coverage of agricultural products under the preferential regime with the EC and under Turkey's other bilateral agreements delays their exposure to greater competition: the products are generally subject to preferential tariff quotas (Chapter III(2)(iii)(e)).

MINING AND ENERGY

The mining and quarrying sector contributed 1.1% to real GNP in 2006 (1.2% in 2002). Turkey has limited reserves of oil and natural gas, but significant proven reserves of lignite, as well as borax, boron, chromite, magnesite, and marble. Renewable combustibles, particularly wood, and the country's water courses are also important indigenous energy resources. The public sector accounts for almost 70% of value added in the mining subsector, while the private sector has increased its role in energy asset management and operations, especially in the generation segment of the electricity market. Local production of energy in Turkey meets approximately 29% of demand.[33]

There have been no major changes to the institutional framework in the mining subsector. Policy issues related to energy and mining are the responsibility of the Ministry of Energy and Natural Resources (MENR), whereas matters related to quarrying are under the Ministry of Interior. The General Directorate of Mining Affairs (GDMA) is responsible for administering the Mining Law on behalf of the MENR, while the Energy Market Regulatory Authority (EMRA) has been the energy market regulator since 2001.[34] The Undersecretariat of State Planning Organization (SPO) evaluates Turkey's general energy needs. Several public institutions are engaged in mining and energy activities, which causes inefficient coordination within the sector, and sometimes makes it difficult to solve problems.[35] However, agencies with responsibility for the sector are liaising, with a view to improving coordination and efficiency.

[30] WTO documents G/AG/R/39 of 16 July 2004; G/AG/R/41 of 17 February 2005; G/AG/R/42 of 25 May 2005; and G/AG/R/44 of 25 November 2005.

[31] WTO document G/AG/R/46, 11 July 2006.

[32] The agricultural component of each good is calculated by multiplying the quantity of primary agriculture products used in processing, according to an agreed set of ratios, by a specific rate charge (basic amount).

[33] Ministry of Energy and Natural Resources online information. Viewed at: http://www.enerji.gov.tr/belge/butce.doc [14 August 2007].

[34] EMRA is in charge of preparing and implementing secondary legislation (e.g. regulations); authorizing market participants by granting licences; approving and publishing tariffs; monitoring and supervising market participants; conducting technical, legal, and financial audits; settling disputes; approving, amending, and enforcing performance standards; and applying sanctions where necessary.

[35] WTO (2003).

Customs tariffs average 0.3% in mining and quarrying (Major Division 2 of ISIC Revision 2), and range from zero on, *inter alia*, sulphur, ores and concentrates, coal, lignite, crude petroleum, natural diamonds and precious stones, to 20% on salt and pure sodium chloride (HS 250100). Imports of electricity are duty free. However, 18% VAT is charged on electricity.

A 0.05% service commission is paid to the Exporters Union for electricity exports realized by TETAS.

MINING

Turkey has a diverse and dynamic mining subsector. Excluding petroleum and coal, it is estimated that there are over 4,400 mineral deposits in Turkey[36], and approximately 77 economically exploitable minerals.[37] In 2005, 53 different minerals were produced.[38] Turkey possesses two thirds of the world's boron reserves, and is the largest producer of boron ore[39]; 6% of the world's chromite reserves; and 40% of world's marble reserves. Known mineral reserves in Turkey are valued at approximately US$2 trillion.[40] During 2003-2004, 1,136 new mining and quarrying companies were established.[41] Mining exports grew by an average of 31% during 2002-06, and constituted 2.4% of Turkey's total merchandise exports in 2006.[42]

Turkey's main objectives in mining are to produce competitive and safe raw materials, and to increase value added by processing. Under Turkish law, "underground resources" are subject to the exclusive ownership and disposition of the State and are not considered as a part of the land where they are located. The State may issue licences to private entities for exploration and operation of mines for specific periods and purposes; royalties must be paid to the State.

Turkey has undertaken a series of reforms in the mining subsector. In 2003, the Parliament enacted a new foreign investment law to encourage both local and foreign investment, including in mining.[43] Foreigners may invest in the mining subsector only through locally incorporated companies (Chapter II(4)). However, exploration and exploitation of baron, uranium and thorium are reserved for the Government.

---

[36] Undersecretariat for the Prime Ministry for Foreign Trade. Viewed at: http://www.igeme.org.tr/eng/turkey/industry.pdf [13 June 2007].

[37] Istanbul Technical University. Viewed at: http://www.humboldt-foundation.de/de/netzwerk/veranstalt/hoersaal/2006_istanbul/oenal.pdf [15 June 2007].

[38] Undersecretariat for the Prime Ministry for Foreign Trade. Viewed at: http://www.igeme.org.tr/eng/turkey/industry.pdf [14 June 2007].

[39] United States Geological Survey report on boron production in the United States. Viewed at: http://minerals.usgs.gov/minerals/pubs/commodity/boron/boronmcs07.pdf [13 June 2007].

[40] Undersecretariat for the Prime Ministry for Foreign Trade. Viewed at: http://www.igeme.org.tr/eng/turkey/industry.pdf [15 June 2007].

[41] Report on the mineral industry of Turkey by the United States Geological Survey for 2003-05. Viewed at: http://minerals.usgs.gov/minerals/pubs/country/2003/tumyb03.pdf ; http://minerals.usgs.gov/minerals/pubs/country/2004/tumyb04.pdf; and http://minerals.usgs.gov/minerals/pubs/country/2005/tumyb05.pdf.

[42] Undersecretariat for the Prime Ministry for Foreign Trade. Viewed at: http://www.igeme.org.tr/introeng.htm.

[43] Undersecretariat of State Planning Organization (2006).

Turkey made several changes to its mining regime, through Mining Law No. 5177 of 2004, which amended Mining Law No. 3213 of 1985. Law No. 5177 categorizes minerals into five groups: (i) sand and gravel; (ii) marble and other similar decorative stones; (iii) salts in solution form that can be obtained from sea, lake, and spring waters; (iv) energy, metal, and industrial minerals; and (v) semi-precious stones and gemstones.

Mining activities are regulated by the GDMA, which also issues mining licences. There are three types of licence: exploration licence/certificate; operation licence; and operation permit. Exploration licences are valid for three years. Mining Licences (or "certificates" for V minerals) may be granted to Turkish nationals or to any foreign company established in Turkey, as they are considered Turkish companies. Prior to the expiry of the exploration licence, the holder must obtain an operation licence: this licence may be granted for periods of five years for certain categories of minerals, and no less than ten years in the case of others, although these terms may be extended. Holders of exploration licences are also obliged to obtain operation permits from the GDMA. Once granted, companies have up to one year to commence mining operations, failing which they are subject to payment of a royalty of 10% of the annual production amount declared in the initial application, for each year of non-operation. Operation licences confer the legal right to use the licensed area, whereas operation permits are evidence of permission to operate a mine. Permits are valid for the same period as licences.[44]

All activities in the subsector are subject to environmental control by the Ministry of Environment and Forestry. Depending on the location of the activities, permission may be required from the Ministries of Health, of Agriculture and Rural Affairs, of Culture and Tourism. Law No. 5177 establishes different royalties for different categories of mineral exploitation.[45] The State's rights over produced minerals are: 4% of the ex-mine sales amount for mineral groups (i) and (v), and for any kind of materials used in construction (such as cover stone), rough construction work, dams, ponds, seaports and roads; and 2% for other groups of minerals. For mining companies that use the ore they produce in their processing activities, the royalty calculation takes into account the amount of ore processed (through a flat 50% royalty reduction). Where mining activities are within state-owned land, licence holders must pay an additional 30% royalty since they will not have to pay to lease state-owned property for mining activities.

In 1985, a Mining Fund was established (Article 34 of Law No. 3213) under the supervision of the MENR to provide financial credits for exploration, technical research, development, project preparation, installation, construction, production, and export activities. The Mining Fund is still in operation, but no new resources are allocated to it; the Fund is only financed under the general budget.[46] Five schemes currently provide credits at well below market rates (Table IV.4).

Table IV.4
Credit schemes, 2007

Scheme	General features	Nominal interest rate
Mine research and development	Maximum three-year credit; no repayment on principal for the first year; amounts cannot exceed 50% of expenditure on exploration and definition of mineral reserves and other properties in the permitted area. If the exploration is done by the	11%

[44] A mining licence may be transferred to those qualified under Law No. 5177 of 2004, and the transfer must be registered at the GDMA (Onder, 2006).
[45] In general, the rate is 4% for the first and fifth groups of minerals, and 2% for the remaining groups (Onder, 2006).
[46] Law No. 5177, and Communiqué of 14 June 2002 published in the *Official Gazette* No. 24785.

Scheme	General features	Nominal interest rate
	General Directorate of Mineral Research and Exploration the amount of the credit can cover 75% of expenditure	
Installations, enlargement, and development	Maximum five-year credit; no repayment on principal for the first two years; amount is proportional to self-source rate; and cannot exceed 50% in normal circumstances. If an incentive certificate is granted it cannot exceed 60%. Credit covers expenditure on expansion of facility, enlargement and renovation investment, and infrastructure in the permitted area	13%
Management (operating) credit	Maximum three-year credit; cannot exceed the working capital; no repayment on principal for the first year	15%
Exports		20%
(i) Export credit	One-year credit; 50% of total expenditure to meet the needs of production and exports (excluding the costs of transportation) of the mineral	13%
(ii) Letter of credit or export certificate credit	Six-month credit period; maximum 50% of the letter of credit; the credit is to supply the finance until the export of the mineral	13%
Stock credit	Maximum 20-40% of the stock cost for minerals produced and prepared	25%
(i) Export stock credit	Maximum 40% of the stock cost for minerals produced and prepared	13%
(ii) Domestic stock credit	Maximum 20% of the stock cost for minerals produced and prepared for domestic consumption	15%

Note: All credits require a bank guarantee letter covering 1.3 times the credit amount.

Source: WTO Secretariat, based on information provided by the Turkish authorities.

ENERGY

Turkey's energy market is among the fastest growing in the world: total primary energy consumption reached 92.6 million tonnes of oil equivalent (toe) at the end of 2006, and is expected to rise to 126 million toe in 2010, and 222 million toe in 2020. According to the authorities, Turkey's energy import dependency is around 71%, with oil representing 46% of total net energy imports, followed by gas (37%), and coal (16%). Domestic production meets 29% of demand. FDI needs in the subsector are estimated at about US$4.5 billion per year until 2010.[47] Electricity demand in Turkey amounted to 174.6 GWH in 2006, and is expected by the authorities to reach between 406 and 499 GWH by 2020.

The main objective of Turkey's energy policy is to ensure supply security. In addition, the authorities aim to, *inter alia*, reform and liberalize the subsector to make it more productive, efficient, and transparent; exploit local energy resources in a sustainable and environment-friendly manner (including from new and renewable sources); reduce public transfers to the SOEs

[47] WTO (2003).

operating in the subsector; and take advantage of the country's geopolitical location to make it a pivotal transit area for international oil and gas trade (East-West energy corridor).[48]

Various SOEs continue to dominate the subsector, including Electricity Generation Company (EUAS), local distribution companies owned by Turkish Electricity Distribution Company (TEDAS), Turkish Electricity Transmission Corporation (TEIAS). Turkish Electricity Trading and Contracting Company (TETAS), Turkish Petroleum Company (TPAO), and Petroleum Pipeline Corporation (BOTAS) (Table IV.5). Some of these companies are in the privatization portfolio, and others have been privatized during the last few years, such as Petrol Ofisi (POAS), Turkey's major petroleum retailer, and the Turkish Petroleum Refinery Corporation (TÜPRAŞ), a monopoly in the petroleum refinery subsector (Chapter III(4)(ii)).

Table IV.5
Selected state intervention in the energy sector, 2007

State-economic enterprise	Market share	Price regulation	Other
Oil & Gas			
Turkish Petroleum Corporation (TPAO): production, exploration, drilling, natural gas storage, pipelines, oil trade and transportation (TPIC-TPAO subsidiary)	Produces 70 % of Turkish oil; owns and operates 18 out of 36 gas fields	Price of crude oil is set in accordance with Article 3/25(a) of Petroleum Law No. 6326 and Petroleum Market Law No. 5015	Oil producers may only export up to 35% of crude oil production onshore and 45% off-shore
Petroleum Pipeline Corporation (BOTAS): natural gas import, transportation, sale and crude oil transportation According to the Natural Gas Market Law, private sector has the right to be involved in the natural gas market activities, and unbundling of BOTAŞ for the above-mentioned activities is foreseen	The monopoly of BOTAS was abolished by the Natural Gas Market Law	Article 11 of Law No. 4646 the types of tariff are: connection; transmission and supervision of conveyance; storage; wholesale; and retail sale to be determined by EMRA. Currently all tariffs (except the CNG sale tariffs) are approved by EMRA until sufficient competition is in place. All tariffs are in the form of price ceilings	
Coal			
Turkish Hardcoal Enterprises (TTK): hard coal	Sole producer of hard coal	Prices set by TTK	Heavily subsidized

[48] Turkey has given priority mainly to two pipeline projects: the Baku-Tbilisi-Ceyhan Crude Oil Pipeline (involving Azerbaijan and Georgia), which was finished in 2006 and can transport 50 million tonnes of oil annually (its first tanker was loaded on 4 June 2006); and the Baku-Tbilisi-Erzurum Natural Gas Pipeline, for regional cooperation in the supply of fuel, which will have capacity to transport 20 billion cubic meters per year. In addition, Turkey has projects under way with other countries, such as the Turkey-Bulgaria-Romania-Hungary-Austria Natural Gas Pipeline (Nabuco); and the South Caucasus Pipeline.

Electricity Generating Corporation (EUAS)[a]	Produces 26% of Turkish lignite	Prices set by EUAS	
Turkish Coal Enterprises (TKI): lignite	Produces 45.8% of Turkish lignite	Prices set by TKI	
Electricity			
Electricity Generating Corporation (EUAS)	Owns 58.5 % of installed electricity capacity	Prices set by EUAS	Private sector may participate in all segments of the market, except for transmission, by obtaining licences from EMRA. Privatization of generation is also on the agenda
Turkish Electricity Transmission Corporation (TEIAS)	Owns and operates the transmission system and also acts as market operator	Methodologies are derived and tariffs are calculated according to the Electricity Market Tariffs Regulation and the related communiqués, and are submitted to EMRA for approval	TEIAS will remain as the sole transmission system operator and asset owner in the long-run
Turkish Electricity Trading and Contracting Corporation (TETAS)	In charge of trading and wholesale of less than 50% of total generation	TETAS submits tariff wholesale price proposals to EMRA for approval	TETAS took over all the public sector purchasing obligations of the previous regime. TETAS may neither sell to new consumers nor sign any new PPAs except for obligations as stated in the EML; its role is intended to diminish over time, once the cost burden is mitigated
20 state-owned, regional distribution companies formed by the restructuring of Turkish Electricity Distribution Corporation (TEDAS), and one private regional distribution company	TEDAS owns the distribution system but distribution and retail sales are undertaken by regional distribution companies	Regional distribution companies submit distribution and retail tariff proposals and the methodologies to EMRA for approval	Privatization of distribution is also on the agenda

a Excluding private companies' production in EUAS's mining field.

Source: WTO Secretariat, based on information provided by the Turkish authorities.

Five new laws have been enacted in the subsector during the review period: (i) Petroleum Market Law (No. 5015), passed by Parliament in December 2003, aims to remove state controls in the subsector, liberalize prices (and domestic content purchase requirements) of oil and oil products, end restrictions on vertical integration, and integrate pipeline, refining, and distribution functions; (ii) Liquefied Petroleum Gas (LPG) Market Law (No. 5307), adopted on 2 March 2005, arranges the supply, distribution, transportation, storage and trade of LPG; (iii) Law on the Utilization of Renewable Energy Sources for the Purpose of Generating Electrical Energy (No. 5346), which came into force on 18 May 2005, promotes and provides for generation of electricity from renewable sources[49]; (iv) Energy Efficiency Law (No. 5627), which came into force on 2 May 2007, aims to encourage the efficient use of energy[50]; and (v) the Law on Geothermal Resources and Natural Mineral Waters (No. 5686), adopted on 13 June 2007, aims to encourage exploration, research, development, and production of geothermal and natural mineral water resources in an environment-friendly manner.

Licences related to exports and imports of electricity, LPG, and natural gas are regulated under Laws Nos. 4628, 5307, and 4646, respectively, and secondary legislation enacted by the EMRA. A licence is also required under Law No. 5015 in order to import petroleum, solvent, and some petroleum products. In the electricity market, licences are issued for up to 49 years, with a minimum term of 10 years, for generation, transmission, and distribution; natural gas market licences are for a minimum of 10 and a maximum of 30 years.[51] Exports of electricity to countries that fulfil the international interconnection requirement are conducted by wholesale licensees, provided it is so stated in their licence. The wholesale licence fees are announced by the EMRA Board annually. For 2007, they are: the electricity market one-time wholesale licence fee of YTL 250,000, plus an annual licence fee of YKr 0.003 per kWh sold[52]; the natural gas wholesale licence fee of YTL 50,000, plus annual licence fee of YKr 0.0005 per kWh sold; the natural gas import licence fee of YTL 75,000, plus annual licence fee of YKr 0.0005 per kWh imported; the natural gas export licence fee of YTL 10,000, and the annual licence fee per kWh exported which is currently zero.

High electricity losses, including theft, have continued over the last few years despite some reductions.[53] The lack of adequate investment, together with large energy wastage, is also becoming a serious problem, and may cause power shortages. Increasing the country's electricity generating capacity continues to be a top priority for the Government, which is turning to the private sector for new investment and restructuring of the subsector. Twelve combined-cycle natural gas power projects, with a total capacity of almost 14,000 MW, are in operation. The operating rights of one thermal power plant and one hydro-power plant have been transferred to the private sector for 20 years and 26 years, respectively. Turkey has announced plans to construct a nuclear power generation plant with a capacity of 5,000 MW by 2015.[54]

---

[49] Under Law No. 5346, EMRA grants a renewable energy resource certificate (RER Certificate), which entitles certain facilities to benefit from the incentives provided by the Law. Wind, solar, geothermal, biomass, biogas, wave, current, and tidal energy resources, together with hydraulic generation plants with a reservoir area of less than 15 square kilometres, are defined as renewable energy resources. Large hydro power plants are also considered as renewable source, but are not included in the support mechanism of the Law.
[50] The other laws pertaining to the energy market are: Electricity Market Law (No. 4628), published in the *Official Gazette* of 3 March 2001; and Natural Gas Market Law (No. 4646), published in the *Official Gazette* of 2 May 2001 (see WTO, 2003).
[51] The licences may be renewed provided that the licensees meet the requirements set out in the laws and secondary legislation.
[52] YKr = 0.01 YTL.
[53] According to the authorities, electricity losses decreased by 17.8% in 2005 and by 15.1% in 2006.
[54] European Commission (2006).

POLICY BY TYPE OF PRODUCT

Oil and natural gas

There are two major SOEs in the oil and natural gas subsector: BOTAS and TPAO. BOTAS is to be split into three SOEs after the year 2009: the one responsible for trading, and the one for storage will be privatized; the one for transmission will not. The two local distributors (ESGAZ and BURSAGAZ), owned by BOTAS, were first corporatized and then privatized in 2004. Under Law No. 4646, and as from 2003, BOTAS has been required to commence tenders to transfer its existing natural gas purchase and sales contracts until its imports fall to 20% of total annual consumption.[55] TÜPRAŞ, privatized on 26 January 2006, remains the only petroleum refining company, with four refineries and a total annual capacity of 27.6 million tonnes. There are 49 distribution companies.

Oil resources are owned by the State, which grants licences for exploration and production.[56] As of July 2007, there were 39 companies in the upstream oil subsector[57], and 107 petroleum and 36 gas fields: 67 of the petroleum fields and 18 of the gas fields are owned and operated by TPAO (responsible for 70% of domestic oil production). Recently, TPAO has also been involved in the storage of natural gas.[58] TPAO's offshore oil and natural gas explorations have increased over the last few years, especially in the Black Sea, including with foreign shareholders (e.g. Petrobras and Chevron).

As in some other members of the International Energy Agency, a stock agency is to be set up to maintain sufficient emergency supply of oil.[59] Under Article 16 of Law No. 5015, the petroleum stock must be equivalent to 90 days of the previous year's net average imports. Distribution and refinery companies are also obliged to hold stocks equivalent to at least 20 days' supply, while big eligible consumers that consume 20,000 tonnes or more of liquid fuel each year, must keep a stock equivalent to 15 days of their consumption (considered as a part of the national petroleum stock).[60] The remainder of the national petroleum stock must be retained by refining undertakings. According to the authorities, price caps are set by EMRA for all products in the subsector and retailers are free to set their prices accordingly. In the natural gas market, all tariffs, except compressed natural gas sale tariffs, are approved by EMRA until there is sufficient competition.

Foreign enterprises may invest in marketing and sales activities without restriction in the oil and natural gas subsector. Companies controlled or owned by foreign States may invest in upstream activities only with the permission of the Council of Ministers.[61] Approval by the EMRA Board is

[55] The first contract release tender was launched on 30 November 2005 and was approved by BOTAS on 30 November 2006; 4 billion cubic meters (bcm) were tendered to four different companies. One of these four companies obtained an import licence from EMRA in July 2007.
[56] To accelerate oil and gas exploration activities, a draft Petroleum Law has been submitted to Parliament.
[57] Oil reserves are located mainly in the south-east of Turkey and Thrace.
[58] Turkey's first underground natural gas facility with a capacity of 2 bcm began operations in July 2007.
[59] For this purpose, a draft National Petroleum Stock Agency Law is being prepared (State Planning Organization, 2006).
[60] An eligible consumer is a licensed consumer whose annual petroleum consumption is more than a threshold set by EMRA, and not less than 5,000 tonnes of fuel oil, heating fuel and diesel per year.
[61] Article 12 of Law No. 6326.

required for investment in refining, transportation through pipelines, and storage.[62] Licences on all petroleum activities are issued by EMRA.[63] Currently, EMRA is processing some private refinery licence applications; however, the places of the refineries have not yet been determined.

EMRA conducts tendering for natural gas distribution. A separate licence is required for each market activity (e.g. wholesale, distribution, import, export, storage), and, where the activity is conducted in more than one facility, for each facility. Since licensing application began in November 2002, 155 licences have been granted for natural gas activities (to August 2007).

Coal

Two main SOEs, the Turkish Lignite Enterprises (TKI), and Turkish Hardcoal Enterprises (TTK), continue to dominate the coal subsector.[64] In the brown coal industry, TKI produces around 46% of all lignite in Turkey, while TTK has a *de facto* monopoly in hard coal production, processing, and distribution. These SOEs set the domestic prices of hard coal and lignite, taking into account world prices. The Government may influence the prices for social and economic reasons. The prices do not allow TTK to recover its costs; it has been operating at a steady loss, whereas TKI became profitable in 1995.

Total financial transfers from the Turkish Treasury to TTK amounted to YTL 571 million in 2006; TKI has not received any direct subsidies since 1995. Since 1993, the Government has aimed to increase productivity and reduce overstaffing in the coal subsector. TTK and TKI are not in the privatization portfolio, but the Government is considering privatization in the medium to long term. So far, only the Cayirhan power plant has been privatized, through a transfer of operating rights (TOOR) procedure. Nonetheless, steps have been taken towards privatization.[65]

Electricity

In 2001, TEAS, a vertically integrated, state-owned undertaking, was unbundled into three companies responsible for different segments of the business: EUAS for generation, TEIAS for transmission, and TETAS for wholesale trade. Regional distribution companies, formed by the restructuring of the Turkish Electricity Distribution Company (TEDAS), are in charge of distribution and retail sales to customers. TEDAS owns distribution assets, while the operating rights for these assets were transferred to regional distribution companies.[66] TEIAS is the sole transmission system operator and is responsible for market operations. Since the mid 1990s, direct private participation has been allowed in all segments (except transmission). With the adoption of Law No. 4628, the regime for private participation shifted from a based concessions-system to bilateral contracts between parties, with a dispute settlement mechanism.

Contracts remaining from the previous regime are of build-operate-transfer, transfers-of-operating-rights, and build-operate-own types. They are for 15-20 years and are subject to power purchase agreements on predetermined quantities and price formula, with the Treasury's

[62] Some of the main private companies operating in the subsector are TUPRAS, Petrol Ofisi, BP, Shell, Total, Opet, and Aygaz.
[63] In 2006, EMRA issued a licence to a private company through a Decree of the Council of Ministers of 10 April 2006.
[64] Turkish brown coal has a low calorific value and a high sulphur, dust, and ash content.
[65] For example, more than 65% of the surface mining preparations in TKI are done by private firms.
[66] TEDAS supplied 73.1% of Turkey's total electricity consumption in 2006, and 78.2% during January-July 2007 (TEDAS, 2005).

guarantee.[67] The system has led to the accumulation of significant contingent liabilities, and implicit subsidization of an already inefficient subsector. TETAS has taken over all purchasing obligations arising from these contracts; benefits from low cost generation by EUAS were used to offset the cost burden.

Network tariffs and tariffs for "non-eligible customers", as well as TETAS's wholesale prices are regulated.[68] Under the Electricity Market Tariffs Regulation and the related communiqués, tariffs must be cost-reflective and calculated on the basis of predetermined methodologies; costs not directly related to market operations must not be taken into account. According to the authorities, cross-subsidies in electricity are allowed until 2010. In general, industrial consumers subsidize households, and Turkey's eastern regions are subsidized by other regions. Once determined by companies, regulated tariffs are subject to review and approval by the EMRA. All tariffs are published in the *Official Gazette* and on the EMRA's website to ensure transparency.

Electricity sale prices have not increased since October 2002[69], despite rising import prices for oil and gas. The consumer price of electricity is subject to four different levies: (i) 1% for the Energy Fund Share; (ii) 2% for Turkish Radio and Television Corporation surcharge; (iii) the aggregated amount of the two preceding levies is then subject to the Municipality Consumption Tax (5% for households and 1% for industrial users); and (iv) 18% VAT.

MANUFACTURING

MAIN FEATURES

Value added Turkey's manufacturing sector increased from US$15 billion in 1980 to around US$45 billion in 2004: the sector grew at an annual average rate of 7.9% during 2001-04 (up from 4.2% over 1990-00). The capacity utilization rate in manufacturing was 80.3% on average in 2005, the highest over the past ten years.[70] As a result, the sector accounted for 25.3% of real GNP in 2006 (24.7% in 2002), and employs about one fifth of formal labour. Private investors have gradually moved into more sophisticated areas, such as consumer electronics and the automotive industry. Some of the main problems facing the sector are: lack of qualified labour and technology; limited production capability in high value-added products; and insufficient investment in emerging subsectors.[71]

Over the last few years, the export structure of the Turkish manufacturing sector has changed somewhat (Table IV.6). Almost one third of Turkey's manufacturing value added is in the textiles and clothing, leather, food and beverages, and tobacco industries. Manufacturing exports account for about 80% of total merchandise exports; the EC and the Middle East are the main markets. Imports of manufactured products represent over 60% of total merchandise imports, and are concentrated in capital-intensive industries, such as machinery and transport equipment and chemicals (Chapter I(3)(i)).

---

[67] Installed capacity under these contracts amounts to 9,200 MW.
[68] Consumers with annual consumption above a threshold set by the Board, consumers purchasing natural gas for power generation, and local natural gas producers are considered as "eligible customers": they acquired the right to choose their suppliers. In 2007, the threshold for eligible elelctricity consumers was reduced to 3 GWh.
[69] TEDAS (2005).
[70] Ministry of Industry and Commerce (2006).
[71] State Planning Organization (2006).

Over the last few years, various state-owned manufacturing companies have been privatized or liquidated, including in some heavy industries (e.g. petroleum refineries, non-ferrous basic metals, chemicals, and iron and steel), while others are scheduled to be privatized soon, such as the tobacco company TEKEL (Chapter III(4)(ii)). Although FDI inflows in the manufacturing sector jumped from US$110 millions in 2002 to US$1,867 millions in 2006, the share of manufacturing in total FDI inflows went from 29% to 10.4% over the same period (Chapter I(3)). FDI inflows in the sector have been mostly allocated to the chemical, beverages and tobacco, electrical machinery, automotive, and textile industries.

Table IV.6
Structure of the manufacturing sector, 2002 and 2005
(% share)

	Production		Exports	
Technology intensity [a]	2002	2005[b]	2002	2005
High	5.1	6.3	6.2	6.0
Mid-high	18.2	25.3	24.3	28.5
Mid-low	26.7	27.0	22.8	26.9
Low	50.0	41.4	46.8	38.7
Total	100.0	100.0	100.0	100.0

a OECD science, technology and industry scoreboard classification is taken as reference.
b Forecasts at 2002 prices.

Source: State Planning Organization (2006), *Ninth Development Plan 2007-13,* Ankara.

POLICY DEVELOPMENTS

Turkey's main long-term objective in the manufacturing sector is to boost its competitiveness and productivity by, *inter alia*, reducing direct state intervention and privatizing SEEs; investing in technological development and innovation[72]; and supporting small and medium-sized enterprises (SMEs).[73] The Ministry of Industry and Trade (MIT), through the Public Agency for the Development of SMEs (KOSGEB), provides various services and support programmes (Chapter III(3)(iv)). Investment incentives are also granted under the Investment Encouragement Programme (IEP) (Chapter III(4)(i)).

The manufacturing sector is the main beneficiary of state aid to domestic producers. In 2006, the sector was granted 52% of total investment incentive certificates (against 65% in 2002): the majority were for textiles and clothing, followed by food and beverages.[74] The sector also receives a large part of duty concessions for exports as well as export credits and guarantees (Chapter III(3)(iv)).

MFN customs tariffs on manufactured goods (Major Division 3 of ISIC Revision 2) average 10.9%; the most tariff protected industry is food manufacturing (Chart IV.1). Specific tariffs are

[72] Technological development and innovation are among the most important components of the Turkish manufacturing policy. A strategic action plan has been set up to promote outward-oriented, technology-intensive, and high-value-added production (Ministry of Industry and Trade, 2006).
[73] SEEs account for around 5% of Turkey's GDP, and about 15% of the value added in the manufacturing sector (European Commission, 2006).
[74] Textiles and clothing, and food and beverages industries are dominated by SMEs: as a result, a relatively high number of incentive certificates are granted to these two subsectors despite their low investment costs.

levied on alcoholic beverages; mixed duties apply to, *inter alia*, carpets, glass and glassware products, and watches; and variable duties to certain manufactured goods, including sugar confectionary, chocolate, malt, and prepared potatoes (Chapter III(2)(iii)(b)). Subject to various incentive schemes (duty and tax concessions in particular), the tariff structure, with mixed escalation, does not encourage investment in certain industries for semi-finished goods, such as in chemical and plastic industries where there is negative escalation (Chapter III(2)(iii)(b)).

MFN tariff quotas for television tubes were opened in January 2007, but were eliminated on 30 June 2007 (Chapter III(2)(iv)). Import licensing applies to some manufactured products, such as motor vehicles, transmission apparatus, and chemicals. Under the CUD, Turkey has introduced quotas on certain textiles and clothing products (section (iii)(a) below). Turkey's anti-dumping measures have mostly affected textile and clothing, base metals, plastics and rubber, and other manufactures such as lighters and pencils (Chapter III(2)(v)(a)).

SELECTED INDUSTRIES

TEXTILES AND APPAREL

Although annual average growth in the textiles and apparel subsector during 2000-05 (1%) was significantly lower than the 5.4% registered by the manufacturing sector over the same period, the subsector still constitutes Turkey's largest industry. It accounts for 4.2% of GDP, 13.3% of manufacturing output, and employs about 22% of workers in manufacturing. A key factor behind the industry's successful performance is Turkey's ample supply of home-grown cotton: Turkey is the world's sixth largest producer of raw cotton. Other factors are the top quality of the raw cotton crops, low wage costs, skilled labour force, and the strong integration between the textiles and apparel industries. The subsector is dominated by the private sector, particularly SMEs. The MFN tariffs on textiles, wearing apparel, and leather products average 7.8%, with rates ranging up to 17%.

Textiles and clothing products contributed 22.7% to Turkey's total merchandise exports in 2006 (against 34.4% in 2002), and the composition of exports has continued to shift towards higher-value-added finished products and ready-made clothing. In 2004, Turkey ranked 4th among the largest apparel exporters in the world with a share of 4.3%, and 9th among textile exporters with a world share of 3.3%.[75] The EC has traditionally been Turkey's largest foreign market for both textiles and apparel, followed by the United States.[76] Over the last five years, about 56% of new spinning investments in the Turkish textile and apparel industry went to the Southeast Anatolia Project (GAP) Region. GAP is the most comprehensive regional development project ever attempted in Turkey; it aims, *inter alia*, to more than double raw cotton production once the project becomes operational.[77]

---

[75] Ministry of Industry and Commerce (2006).

[76] In 2005, Turkey was the EC's second largest supplier of textile and apparel products, with shares of 13.1% and 15.4%, respectively. Turkey was also the 11th and 19th supplier of textiles and apparel to the United States the same year.

[77] GAP covers the provinces of Adiyaman, Batman, Diyarbakir, Gaziantep, Kilis, Mardin, Siirt, Sanliurfa, and Sirnak. The cost of GAP is estimated at about US$32 billion and consists of developing and managing land and water resources for irrigation and for industrial and urban use; improving land use through crop design and agricultural practices; further developing agri-industries and other industries, mainly by relying on locally available resources; and improving social, education, and employment conditions to attract qualified manpower to the region.

The textiles, clothing, and leather industries do not receive any specific incentives. However, these industries are the second most important beneficiaries of the incentives provided under IEP, such as exemption from customs duties and fund levies on imported machinery and equipment; VAT exemption on imported and locally purchased machinery and equipment; and interest rate support in favour of investment projects (Chapter III(2)(iii)(c)).[78] In 2006, investment in the textiles and clothing industries accounted for 11.6% of the investment incentive certificates, down from 26.1% in 2002. Credit and guarantee programmes by Turk Eximbank are also among the more important incentives provided to textile and apparel investors (Chapter III(4)(i)).

The performance of the textiles and clothing industries has suffered from volatile domestic prices of raw cotton in the past few years.[79] To counter this problem, the private sector is working with the Government to establish a futures market in an attempt to stabilize these prices. Another problem for these industries, and many others in Turkey, is the frequent power cuts, as well as high prices for electricity by international comparison (section 3(iii)(b) above).

Under the WTO Agreement on Textiles and Clothing (ATC), Turkey notified that, as from 1 January 2005, it would have integrated all products not previously integrated into GATT 1994.[80] Turkey had retained its right to use the transitional safeguard mechanism under the provisions of the ATC (Article 6), but did not make use of it.[81] Turkey has been involved in the WTO dispute settlement mechanism regarding its restrictions on imports of textile and clothing products from Hong, Kong, China; India; and Thailand (Chapter II(3)(i)).

Turkey introduced import quotas on certain textiles and clothing products under the CUD. It applies quotas under the double checking system on 34 categories of product from Belarus with which an agreement has been reached; and under the single checking system on goods from countries with which an agreement has not been reached, i.e. the Democratic People's Republic of Korea (48 categories of products), Montenegro (12 categories), and Uzbekistan (2 categories). Moreover, Turkey has quotas on 44 categories of textiles and apparel products from China , for example, shirts, jerseys, T-shirts, and gloves.[82] Turkey does not auction its quotas; auctions would have transferred part of the economic "rent" gained by the quota holders to the Government as public revenues. Instead, the largest parts of the quotas are distributed among firms that exported the same category in the previous year; the remainder is allocated to new exporters of the category of goods.[83]

---

[78] The compensation on the interest rate is 5 percentage points for YTL credits, and 2 percentage points for foreign currency credits.

[79] Turkey is a net importer of raw cotton, with annual imports of about 50,000 tonnes and local production of 90,000 tonnes. During the last few years, world raw cotton prices have been very volatile, which has affected domestic cotton prices, and consequently the production cost of the textiles and clothing industry.

[80] WTO document G/TMB/N/480 of 5 July 2004. The subsector was integrated into GATT 1994 in four stages, on 1 January 1995, 1 January 1998, 1 January 2002, and 1 January 2005. In the WTO Council for Trade in Goods, Turkey has requested a work programme to examine the effects of the quota phase-out on production, investment, and trade in the textiles and clothing subsector, arguing that the programme should provide policy options, technical advice, and practical assistance to small-scale producers in need of readjustment strategies.

[81] WTO document G/TMB/N/18 of 6 March 1995.

[82] Communiqué No. 2006/6, published in the *Official Gazette* No. 26386 of 24 December 2006. These quotas are applied under paragraph 242 of the Report of the Working Party on the Accession of China to the WTO, which sets a safeguard mechanism for imports of textiles and apparel products originating in China. WTO document WT/ACC/CHN/49, 1 October 2001.

[83] Turkey's quota distribution system is described in detail in WTO (1998).

IRON AND STEEL

The iron and steel industry has been the backbone of industrialization in Turkey, which is the world's 11th largest crude steel producer (about 2% of world production in 2006).[84] The industry produced 23.3 million tonnes of crude steel in 2006 (up from 16.5 million tonnes in 2002); its estimated capacity is about 27.7 million tonnes (22 million tonnes in 2002). Crude steel production is divided into long steel (84.5% of total production in 2006), flat steel (13.5%), and special steel products (2%). The industry is now operated entirely by the private sector.[85] Tariff rates on iron and steel products average 4.6%, with maximum rates of 23.4%.

Exports of iron and steel accounted for 8.5% of Turkey's total merchandise exports in 2006; the EC and Middle East are the main markets. Turkey's finished steel consumption rose from 8.7 million tonnes in 2001 to 20.8 million tonnes in 2006, mainly due to a construction boom during the period. Turkey imports flat steel products (about US$4 billion in 2006), and special steel (US$1.3 billion), and is one of the biggest scrap iron importers (US$3.8 billion in 2006). Turkey is trying to balance the long/flat ratio by restructuring existing plants to produce more flat steel products. It is estimated that about US$4 billion of investment is necessary for the restructuring of the iron and steel industry.

With the expiry of the European Coal and Steel Communities (ECSC) agreement[86], the five-year period to grant subsidies for the restructuring or conversion of the Turkish steel subsector ended in July 2001.[87] However, Turkey asked the EC for a five year extension to allow its steel companies to benefit from state aid for restructuring purposes (investments related to the conversion and modernization of existing facilities, which will not result in capacity increase). On 31 August 2006, Turkey sent its National Restructuring Programme for the steel industry to the EC; the Programme is being analysed by the EC Commission. Nonetheless, some Turkish companies are already modernizing their facilities according to the framework defined in the Programme.[88]

The iron and steel industries do not enjoy any specific incentives. Also, under the ECSC agreement, investment incentives are not available for the production of iron and steel products. However, the subsector accounts for a small share of investment incentives issued under the IEP (Chapter III(4)(i)). Iron and steel manufactures accounted for 9% of Türk Eximbank's credits in 2006 (against 10% in 2002).

AUTOMOTIVE

The motor vehicle industry in Turkey consists of 15 assemblers and manufactures (some are foreign owned or joint ventures), generally operating under licences, and employing more than 40,000 people directly. In addition, there are about 700 automotive suppliers, employing around

[84] Ministry of Industry and Commerce (2006).
[85] In 2005, Oyak acquired 49.29% of Erdemir's shares through its subsidiary Ataer Holding, for US$2.96 billion. In 2002, Erdemir had bought Isdemir, one of Turkey's long-iron producers, on the condition that Isdemir would start producing flat products within five years.
[86] The Treaty establishing the ECSC entered into force on 23 July 1952 and expired on 23 July 2002.
[87] Articles 7 and 8 of the Agreement between Turkey and the ECSC.
[88] For example, Erdemir has already started the conversion programme from long to flat products at its Isdemir plant (Ministry of Industry and Commerce, 2006).

150,000 workers.[89] In the commercial vehicles industry, 12 companies operate under foreign licence, with a production capacity of over 400,000 units (2006); the passenger car industry is much larger and expanding, with a current production capacity of 796,000 units. Renault (in a joint-venture with Oyak), Toyota, and Fiat (in a joint-venture with Koc Com) accounted for about 89% of car output in 2006 (down from 93% in 2002), and dominated the market for imported licensed parts.[90] Relatively low labour costs and duty-free access to the EC automotive market are some of the main advantages for foreign firms investing in Turkey's automotive component subsector. Nevertheless, as with the rest of the economy, FDI in the industry remains low, albeit increasing.

Automotive (motor vehicles) production in Turkey increased from 347,000 units in 2002 to around 988,000 in 2006. Total automotive exports have also been rising steadily; they reached US$11.7 billion in 2005 (from US$4.3 billion in 2002), to become Turkey's second largest manufacturing export. The share of components in total automotive exports was 31.6% in 2005 (47.8% in 2002). Over 70% of automotive exports go to the EC market, mainly Germany, Italy, and the United Kingdom.

Tariffs on motor vehicles average 6.4%, with a maximum rate of 22%. Other border measures include an import licensing system (Chapter III(2)(iv)). As at the time of the previous Review of Turkey, most motor vehicles (six items at the four-digit level) may only be imported against a pro forma invoice certified by the MIT.[91] According to the authorities, pro forma invoice controls aim to assure the conformity of imported vehicles with EC Directives.

In addition to customs duties, vehicles sold on the domestic market, either through importers or domestic producers, are subject to the highest VAT rate of 18%. The motor vehicle purchasing tax (MVPT) was abolishedon 1 August 2002, together with the environmental fund tax (25% of the MVPT).[92]

Passenger car manufacturers are not granted any specific incentives; however, as for all investors, they have access to incentives under the GIEP (Chapter III(4)(i)), and the export incentive programme (Chapter III(3)(v)).

SERVICES

MAIN FEATURES

Services is a key sector of Turkey's economy, in terms of contribution to both GNP and foreign exchange earning (Chapter I(3)(i)). Since its previous Review, Turkey has taken measures to tackle some of the structural problems in some services subsectors: the monopoly of Turk Telekom (TT) over fixed line, domestic long-distance and international telephony ended in 2004, and the scope of the liberalization and privatization process has been extended in some subsectors (Chapter III(4)(ii)). Nevertheless, various SOEs continue to dominate services activities, and in some cases still operate under monopoly, or hold exclusive rights in certain branches of the services sector, for example, Turkish Postal Administration, and Turkish State Railways.

[89] The Association of Automotive Parts and Components Manufacturers (TAYSAD), established in 1978, is the representative of such industries; it has 189 members, mostly large size companies.
[90] Ministry of Industry and Commerce (2006).
[91] See WTO (1998), Table IV.14.
[92] See WTO (2003).

Under the General Agreement on Trade in Services (GATS), Turkey scheduled commitments in several service categories, and accepted the GATS Fourth and Fifth Protocols on basic telecommunications and financial services, respectively (Table AIV.2).[93] Turkey maintains MFN exemptions under Article II of the GATS, reserving the right to offer more favourable treatment to some WTO Members in some specific areas of business, communication, financial, and transport services (Table AIV.3). Turkey has also tabled its initial conditional offer in the ongoing services negotiations.[94]

Services are not covered by the customs union agreement between Turkey and the EC. Nonetheless, under the pre-accession framework for Turkey, negotiations have started on liberalization of services and opening up public procurement markets, in line with the Turkey-EC Association Council Decision of 11 April 2000.

FINANCIAL SERVICES

(A) BANKING

The banking subsector employs 150,793 workers, and has total assets of US$353.6 billion (December 2006), up from US$303 billion at end 2005. At end 2006, there were 50 banks operating in Turkey: 33 commercial, 13 development and investment banks, and four participation banks. The number has decreased over the last few years mainly due to mergers, and revoked banking licences. In terms of ownership, 21 were private, 21 foreign, and the remainder either state-owned or under the Savings Deposit Insurance Fund (SDIF). Halk Bank and Ziraat are the two largest state banks; privatization of Halk Bank has started[95], while the strategy for Ziraat Bank is to be prepared drawing on the experience with Halk Bank (Chapter III(4)(ii)).

All banks operating in Turkey are universal banks, allowed to carry out almost all types of financial activities. However, only investment and development banks can provide underwriting services. Banks are allowed to engage in equity intermediation activities through their subsidiaries. They do not face any effective competition from other financial institutions; most insurance and leasing companies are affiliated to and/or owned by banks. Foreign and domestic banks are subject to the same rules in terms of establishment, operation, and supervision.

Following its 2000-01 financial crisis, Turkey put into effect the Banking Sector Restructuring Programme (BSRP) to promote an efficient, globally competitive, and sound banking sector, free of distortions.[96] The BSRP is based on four pillars: (i) restructuring of state banks; (ii) prompt restructuring of the SDIF banks; (iii) strengthening of private banks; and (iv) strengthening of the regulatory and supervisory framework by, *inter alia*, creating the Banking Regulation and Supervision Authority (BRSA). The BRSA is the sole authority regulating banking and supervising all banks (as well as the SDIF) in Turkey. To build on progress in bank supervision, the BRSA has recently introduced secondary legislation on systems audit principles; made some organizational changes, including the merger of onsite and offsite supervision; and published its Strategic Plan 2006-09 setting out broad strategic goals. Nonetheless, further improvements

[93] WTO documents WT/LET/199 of 19 November 1997, and WT/LET/288 of 18 February 1999.
[94] WTO document TN/S/O/TUR/Rev.1 of 29 September 2005.
[95] Treasury shares at Halk Bank were transferred to the privatization portfolio, and an initial public offering has been held for 24.98% of the shares.
[96] According to some estimates, the total cost to the Government of restructuring the banking system since the 2000-01 crisis was about US$47 billion (32% of GDP), of which US$6 billion was the cost of compensating depositors after the 2003 failure of Imar Bank, and an estimated US$2 billion for the recapitalization of Pamukbank (OECD, 2006).

seem necessary. For example, the exclusion of non-financial group companies from the banks' consolidated accounts undermines the effective supervision of banks that form part of mixed-holding groups.[97]

In 1999, the SDIF was given the authority and responsibility to restructure banks in financial difficulties, to facilitate their sale, in full or in part, or to liquidate them. The administration and the representation of SDIF were first enforced by the CBRT and then by the BRSA. By end 2007, no banks will remain under the administration of the SDIF.[98] The BSRP also aims to promote a healthier financial situation among private banks through minimum capital requirements.

A new Banking Law (No. 5411) entered into force on 1 November 2005, with the aim of harmonizing Turkish legislation with EC directives and international standards. It reduced the maximum credit limit for parent undertakings to EC standards; introduced risk-based supervision; put an end to the sworn bank auditors' monopoly in onsite supervision; and established a financial services commission to improve cooperation among supervisory authorities.[99]

Under the Law, any bank in Turkey must be incorporated as a joint-stock company and have a minimum capital, paid in cash and free of any collusion, of YTL 30 million.[100] Foreign banks can operate in Turkey by establishing branches, subsidiaries or joint-ventures with banks established or about to be established. The establishment of the first branch of a foreign bank requires BRSA approval. Under Law No. 5411, establishment of a bank to be engaged exclusively in offshore banking, is allowed by Board decision.[101] Cross-border supply of banking services is not legally restricted. According to the authorities, regulations on surveillance of on- and off-balance-sheet risks (including credit risk of banks, measurement of capital adequacy, and internal control) and risk management systems are, to a great extent, in compliance with the Basel principles.

(B) SECURITIES

Inaugurated in 1986, the Istanbul Stock Exchange (ISE) is Turkey's sole securities market, it was established to provide trading in equities, bonds and bills, revenue-sharing certificates, private-sector bonds, real-estate certificates, and foreign securities. The ISE, a public entity, consists of 104 brokerage houses and 40 banks.[102] Margin trading, short-selling, securities lending and borrowing have been regulated by the Capital Market Board (CMB). At the end of July 2007, the ISE comprised 322 companies (286 at end August of 2003), 100 of which are included in the ISE National-100 Index.[103] Total trading in the ISE equities market rose to US$229.6 billion in 2006, up from US$70.8 billion in 2002. The bonds and bills market provides a trading environment for government bonds, treasury bills, bonds issued by the Privatization Administration, private sector bonds, and repo transactions. The "International Bonds Market", within the "ISE Foreign

[97] European Commission (2006).
[98] IMF (2006).
[99] European Commission (2006).
[100] Principles and procedures for the establishment of banks in Turkey are set out in the Banks Act No. 4389 and relevant regulations issued by the BRSA.
[101] This also applies to the opening of a branch in Turkey by offshore banks established abroad, and their fields of activity and financial reporting and audit procedures, as well as details regarding the temporary suspension or revocation of their activities.
[102] Banks cannot operate in the equities market.
[103] In addition, second national markets (with a lower listing requirement), the new economy market (for new technology companies), and the watch-list companies market are available to trading companies that do not fulfil the listing requirements and lack the necessary qualifications for trading in the national market. Moreover, since 2002, in addition to the listed companies, temporarily de-listed companies can be traded off (exchanged in a separate market).

Securities Market", aims to provide a transparent and secure trading environment for listed Turkish Sovereign Eurobonds; it has been active since 16 April 2007.

The legal framework for the capital markets is laid out in the Capital Market Law of 1981 (amended in December 1999). The CMB, established in 1982, has the authority to regulate primary and secondary markets in securities, supervise securities intermediaries and collective investment institutions, and register all public offerings of securities (except government securities). In addition, it has authority to regulate the issuing process of private-sector capital-market instruments. The Turkish stock and bond markets are open to foreign investors without restriction on the repatriation of capital and profits.

The ISE Settlement and Custody Bank (Takasbank), an investment bank owned by the ISE and its members, handles the settlement of equities, bonds, and overnight transactions carried out in the ISE, as well as other related services. The Central Registry Agency (CRA), established as a private entity in 2001 under the Capital Market Law, is the only central depository for all capital market instruments in Turkey. CRA took over the custody function for stocks, on 28 November 2005, from Takasbank.

In February 2005, the Turkish Derivatives Exchange (Turkdex) started operations in İzmir. Turkdex is the sole exchange in Turkey for trading in derivatives instruments. The first private sector corporate bond, since 1999, was issued in July 2006.

(C) INSURANCE

The Turkish insurance market consists of re-insurance companies, insurance companies, and insurance intermediaries (such as brokers and agencies). At end 2006, there were 46 insurance companies (55 in 2002); 35 operate in non-life, ten in life and pension, and and one in pension only There is also one re-insurance company, Milli Reasurans T.A.S. (commonly referred to as Milli-Re), which is a private company owned by Turkiye Is Bank A.S.[104] The State does not have majority shares in any insurance or reinsurance company. At the end of 2006, 29 insurance companies had foreign capital, either directly or indirectly; foreign companies accounted for 32.3% of total premiums. Total assets of insurance and re-insurance companies were US$12.898 million.

The insurance subsector in Turkey is supervised and regulated by the Undersecretariat of Treasury, which reports to the Ministry of State in charge of economic policies. The General Directorate of Insurance is empowered to issue regulations regarding the insurance subsector, and to take measures to protect the insured. The Insurance Supervisory Board is entrusted with supervising, examining, and investigating the subsector. The Insurance Law No. 5684 governs the supervision of insurance and reinsurance companies. All insurance and reinsurance companies, whether foreign or Turkish, are subject to the same legislation.

Insurance or reinsurance companies may be established in Turkey only in the form of joint-stock companies. However, insurance companies may also be established as mutual companies. Foreign insurance and reinsurance companies may also operate in Turkey by opening branches, provided they have not been prohibited in their country of operation. Following establishment,

[104] Milli-Re was set up in 1929 to ensure that local companies could obtain reinsurance on reasonable terms, and to retain reinsurance premiums in the country. The requirement for mandatory cession of domestic insurance business to Milli-Re was terminated on 1 January 2002, although Milli-Re retained a right of refusal on any business to be offered to foreign insurers (about US$40 million annually) until the end of 2006.

insurance and reinsurance companies must obtain a licence from the Undersecretariat; a separate licence is issued for each branch. Subject to specified exceptions, cross-border supply of non-life insurance services is prohibited.[105]

Insurance companies may engage only in insurance business and must perform either life or non-life insurance business, but not both.[106] Export credit insurance is provided by insurance companies and the Turk Eximbank; some private insurance companies cover both short-term export credit and domestic credit risk. Tontines (under which the last survivor of a group of persons acquires the capital invested) are prohibited in Turkey. The minimum paid-up capital requirement for insurance and re-insurance companies is YTL 5 million. The minimum solvency margin for insurance companies is set in terms of premium production and claims figures; the margin varies in life and non-life insurance branches. Compulsory reserves must be invested locally, except for premiums earned abroad in life insurance, as well as statutory and free reserves, which can be invested overseas. There are no restrictions on portfolio composition and risk exposure of insurance companies.

Compulsory earthquake insurance was launched through Decree Law No. 587 on 27 December 1999 and the creation of the Turkish Catastrophe Insurance Pool (TCIP). The TCIP is the only line of insurance business carried out by the public sector and its main aim is to mitigate the risk being borne by public funds.[107] The programme is an example of public-private partnership as the insurance coverage is provided by the TCIP (a public legal entity), whereas insurance policies are distributed through participating insurance companies. The TCIP has the capacity to support insured losses of up to €1 billion: if aggregate losses exceed that level, the excess could fall on the Government and policyholders.

Premiums for compulsory insurance (e.g. third-party motor liability insurance, and earthquake insurance), are set by the Ministry of State. However, for third-party motor insurance, the Undersecretariat sets a band in which companies are free to establish their own premiums (since August 2007). Moreover, for some compulsory insurances, there are minimum premiums, also determined by the Ministry of State. Premiums for the other branches of insurance are set by the insurance companies.

TELECOMMUNICATIONS AND POSTAL SERVICES

Since the last TPR of Turkey, its telecommunications network has continued to grow, notably the mobile market where the number of cellular mobile subscribers has more than doubled (Table IV.7). Similarly, the number of internet users increased from 4.3 million in 2002 to 12.3 million in 2006. All Turkey's villages are connected to the telephone network; at end 2006, there were 18.8 million fixed lines in service, i.e. a teledensity of 25.39 (down from 26.88 in 2002). According to the authorities, the number of fixed telephone subscribers has reached saturation

[105] The exceptions are hull insurance of aircraft, helicopters, and ships purchased through a foreign loan or leased via a financial leasing contract from abroad, provided that the insurance period is limited to the term of the credit or leasing contract; marine liability insurance; transportation insurance for goods imports and exports; and individual accident, sickness, and motor vehicle insurance during any travel abroad.

[106] Companies previously licensed to operate both in life and non-life branches were required to transfer their life insurance portfolio no later than 31 December 1997, failing which they would not be permitted to issue life insurance policies.

[107] It was launched after the 1999 earthquake in Marmara, after which it was found that only a small fraction of the economic loss was insured, and hence the repair burden fell mainly on the Government.

point.[108] Penetration of telephone lines remains below the EC average for both fixed and mobile telephony.[109]

Table IV.7
Selected telecommunication indicators, 2002-06

	2002	2003	2004	2005	2006
Main telephone lines ('000)	18,890	18,917	19,125	18,978	18,832
Main lines per 100 inhabitants	26.88	26.55	26.48	25.93	25.39
Cellular mobile subscribers ('000)	23,323	27,888	34,708	43,609	52,663
Cellular subscribers per 100 inhabitants	33.19	39.14	48.06	59.58	71.00
Internet users ('000)	4,300	6,000	10,220	11,204	12,283
Internet users per 100 inhabitants	6.12	8.42	14.15	15.31	16.56
Internet hosts	154,585	359,188	474,129	474,129	..
Internet hosts per 10,000 inhabitants	22.00	50.41	65.65	65.65	..
ADSL subscribers ('000)	2.9	56.6	452.4	1,539.5	..
Personal computers ('000)	3,000	3,333	3,703	3,703	..
Personal computers per 100 inhabitants	4.27	4.68	5.13	5.13	..

.. Not available.

Source: ITU (2007), *Telecommunication Indicators*, Geneva, and information provided by the Turkish authorities.

The creation of the Telecommunication Authority (TA) in August 2000 put an end to the fragmented regulatory structure.[110] Through Laws Nos. 4502 and 4673, the TA has the power to grant licences and to regulate prices for all telecommunications services. Any company planning to provide telecommunications services or to build telecommunications infrastructure in Turkey has to obtain a licence or authorization from the TA (Table IV.8).[111] Minimum licensing fees for telecommunication services (including GMPCS, internet service provision, premium rate services, satellite platform services, satellite telecommunication services) are set by the TA, subject to approval by the Council of Ministers.[112]

Table IV.8
Licences granted, 2004-06

	2004	2005	2006

[108] Undersecretariat of State Planning Organization (2006).
[109] European Commission (2006).
[110] WTO (2003).
[111] Previously, licences were issued by the Ministry of Transportation.
[112] For details on licensing and the related fees, see the Telecommunication Authority online information. Viewed at: http://www.tk.gov.tr.

Authorization agreements	1	2	2
Concession agreements	3	4	4
Satellite platform operators	3	1	2
Satellite telecommunications services operators	23	24	20
Operators providing mobile telephony services by satellite	5	5	4
Operators performing data transmission over terrestrial lines	14	20	20
Internet service providers	91	74	72
Operators providing long distance telephony services	43	40	35
Operators providing common usage radio services	9	48	48
Infrastructure service operators	0	0	7
Cable platform service operators	0	0	5
Total	192	218	219

Source: Telecommunications Authority (undated), *2005 Annual Activity Report*, Ankara, and information provided by the Turkish authorities.

Since its last TPR, has continued the liberalization process of its telecommunications subsector. The monopoly of TT over fixed line[113], domestic long-distance, and international telephony ended on 31 December 2003.[114] In November 2005, the government sold 55% of its TT's shares to Ojer Telekomünikasyon AS, a consortium consisting of Saudi Oger and Telecom Italia (Chapter III(4)(ii)).[115] As of 1 July 2005, when new regulations on local network sharing came into effect, TT ceased to be the only supplier of ADSL services.

Law No. 5369 on universal services in electronic communication, which became effective in 2005, defines the scope of universal services for: (i) fixed telephone services; (ii) public payphones; (iii) directory enquiry services, printed or electronics; (iv) emergency call services; (v) basic internet services; (vi) transportation services to regions where they can only be made by navigation, and communication services related to emergency and safety in the sea; (vii) service targeting promotion of information technologies, including computer training; and (viii) digital broadcasting services (DVB-T, DVB-S, DVB-C), using different broadcast environments, over terrestrial digital transmitters covering all residential areas in Turkey. Universal service providers are designated among the operators via a tendering method.[116] Turksat and TT are the current universal service providers. The Ministry of Transport is responsible for the application of this law.

In accordance with Directives Nos. 97/33/EC and 2002/21/EC, an "Ordinance regarding the Designation of Operators with significant Market Power" was issued on 7 January 2007, to

[113] TT operates the world's 13th largest installed fixed-line infrastructure. The average daily malfunctions reported in 2005 was 1.15 per thousand (0.5 per thousand in urban areas and 1.15 per thousand in rural areas) (Türk Telekom, 2006).

[114] According to its commitments under the WTO 1997 Agreement on Telecommunications Services, Turkey was due to abolish Turk Telekom's monopoly on basic services by 31 December 2005.

[115] Council of Ministers Resolution No. 2005/9146 (Türk Telekom, 2006).

[116] Any operator may be designated to provide universal services, within the electronic communication sector, at the regional or national levels.

ensure the application of the Tariff Ordinance, and of the Access and Interconnection Ordinance, published in the *Official Gazette* of 14 June 2007.[117] The Ordinance provides for the sharing, by all operators, of infrastructure owned by operators having significant market power (SMP), on a cost, non-discriminatory, and transparent basis. TA set up a detailed dispute settlement procedure and is to publish standard interconnection charges based on log-run incremental costs. If parties fail to reach an agreement, even with the TA's mediation, the TA sets terms, conditions, and prices for access, including interconnection. All SMP operators are required to prepare and send their reference offers on access to the TA for approval. Access (including interconnection) agreements must be made available to the public. In 2002, the TA introduced price-cap mechanisms in the determination of charges for services provided by TT.[118] The TA is required to ensure that cross-subsidization between different services are avoided. It signed a Protocol with the Competition Authority on 16 September 2002 as a further step towards an improved regulatory framework.[119] The TA is also enhancing public participation in the regulatory process through the establishment of a Telecommunication Policy Council comprising operators, consumers, and experts.

A revenue sharing arrangement between two GSM services operators, Turkcell and Telsim[120], and TT, was converted into a 25-year licence in April 1998; both companies paid US$500 million. In 2001, two new GSM operators were licensed: Aria, partly owned by Telecom Italia Mobile, and TT's Aycell. In 2004, these two operators merged into Avea.[121] In addition to GSM services, the TA has been authorizing capital firms to provide some telecommunication services, such as internet service, satellite platform services, and satellite telecommunication services.

Turkcell, the leader of the Turkish GSM market, lowered its intra-network call rates by a third after the creation of Aria, and all its call rates by half since Avea entered the market. Currently, customers in Turkey pay relatively low tariffs, by international standards.[122]

According to the Board of the TA, Turkcell, Telsim, and Avea have significant market power in the mobile call termination market; Turkcell also has it in the mobile access and call origination markets.[123] As a result, an Ordinance on Quality of Service in Telecommunications was published in the *Official Gazette* in March 2005, with the aim of improving various services (e.g. fault repair time, response time for operator services, and bill complaints).

[117] Only tariffs set by legal or physical monopolies, or operators in a dominant position or having significant market power in a relevant product or geographical market are regulated.
[118] Decision No. 246 of 11 May 2005.
[119] The Protocol is currently not in force. Nevertheless, under Article 7 of Law No. 2813, the Competition Authority has to seek the views of the TA in its investigations concerning the subsector, although these views are not binding.
[120] In 2005,Telsim was sold to Vodafone for US$4.5 billion.
[121] AVEA is a GSM service provider currently owned by TT (81%), and Türkiye Iş Bankasi (19%). At end 2005, AVEA controlled about 14% of the mobile market, with 6.2 million subscribers (AVEA online information. Viewed at: www.avea.com.tr).
[122] In May 2007, AVEA's prices were: up to YTL 0.35 (about €0.2) per minute for national calls, and between YTL 0.32 and YTL 2.1 (about €0.19 and €1.1) per minute for international calls. National SMS messages cost up to YTL 0.06 (about €0.03), while the price of international SMS messages were YTL 21 (about €0.12) (AVEA online information. Viewed at: www.avea.com.tr).
[123] The following criteria are used by the Board of the TA to establish if an operator has significant market power: market share; power to influence market conditions; relationship between sales and market share; power to control access devices to last consumer; power to access financial resources; and experience on its products and services in the market (Telecommunications Authority of Turkey, 2006).

In 2007, the TA prepared a Project for Eurasian Cooperation in the field of Telecommunications Regulations in order to, *inter alia*, establish permanent and effective cooperation on telecommunications regulations between countries in the region, and harmonize regulatory activities. With this aim, a coordination study group was created in March 2005.[124] Turkey has signed: the ITU Constitution and Convention; ITU Radio Regulations; ITU International Telecommunications Regulations; Agreement, and Operating Agreement of INTELSAT; Convention, and Operating Agreement of INMARSAT; and Convention, and Operating Agreement of EUTELSAT. Turkey has not signed any bilateral agreements on telecommunications. The ITU Plenipotentiary Conference took place in Antalya in November 2006.

The Turkish Postal Administration, under the Ministry of Transport (MT), is the regulatory and operational body for postal services. According to the postal law[125], its monopoly covers open and closed letters, postcards, and telegraphs for domestic or foreign destinations. The Turkish Postal Administration is carrying out reorganization work and automation of counter services to align the quality of its services on the Universal Postal Union (UPU) standards. In 2004, under the PTT-Bank logo, Turkish Post started offering postal financial services on behalf of banks (e.g. collection of bills and credit card payments), with the aim of making such services available in remote areas.[126]

TRANSPORT

In 2005, under the coordination of the MT, Turkey launched its Transport Master Plan Strategy with the aim of increasing coordination among the various institutions involved in the subsector, and formulating policies in a "balanced and holistic way".[127] One of the key targets of the Plan is to increase, by 2020, the share of railways in total transport to 20% of freight (up from 5% now), and 10% of passengers (up from 2%).[128] Under its Ninth Development Plan 2007-13, Turkey also aims, *inter alia*, to create an efficient transport subsector, giving priority to environmental aspects, and to increase traffic safety in all modes of transport, particular highways (Table IV.9).[129]

Turkey is part of the Euro-Mediterranean Regional Transport Project (EuroMed Transport Project), implemented since 2003, with the aim of contributing to both the development of the Euro-Mediterranean Free Trade Area, and economic integration among the countries in the region. It provides assistance in improving the functioning and the efficiency of the Mediterranean transport system; promotes the harmonization of operational norms and regulations; encourages the coordination of transport policies; and promotes the modernization of the regional transport infrastructure taking into consideration the trans-European networks.[130] In addition, a TINA (Transport Infrastructure Needs Assessment) study has been completed to develop a multimodal

---

124 Telecommunications Authority online information. Viewed at: http://www.tk.gov.tr/eng/pdf/eng-2005.pdf.
125 Law No. 5584.
126 This is under the condition of not offering traditional banking services, such as granting loans and opening saving accounts.
127 In the absence of a master plan, problems regarding all transport activities were being tackled on an *ad hoc*, short-term basis, and without the necessary cooperation and coordination among the different transport authorities that participate in the subsector (WTO, 2003).
128 To alleviate bottlenecks for national and international railway transport through Turkey, major high-speed railways lines and a new Bosphorus underwater railway tunnel are being constructed (UNECE, 2006).
129 State Planning Organization (2006).
130 The other members of the EuroMed transport project are: Algeria, Cyprus, Egypt, Israel, Jordan, Lebanon, Malta, Morocco, the Palestinian Authority, Syria, and Tunisia (EC, 2004).

transport network within Turkey, and to extend the EC's TEN-T (trans-European transport network) into Turkey.[131]

Table IV.9
Freight transport, 2006 and 2013
(Million tonnes-km)

	2006	2013	2007-13 Percentage change
Domestic			
Highway[a]	169,500	248,000	5.6
Railway	8,358	25,400	17.0
Maritime	5,400	8,400	6.5
Airline[b]	468	659	5.0
Pipeline			
Crude oil (million tonnes)	6.1	9.0	47.5
Natural gas (billion m^3)[c]	30.8	37.4	21.4
International			
Railway	1,318	8,248	31.0
Maritime	749,000	1,740,000	12.8
Airline[c]	2,613	4,777	9.0
Pipeline			
Crude oil (transit) (million tonnes)	9.6[d]	120.0	1,150
Natural gas (transit) (billion m^3)	0	14[e]	n.a

n.a Not applicable.

a Transport on the 117 km of motorways and connection roads that were transferred to the Istanbul Metropolitan Municipality is excluded from the beginning of 2005.
b Turkish Airlines' value.
c Not included in total.
d Includes amount transported via Iraq-Turkey crude oil pipeline, and BTC crude oil pipeline.
e Includes amount of gas transported to Europe by Turkey-Greece-Italy and Nabucco natural gas pipeline.

Source: State Planning Organization (2006), *Ninth Development Plan 2007-13,* Ankara, and information provided by the Turkish authorities.

(A) MARITIME TRANSPORT

Turkey's maritime fleet ranking went from 18th in the world in 2000 to 24th in 2005, largely due to problems of financing and flag avoidance.[132] In 2006, Turkey had 61 shipyards (37 in 2002), employing 28,580 persons, and with a capacity of 1.8 million deadweight tonnage (dwt) (550,000

131 The project consists of defining and assessing a multimodal transport network in Turkey, comprising roads, railway lines, seaports, and airports. The final report is yet to be approved by the sponsors, i.e. Ministry of Transport, State Planning Organization, and the European Commission. The ultimate decision-maker of the study, on behalf of Turkey, is the High Planning Council.
132 State Planning Organization (2006).

dwt in 2002); the authorities expect total capacity to reach 6 million dwt in 2010.[133] Maritime transport is important for domestic and international trade, since four of Turkey's main industrial centres (Istanbul-Izmit, Izmir, Bursa, and Adana) are on or near the sea. Total loading and unloading in the maritime subsector rose from about 206 million tonnes in 2004 to over 232 million tonnes in 2006 (Table IV.10). In 2006, container handling reached 3.9 million TEU (twenty-foot equivalent unit), against 2.9 million in 2004. Port facilities are increasingly overcrowded and inadequate to deal with the rise in ship traffic, partly because of delays in some projects (e.g. the North Marmara Port and the Izmir Port dredging and extension projects, as well as in the construction of the Derince Container Port).[134] Some port services in Turkey are also relatively expensive.[135]

Maritime activities are administered mainly by the Undersecretariat of Maritime Affairs, and subject to Turkish Commercial Law No. 6762, Cabotage Law No. 815, Ports Law No. 618, and the International Convention on Standards of Training, Certification and Watchkeeping for Seafarers of 1978 (STCW78).

Table 10 Maritime transport , 2004-06

	2004	2005	2006
Loading (tonnes)	70,041,134	68,639,896	77,908,825
Exports	55,118,561	54,494,224	63,311,978
Domestic	14,922,573	14,145,672	14,596,847
Unloading (tonnes)	136,002,156	140,091,972	154,539,643
Imports	121,043,378	126,169,107	139,406,306
Domestic	14,958,778	13,922,865	15,133,337
Transit	5,491,810	5,261,659	11,144,059
Total	206,043,290	208,731,868	232,448,846

Source: Information provided by the Turkish authorities.

In the last few years, several public ports, operated by the General Directorate of the Turkish Maritime Organization (TDI), have been concessioned[136], and the tendering processes, for the concession of the ports of Bandirma, Derince, İzmir, Samsun, and İskenderun, have been launched (Chapter III(4)(ii)). However, the six largest ports are still operated by a state-owned enterprise, the Turkish State Railways (TCDD).[137] Some of the main problems facing TCDD are

[133] Ministry of Transport online information. Viewed at: http://www.ubak.gov.tr/ubak/en/index.php [21 May 2007].

[134] State Planning Organization (2006).

[135] In 2004, the cost for a twenty-foot container unit in Turkey was, on average, about €330, compared with €70 in Alexandria (Egypt), €210 in Radès (Tunisia), and €370 in Casablanca (Morocco) (*EuroMed Transport Project*, 2004).

[136] The port of Antalya was later returned to the public sector. Ownership of the ports' infrastructure is retained by the State, but the operational rights (including management, facilities, and equipment) are transferred to a private investor for 30 years; TDI remains in charge of supervision and monitoring (*EuroMed Transport Project*, 2004).

[137] All these ports are accessible by railways.

insufficiency of port equipment and infrastructure; lack of computerization, causing delays in tracing cargo, and sometimes their loss; and under-investment with cross-subsidization of railways from port proceeds.[138]

Under Cabotage Law No. 815, merchant maritime transport and passenger services, pilotage, and all other port services can be provided only by Turkish flag ships. Turkey has two ship-register systems, the National Ship Registry and the International Ship Registry. In order to fly the Turkish flag, on the National Ship Registry, shipping companies must be 51% owned by Turkish nationals (Commercial Law No. 6762). First mates and masters of ships must be of Turkish nationality, while up to 40% of the officers of ships engaged in international seaborne transportation (i.e. excluding cabotage) can be foreign nationals.[139] Ships and yachts owned by Turkish and/or foreign persons resident in Turkey and companies incorporated under Turkish legislation, can be registered with the Turkish International Ship Registry in Istanbul, and fly the Turkish flag. National vessels can be authorized to change flag for a period of between one and two years when they are bareboat "chartered out", while foreign vessels can be authorized to fly the national flag for a period of one to two years when they are bareboat "chartered in".

Vessels flying the Turkish flag benefit from a price preference: when bidding for public cargoes to be shipped overseas or carrying strategic raw materials, they are awarded the bids if their quotation is up to 10% higher than the lowest foreign flag vessel quotation. Authorization by the Undersecretariat of Foreign Trade is required for public entities to ship imports under a foreign flag. Foreign flag vessels are used if: (i) Turkish flag vessels' quotations are more than 10% higher than quotations by foreign flag vessels; (ii) loading is at ports not used by Turkish flag vessels; or (iii) the capacity and/or technology used by the Turkish flag vessel is insufficient for the cargo and route.[140]

The tariff system for Turkish ports is based on the principle of non-discrimination between Turkish and foreign flags. According to the authorities, operators freely set their tariffs, and discounts on port dues and charges are linked to the frequency of calls at the port. On 1 August 2003, port fees were reduced by 50%, cabotage carriage fees by 75%, and flashlight fees by 30%. The special consumption tax for fuel used in naval vessels was recently lowered.[141]

Special tax incentives are provided to Turkish investors in the maritime subsector. The wages of seafarers working on ships registered under Turkey's International Ship Registry are exempted from income tax and funds; and revenues from operating and "alienating" ships registered under Turkish International Ship Registry are exempted from personal income and corporate income tax. Profits from non-operation activities are not covered by the exemption. Book profits resulting

[138] Concerns have been expressed about cross-subsidization of the railways by the port's excess profits within TCCD. The cross-subidization suggests overcharging by the port authorities, or inadequate depreciation and maintenance schedules, or both. This is likely to result in inefficiency in the delivery of port services, affecting Turkey's external trade competitiveness through high import costs; it is a strong barrier to new entrants. See also *EuroMed Transport Project*, 2004).

[139] The following ships are considered as Turkish: (i) ships that belong to legal persons, such as bodies, institutions, associations, and foundations set up in accordance with Turkish law, the majority of whose Board of Directors are of Turkish nationality; and (ii) ships that belong to trading companies, the majority of whose managerial staff and representatives are of Turkish nationality and are registered on the Turkish Trade Register (WTO document S/NGMTS/W/2/Add.23/Rev.1, 25 September 1995).

[140] Private importers are free to use foreign or national vessels.

[141] A 20% additional reduction is in place for passengers ships promoting tourism.

from sales of vessels can be deducted from the purchase price of the same kind of replacement vessels within three years and after deducting the realized depreciation amount.[142]

Access to ports, pilotage, towing, tug assistance, provisioning, fuelling and watering, and navigation aids are available to all users of port services. Turkey has no laws and regulations governing the operation of liner conferences. In 2006, the Turkish flag was moved from the Black to the Gray List of the Secretariat of the Paris Memorandum of Understanding on Port State Control.[143] According to the authorities, Turkey has signed all maritime safety international conventions, and is a member of the Regional Marine Pollution Emergency Response Centre for the Mediterranean Sea (REMPEC).[144]

(B) AIR TRANSPORT

In general, Turkey's air transport is still dominated by the state-owned Turkish Airlines (THY) (Chapter III(4)(ii)). In addition to THY, there are 19 air carrier companies. In 2006, 810 aircraft were registered as Turkish. Turkey has 62 airports operated by the General Directorate of the State Airports Enterprise (DHMI)[145], 37 of which are operated by the State Airports Authority; 21 airports are open to international traffic. As of 2007, the operational rights of the main terminals of certain airports (i.e. Atatürk (Istanbul)[146], Antalya, Esenboğa (Ankara), İzmir Adnan Menderes and Dalaman) were concessioned to private enterprises.[147]

Private air carriers have been allowed to establish since the enactment of Public Law No. 2920 on Turkish Civil Aviation in 1983. The MT is responsible for approval of new carriers (pursuant to Law No. 2920 and the Regulation on Commercial Air Transport Operations issued under the law). Air carriers are authorized to schedule domestic services if they are registered in Turkey and operate a minimum of five registered aircraft of at least 100 seats[148]; where there are no

---

[142] Turkish International Ship Registry Law No. 4490 of 16 December 1999, Article 12.
[143] The Black List is composed of flags considered as "very high risk", while the Grey List has "medium to high" risk flags. The White List represents quality flags with a consistently low detention record. Paris MoU, Secretariat report, June 2007. Viewed at: http://www.parismou.org/ParisMOU/Whats+New/News/ News+Detail/xp/selectedcontentitem.2868/default.asp.
[144] REMPEC is a UN body established in the context of the Mediterranean Action Plan. Its main objective is to assist Mediterranean coastal states in the implementation of the Emergency Protocol and Barcelona Convention (REMPEC online information. Viewed at: www.rempec.org/about.asp).
[145] In 2005, all DHMI services (air traffic management, air traffic services, aeronautical communications management, aeronautical information management, and flight inspection services) and DHMI operational services were awarded ISO 9001:2000 in 2005 and 2007, respectively.
[146] The operational rights of the main terminals of the Atatürk Airport were transferred to TAV Airports Holding for 15.5 years (US$3 billion) (General Directorate of the State Airports Authority, 2005).
[147] In April 2005, a new runway and a US$85.5 million terminal, with an annual capacity of 20 million passengers, were open at Antalya International Airport. The new terminal will be managed by a private company, ÇELEBI-IC Antalya Airport Terminal Investment and Management, until 28 September 2009. Antalya Airport International Management is responsible for the operation of the old terminals until 15 September 2007 (General Directorate of the State Airports Authority, 2005). After these dates, the operational rights of domestic and international terminals will be concessioned to the İçtaş-Fraport consortium.
[148] At least three registered aircraft are required in the case of scheduled and non-scheduled domestic flights; the aircraft must have at least 100-seat capacity each.

company-owned aircraft, a bank letter of guarantee for up to US$3 million is required. However, for regional air transport, a carrier should own or lease at least two aircraft registered in the Turkish Civil Aircraft Registry, with a capacity of between 20 and 99 seats.

The majority of a company's executive and authorized representatives must be of Turkish nationality (Article 49 of Law No. 2920) and Turkish shareholders must have voting majority. Hence, the equity participation ratio of foreign shareholders is restricted to 49%. There are no plans to ease the restriction on foreign direct investment. Airlines with a majority of shares controlled by foreigners are not permitted to carry passengers from one national point to another. Technical and financial supervision of existing carriers is carried out by the Directorate General of Civil Aviation. In 2005, Law No. 5431 restructured the Civil Aviation General Management, as a public legal entity with its own budget.

Access to the main national airports is allocated following application to the Turkish Civil Aviation Authority under the rules prescribed in the General and Aerodrome sections of the Turkish Aeronautical Information Publication (AIP), and signature of a contract with a ground-handling company for the provision of services. Landing and take-off rights are allocated on slot time basis. Slot allocation is applied at Atatürk, Antalya, Adnan Menderes, Dalaman, Bodrum, and Esenboga airports, and Kayseri (in the summer). Air carriers operating scheduled services to Turkey are authorized on the basis of reciprocity within the framework of bilateral agreements. Charter services are authorized on the basis of reciprocity under the rules of the European Civil Aviation Commission (ECAC), of which Turkey is a member. Cargo transport is under the provisions of Law No. 2920 and relevant articles of the Regulation on Commercial Air Transport Operations, as well as the applicable provisions of bilateral air transport agreements signed by Turkey.[149] An open skies agreement has been concluded between Turkey and the United States, and a de facto open skies agreement exists between Turkey and Germany.[150] According to the authorities, cabotage in air transport is not to be opened to competition from foreign companies.

Public Law No. 4054 on the Protection of Competition does not grant any special exemptions to the national air transport services industry. No special privileges are granted to state-owned air companies, except, where possible, Turkish civil servants must use the national airline for official travel.

Two private-sector ground-handling companies provide services at all airports open to international civil air traffic. Catering services at the international airports are provided by four catering firms, of which two are entirely owned by Turkish companies, and two are a mixed foreign-Turkish partnership. Airlines may also provide groundhandling services for their own use at all airports (self-handling). The prices for these services are market-determined.

The prices set air carriers operating scheduled services must be formally approved by the MT (Article 25 of Law No. 2920). The government does not intervene in the pricing of non-scheduled or air taxi services. Since 1 January 2004, air tickets have not been subject to the special transaction tax or education contribution payment.

Imports of a wide range of aircraft-related items (78 items at the four-digit level) are only permitted upon approval by the General Directorate of Civil Aviation in the MT. This restriction,

[149] Turkey has signed bilateral air transport agreements with 88 partners. Under these agreements, 63 (may change seasonally) foreign airlines are operating scheduled services to Turkey; THY is operating scheduled services to 77 cities abroad.

[150] Since the Turkish-German market is crucial due to a large Turkish population living in Germany, the air transport agreement between the two countries is an open skies agreement, though it is not named so.

according to the authorities, is to ensure that these imports are used only in the civil aircraft industry.

(c) RAILWAY AND ROAD TRANSPORT

Turkey's railway system consists of 10,984 km of track, of which 8,697 km are main lines.[151] The most important infrastructure problem is that the lines between highly populated cities are not appropriate for high speed travel.[152] As a result, several projects are being developed to improve the infrastructure, including: the Ankara-Istanbul high speed project (€1,955 million); Ankara-Konya high speed project (€377 million); procurement of, *inter alia*, high-speed trains (€253.2 million), locomotives (€374.5 million), and suburban trains (€102.4 million); rehabilitation of existing suburban trains (€44.1 million); and modernization of stations and station buildings.[153]

The Turkish State Railways (TCDD), a state-owned enterprise affiliated to the MT, has a de jure monopoly in providing railway passenger and freight transport services. It owns and operates the whole railway system, together with six ports that have rail access (i.e. Haydarpasa, Iskenderun, Derince, Izmir, Samsun, and Bandirma); five of are under privatization. There are no private rail operators. TCDD is free to introduce fares on a market basis and to increase them, after verbal approval by the MT. The construction of new railway infrastructure and ports is the responsibility of the Directorate General of Ports, Railways and Airports Construction of the MT.

The reorganization of TCDD is one of the key areas for reform under the Ninth Development Plan 2007-13.[154] The main objectives include: increasing the share of rail in total transportation by implementing customer-oriented business strategies, and establishing a sustainable and effective transport infrastructure; enhancing the autonomy of the TCDD; decreasing the consolidated operation ratio (ratio of operating expenses to operating revenues, excluding subsidies) from 4.3 to under 2; cancelling unprofitable local and urban lines; and aligning the domestic railway transport legislation with the *acquis communautaire*. An action plan for the restructuring of TCDD over 2003-08 is also being financed by the EC.[155]

Turkey has a total highway network of 64,195 km (2,431 km of motorway, 31,335 km of state roads, and 30,429 of provincial roads).[156] The share of highway transport in total freight transport increased from 88.7% in 2002 to about 92% in 2006; around 95% of passenger transport is by highway. For the purpose of creating a sustainable transport environment in Turkey, a shift from road traffic to rail and maritime means is to be promoted: bilateral combined-transport agreements are being signed. According to the authorities, transit quota limitations applied by partner countries continue to prevent the efficient use of Turkey's road transport fleet.[157] Other obstacles to the development of the subsector include: traffic congestion and bottlenecks; expensive charges for using transport infrastructure in third countries; difficulties in obtaining

---

[151] State Planning Organization (2006).
[152] Other problems include: about 95% of the railway network is single track; 3,080 km of rails are old (20 years or more); 2,756 km have steel and wooden sleepers; 2,602 km have non-standard curves; 5,586 km of main lines are without signal; and there is insufficient staff (UNECE, 2006).
[153] Information provided by the authorities.
[154] TCDD is the largest money loser among Turkey's public enterprises. The management of ports provides about a third of its revenues, another third comes from rail traffic, and the rest from government subsidies and non-operating revenues (WTO, 2003).
[155] Includes a twinning project with German Railways (European Commission, 2006).
[156] In 2006, approximately 4,366 km of roads (excluding village roads) were still unpaved.
[157] Turkey has the largest truck fleet in Europe, after Italy. In 2004, Turkey's international road transport fleet consisted of some 32,000 vehicles, with a carriage capacity of 1.4 million tonnes (State Planning Organization, 2006).

long-term visas for professional drivers; and border-crossing problems (e.g. outdated technology for customs transactions, different transit regimes, and lack of coordination between customs authorities).[158]

The MT is responsible for regulating road transport to maintain order and safety of transport; to determine the conditions to be applied to carriers agents, brokers, warehouses, and cargo operators; to establish the qualifications, rights, and duties of persons employed in the subsector; and to provide inter-operability of road transport with other modes of transport and efficient use of existing capabilities. Road transport services in Turkey are provided by private companies; an operating licence from the MT is obligatory. The General Directorate of Highways is responsible for the construction, maintenance, and operation of roads. In practice, tariffs in the subsector are set freely by operators and notified to the MT. Cabotage is not permitted in road transport: vehicles registered in a foreign country cannot transport goods or passengers between two points within Turkey. Transport of goods or passengers can be provided to, from, and through Turkey only under bilateral or multilateral (e.g. International Transport Forum) agreements or permits issued by the Council of Ministers.

In February 2004, road transport for intercity passengers and freight was liberalized under the Law on Road Transport.[159] This law and related regulations are aimed at, inter alia, increasing efficiency and safety in road transport activities, developing an insurance system for freight and passenger transport, promoting competition in the subsector through more participation by the private sector, and improving the overall road infrastructure.

In January 2006, the Road Transport Automation (U-NET) system was put into operation. It is a computer-aided system that scrutinizes the road transport subsector, including monitoring and inspecting the market.

TOURISM

Turkey ranks 9th in the world as a tourism earner (against 11th in 2002), with US$18.1 billion of tourism receipts in 2006 (Table IV.11), up from US$11.9 billion in 2002; this is expected to increase to US$36.4 billion by 2013.[160] Tourism activities have continued to expand rapidly during the last few years, especially in Istanbul and on the western and southern coasts. Large numbers of hotels, guest houses, and holiday apartments have been built. There are also important historical sites, and eco-tourism activities are being introduced. The number of licensed tourist beds rose from 619,024 in 2002 to 783,319 in 2006. In 2006, 28.3% of visitors came from Europe and 59.1% from OECD countries (mainly Germany, 19% of the total). The hotels occupancy rate was about 47.3%.

Table IV.11
Selected tourism indicators, 2005-07

	2005	2006[a]	2007[b]	Percentage change 2005-06	Percentage change 2006-07
Incoming tourists ('000)	21,125	20,816	22,339	-1.5	7.3
Turkish tourists abroad ('000)	8,246	8,180	9,000	-0.8	10.0
Tourism receipts (US$ million)	18,152	18,124	19,800	-0.2	9.2

[158] UNECE (2006).
[159] Law No. 4925 published in *Official Gazette* No. 25173 on 19 July 2003.
[160] State Planning Organization (2006).

Tourism expenditure (US$ million)	2,872	2,863	3,200	-0.3	11.8

a Provisional.
b Estimates.

Source: Information provided by the Turkish authorities.

Turkey's tourism policy has three main goals: creating an efficient and internationally competitive subsector with a view to making it more profitable; meeting the requirements of foreign and domestic tourists in terms of overall facilities; and ensuring the continuity of its natural and cultural assets. The Turkish Union of Travel Agencies (TURSAB), established in 1972 under Law No. 1618 and the purview of the Ministry of Culture and Tourism (MCT), is responsible for supervising travel agencies. Within the MCT there is a section responsible for inspection of hotels, holiday villages, yacht enterprises, travel agencies, the professional organization, and professional tourist guides. Under the Tourism Encouragement Law No. 2634 of 1982 (as amended), tourist regions, areas, and centres were designated, and investment in tourism facilities is encouraged. In general, the State is in charge of investment in tourism sites.

The Government remains active in the tourism subsector. It grants incentives for tourism investments in accordance with the Tourism Encouragement Law; provides infrastructure and public services for tourism; defines zones with high tourism potential; promulgates designated tourism centres or areas by decree; elaborates and approves land-use plans; conducts environmental controls; promotes the country abroad; carries out research and collects statistics; and provides vocational training. Local administrations are responsible for similar matters at the local level. Investors in tourism also have access to incentives granted under the Investment Encouragement Programme (Chapter III(2)(iii)(d)).

Foreign companies have increased their role in tourism since the mid-1980s; there is no limitation on foreign investment. Foreign and domestic companies set their own maximum prices. However, the prices must be cleared annually by the MCT. Enterprises are not required to charge uniform prices but cannot exceed their maximum approved prices.

The MCT and local administrations are in charge of classification and certification of hotels and restaurants. According to the authorities, the number of beds certified by the MCT and the municipalities are expected to reach 550,000 and 420,000, respectively.

LEADING EXPORT, INVESTMENT AND BUSINESS OPPORTUNITIES

LEADING SECTORS FOR U.S. EXPORT AND INVESTMENT

OIL AND GAS SECTOR OPPORTUNITIES

Unit: USD millions

	2009	2010	2011 (estimated)	2012 (estimated)
Total Market Size	2,150	2,370	2,700	2,900
Total Local Production	150	190	200	220
Total Exports	70	80	90	100
Total Imports	2,070	2,260	2,590	2,780
Imports from the U.S.	95	110	250	280
Exchange Rate: 1 USD	1.54 TL	1.49 TL	1.54 TL	1.54 TL

Total Market Size = (Total Local Production + Total Imports) – (Total Exports)

Data Sources: Government of Turkey statistics bureau, http://www.x-rates.com/cgi-bin/hlookup.cgi

Surrounding Turkey is 73% of the world's proven oil reserves and 72% of the world's proven gas reserves. This makes Turkey a crucial bridge between energy rich regions and Europe, which spends approximately $300 billion per year for imported energy resources. Turkey spends over $20 billion for oil & gas imports, and there is great demand for exploring and finding indigenous oil and gas resources.

Some companies have found natural gas offshore along the western Black Sea coast of Turkey and started production in Turkey. Companies have explored for oil & gas in only 20% of the potential onshore prospects and 1% of potential offshore prospects so. This means many prospects are waiting to be explored. In 2011, offshore drilling for oil and gas prospects in offshore Black Sea will be one of the major U.S. export opportunities. The state-owned company Turkish Petroleum Corporation (TPAO) has signed JV agreements with Chevron, Exxon Mobil and Petrobras. TPAO has also signed an agreement with Transatlantic Petroleum Corporation for prospects for unconventional oil & gas in Turkey.

TPAO has other important prospect licenses for which they would not hesitate to select a foreign partner as TPAO has limited resources for investment itself. (See www.tpao.gov.tr) TPAO has either established or plans to establish joint ventures for other potential oil & gas prospects in Azerbaijan, Iraq, Kazakhstan, Libya, Syria, Turkmenistan and South American countries.

In addition to TPAO, Aladdin Middle East, Chevron, Edison, Enel, ENI, E.ON Ruhrgas, Exxon Mobil, Genel Enerji, Guney Yildizi, OMV, Pet Oil, Perenco, Petrobras, Shell, Statoil, Total, Transatlantic Petroleum Corporation, Thrace Basin Natural Gas Türkiye Corporation, Tiway Oil, Turcas, and Zorlu are the most active oil and gas upstream companies in Turkey. Some of these companies are also active in downstream operations.

The Baku-Tbilisi-Ceyhan (BTC) oil pipeline started operation in 2006 with 1 million barrels per day (bpd) and approximately 5% of the world's oil supply will be flowing through Turkey. The target is to increase BTC Volumer to 1.6 million bpd of crude. Central Asian oil supply will be blended through BTC. Ceyhan, a harbor on the Mediterranean coast of Turkey, will be the energy hub and in the future supply a crude oil blend of Azeri, Iraqi and Central Asian oil. Ceyhan will also have at least two more new oil refineries and petrochemical plants. Currently, Calik Energy is in the process of developing a design of an oil refinery for which it selected Shaw Stone and Webster Group. Tupras is expected to make new investments in the same region where Azeri and Iraqi oil is received through pipelines.

Another new refinery project is being developed in the Aegean Region. Socar-Turcas received a license to build a new refinery at Petkim's site in Aliaga, Izmir. The refinery will be built adjacent to Petkim's cracker. The refinery will primarily make naphtha to serve as an input into Petkim's processes, but will also produce diesel. Total investment cost will be approximately $4.5 billion. This refinery will treat 10 million tons of crude oil a year and will be operational at the end of 2014. The investment license was issued in July 2010 and the engineering and design services are underway. Request for proposal for turnkey EPC contracting is expected to be issued by the end of 2011.

Currently, the existing refineries owned and operated by TUPRAS meets 60% of Turkey's demand. Therefore, new refineries will help to fill in the demand gap.

Chemical and plastic growth continues to run at about 3 X GDP growths in Turkey. Petkim plans to expand its petrochemical production facilities in the same area. The demand for Polypropylene and PVC are expected to grow in particular, but polyethylene and HDPE also remain strong.

The Turkish Government is supporting the Samsun-Ceyhan Bosporus by-pass crude oil pipeline, to be constructed. Calik Energy and the Italian firm ENI will be investors. Russian energy firms Transneft and Rosneft have also stated they may take 25% shares in the pipeline. The total cost of the project will be $2.5 billion. 6 tender packages are being prepared. U.S. companies may find opportunities with U.S. Eximbank financing. This project will also feed in oil to refinery and petrochemical projects to be implemented in the Ceyhan oil & gas industrial zone.

A natural gas pipeline project to supply Europe from Azerbaijan, Iraq, Egypt and Turkmenistan and potentially Kazakhstan is planned as an alternative resource to Europe. The main source of supply will be the second stage of the Shah Deniz gas field Azerbaijan, coming on-stream in 2017. The Nabucco pipeline will be extended from Turkey to Austria through Bulgaria, Romania, and Hungary. A combination of state-owned and private energy companies from these countries and Germany will be investors in NABUCCO. The Nabucco project is included in the EU Trans-European Energy Network program. The 3,300 Km pipeline is planned to supply 25.5-31 bcma of gas to Europe and is planned to come on line in 2012, pending final approvals. In 2010, tenders for the engineering and survey for the NABUCCO pipeline links have been conducted. Major opportunities will be announced at the NABUCCO web site: http://www.nabucco-pipeline.com/portal/page/portal/en .

Another proposed potential pipeline project to be built in the region is Trans Adriatic Pipeline (TAP) project. The 520km-long pipeline will start in Greece near Thessaloniki, cross Albania and the Adriatic Sea and come ashore in Italy near Brindisi, allowing gas to flow directly from the Caspian basin and Middle East into European markets. The pipeline is part of the European Union-designated Southern Gas Corridor which will link Caspian gas sources to Europe and provide significant reverse flow capacities. The project is designed to expand transportation capacity from 10 to 20 bcm per year depending on throughput. The TAP project also envisages the development of natural gas storage facilities in Albania to further ensure security of supply during operational interruptions of gas deliveries. (http://www.trans-adriatic-pipeline.com/index_.html)

In addition to NABUCCO and TAP, the Interconnection Turkey Greece Italy (ITGI) natural gas pipeline project will probably be another opportunity to be considered. The collaborative agreement to build and manage the pipeline was signed by the representatives of the three countries in July 2007 in Rome. The project will supply natural gas from the Caspian Sea and the Middle East to Europe. The ITGI project includes three segments, including expansion of the Turkish national grid for transmitting natural gas to Italy and Turkey, building a pipeline between Turkey and Greece, and building a further pipeline between Greece and Italy.

The project has been given top priority by the European Commission. The European Union has also proposed to fund €100m for the ITGI project, calling it a "project of European interest" in the European recovery plan. The pipeline between Turkey and Greece is known as Interconnector Turkey Greece (ITG) which is completed and supplying gas to Greece, but may need to be expanded. The pipeline between Greece and Italy is known as Interconnector Greece Italy (IGI). The project will also include a bypass line between Greece and Bulgaria. Known as Interconnector Greece Bulgaria (IGB), it will have a transmission capacity of three to five billion cubic meters of natural gas per annum. The ITGI project is scheduled to be operational by 2015.

Botas, Turkey's pipeline parastatal, has approximately 10,000 Km of natural gas (NG) transmission pipelines within Turkey. Approximately 68 provinces in Turkey received natural gas and this figure is expanding every year throughout the entire country with the private sector investments of NG distribution lines. Maintenance repair and overhaul of these pipelines present opportunities for American firms.

One of the major projects in this sector is BOTAS Petroleum Pipeline Company's Underground Gas Storage project near Salt Lake in Turkey. The World Bank approved a loan of US $325 million to support this Gas Sector Development Project. The gas storage facility will be located in an underground salt formation close to Tuz Lake, a salt lake in Central Turkey. The facility, upon completion, will have a storage capacity of about 960 million cubic meters of working gas and 460 million cubic meters of cushion gas (the portion of gas which is required to remain in the cavern to maintain its integrity). The facility will have the capacity to deliver 40 million cubic meters of gas per day up to 20 days and can be refilled at the rate of 30 million cubic meters per day over a period of 25 days. Calik Energy is developing another underground gas storage project in the same region. The U.S. Trade Development Agency (US TDA) has provided a grant for a feasibility study of this project, which is being conducted by an American firm. The U.S Embassy's Commercial Service is recruiting an oil and gas service/ machinery trade mission to Turkey and Kazakhstan in June 2011; contact our offices for more detail.

As part of the liberalization process in the natural gas (NG) market, the Energy Market Regulatory Agency issues licenses for natural gas distribution, storage, trading (import-export or wholesale) to the private sector. www.botas.gov.tr .

Sub-Sector Best Prospects

Offshore/Onshore Oil and Gas Drilling and Production Equipment and Services;
Turbines, Compressors and Pumps For Pipeline Applications;
Measurement and Process Control Equipment for Pipeline Operations;
Industrial Automation, Control And Monitoring Systems and Other Equipment and Services For Refineries, Gas Processing and Petrochemical Plants;
Seismic Processing and Interpretation;

Petroleum Software Development;
Sulfur Removal and Disposal Technologies;
Well Stimulation;
Field Abandonment Services;
Geothermal Exploration, Drilling, Production and Processing Equipment and Services,
Engineering and Industrial Construction Companies.
Scada Systems,
Pipeline Construction Equipment,
emote Controlled Digital Gas Meters,
ressure Reduction Valves,
CNG Service Station Equipment,
LNG Facilities,
Refinery Equipment and Technology Supply,
Underground Storage Surface and Sub-Surface Facilities

OPPORTUNITIES

U.S. Companies have potential opportunities in the construction of NABUCCO, Samsun-Ceyhan, and Iraq-Turkey natural gas pipelines. Tuz Golu Underground Gas Storage project surface and sub-surface facilities, salt cavern leaching contracts, new refineries, and BOTAS' new main transmission pipeline construction tenders, which include gas turbines and generators. In next 5 years, Botas will require 7 more natural gas compressor stations. Opportunities exist in oil and gas exploration and production offshore Black Sea and in Southeastern Turkey. A new refinery, petrochemical plants and LNG facilities will be other opportunities to consider.

WEB RESOURCES

Botas' Web Site: www.botas.gov.tr
Energy Market Regulatory Agency (EMRA)'s Web Site: www.emra.org.tr
Petroleum Affairs General Directorate (PIGM) web site www.pigm.gov.tr
NABUCCO Web Site:
www.nabucco-pipeline.com
TPAO Web Site: www.tpao.gov.tr
PETFORM Web Site: www.petform.org.tr

For further information on this report and to search more on the potential opportunities, please contact:
Serdar Cetinkaya
Commercial Specialist
U.S. Commercial Service
e-mail: Serdar.Cetinkaya@trade.gov
Web: http://www.buyusa.gov/turkey/en

EDUCATION SERVICES

Unit: Turkish Students

	2009	2010	2011 (estimated)	2012 (estimated)

Total Students Abroad	32,500	32,000	33,000	33,500
Total Students in U.S.	12,148	12,397	12,400	12,600
Undergrad in U.S.	4,008	3,657	3,800	3,900
Grad Students in U.S.	6,320	6,583	6,700	6,750
Other students (Language, training, OPT)	1,820	2,157	1,900	1,950

Data Sources: Turkish Ministry of Education and the Institute of International Education

Turkey's population of 73.7 million is relatively young, when compared with many other countries. About 45 percent of the population is under the age of twenty-five. This young population provides considerable opportunities for international education institutions.

According to the Basic Law on National Education No 1739, the Turkish school system has 4 different levels:

a) Pre-school Education: Pre-school education is not compulsory in Turkey. Most of the preschools are privately owned and some are attached to the state primary schools. They are concentrated in large cities so as to meet the needs of working parents.

b) Primary School Education: In Turkey, primary school education is compulsory which starts at the age of 6 and lasts eight years. 10.92 million students are enrolled at 33,310 primary schools.

c) Secondary Education: Secondary education includes all of the general, vocational and technical high schools that provide four years of education after primary school. The number of high school students is about 4.24 million. There are a total of 8,913 high schools, including the public and private high schools. The public high schools have limited resources and more students in one classroom compared to the private ones.

d) Higher Education: Normally there is 4 years of undergraduate education for the universities, with some fields such as medicine lasting six years. There are also the “Meslek Yuksek Okullari”, literally “higher vocational schools” which offer 2 year of undergraduate study over high school and are very much like the community colleges in the U.S.

As of December 2010, there are 102 public and 52 private foundation universities serving 3 million students in various academic programs. 2009 figures reveal that 1.62 million students are enrolled in undergraduate programs, 109,845 in master’s programs, 35,946 in PhD, 12,292 in doctors in residency programs and 1.14 million in the Open University. Public universities charge a small fee, whereas private university tuition costs range between 10 thousand dollars to 25 thousand dollars per year. A number of outstanding students of limited means are able to attend private universities on merit scholarships.

Entrance into the university is very competitive due to the limited capacity of Turkish universities. Students need to pass a nationwide placement test that takes place once every year in June. Every year an increasing number of students take the exam. In 2010, 1,487,626 high school graduates took the exam and around 24% of these applicants were enrolled in a 4-year program, 19% in a 2-year program, 21% to the Open University (distance education in the various subfields of economics and business administration). The rest were unable to enter any higher education program.

In Turkey, the Ministry of National Education (Milli Egitim Bakanligi) is responsible for administering all educational services in the country, excluding higher education. The Council of

Higher Education (YOK) is a 22-member corporate public body responsible for the planning, coordination and supervision of higher education.

The number of Turkish universities are insufficient to meet the increasing demand for higher education, thus there is a large Turkish student population studying abroad. Many students willing to study abroad, place American universities at the top of the list due to the quality of education and good career prospects. Over 30 thousand students go abroad for university education; U.S. colleges and universities already attract around 13,000 Turkish students for undergraduate, graduate and specialized training. This 40 % plus U.S market share is significant.

The Institute of International Education's Open Doors 2010 Statistics reveal that Turkey, with its 12,397 students is the tenth leading place of origin for students in the U.S., right after Vietnam and surpassing Germany, France and the U.K. Turkey ranks number one among European countries with the number of students in the U.S. Turkish students also constitute the ninth largest student body in the U.S. for intensive English programs.

According to Institute of International Education's Fact Sheet on Turkey for the Academic Year 2009-2010, among 12,397 Turkish students the level of enrollment is as follows:

Undergraduate: 3,657
Graduate: 6,583
Other (Language and Training Courses): 2,157

Sub-Sector Best Prospects

According to the Activity Report prepared by the Turkish Fulbright Commission Istanbul Branch Office in 2010, which is part of the Education USA network of the Department of State, following are the most popular fields of study chosen by Turkish students:

Field	%
1. Business administration and economics (especially MBA programs in finance, marketing and international business)	37 %
2. Engineering, computer science and other technical fields	23 %
3. English as a second language	12 %
4. Short-term certificate programs and/or summer programs (mostly in business ESL)	7 %
5. Social sciences, humanities and arts (mainly psychology, political sciences, architecture and law)	7 %
6. Mass communications (radio-TV, film&video production)	6 %
7. Medicine and other medical fields (for the most part, advanced level residencies)	5 %
8. Natural and physical sciences	2 %
9. Other fields	1 %

Opportunities

There are more students interested in higher education than can be accommodated in the Turkish universities. Thus, good opportunities exist for American universities and colleges to explore a rapidly growing market. The results of the central university placement exam in Turkey are not announced until mid August, so overseas schools that can accept unmatched or dissatisfied students for the second semester/quarter have an advantage.

The Ministry of National Education, the Council of Higher Education and many ministries offer scholarships to hundreds of successful students each year wishing to continue their studies abroad. These students usually apply to top "brand name" universities either in Turkey or abroad. Cost is not a critical factor in their decision-making process as the scholarship sponsors pay for their entire studies. However, these scholarship holders are usually bonded to work with their sponsoring organizations for about 6-10 years after they graduate. Their decisions are based mostly on the reputations of institutions, the faculty, and the programs that these students will be pursuing.

Due to the competitive nature of the Turkish labor market and the significant level of unemployment, many students feel the necessity to have a post graduate/masters degree to be able to find better jobs. These programs are even more competitive, so students seek placement at foreign universities. Graduate studies are the most popular level of enrollment for Turkish students.

Several Turkish universities have cooperation programs with American universities and their students have opportunities to continue their education in the U.S. institutions. Other American institutions may wish to pursue such cooperative agreements as well as student exchange programs to attract qualified Turkish students.

Many students and professionals opt for supplementary English language education to improve their command of English, as fluency in English provides a competitive advantage in job hunting and career prospects. This opportunity gives U.S. firms a chance to compete in the market by providing private English language courses in Turkey and intensive language programs in the United States.

Other opportunities for U.S. educational institutions and companies include the following:

- Professional language training in Law; Business Administration; Marketing; and Technical English in Turkey and abroad
- Graduate and doctorate programs
- Business and certificate courses for professionals in Turkey, particularly computer-based programs
- Distance education programs

Web Resources

The Turkish Fulbright Commission: http://www.fulbright.org.tr/

Ministry of National Education (For General Education):
http://www.meb.gov.tr/english/indexeng.htm

The Council of Higher Education (For Higher Education): http://www.yok.gov.tr/en/

For further information on this report and to search more on the potential opportunities, please contact:

Perim Akguner
Commercial Specialist
U.S. Commercial Service
U.S. Consulate Istanbul, Turkey

e-mail: Perim.Akguner@trade.gov
Web: http://www.buyusa.gov/turkey/en

CONSTRUCTION MACHINERY

Unit: USD millions

	2009	2010	2011 (estimated)	2012 (estimated)
Total Market Size	2,388	2,388	2,791	4,783
Total Local Production	707	707	1,110	1,776
Total Exports	910	910	910	1,138
Total Imports	2,591	2,591	2,591	4,145
Imports from the U.S.	207	207	207	350
Exchange Rate: 1 USD	TL 1.54	TL 1.49	TL 1.54	TL 1.54

Turkish construction machinery market is one of the fastest growing ones in this field in Europe. The Turkish economy has been growing at an average rate of 5-6% every year since 2003 until the last financial crisis of 2008. As was the case in the rest of the world, 2009 was a negative growth year but 2010 proved to be different year for Turkey with a GDP growth rate of approximately 8%. The construction industry was a catalyst to this increase. Turkey houses a population of 75 million people and the country has been experiencing a domestic migration from rural areas to cities in the last 30 years. This created and is expected to keep on creating proper houses for people to live and work in, which eventually led to growth in construction industry.

In addition to strong domestic demand fot construction machinery, the presence of Turkish contractors; Russia, Central Asia, Middle East, the Balkan countries and North Africa also plays a role. According to a report by Engineering News Record, there are 33 Turkish contractors in the "World Top 225 Contractors List" ranked according to the number of contracts granted outside their home/over countries. Turkey ranks after China in the number of contracts granted, which amounted to $23.6billion in 2009.

All of these factors make Turkey an attractive market for U.S. construction machinery exporters in general. Turkey is the sixth largest construction machinery market in Europe, showing signs for room for growth. In 2000, 4,900 units of heavy construction machinery were sold in Turkey; come 2010, the number increased to 7,700 and forecast for 2011 is to close the year with a sales of 10,000 units of heavy construction machinery. According to The Turkish Construction Machinery Distributors and Manufacturers Association's (IMDER) figures, in 2010, there were around 54,000 units of various types of construction machinery in use (not over 7 years of age).

Whereas Italy, France and Germany had 170,000 units, 220,000 units and 210,000 units respectively, The Turkish market has much room for growth.

There are 550 Turkish companies operating specifically in the construction machinery sector. Turkey also manufactures various construction machinery and there are 100 manufacturers. There are 220 companies that are supplying manufacturers and the rest are importers and distributors. Imported products dominate 70% of the market, whereas 30% of market is composed of products manufactured by Turkish companies. These machinery are mainly in the following industries: agriculture, forestry, construction, mining, marble industry, solid waste management, marine and demolition.

Industry sources stated that about 80% of products sold in the market are excavators, loaders backhoe loaders and forklifts. This fact encouraged a number of Turkish companies start their own manufacturing facilities in Turkey in order to meet demand. Eventually, they started exporting, too. The major manufacturers are Cukurova Insaat, Hidromek and Sanko. There are also some global brands operating in this specific area like Caterpillar, JCB, New Holland, Hyundai, Daewoo, Hitachi, Kato Works, Liugong and Volvo. As the value added tax levied on these products is 8% and is less than the 18% levied on other construction machinery, they benefit from this advantage.

The rest of the products, which constitute around 20% of the market, are mainly mobile cranes, tower cranes, crawler cranes, breakers and demolition tools, minining and tunneling machines, drill rigs and rock drills, concrete pumps, cylinders, dozers, road rollers, mixers etc. Global brands that are active in the market in the marketing of these products are Sandvik, Schwing, Stetter, New Holland, Terex, Manitowoc, Demag, Liebherr and Hiab. Within these products, due to fastly growing construction industry and construction of high rise buildings, there is a specific need for tower cranes. There currently are around 1,500 tower cranes in Turkey; in the last few years, about 300 cranes are sold in Turkey annually. In addition to this, use of truck mounted cranes is also increasing, with potential for U.S. companies. It should be noted that Turkey is a major automobile and commercial truck manufacturer and when selling truck mounted cranes to Turkey, sales from U.S. will most probably be less the truck itself.

As for exports of second-hand machinery to Turkey goes, Turkish regulations are not totally aligned with the regulations in European Union (EU). While documentation and certification requirements are the same with EU,Turkey allows for second hand sales of 38 out of 42 construction types sold in Turkey. The four items that are not permitted to be sold second hand are beko loaders, loaders, excavators and forklifts, which are manufactured in Turkey.

There are three groups of buyers of construction machinery in Turkey.

construction companies
rental companies
government/municipalities

Construction companies buy various types of construction machinery to use in their own projects. At times when they are not using them, they rent it to our contractors. It is usually the case that large construction companies have a machine park.

However, in the last few years, in line with the developments in Europe and in the U.S., construction companies started renting their machinery needs from rental companies. There are a number of large size rental companies in the market alongside numerous growing ones. The expectancy is that these rental companies will dominate the market in the coming years and that construction companies will buy less machinery.

One other customer segment is government agencies and municipalities. The State Equipment Office is a government procurement agency and publishes a catalog composed of suppliers that can supply to government entities. Getting into this catalog as a supplier is one way of selling to government entities. However, as government entities and municipalities are now leading towards contracting their infrastructure projects to private construction companies in one package, this means that they are not buying construction machinery directly as much as they used to do.

In order to be able to sell in Turkey, The U.S. Commercial Service recommends U.S. exporters to identify an importer/agent with a strong sales and reseller channel and ability to establish a maintenance service. Selling directly from The U.S. is possible; however, in order to have consistent and growing sales figure in the Turkish market, having representation in the market is advised.

SUB-SECTOR BEST PRODUCTS

As there is a strong manufacturing base and presence of many imported brands for backhoe loaders, loaders, excavators and forklifts, the market is highly competitive for these specific products. However, there are greater opportunities for the manufacturers of the following products:

mobile cranes
crawler cranes
tower cranes (with high ton capacity)
graders
dozers
rollers
rock drills
drill rigs
mining machinery
tunneling machinery
concrete breakers

OPPORTUNITIES

construction sector's being the leading driver of the Turkish economy
growing mining industry
large number of projects Turkish contractors are granted outside Turkey
need for more advanced equipment park to meet advanced construction needs, like high tonage tower cranes
ongoing transportation, metro and infrastructure projects

WEB RESOURCES

IMDER – Construction Equipment Manufacturers and Distributors' Association of Turkey Website: http://www.imder.org.tr/?yenilisan=en

Vincisder – Crane Operators Association of Turkey Website: http://www.vincder.com/

For further information on this report and to search more on the potential opportunities, please contact:

Ebru Olcay
Commercial Specialist
U.S. Commercial Service
U.S. Consulate Istanbul, Turkey
e-mail: Ebru.olcay@trade.gov
Web: http://www.buyusa.gov/turkey/en

DEFENSE EQUIPMENT

Unit: USD millions

	2009	2010	2011 (estimated)	2012 (estimated)
Total Market Size	3,863	4,030	4,390	4,390
Total Local Production	2,319	2,500	2,700	2,700
Total Exports	669	770	893	893
Total Imports	2,213	2,300	2,583	2,583
Imports from the U.S.	400	400	420	420
Exchange Rate: 1 USD	TL 1.54	TL 1.49	TL 1.54	TL 1.54

Turkey has always had a strong military to protect and defend its national borders and interests. Located at the crossroads of Europe, Asia and the Middle East, Turkey and its armed forces must be prepared to deter political conflicts and continue to fight terrorism in the Caucasus, the Middle East and the Balkans. Turkey understands that its role within NATO is to maintain troop strength that will serve as a deterrent, support security and humanitarian operations in the region, support regional crisis management, and operate small scale or limited force deployments. Turkey maintains the second largest land force in NATO and operates the second largest fleet of F-16s, second only to the United States.

The FY 2011 Ministry of Defense (MOD) budget is $ 11.3 billion. This does not include spending by the Ministry of Interior's Gendarmerie, the Coast Guard, defense procurements refunded by the Turkish Treasury and the Undersecretariat for Defense Industry (SSM) Support Fund. The breakdown of the total MOD budget is as follows: 44. 2% personnel expenditures; 8.5% transfers to social security institutions; 45.7% procurement of goods and services; 1.2% current transfers and 0.4% capital expenditures. The total amount allocated to the procurement of goods and services is approximately $ 5.3 billion 50% of which will be spent on modernization activities within the scope of the 2011 Plan for Strategic Targets. Along with MOD spending, $21.3 million is allocated to the SSM proprietary budget. On the other hand, as stated by Defense Minister Gonul, the share of MOD's budget in total GMP has decreased by around 0.8% since 2003.

All procurements for the Turkish Armed Forces (TuAF) are carried out according to certain rules and legislations, through which relevant and authorized institutions and organizations participate. The basis of all procurement activities is the Public Tender Law No. 4734 and the Public Tender Contracts Law No. 4735, which came into effect on January 1st, 2003. Direct military defense procurement is carried out by the Ministry of National Defense. SSM is in charge of all new procurements for TuAF, except for logistics related procurement and certain smaller projects.

The MOD would like to modernize the TuAF to meet operational requirements in a timely fashion. Turkey is aiming to improve its manufacturing capabilities and develop a national industry in the field of defense to become self-sufficient. In order to reach this goal, Turkey is trying to maximize local manufacturing capabilities through R&D and technology transfer. Large scale system integrator companies along with SMEs which develop subsystems for system integrators are playing a key role in building up indigenous solutions for the defense industry.

PROJECTS

Potential Turkish projects include: Demining of Syrian Border, Joint Strike Fighter, Peace Onyx IV Project, F-16 Modernizations, Joint Strike Fighter Program, Attack, Transport, and Police Helicopter Tenders, Development of Turkish National Ship (Milgem), Turkish Frigate 2000

Project, Air Defense Missile Systems, Basic Trainer Aircraft Design, UAV Projects, Satellites, Naval Patrol Craft, Weapon Platforms, Amphibious Vessels, Coastal Surveillance Radar Systems, Turkish National Tank, Armed Tactical Vehicles among many others.

IDEF 2011

The 10th International Defense Industry Fair (IDEF '11) will take place on 10-13 May 2011 in Istanbul. Organized under the auspices of the Ministry of National Defense, IDEF is the premier defense exhibition in Turkey and the region. IDEF is the venue where equipment and service suppliers can meet key decision-makers in order to cultivate and establish business relationships. Kallman Worldwide Inc. is organizing a U.S. Pavilion for IDEF`11 and recruiting U.S. exhibitors. (http://www.kallman.com).

IDEF'11 is certified by the U.S. Department of Commerce and the U.S. Commercial Service Turkey will be present at the U.S.A. National Pavilion during the entire show to assist U.S. companies. If you are interested in learning more about IDEF 2011 please contact Commercial Specialist Ozge Cirika at Ozge.Cirika@trade.gov or +90-312-457-7169.

Opportunities

Although the focus is on developing the national defense industry, due to the size and sophistication level of the upcoming projects there are various opportunities for U.S. companies in the Turkish Market. In the main weapons systems category, about 80% of the defense equipment is presently procured from abroad.

The requirements of TuAF are met through direct purchases from domestic and foreign markets or by their participation in joint production programs. The joint production programs constitute potential export opportunities, as the tendency is to give more emphasis to joint production and joint activities through R&D. Turkey has started taking steps to develop indigenous systems to meet the needs of the TuAF.

The modernization of TuAF will also bring export opportunities to U.S. companies. In the next 20 years, combat weapons and equipment currently in the TuAF inventory will need to be modernized or replaced with systems incorporating new technologies. Other requirements include main battle tanks, wheeled armored vehicles, tank transport and rescue vehicles, artillery upgrades, the pedestal mounted Stinger program, army tactical missile system (ATACMS), combat aircraft, airborne early warning aircraft (AEW), search and rescue helicopters, unmanned aerial vehicles (UAVs), submarines, destroyer class ships, fast patrol boats, mine hunter vessels and maritime patrol and surveillance aircraft.

Web Resources

U.S. Department of Commerce market research: http://www.export.gov/marketresearch.html

SSM www.ssm.gov.tr

MOD www.msb.gov.tr

SASAD www.sasad.org.tr

For further information on this report and to search more on the potential opportunities, please contact:

Ozge Cirika
Commercial Specialist
U.S. Commercial Service
U.S. Consulate Istanbul, Turkey
e-mail: Ozge.cirika@trade.gov
Web: http://www.buyusa.gov/turkey/en -+

HEALTH AND MEDICAL TECHNOLOGIES

Unit: USD millions

	2009	2010	2011 (estimated)	2012 (estimated)
Total Market Size	1,600	1,800	1,870	2,020
Total Local Production	190	200	210	226
Total Exports	190	200	220	240
Total Imports	1,600	1,800	1880	2,034
Imports from the U.S.	260	270	280	305
Exchange Rate: 1 USD	TL 1.54	TL 1.49	TL 1.54	TL 1.54

Turkey has a population of approximately 75 million people and is a growing market for the medical products and services sectors. The Ministry of Health (MOH) is the largest provider of healthcare and the only public provider of preventive services in Turkey. At a national level, MOH is responsible for the country's health policy and health services. In fiscal year (FY) 2011, 17.2 billion TL was allocated to the Turkish Ministry of Health (MOH) by the Government of Turkey (GOT). The MOH budget showed an increase of 40% year over year. A key driver behind Turkey's continued double-digit growth in health expenditure is the country's improved health insurance coverage. The implementation of state-funded health insurance for the lowest earners is expected to make a significant contribution to continued health expenditure growth over the next five years.

More than 50 percent of healthcare expenditures are devoted to medical services, while medical devices constitute a smaller portion of the total overall healthcare budget. Major healthcare services are provided by both public and private hospitals. Approximately 40 percent of in-patient and 56 percent of the outpatient expenses are financed by public funding sources.

There is a strong privatization trend in Turkey's health sector, even though a high percentage of total hospital bed capacity is provided by government agencies. The construction of many private hospitals offers increased sales opportunities and less complicated procurement requirements compared to the confusing tender requirements used by government agencies. The Ministry of Health is also pursuing a number of Public Private Partnership (PPP) projects with Turkish and foreign companies to establish healthcare campuses, large medical complexes with several hospitals, labs and recreational areas, in large cities. These projects are also business opportunities for U.S. medical companies and healthcare service providers, often when teaming with Turkish construction companies.

Another major transformation Turkish healthcare system is undergoing is the introduction of family practitioner practice across the country. Turkey has been educating family practitioner for at least a decade but could not devise the method to utilize these professionals effectively. As of

December 2010, a nationwide system was initiated whereby every Turkish citizen was assigned a family practitioner for primary and preventative medical service.

The Republic of Turkey has a number of private care facilities focused on cardiovascular care, OBGYN, orthopedics and minimally invasive outpatient ambulatory procedures. A number of private hospitals are procuring angio-cath, radiological equipment and advanced surgical and life support technologies. The procurement of air ambulances and diagnostic medical devices is also being considered. The MOH is working to establish a Council of Pharmaceuticals and Medical Devices, which will be independent from the MOH with the authority to regulate and control the medical equipment, pharmaceuticals, cosmetics market in Turkey.

Medical tourism is a new sector developing in Turkey. Increasingly, patients from Europe and the Middle East go to Turkey for medical treatment, as private healthcare is becoming more affordable. Turkey has become a popular destination for health care among these countries because most of the patients have already vacationed in Turkey and are comfortable with the country's infrastructure.

Currently, medical procedures in demand vary from simple procedures to fertility treatment, cosmetic surgery, and laser surgery. The most popular procedures are cosmetic and dental procedures, yet Turkey also has a good reputation in cardiology, ophthalmology, endocrinology, gastroenterology, rheumatology, nephrology, oncology, neurology, dermatology, gynecology/obstetrics, orthopedics, organ transplantation, and otolaryngology (ear, nose & throat). Some of these surgeries have long waiting lists in European countries, which is another reason why Turkey is an attractive country for medical procedures.

Sub-Sector Best Prospects

There are about 6,000 companies in the medical device and disposables market in Turkey, of which about 450 of these are medium to large size companies. There are about 100 medical equipment manufacturers in the country, most of which are manufacturing disposables, prosthetics and hospital furniture.

• Disposable products

• Advanced med/surgery equipment including angio-cath facilities

• Radiology and pathology

• Advanced diagnostics systems

• Optical devices

• Parts and components of medical devices

• Electronic instruments and appliances for physical and chemical analysis

• Vaccines

• Orthotic and prosthetic equipment

• OR/ER systems

• Dental equipment and devices

Opportunities

The total bed capacity in Turkish Hospitals is above 200,000, an increase of more than 10 percent over the past 5 years. The privatization and transformation of the healthcare system, establishment of new healthcare facilities under the PPP model and ongoing hospital projects of the Ministry of Health are export opportunities.

As Turkey continues to expand the number of private and public hospitals, the purchase of advanced medical equipment will continue. There are now some large hospital chains that not only operate in large cities but open private hospitals in parts of the country where only state provided healthcare services. These new hospitals are all state of the art facilities with advanced medical equipment in use.

Web Resources

Ministry of Health http://www.saglik.gov.tr

Health Industry Employers' Association (SEIS) http://www.seis.org.tr/

State Institute of Statistics http://www.tuik.gov.tr/

For further information on this report and to search more on the potential opportunities, please contact:

Ebru Olcay
Commercial Specialist
U.S. Commercial Service
U.S. Consulate Istanbul, Turkey
e-mail: Ebru.olcay@trade.gov
Web: http://www.buyusa.gov/turkey/en

ELECTRIC POWER PROSPECTS

Unit: USD millions

	2009	2010	2011 (estimated)	2012 (estimated)
Total Market Size	2,650	3,330	3,800	4000
Total Local Production	850	980	1,150	1200
Total Exports	120	130	160	180
Total Imports	1,920	2,480	2,810	2980
Imports from the U.S.	410	460	550	650
Exchange Rate: 1 USD	TL 1.54	TL 1.49	TL 1.54	TL 1.54

In accordance with the Turkey's 10 Year Electric Power Generation Capacity Projections prepared by TEIAS and approved by the energy regulator EMRA, Turkey's electricity demand for electricity will grow 5% in 2011, 7.5% until 2017 and 7.4% until 2019 under the high demand scenario. These figures will be 5% in 2011, 6.7% in 2012-2015 and 6.6% in 2016-2019 on annual basis under a low demand scenario. As per the scenario, 62,968 GWh of additional power generation will be added by the private sector while the public sector will add 10,924 GWh with new investments until 2017. If other new investments are not made, Turkey may have an electricity supply shortage by the end of 2016. This presents major opportunities for U.S firms in all aspects of power generation.

Turkey generated approximately 210 billion kWh of electricity from the existing installed capacity of approximately 46,000 MW in 2010. This represents 7.9% increase power generation from that of 2009. 45% of the power generation came from the natural gas combined cycle power plants, almost 25% from hydroelectric, 1.5% from wind energy and the rest from lignite-fired power plants. Turkey also imported electricity from Azerbaijan, Georgia and Iran. In 2010, Turkey's total consumption rose to 212 billion kWh, representing 8.4% growth in electricity consumption. EMRA announced that a total investment of over USD 3.33 billion was inaugurated in 2010, which added 3,810 MW to total installed capacity. 47% of investment was in the renewable energy sector and it provided an investment of USD 1.56 billion.

In case of low demand, Turkey will still require 440 billion kWh and in case of high demand, 480 billion kWh electricity production a year in 2020. This means Turkey will have to increase the total installed capacity over two times of the existing capacity until 2020. Turkey will require the following new power generation investments through 2020 in the electric energy sector:

US$ 20.1 billion; US$ 4 billion per year between 2011 – 2015

US$ 27.5 billion; US$ 5.5 billion per year between 2016 – 2020

The Turkish government has focused on the development of nuclear power plant projects as Turkey pays over USD 20 billion for oil and gas imports every year. Turkish and Russian Governments signed a bilateral agreement to build Turkey's first nuclear power plant. The Russian Federal Atomic Energy Agency (Rosatom) and Energy and Natural Resources Ministry will be the representatives of the two sides in the agreement. A Russian consortium will initiate work for the establishment of a company to carry out the construction project within three months. The plant will have the total capacity of 4,800 megawatts (MW) in four units. The company that will be established to carry out the project will be the owner of the power plant as well as all of the electricity produced. Russian companies will not have less than a 51 percent share in this new company. Turkey will start receiving 20 percent of the company's net profit 15 years after each unit begins operating. The first unit is expected to be built and start operations within seven years of construction. The Turkish Electricity Trading and Contracting Company (TETAŞ) will sign an agreement with the company to be established; giving a power purchase guarantee of 12.35 cents per kilowatt hour (kWh). A consortium led by state-controlled Russian builder AtomStroyExport will construct the plant in Akkuyu, undertaking the entire cost of construction, estimated at around $20 billion. The first nuclear power plant will be operational by 2018.

Considering the high demand, Turkish Minister of Energy Yildiz announced Turkey will need three functioning nuclear power plants by 2023, in an effort to diversify the supply of energy in the country. Japan is interested in implementing a similar project in Sinop province.

The Ministry of Energy expects renewable energy power generation to meet 30% of Turkey's electricity demand in 2023 (100th year anniversary of Turkish Republic.) The current wind power generation capacity of 1044 MW (as of June 2010) is expected to increase to 10,000 MW by the end of 2015. In this regard; the Turkish Parliament passed an amendment to the existing Renewable Energy Law No. 5346. The New Law No. 6094 came into force on January 8, 2011, which set different feed-in tariffs for different renewable energy resources as follows:

7.3 dollar cents for hydroelectric,

7.3 dollar cents for wind,

10.5 dollar cents for geothermal,

13.3 dollar cents for biomass,

13.3 dollar cents for solar energy.

These figures are envisaged to apply only for power plants, to be commissioned on or before 31 December 2015. Extension of the deadline is subject to Council of Ministers' decrees. Companies are free to select these feed-in tariffs or sell electricity to the PMUM pool system at the daily and hourly proposed prices, which includes peak hours. Companies have to make this election on a yearly basis.

The new law provides incentives for domestic production of renewable energy equipment. By manufacturing some parts of the renewable energy equipment, investors will receive higher feed-in tariff rates for the next five years.

Turkey also has an Energy Efficiency Law, which sets strategies and prepares energy efficiency plans and programs. The law assigns an Electricity Affairs Survey Administration (EIE) as the authorized agency for issuing Energy Service Company (ESCO) licenses. The law stipulates that industrial facilities will be asked to employ ESCOs and energy efficiency projects will receive incentives after approval by the EIE and the Energy Efficiency Coordination Board.

The Turkish Parliament also passed a Law (# 5836), which approved Turkey's participation in the Kyoto Protocol agreement, which was followed by the Council of Ministers Decree No. 2009/14979 also approving the Protocol. The law and decree will force manufacturing companies, thermal power plants and others major carbon emission producers to support renewable energy projects and obtain carbon credits.

The private sector plans to invest in wind power projects over the next 5 years at a total capacity of 5000 MW. The EIE has developed a Turkey specific wind energy atlas including information on the availability of transmission lines and substations. The study demonstrates that Turkey has at least 48,000 MW of wind energy potential. The Energy Market Regulatory Authority (EMRA) started issuing new licenses for wind power projects. EMRA is also tendering new licenses for wind power project locations, which received more than one application for a certain region.

Turkey has high solar energy potential. The average annual sunshine exposure is 2,640 hours (daily total 7, 2 hours) and average annual solar radiation is 3.6 kWh/m2-day (1311 kWh/m2-year). A recent solar atlas study calculated the total solar electricity capacity to be approximately 380 billion kWh (56,000 MW thermal power). According to the Turkish Ministry of Energy, Turkey is ranked as the second best country in Europe after Spain for solar power generation investments. According to the new renewable energy law (6094) the total established capacity of the solar energy based power plants, which will connect to the transmission system by 31 December 2013, shall not exceed 600 MW. A recent regulation became effective allowing any power generation facility investment including solar will not require a license if the total installed capacity is less than 500 kW.

Biomass potential is estimated at approximately 8.6 million TOE. Some of the agricultural area used for beet and wheat farming can be allocated for bioethanol production. Approximately 1.5 million tons of biodiesel and 3.5 million tons of bioethanol can be produced in these areas.

Many Turkish companies are investing in small hydroelectric projects and seeking financing. However, not many U.S. manufacturers are active in this field in Turkey. U.S. companies can probably find major opportunities in geothermal projects and biomass projects in addition to wind energy projects.

Turkey is first in Europe and 7th in the world in geothermal energy resources. The overall geothermal energy potential of Turkey is estimated to be 35,000 MW. Current geothermal production is approx 2 Mtoe and expected to increase to 6.3 Mtoe by 2020. Several companies have obtained operating rights from the Minerals Research Exploration Institute (MTAE) of Turkey for proven reserves of geothermal energy. Others are exploring geothermal resources. Turkish companies will therefore require lots of drilling services as well as insurance and financing for such services. Engineering and survey firms for geothermal energy as well as design firms and equipment suppliers will find a good market In Turkey.

After the renewable energy bill passed, large companies in Turkey like Koç, Sabancı, Zorlu, Aksa, Anadolu Group, MMEKA, Polat, and Bilgin Energy announced their renewable energy investment plans. Sector representatives assume that at least $30 million in investments will be made in the renewable energy sector in 2011.

The U.S. Department of Energy (DOE), in coordination with other U.S. agencies, is launching the Near-Zero Zone project, a demonstration project for industrial energy efficiency in Turkey. This interagency project, which has the support of the Turkish government and business organizations, will help industrial companies operating within the Izmir Ataturk Organized Industrial Zone (IAOSB) to reduce their energy usage through a series of cost-effective efficiency upgrades. The project aims to demonstrate the impact that reducing energy consumption can have on companies' profitability, promote bilateral trade and investment, and serve as a replicable model for companies and industrial zones throughout Turkey. A fall 2011 Trade Mission in Renewable Energy and Energy Efficiency, led by a senior U.S Department of Commerce official, will focus on such opportunities.

Sub-Sector Best Prospects

Supply of:

- Wind turbines and generators
- Geothermal power plant equipment
- Engineering and design of geothermal power plants
- Geothermal survey service
- Solar energy power generation engineering and design services
- Concentrated solar power generation systems
- Thin-film PV panels supply and manufacturing equipment
- Energy storage systems
- Energy Efficiency systems
- Smart Grid Systems such as SCADA, remote metering, loss control systems,
- Biomass, ethanol, biodiesel, energy efficiency services and equipment
- Hydroelectric turbines and coal gasification systems.
- Nuclear consultancy and nuclear power plant equipment

Opportunities

There are opportunities in wind energy projects, waste to energy and biomass projects and geothermal energy projects. US DOE supported Near Zero Zone project will create business opportunities for U.S. companies in the energy efficiency sector. Smart Grid applications at 21 electricity distribution companies and Turkish Electricity Transmission Company (TEIAS) will create major opportunities. Estimated investment in smart grid applications is expected to be in the range of USD 5-6 billion. There will be opportunities for U.S. nuclear energy consultancy and engineering firms as well as equipment suppliers.

Domestic manufacturing of some parts of renewable energy equipment may create some advantages over the competitors. The resources of US TDA, U.S. EXIM Bank and OPIC are available in Turkey to finance new renewable energy and energy efficiency projects. U.S. EXIM Bank provides financing for renewable energy projects with repayment period of 18 years after the post commissioning.

Web Resources

Ministry of Energy and Natural Resources' Web Site: www.enerji.gov.tr

Energy Market Regulatory Agency Web Site: www.epdk.org.tr

Turkish Electricity Trading Company Web Site: www.tetas.gov.tr

Turkish Electricity Transmission Company Web Site: www.teias.gov.tr

Turkish Electricity Distribution Company Web Site: www.tedas.gov.tr

Solar Atlas of Turkey (GEPA): http://www.eie.gov.tr/MyCalculator/Default.aspx

Wind Atlas: http://www.eie.gov.tr/duyurular/YEK/YEKrepa/REPA-duyuru_01.html (province by province)

For project financing, please see:

http://www.exim.gov/
http://www.opic.gov/
http://www.ustda.gov/
www.worldbank.org.tr
http://www.ifc.org/ifcext/eca.nsf/Content/Turkey_Home
http://www.ebrd.com/country/country/turkey/index.htm
www.tskb.com
http://english.kalkinma.com.tr
http://www.teias.gov.tr/apkuretimplani/sonuclar.htm#_Toc86219442
http://www.bugun.com.tr/haber-detay/137659-2011-de-enerjiye-68-milyar-yatirim-haberi.aspx

For further information on this report and to search more on the potential opportunities, please contact:

Serdar Cetinkaya
Senior Commercial Specialist

U.S. Embassy Turkey
U.S. Commercial Service
Serdar.Cetinkaya@trade.gov
Web: http://www.buyusa.gov/turkey/en

INFORMATION AND COMMUNICATION TECHNOLOGIES

IT SECTOR (EXCLUDING TELECOMMUNICATIONS):

Unit: USD millions

	2009	2010	2011 (estimated)	2012 (estimated)
Total Market Size	5,600	6,160	6,776	7,454
Total Local Production	2,300	2,530	2,783	3,061
Total Exports	1,200	1,320	1,452	1,597
Total Imports	4,500	4,950	5,445	5,990
Imports from the U.S.	1,950	2,145	2,360	2,596
Exchange Rate: 1 USD	TL 1.54	TL 1.49	TL 1.54	TL 1.54

Telecommunications Sector (excluding IT):

	2009	2010	2011 (estimated)	2012 (estimated)
Total Market Size	19,300	21,000	23,100	25,410
Total Local Production	12,800	14,000	15,400	16,940
Total Exports	2,900	3,500	3,850	4,235
Total Imports	9,400	10,500	11,550	12,705
Imports from the U.S.	490	560	616	677
Exchange Rate: 1 USD	TL 1.54	TL 1.49	TL 1.54	TL 1.54

Turkey's Information Communication Technologies (ICT) market size is estimated to have reached $27.3 billion in 2010, with a breakdown of $20 billion in Telecommunications and 7.3 billion USD in Information Technologies. (ref. Interpro). The Turkish ICT market continues its rise as one of the key growth markets in Turkey with an estimated growth of 8-10% for 2011, despite the economic global crisis.

Although the industry has shown slower growth than in the past (with the exception of the 2002 crisis) investors still see the Turkish ICT market as a significant growth opportunity and increased investment in channels and local production and set ambitious sales targets.

Current PC penetration levels are estimated at 15%, but the Government aims for computer ownership at 51% and internet usage at 48% by 2013. Meanwhile, a survey of Turkish primary and secondary schools showed that in 40% of schools, computers are still not integrated into education. This is expected to significantly increase as the Ministry of Education plans to increase the number of computers and internet connection. Schools in remote areas are to be connected to the net through satellite with the cooperation of the Turkish satellite company Turksat.

There has however, been a recent shift in the driving forces behind the IT industry in Turkey. Although until recently the driving force behind the industry was desktop and notebook sales, the consumer electronics market has significantly caught up and increased its share in the market.

The consumer electronics market in Turkey is estimated at 3 billion USD. While the rest of the world averaged an increase of 10% in the consumer electronics market, Turkey averaged 35% annual growth in 2010.

Traditionally significant PC sales were confined to Istanbul, Ankara and Izmir but now PC sales have received new momentum as the focus of demand shifted towards the Anatolian region; this is expected to continue as the rate of PC penetration rises. The PC penetration has ripple effects to sense of other items being purchased such as ADSL subscription, modems, software and other IT products and services.

In the Telecommunications market, Turk Telekom has 17.3 million fixed line subscribers, 6 million ADSL lines and 12.4 million GSM mobile subscribers through AVEA. Turk Telekom owns 99.9% of TTnet, Argela, Innova, Sebit, Sobee ve AssisTT companies. It also owns 81% of AVEA, one of the three GSM mobile operators in Turkey. Turk Telekom is the minority share of ALBtelecom in Albania. 55% of the shares of Turk Telekom belong to Ojer Telecom Inc. and 30% belongs to the Turkish Treasury. The remaining 15% is floated in the Istanbul Stock Exchange (IMKB). The value of Turk Telekom was over US $15 billion in 2010.

The three GSM cellular operators, Turkcell, Vodafone and AVEA and the fixed line operator Turk Telekom invested in equipment and services at a total value of $2-3 billion to expand their services. Turkcell has almost 36 million subscribers (56.6 % of the total GSM cellular subscribers), Vodafone has 15 million (24.5% of the subscribers) and AVEA has 12 million almost 18.9% of the subscribers).

The total number of GSM cellular service subscribers reached almost to 64 million with an approximate penetration rate of almost 89 %. The total telecom equipment and service market grew to $19.3 billion and is expected to expand in 2010 as the GSM sector is the driving force and the subscribers are expected to use more and more 3G services. Total number of 3G subscribers reached to almost 6 million while 2G subscribers decreased to 58 million. Fixed line subscribers are almost 17 million, reaching almost 100% penetration per house basis. Subscriber penetration for fix line is 23.5% and is not expected to increase anymore due to hard competition from the GSM cellular operators.

With the introduction of 3G last year; IPTV, online services, content and media services, E-business, personalized services, music download, games, multi-play, video services, and other mobile entertainment, has been developing rapidly, creating new business areas and revenues. BTK (Turkish Telecom Authority) is expected to conduct tenders for WiMax licenses in 2011.

Turk Telekom will continue to be the major buyer of fixed-line telecommunications equipment. Turk Telekom with approximately 17 million subscribers may invest in new technologies in 2010. Turk Telekom's revenues during first 6 months of 2009 had a growth rate of 3.5%. Main growth came from the ADSL revenues as 29% and from the mobile revenues as 14% through AVEA. Turk Telekom introduced a new technology, which provides fixed line services through GSM mobile phones that have Wi-Fi capability. Consumers can now use both fixed line services and mobile GSM services through same mobile phone by uploading special software. Turk Telekom will also introduce 3N technology through fixed Internet and other ISPs by using its Wi-Fi capabilities spread around the country. 3N technology will provide mobile Internet services. AVEA actually started introducing this technology through road shows. AVEA has been distributing Blackberry phones rather successfully in Turkey.

Turk Telekom will invest $3.42 billion thru 2011 for its Next Generation Network (NGN) project and will also replace its rural area switches with small telephone switches over 10,200 switch centers. Turk Telekom is in the process of introducing IP TV. Fixed line subscribers can now change their operators without changing their phone numbers as a result of the fixed line number portability regulation, which came into force in September 2009.

Over 40 private long distance telephone companies have been also operating over the last 5 years, mostly using VoIP via an interconnection agreement with Turk Telekom. Some of these companies have established or continue to establish their own network.

BTK has registered over 60 million GSM cellular phone handsets in Turkey. BTK estimates that Turkey imports approximately 10 million mobile handsets every year. Many subscribers continuously change their cell phones with new models sustaining consistent growth in the handset market.

GSM cell phone sets suitable for video downloading and TV broadcasting equipped with wide band Internet access will be the driving force for growth in this sector. These new technologies will be the basis for the 3G and 4G operations.

In Turkey, Northern Telecom, Alcatel, Siemens, Ericsson and NEC supply majority of the fixed lines switches, trans-multiplexers, and other telephony equipment. U.S. companies can be competitive in software programs required for customer databases, emergency call services, corporate management and intelligent network operation centers. Motorola, Nokia, Ericsson and Siemens are the main GSM switch and base station suppliers. U.S. companies can be competitive in new software products required by GSM cellular operators to provide new services to their clients and better corporate and client management.

The government's E-Government projects still continue to move forward, although slower in 2010 than in recent years. The Turkish IT market is far from being saturated and still has significant growth potential as the technology driven young population continues to invest in computers, consumer electronics, software and IT services. The IT market has grown every year and even in times of global crisis the growth has only dropped slightly, a good indicator that the IT industry remains an attractive industry in Turkey. (UNDP, Harnessing ICT for Development in Turkey)

This attractive consumer electronics trend has lured many international and national electronic retail supermarkets to establish themselves in the market. German Mediamarkt, British Electro World, Turkish Teknosa, Vatanbilgisayar and Gold Bilgisayar have been competing for a number of years in Turkey. However, in early 2011, the U.S consumer electronics giant Best Buy announced it would close its Turkey operations as part of a global restructuring.

Sub-Sector Best Prospects

- Consumer Electronics
- Notebook PC's
- Audio Visual Equipment
- Wireless equipment / services
- IPTV
- WiMax (awaiting law)
- VDSL
- 3 G related technologies/services

IPTV, WiMax, VDSL technologies and services will be in great demand. 3G related technologies and services, 3G compatible handsets, online services, content and media services, E-business, personalized services, music download, games, multi-play, video services, and other mobile entertainment, will be the best prospects.

The young population and new home statistics, as anticipated has invested considerably in consumer electronics. Consumer electronics now rival the traditional leader of notebook and pc sales. Regarding the number of TV channels, Turkey ranks in the top five worldwide behind USA. Market research shows that 97% of Turkish families see television as their prime source for entertainment and news.

Opportunities

Cebit Bilisim Eurasia, Istanbul, Turkey. IT and Telecom solutions trade fair. Details: www.cebitbilisim.com The young population and new home statistics, will continue to invest considerably in consumer electronics, pc/notebook and audio/visual sales.

GSM companies will be procuring new network equipment and software to expand their services and provide better quality service to their clients. Turk Telekom's potential investment of over $2-3 billion for its Next Generation Network (NGN) project and other technologies and services will be a major opportunity. TT's plans to change its rural area switches with small telephone switches in 10,200 switch centers. U.S. companies should consider this large telecom market as a hub for the region and consider establishing joint venture companies to supply to the EU markets as Turkey is already in the European Customs Union and a candidate to join the EU.

Wimax will open an era of opportunity once licenses are issued by the Telecommunications Authority (BTK).

Web Resources

ref: http://www.gfmag.com/gdp-data-country-reports/157-turkey-gdp-country-report.html#axzz1Cz1kMJe7

For further information on this report and to search more on the potential opportunities, please contact:

Ihsan Muderrisoglu
Commercial Specialist
U.S. Embassy Turkey
U.S. Commercial Service
Ihsan.Muderrisoglu@trade.gov
Web: http://www.buyusa.gov/turkey/en

PLASTICS MATERIALS AND PROCESSING MACHINERY

Unit: USD thousands

	2009	2010	2011 (estimated)	2012 (estimated)
Total Market Size	19,996	24,223	27,800	30,600
Total Local Production	15,765	18,040	20,700	22,800
Total Exports	3,159	3,671	4,200	4,600
Total Imports	7,390	9,854	11,300	12,400

Imports from the U.S.	107	140	160	175
Exchange Rate: 1 USD	TL 1.54	TL 1.49	TL 1.54	TL 1.54

The plastics industry is one of the youngest and most rapidly developing in Turkey. On average, the industry grew by 15 percent every year from 2002 – 2007. The sector then decreased by 4 percent in 2008 due to the impact of the global economic crisis and the resulting fall in exports, which also impacted purchases of raw materials and machinery. However, the Turkish economy in general, and with it the plastics industry, is expected to recover quickly. This recovery is already seen in the plastics industry with a 20% increase in the local market in 2010 compared to the year before.

The Turkish plastics industry holds a 1.6 percent market share in the international plastics industry. Turkey is 2nd in synthetic fiber production, 3rd in PVC (polyvinyl chloride), and 5th in total plastics processing capacity in Europe. Many industry experts predict that the Turkish plastics industry will soon rank 3rd among EU countries.

The industry currently employs more than 200,000 people. Nearly 7,000 companies work in the plastics industry, of which 98 percent are SMEs. One hundred and thirteen of these firms have foreign capital, and almost half (46%) are of EU origin. German companies lead with 21 percent of the total, followed by the Netherlands (11%) and the USA, France and Italy with 7 percent.

Plastic Raw Materials Market

In Turkey, local production meets 15 percent of the total demand for plastics raw materials. Turkey has one major petrochemical production facility, Petkim, which supplies materials to the plastic processing industry. Petkim provides 85 percent of local production. It was state-owned, but was privatized a few years ago and was sold to the TransCentralAsia Petrochemical Holding consortium. Industry experts expect Petkim to make new investments and increase market share from 15 to 50 percent. In addition, more investments are expected from countries in the region (i.e. Iran, Saudi Arabia). Other manufacturers include SASA and Baser.

The following plastic raw materials make up the market in Turkey:

-PP (Polypropylene), which is used in the production of carpet yarns, big bags, woven sacks, oriented films, sanitary piping and household items, has the largest share in the market with a share of 27%. Local production meets the nine percent of the market need.

-LDPE (Low-density Polyethylene). Petkim is the sole Turkish producer, but is currently capable of meeting only 75 percent of market demand. Primarily used in film production (90%), injection molding (2%), cable production (3%), and blow molding (5%) industries in Turkey.

-LLDPE (Linear Low Density Polyethylene), all of which is imported.

-HDPE (High Density Polyethylene), for which Petkim is the sole local producer. The majority is imported.

-PVC (Polyvinyl Chloride), for which Petkim is again the sole domestic producer, supplying 18 percent of local demand. PVC is used primarily in electric, automotive, toys, profiles, cladding, pipes, packaging films, and artificial leather and health products.

-PS (Polystyrene), produced locally by Baser Kimya, again with the majority imported (58%). PS is used primarily for packaging insulation and appliances.

-PET (Polyethylene Terephthalate), with a market share of seven percent among the plastic raw materials, is produced locally by SASA, the largest polyester fiber and filament producer in Europe and the Middle East, and is used for PET bottles and engineering plastics in electrical and automotive applications.

-ABS (Acrylonitrile-butadiene-styrene), with a market share of two percent, is one of the major thermoplastic products, and is supplied entirely by imports.

The top 10 supplier countries of plastic raw materials in the first nine months of 2010 were Saudi Arabia, Germany, Belgium, Netherlands, Italy, South Korea, France, Iran, United States and Spain supplying over 63 percent of Turkish imports in plastics raw materials.

Plastic Processing Machinery

Recently, cheap Chinese machinery and molds began entering into the Turkish market and taking market share from local machinery manufacturers. Local manufacturers tried to survive by exporting their products, but the same Chinese competition is present in export markets. This is a serious threat to Turkish plastics processing machinery manufacturers.

Turkish plastics production machinery imports are dominated by injection machinery (27%), followed by cutting, splitting and shaping machinery (26%) and extrusion machinery (21%). The top supplier countries of plastics production machinery in 2009 were Germany, Italy, China, Taiwan, Austria, Japan, Switzerland, U.S.A., France, and South Korea. The first three of these, Germany, Italy, and China supplied over 60 percent of Turkish plastic machinery imports.

Currently, there are no significant trade barriers against U.S. imports. Turkey's imports are regulated by an annual import regime published by the Undersecretary for Treasury and Foreign Trade (UTFT). The Import Regime sets forth import rules and regulations for the year, customs duties and surcharges on imported products, and lists of "investment" capital equipment machinery, the importation of which is encouraged by the government since it adds value for Turkish exports.

Turkey's accession to the European Union's customs union in January 1996 resulted in zero duties for imports from EU countries and the same agreement led to general reductions in duty rates assessed to non-EU third-country imports. All plastic processing machinery is subject to a 1.7 percent customs duty, and almost all plastics raw materials have a 6.5 percent import duty based on CIF (Cost, Insurance, and Freight) value for imports from non-EU countries, including the United States.

Sub-Sector Best Prospects

Plastics Raw Materials:

Materials with shortages in local production (PP, HDPE, PVC, PS) are considered best prospects as well as materials with no local production (LLDPE, ABS).

Plastic Production Machinery:

Cutting, splitting, and shaping machines, injection machines, and extrusion machines have the best chance for success in the Turkish market.

Opportunities

Turkish and European trade shows are international platforms for U.S. firms seeking to network with Turkey and international buyers/distributors and to assess their competitors' lines and market situation. Upcoming shows in related sectors:

Web Resources

PAGDER-Plastik Sanayicileri Dernegi (Plastic Industrialists Association)
http://www.pagev.org.tr/pagder/main.asp

PAGEV-Turk Plastik Sanayicileri Arastirma Gelistirme ve Egitim Vakfı

(Fountation of the Turkish Plastic Industrialists Research, Development and Education)
http://www.pagev.org.tr/

For further information on this report, please contact:

Berrin Erturk
Commercial Specialists
U.S. Embassy Turkey
U.S. Commercial Service
Berrin.erturk@trade.gov
Web: http://www.buyusa.gov/turkey/en

AUTOMOTIVE PARTS AND EQUIPMENT

Unit: USD millions

	2009	2010	2011 (estimated)	2012 (estimated)
Total Market Size	11,200	10,100	10,900	12,200
Total Local Production	7,000	7,500	8,000	9,000
Total Exports	4,800	5,300	5,800	6,400
Total Imports	9,000	7,900	8,700	9,600
Imports from the U.S.	75	80	85	95
Exchange Rate: 1 USD	TL 1.54	TL 1.49	TL 1.54	TL 1.54

Most international vehicle producers already have production in Turkey. Presently, there are 19 international vehicle producers in the Turkish market including; Ford, Toyota, Renault, Fiat, Chrysler, Opel, Honda, Hyundai, Peugeot, MAN, Mercedes, Isuzu, Mitsubishi, through joint venture (JV) partnerships with local firms, direct investment, or license agreements. Moreover some other producers are about to start their operations in Turkey, for example Chery Automobile Co. of China committed to build a factory in Turkey last month. Cherry will be building vehicles for the European market. Also Ford and Renault's local partners are expanding their operations recently. German Daimler is another firm, which started producing buses in Turkey with its Turkish partner.

Turkish automotive production capacity reached 1.2 million units, and is targeting 1.5 million in 2015. 70% of the vehicles made in Turkey are exported and this stands for 20% of Turkish exports. According to forecasts of The Wall Street Journal, Turkey is going to overtake the Czech Republic and Slovakia, as the biggest car makers in Eastern Europe. Unlike the Czech Republic and Slovakia that are mainly gearing towards exports to European markets, with Germany being the main market, Turkey is increasing its exposure to markets beyond Europe, in the Middle East and North Africa. Turkey ranks as the following among European Union countries:

- The largest bus producer

- Third largest LCV producer

- Third largest truck market

-Turkey is the 17th largest automotive producer on the world.

The Turkish automotive parts/service equipment industry has expanded as Turkish automotive production and imports have increased. Today, the Turkish automotive and parts industry have become an integrated part of the global automotive and parts industry. With its high production capacity, high standards, and a wide variety of products manufactured, automotive exports in Turkey now rank first in total exports of the country ahead of the traditional exports such as textiles and apparel.

Most industry leaders, such as Delphi and Bosch have direct investments or JV partnerships with Turkish manufacturers. Currently, there are 250 foreign investors in the parts industry. German auto-parts supplier Mann & Hummel Group said they would start production in Turkey in two years.

Furthermore, the American diesel motor producer Cummins started a new investment in Turkey to build a new factory to manufacture filters immediately and generators and alternators for the automotive industry in 2011.

The total number of auto parts manufacturers in Turkey is 4,000, and 70 percent of these are SMEs. Today, the Turkish parts industry produces almost all parts and components, including engines and parts, brakes and clutches and parts, suspension systems, batteries, rubber and plastic parts, power train parts and components, security systems, auto glass, seats, etc. This sector provides parts for new vehicles as well as the existing Turkish automobile fleet that exceeds 10 million units. Of the locally produced parts industry, 90 percent either are used in the production of vehicles that are exported or directly go to world parts market. Seventy percent of Turkish exports go to European Union countries.

The following products are imported in the highest volumes: diesel and semi-diesel engines, body and parts for the assembling industry, gear boxes, engine parts, tires, internal combustion engines, steering wheels, brakes and servo brakes.

The Turkish import regime prohibits the importation of remanufactured, rebuilt, used, reconditioned vehicles. Only the current year or the following year models can be imported. This rule also applies for parts, too. The Turkish import regime also prohibits importation of remanufactured, rebuilt, used or reconditioned parts. They can only be imported for use as scrap iron for iron and steel production.

Sub-Sector Best Prospects

Tires
Brake linings
Gearboxes
Clutches
Power steering hydraulic systems
Bearings
V-belts
Shock absorbers
Brakes
Clutch rings
Filters
Bumpers
Lights, and signaling equipment

Opportunities

As Turkey continues to move towards European Union integration, equipment meeting stricter EU guidelines from emissions control for automobile safety and standards tests, will equate to increased sales of high tech auto parts. The privatization of the vehicle inspection centers could also provide opportunities for U.S. service equipment suppliers, because these centers need to meet some guidelines in order to be authorized inspection centers. As a result of stricter inspections, parts market is also estimated to bring new opportunities to the parts suppliers.

Web Resources

Automotive Distributors' Association www.odd.org.tr

Automotive Manufacturers' Association www.osd.org.tr

Authorized Automobile Dealers Association www.oyder-tr.org

Association of Automotive Parts & Components Manufacturers www.taysad.org.tr

For further information on this report and to search more on the potential opportunities, please contact:

Berrin Erturk
Commercial Specialist
U.S. Commercial Service Izmir
Berrin.Erturk@trade.gov
Web: http://www.buyusa.gov/turkey/en Agricultural Sectors

COTTON

Unit: '000 Metric Ton

	2009	2010	2011 (estimated)	2012 (estimated)
Total Market Size	1336	1235	1410	1410
Total Local Production	380	460	580	580

Total Exports	10	25	20	20
Total Imports	966	800	850	850
Imports from the U.S.	499	500	550	550

Turkey continues to be one of the leading markets for U.S. cotton. Turkey's textile industry remains important to Turkey's economy in terms of investment, employment and exports. U.S. cotton has a very good reputation in Turkey, which is reflected in the continued high U.S. market share. Turkey is expected to remain a significant importer in the coming years due to the quality of U.S. cotton and the availability of the GSM-102 Export Credit Guarantee Program. Imports increased in the previous marketing year due to stronger demand for textiles in export markets, which is expected to continue in the coming marketing year. Total Turkish imports of U.S. cotton were valued at $862 million in 2010, up from $487 million in 2009 and $$536 million in 2008.

United States Department of Agriculture

Agricultural Affairs Office Turkey Agankara@fas.usda.gov

SOYBEANS

Unit: '000 Metric Ton

	2009	2010	2011 (estimated)	2012 (estimated)
Total Market Size	1190	1265	1310	1310
Total Local Production	40	65	60	60
Total Exports	0	0	0	0
Total Imports	1150	1200	1250	1250
Imports from the U.S.	800	600	650	650

Soy based foods are not popular in Turkey; however the poultry sector is dependent on soybeans as a major feed ingredient. The poultry and feed industry has been investing in modern crushing facilities and is continuing to expand its capacity. While domestic poultry consumption is increasing, new export markets such as Iraq and other neighboring countries which will further increase the demand for soybeans by Turkey's feed industry. The U.S. continues to be a leading supplier of soybeans for the Turkish market, however new regulations on biotechnology have interfered with the market periodically since October 2009. As a result, imports of soybeans are expected to decrease further in the coming year due to uncertainty and risk of rejection for unapproved biotech contamination. 2010 Turkish imports of U.S. soybeans were worth $250, down from $342 million in 2009.

United States Department of Agriculture

Agricultural Affairs Office Turkey Agankara@fas.usda.gov

LIVE CATTLE

Unit: '000 Head

	2009	2010	2011 (estimated)	2012 (estimated)
Total Market Size	10,004	10,240	10,450	10,450

Total Local Production	10,000	10,100	10,300	10,300
Total Exports	0	0	0	0
Total Imports	4	140	150	150
Imports from the U.S.	3.8	16	20	20

U.S. exporters are increasingly taking advantage of a recent market opening for live breeding cattle and breeding bulls coupled with strong demand in response to the need for larger and better herd stock in Turkey. USDA and the Government of Turkey agreed to a protocol for U.S. shipments of live breeding cattle in May 2007 and for live breeding bull on September 2009. Since then, the Turkish government increased its support payments to the livestock industry, which include a program offering reimbursement of 30-40% of cattle purchase and infrastructure costs for livestock investments in certain regions of the country. U.S. exports of live cattle reached over $70 million in 2010 and strong demand for live breeding cattle is expected to continue.

United States Department of Agriculture

Agricultural Affairs Office Turkey Agankara@fas.usda.gov

RICE

Unit: '000 Metric Ton

	2009	2010	2011 (estimated)	2012 (estimated)
Total Market Size	832	850	890	890
Total Local Production	400	450	470	470
Total Exports	26	50	50	50
Total Imports	458	450	470	470
Imports from the U.S.	165	250	260	260

The government eliminated most import barriers in 2007 after a WTO dispute settlement and now produces about one half of its rice needs and imports the other half. However,

Turkish rice production has increased significantly in recent years due to government incentives. Turkey had a record crop in 2009 of 715,000 MT of paddy rice (429,000 MT of rice). The Turkish rice market is extremely price sensitive. Most of the rice in 2007 has been imported from Egypt and the remainder from Italy. This is milled rice. Turkey typically imports paddy rice from the United States but also imports from Egypt. In the

Official Gazette dated December 31, 2009; the Government of Turkey allocated a duty free rice import quota of 100,000 MT to the Turkish Grain Board (TMO), available until

December 31, 2010. Turkish imports of U.S. rice in 2010 reached a record $185 million, more than double the value of the previous record of $76 million in 2008.

United States Department of Agriculture

Agricultural Affairs Office Turkey Agankara@fas.usda.gov

INDUSTRY CONTACTS

Turkish Farmers Union www.tzob.org.tr

Turkish Dairy, Meat, Food Industry and Producers Union www.setbir.org.tr

Poultry Industrialists' and Breeders Association www.besd-bir.org

Turkish Flour Industrialists' Federation www.usf.org.tr

Turkish Feed Millers Association www.turkiyeyembir.org.tr

Turkish Seed Industry Association www.turkted.org.tr

Federation of Food and Drink Industry Associations of Turkey http://www.tgdf.org.tr/english/

United States Department of Agriculture

Agricultural Affairs Office Turkey Agankara@fas.usda.gov

TRADE REGULATIONS, CUSTOMS AND STANDARDS

IMPORT TARIFFS

Import duties are calculated on the C.I.F. (cost, insurance and freight) value. Turkey is a signatory to Article VII of the General Agreements on Tariffs and Trade (GATT). The agreement stipulates that the customs valuation is the transaction value (the price that is actually paid or payable plus costs and expenses). Turkey is also obliged to comply with other Article VII provisions including the rapidity of clearance of goods, currency convertibility, and appeal privileges and rights. Turkish regulations do not allow for advance rulings on customs HS classification or on the applicable import duties on particular products.

Customs surcharges including a value-added tax (VAT) being levied on most imported, as well as domestic, goods and services. The importer is responsible for paying the VAT. The VAT is calculated on a C.I.F. basis plus duty rate and any other applicable charges levied before the goods clear customs. The VAT for most agricultural products (basic food) ranges from one to eight percent and can reach up to 18 percent for some processed products. Capital goods, some raw materials, imports by government agencies and state owned enterprises, and products for investments with incentive certificates are exempt from import fees. Information on Turkish Customs procedures and regulations can be seen at:
http://www.gumruk.gov.tr/ENG/homepage/Pages/default.aspx

Turkey applies the European Union's common external customs tariff to third-country nonagricultural imports (including from the United States) and imposes no duty on nonagricultural items from EU and European Free Trade Association (EFTA) countries. Turkey's average applied tariff rate in 2007 for nonagricultural product imports was 5 percent; however, only 36 percent of Turkey's nonagricultural tariff lines are bound in Turkey's World Trade Organization (WTO) tariff schedule.

U.S. companies can also calculate the Turkish duty by visiting:
http://www.gumruk.gov.tr/ENG/homepage/Pages/default.aspx

Please review Turkey's Harmonized Tariff Schedule by commodity, chapter or sub heading.

TRADE BARRIERS

On October 3, 2005, the European Commission began EU accession proceedings with the Republic of Turkey. The process of EU membership is expected to take between ten and fifteen years. Prior to beginning its move towards EU accession, on January 1,

1996, Turkey and the EU formed a customs union. The agreement covers industrial products and processed agricultural goods. The Republic of Turkey adopted the EU's common external tariff (CCT), resulting in lower duties for imports from third countries, including the United States. The union establishes zero duty rates and no quotas for non-agricultural items of EU and European Free Trade Association (EFTA) origin. The current import regime is organized in five chapters that list more than 20,000 items, identified with 12 digit harmonized tariff system numbers.

The Government of Turkey (GOT) estimates that as a result of its accession to the

European Customs Union, the average duty rate for imports from the European Union and EFTA countries has dropped from approximately ten percent to zero. For products imported from third countries, including the United States, the average duty rate has dropped from ten percent to approximately 4.1 percent. Turkey has reserved some exempted categories for sensitive products with tariffs on these items generally much higher than the CCT. Some agricultural goods will remain protected by steep tariffs.

Turkey is a member of GATT/WTO and regulates its customs in line with GATT requirements. While generally in compliance with the WTO agreement, Turkey often fails to notify the WTO of changes to import requirements. Applications of non-tariff barriers, such as implementing a reference price system and not issuing control certificates on occasion, continues from time to time and poses problems for imports of agricultural products. For instance, Turkey has not provided any control certificates for beef for years.

In November 2005, the United States brought a dispute against Turkey in the WTO arguing that, inter alia, Turkey's tariff-rate quota (TRQ) scheme for rice, which contains an onerous domestic purchase requirement, and its refusal to issue import licenses for rice outside the TRQ, are inconsistent with Turkey's WTO obligations. In September, 2007, the dispute settlement panel agreed with the United States that Turkey's failure to grant licenses to import rice and its operation of a discretionary import licensing system for rice are in breach of Turkey's market access obligations under the WTO Agreement on Agriculture. The panel also agreed with the United States that Turkey's domestic purchase requirement, under which Turkey required importers to purchase large quantities of domestic rice in order to import rice at preferential tariff rates, is in breach of the national treatment provisions of the WTO.

The reasonable period of time for Turkey to bring itself into compliance with the WTO's rulings and recommendations expired at the end of April 2008.

IMPORT REQUIREMENTS AND DOCUMENTATION

IMPORT LICENSES

The 1996 Turkish import regime abolished the requirement that every importer needs an import license and that the importer must obtain an import authorization from a bank. An importer only needs a tax number to import all but restricted items, e.g., firearms, hazardous materials, etc., which can be imported only by authorized establishments, or for which the approval of the Directorate General of Security is required. All agricultural imports require control certificates, which are issued by the Ministry of Agriculture and Rural Affairs' General Directorate of Protection and Control.

IMPORT DOCUMENTATION

Turkish documentation procedures require a commercial invoice and a bill of lading or airway bill to accompany all commercial shipments. Depending on the type of the product importers may be required to submit a Certificate of Origin. Import licenses and phytosanitary certificates are necessary for food and agricultural commodity imports.

Commercial Invoice: The commercial invoice must be submitted in triplicate, including the original copy; and must contain a complete description of the goods and all required payment terms. The exporter must endorse the original as follows: "We hereby certify that this is the first and original copy of our invoice, the only one issued by our firm for the goods herein mentioned." It is advisable to have the Turkish Embassy or Consulate in the United States certify the document. At least one copy of the invoice should accompany the goods, and the original should be sent to the importer through the correspondent bank.

Certificate of Origin:

The certificate of origin is to be prepared in duplicate. No corrections are permitted on this document, which is to be prepared in English by a local chamber of commerce. The Turkish Embassy or Consulate in the United States must certify the certificate of origin. One copy of the document must be surrendered to the customs authorities at the time of importation.

Bill of Lading/Airway Bill:

Details in the bill of lading should correspond exactly to those given in other shipping documents. The original bill of lading should be submitted in triplicate along with 3 copies.

Proforma Invoices:

The proforma invoice must not be more than six months old at the time of application. It must contain an unexpired option (if appropriate), indicate freight and insurance charges separately, and bear the importer's name. Products falling under the European Union New Approach Directives must be accompanied by either a self-declaration of conformity or a notified body's issued certificate of conformity to be allowed entry into the Turkish market. Please see the standards and CE mark section below.

Health Certification:

Special health certificates are required for imports of plants, seeds, animals and animal products. Plants, including fruits and vegetables, must be substantially free from pests and diseases and must have been grown in an area substantially free from prohibited pests and diseases. Additional information may be obtained from the U.S. Department of Agriculture's Animal and Plant Health Inspection Service (APHIS) at Tel: (301) 734- 7885 or Fax: (301) 734-6402 (Veterinary Services) and Tel: (301) 734-8537 or Fax:

(301) 734-5786 (Plant Protection and Quarantine). APHIS inspects and certifies that plants, plant products and live animals conform to health and sanitary requirements as mandated by the Turkish government. U.S. exporters are encouraged to obtain information from the importer prior to shipment because of the complexity of phytosanitary regulations.

SPECIAL IMPORT REQUIREMENTS:

Alcohol can be imported by the private sector by obtaining license and permission from the Tobacco, Tobacco Products and Alcoholic Drinks Market Regulatory Authority (TAPDK), which is an independent regulatory body. Despite these changes, non-tariff barriers, arduous document requirements, and high duty rates continue to limit trade in alcoholic beverages. Cigarettes can only be imported by TEKEL and cigarette producers, which are permitted by the government under a special decree (such as Philip Morris, RJ Reynolds, British Tobacco, etc.). The Tobacco Law was enacted in 2001, however privatization of Tekel's tobacco production has yet to be completed.

Medical X-ray films can only be imported into Turkey by the Red Crescent Association that is a sister organization to the Red Cross.

The importation of precious metals (gold, silk, and platinum) can only be done by members of the Istanbul Gold Exchange. The Istanbul Gold Exchange consists of domestic or foreign banks, precious metals companies, currency offices, precious metals producing and marketing companies and precious metals refineries are members of the exchange. In 2003, Turkey signed an agreement to become a participant of the

Kimberley Process Diamond Certification Scheme, which is a joint government, international diamond industry and civil society initiative to stem the flow of conflict diamonds. On 14 August 2007 Turkey officially became a member of the Kimberley Process Certification Scheme. Information on the regulations pertaining to the importation of precious metals and stones can be found at: http://www.iab.gov.tr/

Importing products such as pharmaceuticals; organic chemicals, especially those used to produce medicines and medical products; vaccines for both humans and animals; cosmetic products; chemicals used in cleaning and the food industry; live animals and plants; grains and plant seeds; and hormones require control certificates from the Directorate General of Curative Care Service of the Ministry of Health and Agriculture.

The following documents must be submitted to the relevant Ministry to obtain the control certificates: pro forma invoice, health certificate, certificate of analysis, formula or list of contents of the product, pedigree certificate, and radiation analysis report. All documents must be obtained from and/or approved by the relevant authorities in the country of origin. Documents must be submitted in the original language with a translation into Turkish. Control certificates must be presented to customs authorities upon import.

Products requiring after-sales service such as motor vehicles, household electrical goods, office equipment and computers, cash registers, TV and video equipment, heaters, gas-fired burners, industrial machinery, automobiles, and wireless equipment require an import permit from the Ministry of Industry and Trade. In order to obtain such a permit, importers must guarantee that they will provide service and spare-parts either by establishing offices or by signing agreements with existing service/parts firms. The penetration of maintenance facilities over the country depends on the type of the product. Particular product groups that are being frequently used require a wide spread network of maintenance facilities in each of Turkey's seven geographic regions. In July 2001, the GOT codified a regulation, which requires additional maintenance facilities to be established for companies importing automobiles into the Turkish Republic.

Telecommunications equipment such as all wireless equipment, automatic data processing machines, electrical apparatus for line telephony or telegraphy, and telephone answering machines need type-approval of the Telecommunications Regulatory Authority.

Under a regulation published in the Turkish Official Gazette of December 31, 2007 (No. 26743-supplementary issue) importers are required to obtain a control certificate from the Ministry of Environment for materials considered detrimental to the environment.

Such materials include hard coal, lignite, petrocoke, petroleum, arsenic, mercury, lead sulfides and carbonates, fluorocarbons, other chemicals and scrap metals.

U.S. EXPORT CONTROLS

The Bureau of Industry and Security is charged with the development, implementation and interpretation of U.S. export control policy for dual-use commodities, software, and technology. Dual-use items subject to BIS regulatory jurisdiction have predominantly commercial uses, but also have military applications. In order to accomplish this objective, BIS seeks to promulgate clear, concise, and timely regulations. This section of our Web site provides a link to the Bureau's regulations governing exports of dual-use items (the "Export Administration Regulations"), codified at 15 Code of Federal Regulations, Chapter 7. It also provides discussions of certain key regulatory policy areas; including policies governing exports of high performance computers, exports of encryption products, deemed exports, U.S. antiboycott regulations, and special regional considerations, the multilateral export control regimes, and the technical advisory committees.

In addition to the U.S. export control policy for dual-use items, the Bureau of Industry and Security is also charged with the development, implementation and interpretation of the antiboycott provisions of the Export Administration Act. The antiboycott provisions encourage, and in some cases require, U.S. persons to refuse to participate in foreign boycotts that the United States does not sanction. U.S. persons are also required to report receipt of boycott-related requests. http://www.bis.doc.gov/

TEMPORARY ENTRY

Goods may be temporarily imported into Turkey without payment of duties and tax if they are to be used in the production or manufacture of a product that is to be exported. The importer gives security in the form of a bank guarantee (temporary import bond) in the amount of applicable duties and taxes. Upon exportation of the finished product, the guarantee is remitted. Temporary admission of goods intended for re-export in their original form is permissible free of import duties and taxes with the approval of the Undersecretariat for Foreign Trade.

Turkey is a signatory to the International Convention to Facilitate the Importation of Commercial Samples and Advertising Material. Samples of no commercial value are admitted duty-free. Other samples are assessed duties and taxes at the time of import, but these are refunded if the samples are re-exported within six months from the date of import. A letter of guarantee will be provided to Turkish Customs for a temporary import, with the guarantee being returned at the time of re-export. Samples should be listed on an invoice. Books, newspapers, magazines, catalogs, pamphlets, brochures, and similar advertising materials are exempt from customs duty.

U.S. traders may also wish to consider a more simplified procedure in the form of an "ATA Carnet." Carnets are international customs documents permitting the holder to temporarily import products as samples without paying customs duties or posting bonds.

Virtually all goods, personal and professional, including commercial samples, professional equipment, goods intended for use at trade shows and exhibitions, computers, tools, cameras and video equipment, industrial machinery, automobiles, apparel and even jewelry are covered under a carnet.

The reader may wish to check the "General List" to see if the goods are covered by ATA

Carnet guidelines or call the Carnet-Help-Line at (800) 5-DUTYFREE or visit the web site for clarification: http://www.uscib.org

Normal processing of an ATA Carnet is five working days; expedited service is available at an extra charge. In the United States, carnets are sold by the U.S. Council for International Business and Roanoke Trade Services at the following locations:

New York, NY, (212) 708-5078; Long Beach, CA, (800) 421-9324 or (562) 628-9306; Schaumburg, IL, (800) 762-6653 or (847) 969-8211; San Francisco, CA

(800) 255-4994 or (415) 732-5480; Miami, FL (also serves Houston) (800) 468-5467 or (305) 593-5583; Hunt Valley, MD (800) 422-9944 or (410) 771-6100 x 12; Boston, MA (800) 233-3620 or (617) 368-9907; and Houston, TX (pick up site only) (800) 456-0422 or (713) 582-6464 x 102.

With the carnet, goods may be imported without payment of duties and taxes. Carnets are valid for one year.

LABELING AND MARKING REQUIREMENTS

All packages, cases, and bales must bear shipping marks, numbers, dimensions, and the gross weight of the merchandise. Packages along with accompanying bills of lading for goods to be shipped through Turkey must be marked "In Transit." All goods entering Istanbul or any other entry port in Turkey (Ankara, Iskenderun, Izmir, Antalya, Mersin,

Sinop, Samsun, and Trabzon) will be cleared through customs, and full payment of duty will be required unless the packages and bills of lading are marked "In Transit." If so marked, the goods may be cleared for entry and reshipment.

PROHIBITED AND RESTRICTED IMPORTS

Importation of certain product groups like narcotics is prohibited. A list of all prohibited or restricted products for Turkey can be viewed at the Turkish Customs Service Website at http://www.gumruk.gov.tr/ENG/homepage/Pages/default.aspx

Customs Regulations and Contact Information

The Turkish Customs can be reached via
http://www.gumruk.gov.tr/ENG/homepage/Pages/default.aspx

STANDARDS

The Government of Turkey's Undersecretariat for Foreign Trade announced the implementation of twenty-three European Union industrial directives, which would affect an estimated 70 percent of the manufactured products imported into Turkey.

The Undersecretariat for Foreign Trade has adopted the EU's Low Voltage Directive, the Simple Pressure Vessels Directive, the Gas Appliances Directive, the Hot Water Boilers Directive, the EMC, the Machinery Directive, the Civil Explosives Directive, the Weighing Instruments Directive, the Equipment and Protective Systems Intended in Explosive Atmospheres Directive, the Lifts Directive (elevators), the Household Refrigerator/Freezer Directive, the Pressure Equipment Directive, the Noise Emission Directive, the Energy Efficiency for Ballast for Fluorescent Lighting Directive, the Active Implantable Medical Device Directive, the Medical Device Directive, the In Vitro Diagnostics Device Directive, the Toy Directive, the Recreational Water Craft Directive, the Construction Equipment Directive, the Personal Protective Equipment Directive, the Radio and Telecommunications Terminal Equipment Directive and the Cableway Directive (ski lifts and gondolas).

Equipment meeting the directive definition of products needing to conform to EU technical regulations must have evidence of meeting the requirements either through verified laboratory testing conducted by an EU approved notified body or by manufacturer's self-declaration if the directive dictates. Companies selling to the Turkish market must submit evidence of conformity (CE Mark) either by providing a notarized/consularized conformity certificate from a notified body or a manufacturer's issued certificate of conformity, which declares compliance of all relevant directives.

The CE Mark was established by the European Union to ensure the free circulation of products in Europe.

The directives that were entered into effect under a system called the "New Approach," were established to ensure, health and safety, consumer and environmental protection. The "New Approach" identifies level of risk and hazard.

Annexes to the various EU directives will specify levels of risk and types of products that would need to be either certified by a notified body or if the product can be certified by the manufacturer as conforming to the particular directive(s). The EU's laws and regulations made it compulsory to comply with the directives when goods are sold in the territory of the European Union and the European Economic Area (EEA). Companies must show evidence of product compliance by maintaining or presenting a technical file that includes product specifications, technical drawings and standards applied per the appropriate directives and corresponding annexes.

U.S. companies have reported that products of U.S. origin bearing the EU certificate of conformity (CE mark), particularly medical devices, have been detained by Turkish customs authorities for inspection related to a variety of Turkish requirements. Both U.S. companies and Turkish

Government officials have acknowledged that products of EU origin bearing the CE mark, regardless of their point of origin, are not subject to inspection and therefore Turkish customs authorities have been unfairly singling out U.S. products. In some cases, U.S. products apparently have been subjected to additional tests, despite their CE marks. U.S. products which have previously entered the EU

Customs Union, with all required documentation including A-TR certificates, are still subject to inspections and in certain cases, further testing if deemed necessary by Turkish customs officials. The Embassy raised this issue on several occasions with the Foreign Trade Undersecretariat and the Turkish Standards Institute. They have argued that the policy is necessary because Turkey does not have an aftermarket monitoring system in place to ensure consumer protection.

Beginning in early 2009, U.S. companies reported a sharply increased incidence of delays in the entry of U.S. goods from the EU into Turkey, even though those goods complied with EU requirements and traveled freely to all other EU Customs Union member countries. Without prior notice, the Turkish Government published communiqués in January and April 2009 (2009/9, 2009/10, 2009/11, 2009/15, 2009/16, among others) outlining the standard procedures to be followed by importers/manufacturers of toys, personal protective equipment, batteries and medical equipment. Products manufactured in the EU are exempt from these inspections.

Standards Organizations

NIST NOTIFY U.S. SERVICE

Member countries of the World Trade Organization (WTO) are required under the Agreement on Technical Barriers to Trade (TBT Agreement) to report to the WTO all proposed technical regulations that could affect trade with other Member countries. Notify U.S. is a free, web-based e-mail subscription service that offers an opportunity to review and comment on proposed foreign technical regulations that can affect your access to international markets. Register online at Internet URL: https://tsapps.nist.gov/notifyus/data/index/index.cfm

Conformity Assessment

The European Commission does not have a list of products to which their directives apply. Thus the manufacturer is to determine the applicability of relevant directives to any given product. Conformity Assessment is a mandatory step for the manufacturer in the process of complying with specific EU legislation. As the initial step to obtain the CE marking manufacturers need to identify all applicable EU directives and determine the essential requirements indicated in the directives. This is followed by the selection of the appropriate conformity assessment module, which determines the relevant procedures to demonstrate conformity. For low risk profile products the process is relatively simple as manufacturers are allowed to self certify without a third party involvement. The high-risk group products are certified via an accredited testing laboratory, which is referred to as a "Notified Body". The risk level of the product determines the scope of the notified body involvement during the conformity assessment process. A notified body may be involved in the design, the production phase or both. CE marking shall be followed by the identification number of the notified body if it has any involvement in the production phase. It is also possible to have multiple notified bodies involved in the conformity assessment process for those products, which fall under more than one directive. There are competent notified bodies in the U.S. to perform tests on products and an updated list is maintained by the U.S. Department of Commerce. You can find conformity assessment bodies in individual member state country in this list by the European

Commission http://europa.eu.int/comm/enterprise/nando-is/home/index.cfm. To promote market acceptance of the final product, there are a number of voluntary conformity assessment programs.

Turkish Standards Institute, Turkish Cement Manufacturers Association and Turk Loydu

Vakfi Iktisadi Isletmesi have been recognized as notified bodies in Turkey responsible for carrying out the conformity assessment procedures referred to in the applicable New

Approach directives indicated below:

Turkish Standards Institute (Notified Body Number: 1783)

-89/106/EEC Construction Products

-90/396/EEC Appliances Burning Gaseous Fuels

-95/16/EC Lifts

-97/23/EC Pressure Equipment

Turkish Cement Manufacturers Association (Notified Body Number: 1784)

-89/106/EEC Construction Products

Turk Loydu Vakfi Iktisadi Isletmesi (Notified Body Number: 1785)

-90/396/EEC Appliances Burning Gaseous Fuels

-97/23/EC Pressure Equipment

Products that fall under the Active Implantable Medical Device Directive, the Medical

Device Directive, the Low Voltage Directive, the EMC Directive and the Machinery Directive are inspected by the Turkish Standards Institution, in terms of CE compliance.

The inspection procedure in TSE, for CE compliance, starts with the examination of the declaration of conformity. The declaration of conformity must mention the applicable directive(s), the name of the manufacturer or his authorized representative, the name of the notified body (if involved), product information and reference to harmonized standards. If the notified body is also involved in the process, the type examination certificate should also be submitted.

Following the initial phase, the products are examined in terms of the way CE Mark is affixed. The examination process is conducted by a committee set up by the Turkish

Standards Institute. CE Mark must be affixed to the data plate or to the product. If not, it should be placed on packaging and accompanying documents. It must be affixed visibly, legibly and indelibly. It must be in compliance with the predetermined proportions. If the committee decides that CE mark is affixed properly to the product, TSE issues another declaration of conformity.

For products falling outside of the scope of the European Union New Approach

Directives and where the Government of Turkey has established a directive or standard, then that standard or directive would apply. At this point, certification of compliance with

TSE standards would be required. Turkish Standards Institute contact information is provided below in the website portion of this chapter.

The manufacturers are required to submit a declaration of conformity for each applicable directive and prepare a technical file. Following this step the CE mark can be affixed to the product in accordance with the Directive 93/68/EEC

PRODUCT CERTIFICATION

To sell their product to Turkey, the EU as well as Norway, Liechtenstein and Iceland,

U.S. exporters are required to apply CE marking whenever their product is covered by specific product legislation. CE marking product legislation offers manufacturers a number of choices and requires decisions to determine which safety/health concerns need to be addressed, which conformity assessment module is best suited to the manufacturing process, and whether or not to use EU-wide harmonized standards.

In the 1980s, the New Approach was launched to overcome the lengthy adoption process of "old approach" type legislation. The goal of the European Union's harmonization program under the New Approach is to streamline technical harmonization and the development of standards for certain product groups, including, among others, machinery, toys, construction products, electromagnetic compatibility, personal protective equipment, non-automatic weighing instruments, medical devices, gas appliances, hot water boilers, and radio and telecommunications terminal equipment (RTTE). Under the New Approach, Directives cover essential safety, health and environmental requirements. The three regional European standards organizations,

CEN, CENELEC and ETSI, are mandated by the Commission to develop technical standards that are consistent with the essential requirements of EU Directives.

Products manufactured to standards adopted by CEN, CENELEC and ETSI, and published in the Official Journal as harmonized standards, are presumed to conform to the requirements of EU Directives. The manufacturer then applies the CE Mark and issues a declaration of conformity. With these, the product will be allowed to circulate freely within the European Union.

A manufacturer can choose not to use the harmonized EU standards, but must then demonstrate that the product meets the essential safety and performance requirements. Trade barriers occur when design, rather than performance, standards are developed by the relevant European standardization organization, and when U.S. companies do not have access to the standardization process through a European presence.

The CE mark addresses itself primarily to the national control authorities of the Member States, and its use simplifies the task of essential market surveillance of regulated products. Although CE marking is intended primarily for inspection purposes by EU

Member State inspectors, the consumer may well perceive it as a quality mark.

The CE mark is not intended to include detailed technical information on the product, but there must be enough information to enable the inspector to trace the product back to the manufacturer or the authorized representative established in the EU. This detailed information should not appear next to the CE mark, but rather on the declaration of conformity, the certificate of conformity (which the manufacturer or authorized agent must be able to provide at any time, together with the product's technical file), or the documents accompanying the product

Accreditation

Independent certification bodies have been officially accredited by competent authorities to test and certify to EU requirements. However, under the U.S./EU Mutual Recognition

Agreements (MRAs), notified bodies based in the United States and referred to as conformity assessment bodies, will be allowed to test in the United States to EU specifications, and vice versa. The costs will be significantly lower and U.S. products will, as a result, become more competitive. At this time, the U.S./EU MRAs cover the following sectors: EMC (in force), RTTE (in force), medical devices (in transition), pharmaceutical (in transition), and recreational craft (in force). This link lists to American and European Conformity Assessment bodies operating under a mutual recognition agreement. http://ts.nist.gov/ts/htdocs/210/gsig/mra.htm .

Accreditation is handled at member state level. "European Accreditation" (http://www.european-accreditation.org/content/home/home.htm) is an organization representing nationally recognized accreditation bodies. Membership is open to nationally recognized accreditation bodies in countries in the European geographical area that can demonstrate that they operate an accreditation system compatible with EN45003 or ISO/IEC Guide 58.

As previously stated, Turkish Standards Institute, Turkish Cement Manufacturers Association and Turk Loydu Vakfi Iktisadi Isletmesi have been recognized as notified bodies in Turkey responsible for carrying out the conformity assessment procedures referred to in the applicable New Approach directives The Turkish Standards Institute is the accredited authority in the Republic of Turkey for all matters related to ISO, EN ISO and TSE standards and directives.

Publication of Technical Regulations

The Turkish Standards Institute publishes all Turkish standards and directives and documents are available for purchase.

Turk Standartlari Enstitusu (TSE)
Necatibey Caddesi 112
Standart Hazirlama Baskanligi
06100 Bakanliklar
Ankara, Turkey
Tel: [90] (312) 417-0020
Fax: [90] (312) 425-4399
Web site: http://www.tse.org.tr/english/tsedefault1.asp

LABELING AND MARKING

All packages, cases, and bales must bear shipping marks, numbers, dimensions, and the gross weight of the merchandise. Packages along with accompanying bills of lading for goods to be shipped through Turkey must be marked "In Transit." All goods entering Istanbul or any other entry port in Turkey (Ankara, Iskenderun, Izmir, Mersin, Sinop,

Samsun, and Trabzon) will be cleared through customs, and full payment of duty will be required unless the packages and bills of lading are marked "In Transit." If so marked, the goods may be cleared for entry and reshipment.

Contacts The Turkish Customs can be reached via http://www.gumruk.gov.tr/ENG/homepage/Pages/default.aspx

TRADE AGREEMENTS

Turkey has been in accession negotiations since December 17, 2004 and continues to reap the benefits of its 1996 customs union agreement with the EU, particularly in terms of improved economic efficiency. The customs union commits Turkey to adopt the EU's common external tariff and a commercial policy "substantially similar" to that of the EU, including adoption of the EU's preferential trade regime with third countries. Turkey has already signed Free Trade Agreements with the EFTA member countries and is in the process of finalizing agreements with the other EU applicant countries.

Turkey is a founding member of the Black Sea Economic Cooperation (BSEC) in which the governments of Albania, Armenia, Azerbaijan, Bulgaria, Georgia, Greece, Moldova,

Romania, Russia, Turkey and the Ukraine are nurturing multilateral cooperation among the members on a number of issues including trade. Turkey, along with Pakistan and Iran, is a founding member of the Economic Cooperation Organization (ECO). ECO, whose membership beyond the founders includes Afghanistan, Azerbaijan,

Turkmenistan, Uzbekistan, Kyrgyzstan, Tajikistan and Kazakhstan has had limited success in improving trade cooperation. Turkey is a founding member of the Southern

Europe Cooperative Initiative (SECI); a regional association aimed at encouraging cooperation among its member states on a variety of issues including customs, transportation and anti-crime efforts. SECI member states include Albania, Bosnia &

Herzegovina, Bulgaria, Croatia, Greece, Hungary, the Former Yugoslav Republic of Macedonia, Moldova, Romania, Slovenia and Turkey.

Turkey has free trade agreements (FTA's) with the following countries:

Chile
Serbia
Montenegro
EFTA countries (Norway, Switzerland, Iceland and Liechtenstein)
Israel
Macedonia
Croatia
Bosnia Herzegovina
Morocco
The Palestinian Authority
Tunisia
Syria
Egypt
Georgia
Albania

Jordan

WEB RESOURCES

The United States Embassy's Commercial Section has been assisting U.S. companies, which meet EU directives conformity, in having products clear Turkish Customs as expeditiously as possible. The Commercial Section is also working to have the Government of Turkey accept CE conformity certification from U.S. corporations or U.S.-based Notifying Bodies, without having U.S. companies face additional bureaucratic delays at customs and additional testing at the Turkish Standards Institute. For additional assistance in managing the new CE Mark regulations in Turkey, please contact Commercial Specialist Ozge Cirika at Ozge.Cirika@trade.gov

For additional information on the European Union Directives and European standards, please contact:

U.S. Mission to the E.U.
Foreign Commercial Service
Rue Zinner 13
B - 1000 Brussels, Belgium
Fax: 32 2 513 1228
http://www.buyusa.gov/europeanunion/

CE Websites
http://gsi.nist.gov/global/index.cfm/L1-3
http://ec.europa.eu/index_en.htm
http://www.newapproach.org/
Standards Websites
http://www.cen.eu/cen/pages/default.aspx
http://www.cenelec.eu/Cenelec/Homepage.htm
http://www.etsi.org/WebSite/homepage.aspx
http://www.ansi.org/

TRADE AND PROJECT FINANCING

METHODS OF PAYMENT

GENERAL FINANCING AVAILABILITY

Traditionally, Turkish corporations have satisfied most of their financing requirements through the banking industry. Corporate/banking relationships are close. However, given the continuing gap between Turkey's extensive needs and its limited internal resources external financing of public and private project investment is a crucial factor in the and coming years. Exporters are advised to provide financing for their exports. In addition to short and medium-term credits available from commercial banks in local and foreign currencies, lower-cost TL credits are also available from Turkish Exim bank.

HOW TO FINANCE EXPORTS AND METHODS OF PAYMENT

Letters of Credit (LCs) are traditional import instruments for private-sector transactions.

LCs should be irrevocable and confirmed by a prime U.S. bank. As Turkish importers develop long-term contacts and prove their credit-worthiness, suppliers may be willing to accept documents against payment (d/p) or documents against acceptance (d/a). Deferred payment schedules are not common except in cases of large transactions where supplier financing plays a role.

Turkish banks continued to have seen some tightening in their access to international credit, though the major banks borrow internationally. Suppliers should consider unconventional project financing packages (e.g., forfeiting, factoring and utilization of third-country export credits) when bidding on major government infrastructure projects.

Exporters should be flexible and try to accommodate customers' needs, building any additional associated cost into the offer price.

Firms bidding on GOT contracts should pay careful attention to the way proposals are prepared and should strictly follow the administrative specifications. Financing costs and foreign exchange rate risks, wherever applicable, should be factored into the bid price.

Bids, which do not comply with administrative specifications (which include financial criteria), are generally rejected. Generally, validity of a proposal is required to be three to six months from the bid date. Government tenders often involve bid and performance bonds. Bid bonds are normally equivalent to three percent of the value of the tender, while performance bonds are usually equivalent to six percent of the contract value. The government only calls these bonds in cases of substantial non-performance. All bonds have to be counter-guaranteed by a Turkish national bank.

A number of leasing companies operate in Turkey, most owned by Turkish banks. They finance purchases of expensive capital goods such as aircraft, auto fleets, construction equipment and other special equipment. Turkish financial leasing in capital expenditures still only accounts for a fraction of capital expenditures in developed countries. The terms of leasing are usually four years, with a balloon payment at the end. Turkish leasing companies are eager to work with U.S. counterparts.

Turkish factoring companies (again, usually offshoots of banks) generally belong to the

International Factors Group based in Belgium. Like leasing companies, all factoring and forfeiting companies are having funding difficulties. Both factoring and forfeiting maximize cash flow, reduce transaction risks, and may enhance competitiveness by offering flexible payment terms to the buyer. All U.S. banks active in Turkey know and deal with at least one of the major leasing and factoring companies.

HOW DOES THE BANKING SYSTEM OPERATE

The banking sector plays less of a financial intermediary role than one would expect in an economy of Turkey's size and sophistication. The three state -owned commercial banks plus the six largest private banks hold nearly a two-thirds share of total bank assets (information on banks, the listing of banks licensed in Turkey and statistics on the

Turkish banking sector can be viewed at (www.bddk.org.tr). Turkish banks engage in core banking services, securities brokering and other businesses. In terms of trade finance, treasury operations, electronic banking, and information management, the dozen leading Turkish banks are as sophisticated as their other OECD counterparts.

The Istanbul Stock Exchange, formed in 1986, is becoming one of the major players in the capital market. In 1995, the Istanbul Gold Exchange opened for trading. The Capital

Market Board, based in Ankara, is responsible for overseeing the activities of capital markets. The Central Bank of the Republic of Turkey is headquartered in Ankara and together with Turkish Treasury is responsible for the integrity of the banking system. In 1994, the Central Bank became an autonomous body but is not independent.

The Central Bank and BDDK (Banking Regulating and Auditing Commission) supervises bank activities in order to guarantee that they meet liquidity requirements and operates in a responsible fashion. While the Central Bank's Bank Supervision Division acts as the government's supervisory authority, the Undersecretariat of the Treasury is responsible for the enforcement of banking laws. The BDDK also determines the disposition of insolvent banks.

Net foreign direct investment inflows amounted to USD 18.3 billion in 2008 and USD 8.3 billion in 2009 (source: ISPAT). Turkey remains reliant on foreign financing to drive capital investments, but experts predict that although the economy bounced back from the financial crisis in 2009, net FDI inflows will not return to 2006 and 2007 figures ($20 billion) in 2010.Turkey's stand-by deal with the IMF expired in May 2008.

FOREIGN-EXCHANGE CONTROLS

There are no GOT foreign-exchange limits for importers, and there are no restrictions on the transfer of funds in or out of the country. Although the Turkish Lira (TL) is fully convertible, most international transactions are denominated in U.S. dollars or Euros due to these currencies' universal acceptance. Banks deal in foreign exchange and to borrow and lend in foreign currencies. Foreign exchange is freely traded and widely available. Foreign investors are free to convert and repatriate their Turkish lira profits.

U.S. Banks and Local Correspondent Banks

U. S. and U.S.-affiliated investment and commercial banks present in Turkey include: Citibank, JP Morgan Chase, American Express, Wells Fargo and the Bank of New York Mellon

PROJECT FINANCING

Project financing is available through a multitude of sources including Turkish and foreign commercial banks and investment banks. OPIC is another source for project financing for U.S. investors. Interested U.S. companies should note that American banks active in Turkey are among the leaders in project financing.

Turkey offers numerous major project opportunities in telecommunications, energy, transportation, and building of infrastructure projects such as dams, airports, harbors, roads, and water and sewerage systems. Supplier financing is the key to winning these large projects. U.S. Ex-Im bank financing, along with OPIC and TDA programs, are available to U.S. suppliers. The World Bank /International Bank for Reconstruction and

The Overseas Private Investment Corporation (OPIC) has established small business centers to assist qualified small businesses the opportunity to utilize OPIC's resources with improved customer service and easier access through a streamlined approval process. OPIC stands ready to assist small and medium sized business grow through investments in over 150 emerging markets around the world. The Small Business Centers will support the financing and political risk insurance needs to eligible small business.

To support small and medium sized business enterprises in their international trading activity, the United States Commercial Service and the Overseas Private Investment

Corporation entered into a partnership that combines the strength of the Commercial

Service's network of 105 offices in the United States and 150 offices overseas with the investment finance and political risk insurance support of the Overseas Private Investment Corporation. This cooperation agreement has been established to better assist small and medium sized business enterprises. These businesses account for ninety-seven percent of all U.S. exporters, and small business continues to be the bulwark of the U.S. economy.

Leasing issues and licenses are regulated via the Banking Regulating and Auditing

Commission also known as the BDDK. Presently there are 75 leasing firms in Turkey.

Leasing firms can only offer leasing and are not allowed to make any other financial transactions. There are no limits on foreign investment or international leasing firms provided they obtain a license to operate in Turkey from BDDK: http://www.bddk.org.tr/WebSitesi/English.aspx

Leasing terms are 4 years and in very exceptional cases 2 years. The equipment leased will be owned by the leasor after the period of the lease. A definite advantage of the leasing process was the VAT reduction from 18 to 1 percent during the lease time.

However, recently the government has raised the rate back up to 18 percent. Industry groups have complained about this change and are seeking to overturn this decision and at a minimum be to 8 percent.

WEB RESOURCES

Export-Import Bank of the United States: http://www.exim.gov

Country Limitation Schedule: http://www.exim.gov/tools/country/country_limits.html

OPIC: http://www.opic.gov

Trade and Development Agency: http://www.tda.gov/

SBA's Office of International Trade: http://www.sba.gov/oit/

USDA Commodity Credit Corporation: http://www.fsa.usda.gov/ccc/default.htm

U.S. Agency for International Development: http://www.usaid.gov

BUSINESS TRAVEL

BUSINESS CUSTOMS

The Turkish people take pride in their traditions and culture. However, having ties with western countries, Turkish people in major cities have adopted a western way of life. A foreigner visiting any one of the large cities in Turkey will find himself or herself in an atmosphere similar to that of a contemporary western city. Turks are extraordinary hospitable people and visiting businessmen will do well to offer normal courtesies, respect, and to take the time to know your Turkish counterpart. In general, a personal relationship is an important basis for a successful business relationship in Turkey. It is usually important to allow time for friendly conversation before commencing with a business agenda. Business cards are almost always exchanged, and visitors are usually offered a glass of tea or a cup of Turkish coffee and it is customary to accept the offer.

VISA REQUIREMENTS

U.S. citizens are required to obtain visas before entering Turkey. A passport and visa are required. Holders of all types of passports can purchase a 90-day sticker visa at the port of entry for $20, if they are traveling to Turkey as tourists. For further information, travelers in the U.S. may contact the Embassy of the Republic of Turkey at 2525 Massachusetts Avenue, NW, Washington, D.C. 20008, telephone: (202) 612-6700, or the Turkish consulates general in Chicago, Houston, Los Angeles, or New York.

Information may also be found at Internet address http://www.turkey.org

Overseas, travelers may contact a Turkish embassy or consulate. Holders of official and diplomatic passports on official business must obtain a visa from a Turkish embassy or consulate before arrival in Turkey. Holders of official and diplomatic passports on private travel may receive a visa free of charge from a Turkish embassy or consulate, or obtain one upon arrival at the port of entry for $20. All those who are planning to stay more than three months for any purpose are required to obtain a visa from a Turkish embassy or consulate. Such travelers must also apply for a residence/work permit or Turkish ID card within the first month of their arrival in Turkey. For example, this would include anyone who plans to spend more than three months doing research, studying, or working in Turkey.

All travelers are advised to obtain entry stamps on the passport page containing their visa at the first port of entry before transferring to domestic flights. Failure to obtain entry stamps at the port of entry has occasionally resulted in serious difficulties for travelers when they attempt to depart the country.

In an effort to prevent international child abduction, many governments have initiated procedures at entry/exit points. These often include requiring documentary evidence of relationship and permission for the child's travel from the parent(s) or legal guardian not present. Having such documentation on hand, even if not required, may facilitate entry/departure.

The loss or theft abroad of a U.S. passport should be reported immediately to the local police and the nearest U.S. Embassy or Consulate. Travelers are encouraged to carry a photocopy of their passport, to assist in getting a replacement passport if the original is stolen. U.S. citizens may refer to the Department of State's pamphlet, A Safe Trip Abroad for ways to promote a trouble-free journey.

U.S. Companies that require travel of foreign businesspersons to the United States should allow sufficient time for visa issuance if required. Visa applicants should go to the following links.

State Department Visa Website: http://travel.state.gov/visa/index.html

United States Visas: http://www.unitedstatesvisas.gov/

U.S. Embassy Ankara: at http://www.usemb-ankara.org.tr

U.S. Companies that require travel of foreign businesspersons to the United States should be advised that security options are handled via an interagency process. Visa applicants should go to the following links.

State Department Visa Website: http://travel.state.gov/visa/index.html

United States Visas.gov: http://www.unitedstatesvisas.gov/
http://turkey.usembassy.gov/us_consulates.html

TELECOMMUNICATIONS

In 2010, there were 76.5 million GSM users in Turkey, up from 23 million in 2002. The telephone system in Turkey's major cities is good. E-mail and faxes are widely used in international business. Travelers and businesspersons can utilize GSM cellular service prepaid cards and hire a GSM mobile/cell phone in Turkey. I-phone and Blackberries are increasingly common. Coverage is nationwide.

TRANSPORTATION

The national flag carrier, Turkish Airlines (THY), together with its subsidiaries, dominates air passenger service and flies non-stop daily to most major European, Middle Eastern,

Asian cities and U.S. gateways including Tokyo, London, Frankfurt, Paris, New York and

Chicago. Major European airlines have also frequent non-stop flights to Turkey. Delta Airlines serves Istanbul direct from its New York Kennedy hub. THY joined the Star Alliance in 2008. United Airlines and Lufthansa offer code-share service with Lufthansa serving Istanbul, Izmir and Ankara from its Star Alliance Frankfurt and Munich hubs.

Though Turkish Airlines dominates domestic air travel within Turkey, the Government has liberalized domestic air service, and new airlines are also serving the domestic market. Rail transportation is also available between most of the major cities.

Comprehensive networks of long distance buses, which are inexpensive, operate between the major cities. Car rental is relatively expensive. Public transportation is available in the cities. However, businessmen are advised to use taxis.

Lodging: Medium to luxury-type hotels, including international hotels such as the Hilton,

Sheraton, Hyatt, Holiday Inn, Conrad, Four Seasons, Ritz Carlton and Swissotel, are available in major cities. Apartment rents in Istanbul are expensive. Rents in Ankara and Izmir are more reasonable. Payment on an apartment rental, in a popular area of a city, is usually made in a foreign currency. Generally, six months to one year's rent is expected in advance.

Please see a list of business service providers for more information at http://www.buyusa.gov/turkey/en/business_service_providers.html

LANGUAGE

The official language spoken by more than 90 percent of the population is Turkish. Most educated Turks have a command of at least one foreign language, with sufficient fluency to carry out business transactions. Most company executives were educated in western countries. English is the dominant language for international business.

HEALTH

Medical facilities are available, but may be limited outside urban areas. Food and water borne diseases are present in Turkey. Anyone coming to Turkey should have comprehensive medical insurance. Useful information on medical emergencies abroad, including overseas insurance programs, is provided in the Department of State's Bureau of Consular Affairs brochure, Medical Information for American Traveling Abroad, available via the Bureau of Consular Affairs home page at www.travel.state.gov

Vaccines: Vaccines recommended for Turkey are all childhood immunizations, Typhoid, Hepatitis B, Hepatitis A (or Immune Globulin as an alternative). Visitors who will visit rural areas, or go on hiking, or trekking trips in the country may wish to get Rabies vaccine although this is not required.

Information on vaccinations and other health precautions can be obtained from the

Center for Diseases Control and Prevention's (CDC) hotline for international travelers at 1-877-FYI-TRIP (1-877-394-8747), fax 1-800-CDC-FAXX (1-800-232-3299), or via

CDC's Internet site at http://www.cdc.gov

Food: Turkish cuisine is characterized by the freshness of its ingredients and most

American business travelers have no trouble finding a good meal. All major hotels have at least one restaurant serving continental cuisine. Several European and ethnic restaurants are also available in major cities. Prices at these places are usually moderate-to-expensive. Good food is available not only at expensive restaurants but also at moderately priced establishments. One also has the choice of fast food restaurants such as McDonald's, Wendy's, Kentucky Fried Chicken, Burger King and their Turkish kebap equivalents. A variety of fresh fruits and vegetables are available throughout the year.

Local Time, Business Hours, and Holidays

Time in Turkey is Universal Time Coordinated/Zulu + 2 hours (Zulu is London UTC). In comparison, Eastern Standard Time is Zulu –5 hours, Central Standard Time is Zulu –6 hours and Pacific Standard Time is Zulu –8 hours.

Business Hours are from 08:30 to 17:30 Monday through Friday except holidays.

Turkish Holidays

DATE NAME OF HOLIDAY

January 1: New Year's Day (Yılbaşı)

April 23: National Sovereignty and Children's Rights Day (Ulusal Egemenlik ve Çocuk Bayramı)

May 1: Labor Day

May 19: Commemoration of Ataturk,Youth and Sports Day (Atatürk'ü Anma,Gençlik ve Spor Bayramı)

August 30: Victory Day(Zafer Bayramı)

August 29(half day) &
August 30 - September 1: (End of the Islamic month of fasting-the Ramadan) Ramadan Feast (Ramazan Bayramı or Şeker Bayramı)

October 28(half day) &
October 29: Republic Day (Cumhuriyet Bayramı)

November 5(half day) &
November 6-9: (70 days after Ramadan) Sacrifice Feast (Kurban Bayramı)

TEMPORARY ENTRY OF MATERIALS AND PERSONAL BELONGINGS

Travelers entering Turkey on a temporary basis and carrying items such as laptop computers and accessories, display and exhibit materials are permitted to bring these items into Turkey duty free. Customs officials register the items to the traveler's passport and subsequently cancel them as the traveler exits the country with the same items. Catalogs, brochures, pamphlets, and similar advertising materials are exempt from customs duty. For additional information about temporary entry, please see VI. Trade Regulations and Standards, Temporary Entry section. Customs regulations may be found at www.gumruk.gov.tr

Web Resources

Department of State Travel Information: www.travel.state.gov

Center for Diseases Control Health Info: http://www.cdc.gov

State Department Visa Website: http://travel.state.gov/visa/index.html

United States Visas.gov: http://www.unitedstatesvisas.gov/

U.S. Embassy Anakara: at http://www.usemb-ankara.org.tr

CONTACTS

U.S. Mission Trade-related Personnel

Commercial Affairs http://www.buyusa.gov/turkey/en/

United States Department of State http://ankara.usembassy.gov/

United States Department of Agriculture

Agricultural Affairs Office Agankara@fas.usda.gov

WASHINGTON-BASED U.S. GOVERNMENT COUNTRY CONTACTS

U.S. Department of Commerce
Ms. Kristin Nadji
Turkey Desk Officer
Kristin_Nadji@ita.doc.gov
U.S. Department of State
Victoria J. Taylor
Turkey Desk
Office of Southern European Affairs (EUR/SE)
TaylorVJ@state.gov
Trade and Development Agency
www.ustda.gov
Mr. Carl Kress
Regional Director for Russia, NIS, and Turkey
ckress@ustda.gov
U.S. Department of Agriculture, Foreign Agricultural Service
www.fas.usda.gov
Ms. Kathleen Wainio
kathleen.wainio@fas.usda.gov
Export-Import Bank of the United States
www.exim.gov
Mr. Brian Santangelo, Business Development Officer
Brian.Santangelo@exim.gov
Mr. Craig O'Connor, Director of the Office of Environmental Exports and Renewable Energy
Craig.Oconnor@exim.gov
Overseas Private Investment Corporation
www.opic.gov
Peter Ballinger, Director of Business Development
Pball@opic.gov
For Linkedin:
http://tr.linkedin.com/pub/commercial-service-turkey/30/852/a67
For Twitter:
http://twitter.com/#!/CommmercialUS
For Facebook:
www.facebook.com

U.S Banks Operating in Turkey:
Citibank Ms. Neslihan Serra Akcaoglu, General Manager
http://www.citibank.com.tr

JP Morgan Chase
Ms. Belma Ozmen, Chairman
http://www.jpmorgan.com/pages/international/turkey

Bank of America Merrill Lynch Investment Bank
Osman Nihat Kokmen, General Manager
http://www.ml.com.tr

U.S Banks with Representative Offices in Turkey
Wells Fargo Bank
Ms. Dilek Mutus, General Manager
dilek.mutus@wellsfargo.com

Bank of New York Mellon
Mr. Michel Sidier, General Manager michel.sidier@bmymellon.com

TURKISH GOVERNMENT CONTACTS:

AGRICULTURE AND RURAL AFFAIRS
Ministry of Agriculture and Rural Affairs, General Directorate of Agricultural Production Development
www.tarim.gov.tr

COMMUNICATIONS
Ministry of Communications and Transportation www.ubak.gov.tr
Telecommunications Authority www.tk.gov.tr

DEFENSE AND NATIONAL SECURITY
Ministry of National Defense, Foreign Procurement Department
www.msb.gov.tr

Undersecretariat for Defense Industries www.ssm.gov.tr

EDUCATION
Ministry of National Education www.meb.gov.tr
Higher Education Council www.yok.gov.tr

ENERGY AND NATURAL RESOURCES
Ministry of Energy and Natural Resources www.enerji.gov.tr

ENVIRONMENT AND FORESTRY AFFAIRS
Ministry of Environment, General Directorate of Environmental Impact, Assessment and Planning www.cevreorman.gov.tr

HEALTH
Ministry of Health, Foreign Relations Department www.saglik.gov.tr

TRADE AND ECONOMY
State Planning Organization-SPO www.dpt.gov.tr
Undersecretariat of the Treasury www.treasury.gov.tr

Undersecretariat of Foreign Trade, General Directorate of Imports www.dtm.gov.tr

Prime Ministry, Privatization Administration www.oib.gov.tr

Turkish Institute of Standards, Standards Preparation Department www.tse.org.tr

TRANSPORTATION
General Directorate of State Highways www.kgm.gov.tr

State Airports Administration www.dhmi.gov.tr
General Directorate of State Railways Administration
www.tcdd.gov.tr

TRAVEL AND TOURISM
Ministry of Culture and Tourism www.kulturturizm.gov.tr

BUSINESS/TRADE ASSOCIATIONS
American Chamber of Commerce in Turkey
http://www.abft.net/

Turkish-American Business Association
http://amcham.org.tr/

Foreign Economic Relations Board-DEIK
www.deik.org.tr
Turkish Industrialists' and Businessmen's Association-TUSIAD
www.tusiad.org.tr

Union of Chambers of Commerce, Industry, Maritime Commerce and Commodity Exchanges of Turkey (TOBB) www.tobb.org.tr

EDUCATIONAL
Fulbright Commission www.fulbright.org.tr
E-mail: fulb-ank@itu.edu.tr

FRANCHISING
Turkish National Franchising Association www.ufrad.org.tr

STRATEGIC INVESTMETN OPPORTUNITIES AND CONTACTS

TURKEY: PACKAGING INDUSTRY

The Packaging industry is considerably developed in Turkey. There is a trend towards innovation and environmentally friendly production in recent years. New packaging formats are improved according to quality, size and appeal of products. Growth in population and living standards, urbanization, diversification of consumer goods, increase in the number of women in labor force and increase in exports have all resulted in higher demand for packaged products.

Packaging consumption in Turkey is 5.5 million tons of which 39% is for paper, carton and corrugated board packaging and 33% for plastic packaging. Likewise, these two sub-sectors have the biggest share in imports. Import of packaging materials of Turkey in 2011 was around 3 billion dollars and has increased around 7.8% compared to year 2010. The U.S. is one of the largest suppliers of packaging material to the country.

Turkey is a promising market for international companies with its young and large population, lack of market maturity, favorable long-term economic structure and increasing GDP per capita. European Union companies dominate the import market due to geographical proximity and the Customs Union Agreement. American companies can increase market share in this developing market by finding qualified distributors. Additionally, they can take advantage of Turkish companies' expertise in surrounding countries by forming partnerships.

MARKET OVERVIEW

Packaging is a vital component of all manufacturing industries in Turkey with regard to domestic and international marketing of products. The World Packaging Organization considers packaging as an indication of welfare. Packaging sector development and per capita packaging consumption in a country is often evaluated as a measurement of life standards and economic activities. Packaging has an increasingly important place in the marketing of various agricultural and food products and other non-food products in Turkey and shows an inclination for development in recent years, especially in export goods. Despite the recent worldwide economic recession in manufacturing sectors, the developments in packaging including the preference in quality, and the rationalization and environmental adaptation precautions in main and side items used continue in Turkey as well as in world markets. In fact, as manufacturing industry gains new production facilities, the Turkish packaging sector is developing faster than EU countries whose packaging markets are relatively saturated.

Turkey's European Union accession process also contributes to the development of the packaging industry. Legal arrangements on public health and consumer protection such as food law, packaging wastes and legal regulations on prepackaged products are all contributors to the sector.

Growths in population and living standards, rapid urbanization and diversification of consumer goods have resulted in higher demand for packaging products. Growth in domestic demand has enabled packaging companies to continue to increase their profits and focus on investment plans. Due to increases in average per capita income in Turkey since last decade, life standards have experienced important changes. Increasing urbanization, increased average life span, rise in female population active in business life and the change in consumer expectations have developed self-service methods in consumption centers, and have encouraged the dispersion of direct selling hypermarkets, supermarkets and market chains around the entire country. These factors have raised awareness for packaging catering to buyer groups with different demographic characteristics. Preference for homemade food types have been decreasing as a result of increase in working life in big cities and more packaged products have been manufactured due to the increase in convenience food and fast food sectors.

Retail sales systems support the development and use of portion style packaging. Consumers can find more variety, cheap, good quality and trustworthy products, as well as price and quality balance in. In addition to this, factors such as customer service, promotions at sales points, special discounts, and free product coupons direct the customer to shop at the market. In short, chain retailing and shopping malls have significantly increased the demand for packaged product.

Mass retailing in Turkey began towards the end of 1980s. With the opening of the first shopping mall in 1987, the retail sector in Turkey entered a new era following chain stores. Projects that consecutively developed have shown a rapid growth especially after 2006. According to Shopping Malls Investors Association data, by March 2011, the active number of malls is 276 and total rentable area is 6,800,000 m2.

In the early 2000s, organized retail trade rate was just over 20% and now it has exceeded 40%. Despite this impressive growth, this rate is still low compared to European Union and North American countries, which have a rate of over 80% but it is believed that the demand for packaged goods will increase in importance in Turkey.

A general increase is observed not just in the number of new malls, but also in seasonal fluctuations in the amount of shopping/bill number in malls during the year and this should be evaluated as a measurement of retail trade being oriented towards organized trade.

Retail trade in Turkey is expected to reach 948 billion TL in 2013 (approximately $520 billion) and organized retail within this number is expected to reach 448 billion TL (approximately $246 billion), which is 47%.

Another trade channel that feeds packaged good demand is e-commerce. With the aid of developments in Turkey's internet infrastructure in the last 5 years, 15 companies that deal in electronic trade have reached total revenue of 607 million dollars. Based on declarations made by the Electronic Trade Administrators Association, a total of 10 billion TL worth of sales requiring packaging for primary and secondary transportation is realized in 2011 and 2012.

The factor that affects sales of packaged goods the most is the development in household and per capita national income. Per capita national income development calculated based on Turkey Purchasing Power Parity points to optimistic results.

Following world trends, packaging consumption in Turkey has increased rapidly. The packaging sector does not normally produce for stock. Production is done based on orders. Therefore, production and consumption may be considered as similar quantities. The amount of production in all branches of packaging (paper, cardboard, corrugated cardboard, plastic, metal, glass and wood packaging) was 6 million tons and total revenue was 12 billion dollars in 2011. In the context of production capacity, for example, one of the Turkish glass packaging companies ranks in the world's top 15. The Turkish Packaging Industry was affected by the global crisis in 2009, but it rebounded in 2010, and increased its production and revenue by 8% and 14% respectively in 2011.

The value of the Turkish Packaging Sector reached 12 billion dollars in 2011. When foreign trade measurements are taken into account, the size of packaging sector reached 14-15 billion dollars by the end of 2012. Average growth rate of the industry in Turkey has been 6% in past years, and this trend is estimated to continue. The breakdown of consumption, which is at 5.5 million tons, is 39% for paper, carton and corrugated board packaging, 33% for plastic packaging, 13% for glass packaging, 8% for wood packaging and 7% for metal packaging.

The Packaging sector contributes to the marketing of industrial and agricultural products. Generally, the value of packaging is 3-5% of the sales value of the product in daily conveniences and around 10% in relatively luxurious goods that are less active. Around 50% of packaging production is mostly food products and around 20-30% is other non-food consumption goods. Based on values provided by the World Packaging Organization, 20-30% of packaging production is for industrial packaging.

When sub-sectors of packaging are analyzed, it is evident that Turkey is one of the largest production and consumption centers of **paper and cardboard packaging**. Produced paper and cardboard packages comprise 80% of the packaging market in Turkey. When packaging materials are examined on the basis of turnover, the share of paper packages is 17%, cardboard packages is 17% and corrugated paperboard packages is 9%. Turkey is the sixth largest production center in the world, with a production capacity of 2 million tons dedicated to paper, carton and corrugated board products. There are 8 paper packaging companies which are among Turkey's top 500 companies. Turkey is one of the two countries in the world that has achieved 50% growth and 100,000 tons production increase in paper-cardboard packaging in the last 5 years. Raw material requirement of paperboard, except NSSC Fluting, is met by local production. Recycling of corrugated paperboard is performed at a high level of around 70-75%.

Plastic packaging applications produced in Turkey include stretch films, shrink films, pallet covers, bags, sachets, big bags, threads, solid and liquid thermoform food-beverage containers, bottles for carbonated and non-carbonated beverages, industrial barrels, containers for detergents and cosmetics, foam containers and packaging forms. Measured by volume, 55% of these packaging products are flexible and 45% are hard. Plastic packaging is really taking off, and its use is constantly increasing. Turkey is the world's second largest exporter of FIBC (Flexible Intermediate Bulk Containers). The total capacity of the plastic packaging sector in Turkey is 1 million tons. There are 11 plastic packaging companies which are among Turkey's top 500 companies. Most companies in this segment are small and medium sized.

Turkey has a very well-developed **glass industry**. There is a group of companies, namely "Turkiye Sise ve Cam Fab. A. S." in the glass industry that dominates the domestic market and ranks 12th among the top 15 firms in the world. The Group consists of 26 companies which produce almost every kind of glass product, and Anadolu Cam branch of the company produces glass packaging. Turkey has a glass production capacity of 2.2 million tons in total. Approximately one third of this capacity, which is about 750,000 tons, is for glass packaging products.

Wooden packaging consists mainly of products used for packaging agricultural products such as fresh fruits and vegetables, standard and non-standard pallets used in warehouse stacking and logistics, demountable transportation boxes and containers. Total capacity is estimated to be 600,000 tons per year and the production of various wooden packaging materials is about 500,000 tons per year.

Based on 2011 values published by the Turkish Statistical Institute, packaging sector exports are valued at 2.95 billion dollars. In addition, it should be taken into account that a large amount of packaging has been exported indirectly as export good packaging. Packaging sector exports have increased 24% compared to the previous year.

The Turkish Packaging Sector exports products to 191 countries, with a focus on the EU countries. In 2011, Germany, the United Kingdom, Iraq, France, Iran, the Netherlands, Italy, Israel, Russian Federation and Greece were the top 10 importers of Turkish packaging. Plastic packaging products rank highest, with an export share of 68% in 2011. Another important packaging group for exports is paper/cardboard/corrugated cardboard packaging products with 19% export share. Other packaging groups with high export share are metal packaging products at 10%, wood at 1.5% and glass at 1.5%. Turkish packaging exports are characterized as high-quality products sold at competitive prices. American companies can take advantage of Turkey's expertise in the surrounding countries of Middle East, North Africa, Central Asia and Caucasus countries by forming partnerships with big Turkish companies in the market.

Turkey's imports of packaging materials in 2011 were around 3 billion dollars, an increase of around 7.8% compared to year 2010. Plastic packaging (48% of packaging imports), and paper/cardboard/corrugated cardboard packaging (42% of packaging imports) are the most important import items. However, a major amount of imports are raw materials or intermediate-product imports. Due to a lack of cellulose production used in paper/cardboard manufacturing in Turkey, the raw material of industrial packaging made of corrugated cardboard used in transport packaging is almost entirely imported. Main countries of import in packaging materials are Germany, Italy, USA, China, France, South Korea, the United Kingdom, Finland, Spain and Belgium.

The import market is dominated by European Union (EU) countries due to geographical proximity and Turkey's accession to Customs Union of the EU, which resulted in zero duties for imports from these countries. There are no significant trade barriers for U.S. imports. Turkey's imports are regulated by an annual import regime published by the Undersecretariat for Foreign Trade. The import regime sets forth import rules and regulations, customs duties and surcharges on imported products.

Acquisitions and mergers have taken place among packaging manufacturing companies, and this trend is expected to change the overall competition and packaging dynamics in Turkey. In paper-based packaging, Olmuksa International Paper Sabanci Ambalaj Sanayi ve Ticaret increased its market share considerably by acquiring the entire share capital of DS Smith Copikas Kagit ve Oluklu Mukavva Kutu Sanayi, worth €5.5 million as of October 2010. In glass packaging, Anadolu Cam acquired an existing glass company in Ukraine in 2011 and became the fifth largest European glass packaging company. In flexible packaging, there is a possible takeover of Asas Ambalaj by Constantia Packaging, an Austrian company which invests in medium-sized industrial and related services companies. Crown has announced a TL100 million (approximately $55 million) investment in Turkey. Koksan has announced that it will invest in a PET resin plant with a capacity of 432,000 tons per year. Sarten Ambalaj announced plans to invest in Jordan and Syria and installed a new line for plastic packaging in order to satisfy plastic packaging demand of regional customers.

Top 10 countries for packaging imports in 2011 (x$1,000)

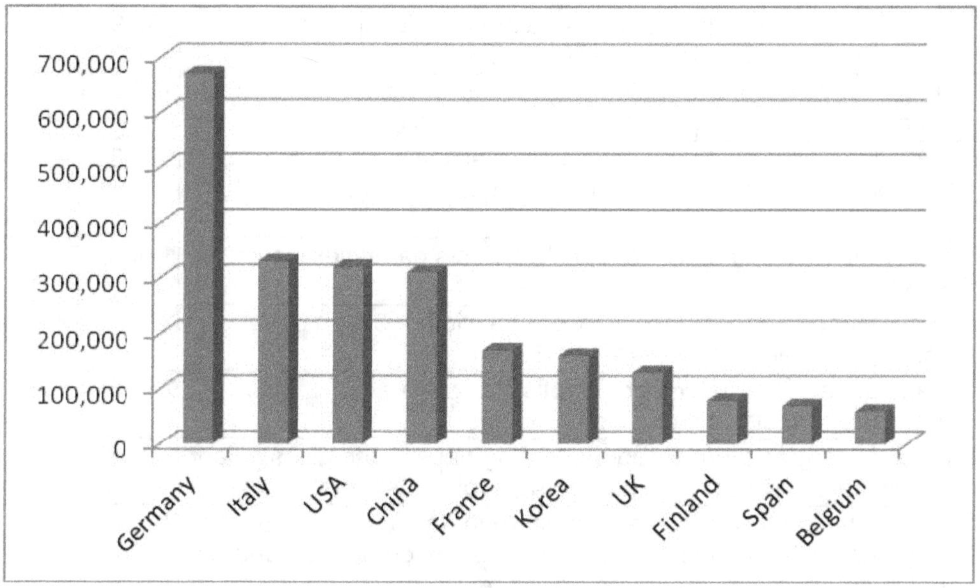

Import Amounts According to Packaging Materials (Years 2010 and 2011)

	Imports according to material type USD and weight (2010)	Average price $/ton	Imports according to material type USD and weight (2011)	Average price $/ton	$(%) compared to 2010	Kg(%) compared to 2010		
	$ (x 1,000)	Kg(x1,000)		$(x1,000)	Kg(x1,000)			
WOOD	8,619	9,683	890	8,318	8,416	988	-3.5	-13.1
GLASS	68,839	89,757	767	63,275	65,269	969	-8.1	-27.3
METAL	160,914	32,322	4,978	197,653	35,401	5,583	22.8	9.5
PAPER/CARDBOARD	1,386,170	1,569,853	883	1,286,890	1,135,511	1,133	-7.2	-27.7
PLASTIC	1,181,255	285,673	4,135	1,469,383	319,436	4,600	24.4	1.18
TOTAL	2,805,797	1,987,290	1,412	3,025,529	1,564,035	1,934	7.8	-21.3

Turkey's Imports of Packaging Materials in 2012 by HS code (provisional)

HS Code	Description	$ amount
3919	Self-adhesive plates, sheets, film, foil, tape, strip and other flat shapes, of plastics, whether or not in rolls	244,341,514
3920	Plates, sheets, film, foil and strip, of non-cellular plastics, not reinforced, laminated, supported or similarly combined with other materials	770,296,193

3921	Plates, sheets, film, foil and strip, of plastics, reinforced, laminated, supported or similarly combined with other materials	199,925,075
3923	Articles for the conveyance or packaging of goods, of plastics; stoppers, lids, caps and other closures, of plastics	182,294,373
4415	Packing cases, boxes, crates, drums and similar packings, of wood; cable-drums of wood; pallets, box pallets and other load boards, of wood; pallet collars of wood	8,223,222
4416	Casks, barrels, vats, tubs and other coopers" products parts thereof, of wood, incl. staves	1,093,375
4804	Uncoated kraft paper and paperboard, in rolls of a width > 36 cm or in square or rectangular sheets with one side > 36 cm	326,552,641
4805	Other paper and paperboard, uncoated, in rolls of a width > 36 cm or in square or rectangular sheets with one side > 36 cm	239,044,568
4806	Vegetable parchment, greaseproof papers, tracing papers and glassine and other glazed transparent or translucent papers, in rolls or sheets	25,818,956
4807	Composite paper and paperboard "made by sticking flat layers of paper or paperboard together with an adhesive", not surface coated or impregnated, whether or not internally reinforced, in rolls or sheets	10,459,799
4808	Corrugated paper and paperboard "with or without glued flat surface sheets", creped, crinkled, embossed or perforated, in rolls or sheets	7,150,722
4811	Paper, paperboard, cellulose wadding and webs of cellulose fibres, coated, impregnated, covered, surface-colored, surface-decorated or printed, in rolls or rectangular (including square) sheets of any size	311,014,806
4817	Envelopes, letter cards, plain postcards and correspondence cards, of paper or paperboard; boxes, pouches, wallets and writing compendiums of paper or paperboard, containing an assortment of paper stationery	1,073,299
4819	Cartons, boxes, cases, bags and other packing containers, of paper, paperboard, cellulose wadding or webs of cellulose fibers; box files, letter trays and similar articles, of paper or paperboard of a kind used in offices, shops or the like	61,918,130
4821	Paper or paperboard labels of all kinds, whether or not printed	36,813,526
4823	Paper, paperboard, cellulose wadding and webs of cellulose fibres, in strips or rolls of a width <= 36 cm, in rectangular	55,692,212
6305	Sacks and bags, of a kind used for the packing of goods, of all types of textile materials	7,560,332
7010	Carboys, bottles, flasks, jars, pots, phials, ampoules and other containers, of glass, of a kind used for the conveyance or packing of goods; preserving jars of glass; stoppers, lids and other closures of glass	53,135,257
7309	Reservoirs, tanks, vats and similar containers, of iron or steel, for any material "other than compressed or liquefied gas` of iron or steel, of a capacity exceeding 300 l , whether or not line or heat insulated, but not fitted with mechanical or thermal equipment.	28,901,287
7310	Tanks, casks, drums, cans, boxes and similar containers, of iron or steel, for any material "other than compressed or liquefied gas` of iron or steel, of a capacity exceeding 300 l , whether or not line or heat insulated, but not fitted with mechanical or thermal equipment.	17,923,666
7612	Casks, drums, cans, boxes and similar containers, incl. rigid or collapsible tubular containers, of aluminum, for any material "other than compressed or liquefied gas` of iron or steel, of a capacity exceeding 300 l , whether or not line or heat insulated, but not fitted with mechanical or thermal equipment.	39,424,378

7613	Aluminium containers for compressed or liquefied gas	1,911,064
8309	Stoppers, caps and lids, incl. crown corks, screw caps and pouring stoppers, capsules for bottles, threaded bungs, bung covers, seals and other packing accessories, of base metal	85,437,183
Total		2,716,005,578

Source: Turkish Statistical Institute

Per capita packaging consumption tends to increase as a country becomes more developed. In 2010, the world average was $110 per person. In Turkey, there is a long road ahead when compared to North America, with a per capita packaging consumption valued between $350 and $400, Western Europe between $250 and $300 and Japan at $550. Per capita packaging consumption in Turkey was $140 in 2010 $160 in 2011, which is above the world average but still much lower than developed countries. The estimate for per capita consumption in 2023, the centennial of the foundation of Republic of Turkey, is that it will be over $300.

The fact that Turkey has a lower consumption level than developed countries is not due to shortcomings in the capacity of packaging industry or the technological level of development in the industry, but rather due to the fluctuations in the manufacturing industry. The Turkish packaging industry is not lacking in the implementation of standards and technology compared to developed countries. On the contrary, it has some newer implementations than certain EU countries and USA. Production quality has rapidly adapted to the requirements of end users, ISO 9000, ISO 14001, ISO 22000, ISPM 15, recycling certifications, HCCP certifications and European standards are already widely applied. This is why the packaging industry is one of the most developed sectors in Turkey.

Research and development activities and packaging product designs also have world-scale reputation. Rationalization of manufacturing and the environmental measures are the other issues handled in conformity with the global trends in the sector. Turkish packaging manufacturers closely follow recent national and international developments in environmental issues and comply with environmental legislation and regulation. All types of packaging wastes, including those imported and produced in Turkey are controlled under the `Packaging and Packaging Waste Management Legislation'. Additionally, there is legislation for the control of food packaging production and articles in direct contact with food materials. These legislative adjustments aim to reach a compliance with European Union regulations.

As new necessities marketed via imports due to both foreign trade policies and low exchange rates are started to be produced in Turkey, "life standard measurement" will also rise. This is because the Turkish packaging sector has the capability to meet the requirements of domestic manufacturing industry both structurally and technologically, however, the necessities imported today come with their own packaging. As new products start to be produced in Turkey, their packaging will also be produced in Turkey and the market size will develop in connection to this.

It is estimated that around 90,000 – 100,000 people work in the packaging sector in Turkey. The sector is not labor intensive but technology intensive. Packaging companies are fairly closely located to production industries. They are concentrated in Western Turkey with a majority in the area of Istanbul in the Marmara Region and in Izmir/ Manisa in the Aegean Region. Other important cities with packaging company concentration are Kocaeli, Bursa, Ankara, Konya, Gaziantep, Adana and Kayseri. The geographical breakdown of the number of packaging companies in major cities of Turkey is as follows:

REGION	CITY	No. of COMPANIES
Marmara	Istanbul	1,881
	Bursa	126
	Kocaeli	74
Aegean	Izmir	234
	Manisa	28
Central Anatolia	Ankara	112
	Konya	100
	Kayseri	44
Southern Turkey	Gaziantep	65
	Adana	56

There are 5,000 companies that produce packaging materials, equipment and related supplies in Turkey, mostly comprised of small and medium sized companies and some large companies. The Turkish packaging industry is developing rapidly at an average annual growth rate of 10% in the past two years. According to Istanbul Chamber of Commerce's (ISO) annual top 1,000 Turkish companies list, 55 industry institutions active in packaging have been placed on the list. These 55 companies made sales from production of 10.45 billion TL in year 2011. The production value done by these 55 companies rose by 26%, their period profits rose by approximately 24%, their exports rose by approximately 2%, and their number of employees fell by approximately 10% compared to 2010. Packaging companies constitute 2.8% of sales from production, 2.3% of period profits, 1.9% of exports and 2.4% of number of employees of all ISO 1,000 companies. American companies are advised to identify distributors/representatives in Turkey to take advantage of this developing market and form partnerships in third countries in the region.

ASSOCIATIONS

- Packaging Manufacturers Association *www.ambalaj.org.tr*
- Corrugated Board Manufacturers Association *www.omud.org.tr*
- Label Manufacturers Association *www.esd.*org.tr
- Carton Board Packaging Manufacturers Association *www.kasad.org.tr*
- Flexible Packaging Manufacturers Association *www.fasd.org.tr*
- Packaging Machine Manufacturers Association *www.amd.org.tr*
- Association For Recyclable Packaging Materials Collectors And Separators *www.tudam.org.tr*
- Rigid Plastic Packaging Manufacturers Association *www.sepa.org.tr*

PLASTIC RAW MATERIALS MARKET IN TURKEY

The plastics industry is one of Turkey's emerging industries, but continues to grow at over 12 percent per annum. This growth rate is almost the double of the GDP growth rate of the country.

The Turkish plastics industry has 1.6% market share in the international plastics industry, and it ranks 3rd in Europe, following Germany and Italy.

The Turkish plastics industry relies heavily on imported down-stream petrochemical components and foreign technologies to manufacture finished plastic products for the domestic and Central Asian markets. Turkey ranks 16 in plastic raw materials importation in the world with a share of two percent.

Plastic consumption in Turkey was 5.5 million metric tons in 2011. This indicates an increase of 10% compared to the year before. Turkish consumption of the 5.5 million tons is broken down as follows: PE 27.9%; PP 28.7%; PVC 17.7%; PET 5.1%; others 20.6%.

Over six thousand companies are engaged in the plastics industry, 97% of these being SMEs. Again, of these, 113 are firms with foreign capital shares, and of the 113, 43% are of EU origin. 63% of all the firms in the industry are plastic product manufacturers, 16% are machinery and equipment producers, and 12% are raw material and auxiliary material manufacturers.

In Turkey, more than 81% of plastic raw material production is realized by Petkim. SASA, Baser, Artenius, Advansa, and Meltem Kimya are other manufacturers.

As the domestic plastic raw material production fails to fulfill demand, the majority of raw material is imported, amounting to $ 9.9 billion and 5.2 million tons in 2011. This represents nearly 94.5% of the domestic raw material need. Of the plastic raw materials imports, 27% is PP, 21% is PE, 14% is PET, and 11% is PVC. 27% is others.

Saudi Arabia, South Korea, Iran, and EU firms dominate the market, benefiting from geographic closeness to the Turkish market. However, American firms, which rank tenth as suppliers, can increase its market share in this growing market by establishing a distribution center, preferably at the free zones to be able to import into the country as needed or ship to surrounding countries to benefit from the geographic location of the country.

MARKET OVERVIEW

Turkish end users started to use plastics as an alternative to iron, glass, paper or wooden products as in the rest of the world. This trend resulted in a more than 10% yearly increase in the market since the 1990s. Consumption of plastics per capita is almost 48 kg in Turkey, whereas this figure climbs to 70-90 kg in most developed countries. Considering the development projects of the country, growth expectations in most industries, and increase in population show the potential growth in the petrochemical industry.

Domestic production meets only the 5.5 percent of the demand for plastic industry raw materials meaning 94.5% is imported. Average growth of the plastics industry for the last 5 years: 12%

Plastic consumption in Turkey comprise of commodity plastics as follows:

	Percentage in Total Consumption (%)	Percentage of Local Production in Total Supply (%)
PE	27.9	23.7
PP	28.7	7.9
PVC	17.7	15.2
PET	5.1	40.0

Others	20.6	0	

Source: TUIK

PE, PP, PVC, and PET are manufactured locally. However, local production can only meet some portion of the demand. Others, including styrene, vinyl polymers, acrylic polymers, polyacetals, polycarbonates polyamides, etc. are all imported only.

MARKET TRENDS

The plastic raw materials market grows parallel to the growing plastic products market in Turkey. The plastic products suppliers find a niche in:

- The growing automotive industry and the white goods industry in Turkey: Most OEMs in the automotive industry established their production facilities in Turkey to be closer to the market, especially the European market. The plastics industry manufactures intermediate products for growing industries with a high added value, automotive and white goods being two of these. Turkey has already become an important production and exports base for these industries.

- The existing and planned pipelines of petroleum and natural gas market: Turkey aims to become an energy terminal with existing and planned natural gas and crude oil pipe line products. It acts as a bridge connecting the newly commissioned giant-sized petrochemical plants in the Middle East and the large scale markets in the west.

- The growing packaging industry: Increase in trend of packaging of goods to comply with the EU standards and increasing consumer awareness to packaging.

- The increasing investments in construction and building industries

Petkim is the sole producer of LDPE (3901.10.90.00.11) in Turkey, and with the new investment, it currently is capable of meeting the 80% of the total market demand in LDPE. Its production capacity reached 330,000 tons per year. LDPE is primarily used in the film production – 90%, injection molding – 2%, cable production – 3%, and blowing molding -5% industries in Turkey.

There is no Linear Low Density Polyethylene (LLDPE) production in Turkey. All is imported – 3901.10.10.00.00.

Petkim is again the sole producer of High Density Polyethylene (HDPE, 3901.20.90.00.11) in Turkey. Its capacity is 96,000 tons per year, and Petkim only meets the 15% of the total demand in Turkey.

Again, Petkim is the sole producer of Polyvinyl Chloride-PVC- (3904.21.00.00.00, 3904.22.00.00.00) and it meets the 15% of the market demand. Its production capacity is 150,000 tons per year. PVC is used primarily in building, agriculture, electric, automotive, toys, and health industries.

Petkim is the sole producer of another item, Polypropylene –PP- (3902.10.00.00.00). Even with the latest investments to increase its production capacity of PP to 144,000 tons, it can only meet the 12 percent of the market.

Polystyrene (3903.19.00.00.11-crystal, and 3903.19.00.00.12 – antishock) is produced by Baser Kimya (annual production capacity - 40,000 tons). Again, demand is above the total domestic production capacities. Rest is met by imports. Total imports of polystyrene reached $985 million.

Acrylonitrile-butadiene-styrene (ABS) copolymer (3903.30.00), one of the major thermoplastic items, is only met by imports.

There are three other firms in Turkey, Baser Kimya, Artenius, and Advansa that manufacture PET. There's a new investment that will start production in the southeast part of Turkey.

Investments of European petrochemical producers started moving to Middle East countries, due to environment concerns and to be able to be closer to the petroleum resources.

Products covered in this report encompass industrial organic chemicals under the following Harmonized Tariff Numbers:

HS CODE PRODUCT DESCRIPTOR

3901 Polymers of Ethylene in primary forms

3902 Polymers of Propylene or of other olefins in primary forms

3903 Polymers of Styrene in primary forms

3904 Polymers of Vinyl Chloride or other halogenated olefins in primary forms

3905 Polymers of Vinyl Acetate or of other vinyl esters in primary forms; other vinyl polymers in primary forms

3906 Acrylic polymers in primary forms

3907 Polyacetals, other polyethers, and epoxide resins, in primary forms; polycarbonates, alkyd resins, polyallyl esters and other polyesters, in primary forms

3908 Polyamides in primary forms

3909 Amino-resins, phenolic resins, and polyurethanes, in primary forms

3910 Silicones in primary forms

3911 Petroleum resins coumarone-indene resins, polyterpenes, polysulfides, polysulfones, and other products in primary forms

3912 Cellulose and its chemical derivatives in primary forms

3913 Natural polymers, and modified natural polymers in primary forms

3914 Ion-exchangers based on polymers in primary forms

3919 Waste, parings and scrap of plastics

IMPORT MARKET

Statistical Data

	2010 ($ million)	2011 ($ million)	2012 (Estimated) ($ million)
Import Market	7,621.9	9,932.1	10,900.0
Local Production	1,400.0	1,650.0	1,950.0
Exports	705.1	894.5	1,000,0
Total Market	8,316.8	10,687.6	11,850.0
Imports from USA	352.6	380.0	420.0

Estimated future inflation rate: 10% plus

2011 import market share: Saudi Arabia: 14%, Germany: 10.5%, Belgium: 7.3%, The Netherlands: 5.0%, South Korea: 4.9%, Spain: 4.8%, Italy: 4.7%, Iran: 4.5%, France: 4.2%, U.S.A.: 3.8%

Sources: The Turkish State Institute of Statistics, "Dunya" Newspaper, various publications by the related associations, and CS estimates based on discussions with local contacts and businesspersons active in the industry.

o Best Prospects

All plastic raw materials are among best prospects, especially the ones where there is shortage in local production (HDPE, PVC, PP, PE), or no production at all (LLDPE, PS, ABS).

COMPETITION

o Local Production

Petkim, Artenius, Advansa, Sasa and Meltem Kimya are the major local producers of plastic raw materials.

Among these, Petkim is the sole producer in basic petrochemicals, and the major one, in thermoplastics with its share of more than 81 percent of the total local production. In 1965 Petkim was part of the Turkish government, and supplied petrochemicals to the country as the sole producer for long years. In 2008, 51% of its shares were sold to the Azerian Socar & Turcas company under privatization program. These days another 10.32 percent, which belongs to the Privatization Administration, is again under privatization process. With the privatization of the company, investments both to increase the production capacity and to renew the existing technology of the facilities were possible, and the company took important steps in doing this.

The average capacity utilization rate in plastic raw material production is around 85%. Petkim, recently, increased its annual production capacity for LDPE to 330,000 tons from 200,000. With this new investment, Petkim overcame the shortage in production in LDPE. Currently, Petkim meets the 25% of the total market demand.

Production capacities of Petkim in 2011 included the following:

PVC: 150,000 tons, LDPE: 330,000 tons, HDPE: 96,000 tons, and PP: 144,000 tons, PVC: 150,000 tons. With recent investments in several lines, Petkim increased production capacities in the following lines: 30% in ethylene, 63% in LDPE, and 80% in PP.

Sasa produces DMT and PET per year. Its annual capacity to produce DMT is 240,000 tons.

Baser Kimya produces 40,000 tons of PS per year. The three producers, Advansa, Artenius, and Meltem Kimya produced 150,000 tons of PET in 2011, and a new facility is under construction in the Antep region to produce PET. Another producer, SASA, produces DMT.

Local production of plastic raw materials in Turkey in 2011 is around 1,100,000 tons. Its distribution is given in the below table:

	2011 (tons)	Produced by
LDPE	185,000	Petkim
LDPE-T	121,000	Petkim
HDPE	84,000	Petkim
PVC	153,000	Petkim
PP	127,000	Petkim
PS	40,000	Baser Kimya
DMT	240,000	Sasa
PET	150,000	Advansa, Artenius, Meltem Kimya
TOTAL	1,100,000	Advansa, Artenius, Meltem Kimya

Source: PAGEV

o Third Country Imports

In 2011, share of imported materials in the plastic raw materials supply reached 86%. Share of importation in different items in total supply are given in the below table:

	Share of Imports (%)	Share of Locally Produced Items (%)
PE	76	24
PP	92	8
PVC	85	15
PET	61	39
Others	100	0
Total	86	14

As can be seen from the above table, importation is high in items where there is shortage in local production, as in PE and PVC, and PET. All other items that are not produced locally are imported.

While Turkey imports plastic raw materials from almost 100 different countries, it imports 63% of the total imports from the first ten supplier countries (Saudi Arabia, Germany, Belgium, Holland, South Korea, Spain, Italy, Iran, France, and the United States).

Dow Plastics, BASELL, and SABIC are major foreign players in the Turkish market.

The following table provides a breakdown of the main sources of imports (in USD millions):

Countries	Million $	Percentage in Total Imports
Saudi Arabia	1,398	14.1
Germany	1,041	10.5
Belgium	728	7.3
Holland	492	5.0
South Korea	490	4.9
Spain	474	4.8
Italy	464	4.7
Iran	450	4.5
France	417	4.2
U.S.A.	380	3.8
Other Countries	3,597	36.2
Total	9,932	100.0

U.S. Market Position

United States is not a major foreign supplier of plastic raw materials in Turkey, with its 3.8% market share. European suppliers benefit from the geographic closeness to the market. However, American firms establishing warehouses in the local market will have a very high chance of selling in this growing market. The best would be to establish these centers at free zones to be able to clear the products from the customs as they are sold in the market. As can be seen from the below given table, PVC is one of the materials that American firms have a remarkable share in the market. Items with significant shares are given in the below table:

HS	**Product**	**(million $)**	**Share of the U.S. in the Total Imports of the Subject Item (%)**
3904	Polymers of Vinyl Chloride or other halogenated olefins in primary forms	183.5	17.2
3908	Polyamides in primary forms	43.9	16.8
3901	Polymers of Ethylene in primary forms	78.0	
3911	Petroleum resins coumarone-indene resins, polyterpenes, polysulfides, polysulfones, and other products in primary forms	7.0	8.6
3905	Polymers of Vinyl Acetate or of other vinyl esters in primary forms; other vinyl polymers in primary forms	6.8	6.9
3913	Natural polymers, and modified natural polymers in primary forms	1.5	6.9

Far East products do not meet the quality needs of the market, even though their prices are incomparably inexpensive compared to Petkim's prices. The average import price of these materials was around $1903 per ton in 2011. During the same period, export average unit price was $1817.

END USERS

In Turkey, as throughout the world, the main industries influencing plastic consumption are the packaging and construction materials industries. Distribution is as follows:

End users	Share (%)
Packaging	40
Construction materials	22
Electricity	10
Agriculture	6
Clothing and shoes	4
Automotive	4
Other	14

For further potential end-users, the catalogs of pertinent industry associations serve as good sources of information. Addresses for such associations are given in the 'Trade Associations' section at the end of this report.

MARKET ACCESS

Turkey's January 1, 1996 accession to the European Union's customs union has resulted in zero duties for imports from the EU countries and the same agreement has led to general reductions in duty rates assessed to non-EU third-country imports. Almost all items subject to this report have 6.5% import duties built on CIF prices on each item for imports from non-EU countries, including the United States. Small number of items is exempt from import duties.

All products, both imported and locally manufactured, are subject to an additional 18 percent value-added tax (VAT). VAT is calculated based on the CIF value for imported products.

Most items in this report are subject to the following procedures during importation:

- A control document from the Workers' Health and Work Security Department is required

- A laboratory test will be done, if the item is not in solid form

- A control certificate from the Ministry of Environment for materials considered detrimental to the environment

- A control document from the Ministry of Agriculture and Rural Affairs (MOA) is required for chemicals that will be used in producing food products or for products touching food products

- Need special order in the temporary warehouses

Currently, there are no significant trade barriers against U.S. imports. Turkey's imports are regulated by an annual import regime published by the Undersecretary for Treasury and Foreign Trade (UTFT). The Import Regime sets forth import rules and regulations for the year, customs duties and surcharges on imported products, and lists of investment products, the importation of which is encouraged by the government.

o Distribution Channels

Suppliers' distributors play an essential role in marketing and sales to the more than 6000 end users. Good contacts with each customer are essential tools in selling practices in Turkey. American companies are encouraged to identify aggressive agents who could help them establish these. U.S. firms can take advantage of U.S. Commercial Service programs to identify appropriate agents/distributors overseas. More information on these services is available at www.buyusa.gov/turkey . Regional warehouses that will help the demand to be met timely is another key factor, therefore, distributors with this ability will increase competitiveness in the market. Nearly all major foreign players established warehouses in the free zones in Turkey, and they sell into Turkey or send to neighboring markets from these points easily.

In Turkey, agency/representation/distributor agreements are private contracts between agents and their foreign suppliers. There are no unusual regulations, which govern commission rates, termination, etc.

o Financing strategies

The most common payment method is by letter of credit. Importers generally provide letter of credit at sight. Foreign suppliers usually work with brokers. Brokers, then, provide deferred payments to local buyers, up to 360 days. Some suppliers even work with Cash Against Documents, however, usually ask for 15-20% down payments to ensure the sale.

WOODWORKING EQUIPMENT MARKET

There is a potentially strong market for U.S. woodworking machinery and equipment in the rapidly developing Turkish market. Turkey is a strong manufacturer and exporter of this type of machinery; however, due to its growing furniture, construction and yacht building industries, Turkey is importing high-end equipment predominantly from the European Union (EU) countries. Turkey is a candidate country for EU membership and has customs union with this institution. This implies that many of the certification and standards required in Europe of equipment and machinery are required in Turkey, too. U.S. manufacturers that already are ready to sell in the EU and have taken the decision to work with a local representative to market their products have a strong chance to build market in Turkey.

Turkey is one of the fastest growing emerging market economies in the world Turkey. This is a result of many factors. Turkey has:

a young population composed of 75 million people with rising consumption,
real GDP growth over global average which is expected to continue in the coming years,
growing industrial production and new industrial investments,
decreasing inflation and interest rates which trigger investments,
an increasing level of Foreign Direct Investment which and
active participation in international trade with strong exports and imports.

One of the leading industries in the economy is the construction sector whose growth is triggered by shortage of proper housing and commercial buildings across the country and also by the size of the young people in the population. As a subsector contributing to the construction industry is the furniture industry, which grew at fast pace in the last decade. These two factors led to investments in these industries and eventually increase in the amount of forest products and woodworking machinery produced and manufactured in Turkey and also imported into Turkey.

Turkey's imports of forest products had been increasing each year due to the said factors and also due to the growth in the yacht building and paper industries. Even though imports of forest products slowed down in 2009 as a result of worldwide economic slowdown, imports in all types of forest products showed remarkable increases in the first two months of 2010. Total imports of logs were 0.9 million cubic meters (mm3), of lumber were 454,000 m3, of wood chips and scrap were 1.6 MMT and of wood pulp were 612,000 MT. Although Black Sea countries enjoy a price advantage for logs and lumber due to their geographic proximity, the United States has been an important supplier of hardwood logs and lumber, veneer and veneer logs, wood chips and wood pulp.

Turkey produces 7 mm3 of logs and 2.5 mm3 of industrial wood annually, while annual demand for logs is around 10 mm3. Turkey.

The following HS Codes 'under woodworking machinery category' have been the base of imports and exports figures between Turkey and U.S. in this report. The source of information is U.S. Census and Turkish Statistics Institute:

		Turkey Imports from U.S.A. ($)			U.S.A. Imports from Turkey ($)			Total Turkey's Total Imports ($)		
HS Code	Description	2007	2008	2009	2007	2008	2009	2007	2008	2009
8465.10	Machines for working certain hard materials which can carry out different types of machining operations w/o tool change between operations	$817,026	$643,993	$0	$52,800	$18,503	$0	$16,119,229	$40,268,940	$8,782,558
8465.91	Sawing machines for working wood, cork, bone, hard rubber, hard plastics or similar hard materials	$0	$14,966	$14,531	$212,466	$102,197	$74,925	$14,165,153	$11,939,181	$6,767,685
8465.92	Planing, milling or molding (by cutting) machines for working wood, cork, bone, hard rubber, hard plastics or similar hard materials	$660,872	$6,279,182	$347,335	$58,648	$43,610	$25,150	$11,961,594	$15,107,775	$5,739,632
8465.93	Grinding, sanding or polishing machines for working wood, cork, bone, hard rubber, hard plastics or similar hard materials	$19,400	$0	$92,004	$0	$0	$0	$12,405,680	$14,199,342	$6,670,159
8465.94	Bending or assembling machines for working wood, cork, bone hard rubber, hard plastics or similar hard materials	$68,790	$52,343	$0	$17,758	$29,837	$40,500	$9,546,028	$29,124,899	$7,837,233
8465.95	Drilling or mortising machines for working wood, cork, bone, hard rubber, hard plastics or similar hard materials	$0	$93,572	$0	$0	$0	$2,014	$8,410,732	$8,845,273	$3,602,857
8465.96	Splitting, slicing or paring machines for working wood, cork, bone, hard rubber, hard plastics or similar hard materials	$108,623	$0	$0	$0	$0	$0	$8,791,441	$35,278,427	$21,719,252
8465.99	Machine tools for working wood, cork, bone, hard rubber, hard plastics and similar hard materials	$389,169	$188,646	$11,612	$0	$0	$0	$42,599,709	$30,920,567	$17,254,061

		Top 3 countries in Turkey's imports		
HS Code	Description	2007	2008	2009
8465.10	Machines for working certain hard materials which can carry out different types of machining operations w/o tool change between operations	Germany, Italy, Greece	Germany, Italy, Austria	Germany, Italy, Spain
8465.91	Sawing machines for working wood, cork, bone, hard rubber, hard plastics or similar hard materials	Germany, Italy, Austria	Germany, Italy, China	Germany, China, Italy
8465.92	Planing, milling or molding (by cutting) machines for working wood, cork, bone, hard rubber, hard plastics or similar hard materials	Germany, Italy, U.S.A.	Germany, Italy, U.S.A.	Germany, Italy, China
8465.93	Grinding, sanding or polishing machines for working wood, cork, bone, hard rubber, hard plastics or similar hard materials	Italy, Switzerland, Germany	Italy, Germany, Switzerland	Switzerland, Italy, Germany
8465.94	Bending or assembling machines for working wood, cork, bone hard rubber, hard plastics or similar hard materials	Germany, Austria, Italy	Germany, Italy, Austria	Germany, Italy, Austria
8465.95	Drilling or mortising machines for working wood, cork, bone, hard rubber, hard plastics or similar hard materials	Italy, Germany, Austria	Italy, Germany, China	Italy, Germany, China
8465.96	Splitting, slicing or paring machines for working wood, cork, bone, hard rubber, hard plastics or similar hard materials	Germany, Italy, China	Germany, Italy, China	Germany, China, Brazil
8465.99	Machine tools for working wood, cork, bone, hard rubber, hard plastics and similar hard materials	Italy, Germany, Taiwan	Italy, Germany, Taiwan	Italy, Germany, Taiwan

As Turkey's construction and furniture market are two of the leading locomotives of the economy in the foreseeable future, there is market potential for all types of equipment that can be used in the woodworking process and automation of the manufacturing process. The important factor is to have local representation so that the products can be marketed in Turkey effectively.

The types of woodworking machinery and equipment that are manufactured in Turkey for domestic use and exported to other countries from Turkey are as follows:

Profiling and planning machines
Hydraulic presses
Glue spreading machines
Veneer sawing machines
Machine for flooring production
Profiling machines
Carpentry machinery
Furniture production machinery
Sanding machinery
CNC machinery
Panel sizing machines
Edge bending machines
Thin cutting frame saw

As far as imports are concerned, these are the types of machinery that are imported from various countries around the world:

Tilting circular saw
CNC machines and CNC control unit

CNC machines for foors and frames
Panel sizing machines
Edge bending machines
Panel blade machines for solid wood and flooring
Automatic vacuum press machines
Hydraulic cross cutting, wrapping guillotines
Roller coater machinery
Fingerjoint manufacturing machinery
Double end tenoner
Workstation for doors/frames
Multi ripsaw machines
Automatic profile router machines
Timber drying kilns
Sanding machines
Packaging machines
Membrane cutting and trimming machines

Suppliers from EU countries and Far East, mainly China, have a strong position in this market mainly due to:

proximity of EU counties to Turkey geographically,
costs associated with importing a product being typically less from EU countries. The 1996 Customs Union agreement between Turkey and the EU means that products originating from EU countries are not charged any import taxes. EU companies prefer to open direct offices here in Turkey or to assign agents to monitor developments and to report on local tender announcements.
Products from Far East are relative less expensive making them more affordable.

Some of the international brands that are in the market are:

- Wilhelm Altendorf GmbH - http://www.altendorf.de/
- BIESSE SPA- http://www.biesse.it/home_IT.asp
- Saom Srl - http://www.saomsrl.com/
- Harwi Machinefabriek Bv - http://www.harwi.nl/
- Steton S.P.A - http://www.steton.it/
- Blue Steel Machinery- http://www.highpointtools.com/
- Roberto Bürkle GMBH- http://www.buerkle-gmbh.de/
- Casati- http://www.casatisnc.it/
- Cattinair Finishing- http://www.cattinair.com/
- Cheng Kuang Wood Machinery -http://www.ckmtw.com.tw/
- Spanevello Srl- http://www.spanevello.com/

- GMC - http://www.gmcservice.com/
- Framar - http://www.framarcarpi.com/
- Kuang Yung Machinery- http://www.kuangyung.com/
- Paul Machinenfabrik Gmbh - http://www.paul.eu/
- Leadermac Machinery Co.,Ltd -http://www.leadermac.com/
- Tecno Azurra- http://www.tecnoazzurra.it/
- Incoplan SRL – http://www.incoplan.it/
- Loewer Gmbh & Co. Kg- http://www.loewer-online.com/
- Vertek Group – http://www.vertekgroup.it/
- Process s.r.l- http://www.process.it/
- Sittex s.r.l
- Dubus Industries- http://www.dubus-fr.com/

Main buyer group of wood working machinery in Turkey are furniture manufacturers which are spread all around the country. There are some cities like Kayseri and Inegol where there are larger factories that manufacture mass and which might be potential buyers of more advancedd and automated systems. However, please note that there are small manufacturers not confined to these cities but all over the country.

Other groups of potential buyers are lumber, flooring, door, frames and moulding manufacturers which process solid wood.

Construction sector is the locomotive industry in the country and projects these companies undertake all kinds of projects in the range of residential, office and commercial developments like hotels, shopping malls etc. Especially in the hotels, there is a lot of wood work used which are not necessarily manufactured by large industrial plants but boutique workshops some of which also have retail stores to display and market their own line of furniture.

SAFETY AND SECURITY QUIPMENT MARKET

The total market for safety and security equipment and services in Turkey is estimated to be $3.73 billion in 2012. Physical security services, meaning private security guards, patrols, and security training services captured around $3 billion of the total market, electronic security methods $500 million, and cash in transfer services (C.I.T., cash and valuables) $180 million. As these figures indicate, the safety and security sector in Turkey is heavily weighted towards physical security services, due to the advantages of comparatively lower labor costs in Turkey. It can be expected that as the Turkish economy advances further, a shift towards electronic security systems will take place.

PRODUCT GROUP	% OF MARKET
Surveillance Systems (CCTV, IP cameras etc.)	55%
Fire Protection & Control	12%
Alarms & Warning Systems	14%
Access Control & Perimeter Security Systems	8%
Other	11%
Total:	100%

Source: A&S Magazine Turkey

*The numbers are estimates out of interviews with the major players of the market. The reason for that is the products that enter the country unrecorded or with different GTIP numbers. It is predicted that 30% of the total sales is installation and services.

Turkish economy has a serious dynamism and a growth rate which cannot be seen much in Europe and this positively affects the sector. 2011 was a year of growth for Turkish economy and the sector. In 2012 growth continued however slowed down. The investments in Turkic republics even though affected the sector in a positive manner, the riots that took place in Libya and the North Africa and the debt crisis in Europe have adversely affected the investments in these regions. Moreover the sudden increase in the parity of dollar towards the end of 2011 was a negative effect.

For many subsectors of the sector, construction environment in the country and the region is deeply related to the growth. As the construction sector kept its steady growth, the safety and security sector was affected positively. As urban revitalization and city transformation projects continued in 2012, especially in big cities there were positive reflections on the market. Fire warning systems, intercom systems were heavily used in the new buildings. Perimeter security and CCTV systems were installed. One of the decisive concepts for the sector will be green and smart buildings which are used more often.

MARKET ENTRY

U.S. suppliers enjoy an excellent reputation for quality, reliability, timely delivery and after-sales service. Aggressive marketing, accompanied by suitable financing packages, can increase the U.S. market share further. U.S. companies should also focus on training the local distribution and sales network. This will ensure that end users will take full advantage of the capabilities of the newly acquired technology.

Imports are carried out by specialized importers/distributors, local subsidiaries of international manufacturers, or domestic manufacturers with a distribution network seeking compatible products to broaden their lines. Interested U.S. firms with expertise in high-tech equipment may consider joint ventures with locally based security companies seeking diversification.

To bid on government contracts, foreign firms must either be legally established, or have an authorized representative in Turkey prior to bidding, which is another reason to consider teaming with a reputable local agent/distributor.

U.S. firms can take advantage of U.S. Department of Commerce services to find an appropriate representative through the International Partner Search (IPS) and Gold Key Services (GKS). For more information on these, please refer to our website, http://export.gov/turkey/

CURRENT MARKET TRENDS

Major suppliers of the electronic security systems market in Turkey are from the U.S., Germany, the U.K., Israel, Japan, Taiwan, China, South Korea, Italy and Canada.

In the less sophisticated security products sector, Turkey offers 100 percent local production of equipment like protective apparel, locks and lock subassemblies, steel doors, laminated safety glass, portable fire extinguishers, safes, safety vaults, alarms and security panels. In the case of more advanced production, primarily imported components are used.

In the IT security sector, the most widespread and the most popular technologies in providing information security include encryption (cryptography), digital signature and PKI, network segmentation and firewalls, back up, attack detection and tracking, access control, security depth and anti-virus. Rising user awareness with security training will minimize the possibility of security gaps or other risk factors.

Prominent technologies regarding the gathering, storing, and distribution of information are among the top priorities of Turkey's private sector. Despite the global economic crisis that led to less spending on information technology infrastructure and upgrades, the IT security industry has been one of the few industries to remain in constant growth throughout the crisis. The same holds true in Turkey.

Corporate and government IT security systems are a particular focus in the Turkish market. Security of information leaving the company as well as identity theft, network security against attackers, viruses, trojans and storage of network activities are among the top priorities with particular emphasis on providing legally sustainable evidence used in courts of law.

Sensormatic Chairman of Board Mr. İsmail Uzelli emphasizes while IT companies try to become security companies as a result of using the same materials, the security companies have become significant server and switch providers due to the increase in their sales in this field. (Source A&S Magazine)

MAIN COMPETITORS

Please see below some major players in the sector. You will see both local and foreign (including US) names working in many subsectors.

Bosch Security Systems www.tr.boschsecurity.com/

Senkron Security and Communication Systems www.senkronguvenlik.com.tr/

Öncü Security Systems www.oncuguvenlik.com.tr/

Sensormatic Security Systems www.sensormatic.com.tr/

UTC Climate, Controls & Security Systems www.utcclimatecontrolssecurity.com/

Okisan Security Systems www.okisan.com.tr/

Bilmak Security Systems www.bilmak.com.tr/

Bilgi Electronic www.bilgielektronik.com.tr/

Videofon Security Systems www.videofon.com.tr/

Pelco Security Cameras & Surveillance Systems www.pelco.com/

Honeywell Turkey www.honeywell.com.tr/

Siemens www.siemens.com.tr/

Pronet Security www.pronet.com.tr/

Ateksis www.ateksis.com/tr_Default.aspx

Kekova Security Systems www.kekova.com.tr/

NFS Security www.nfsteknoloji.com/

Profilo Security Systems www.profiloguvenlik.com/

CURRENT DEMAND

All around the world, including Turkey, the U.S. electronic security products have set the standard, as most of the industry R&D and technological innovations are realized in the U.S.

Best prospects for U.S. companies include:

- **Closed circuit television systems**
- **IP based surveillance systems**
- **Full HD products**
- **Fiber optic cable or linear cable fire detection systems**
- **Biometrics applications**
- **Microwave detectors**
- **Anti-aggression and anti-hold-up devices**
- **Anti-shoplifting equipment**
- **Systems for automation of homes and buildings**
- **Remote positioning devices**
- **X-ray machines**

- **Forensics equipment**
- **Card access systems**
- **Integration applications between the systems**
- **Mobile DVR**

An important market trend in Turkey is the demand for integrated security solutions marketed by independent security consultants. These integrated solutions cover on-site and immediate response personnel, electronic security and alarm systems, and fire-related security all in one package. U.S. companies can find opportunities in the turnkey design of integrated security projects.

The Turkish Government has increased its expenditures in hardware, software and education in battling cyber threats. In order to implement these defenses the Departments of Justice, Interior, the Turkish National Police, and the Turkish military have all updated their information security technologies. All governmental and military institutions have been training their personnel up to international standards and have been inviting expert professionals from abroad to provide further training. Resources indicate that the Turkish government and private sector institutions are looking at new technologies to enhance their IT security systems. Given that there are 15 major cities in which the national police have established crime laboratories, it is expected that the government spending on digital IT investigations will increase.

The pick-up in the construction sector accelerated the housing, hospital, shopping center and residence projects in the private sector; however, the biggest consumer this year is again the public. In the public sector, the projects at the fore were city surveillance, transportation projects (airports, undergrounds, tunnels, etc.) and public buildings. In addition to these, the security projects conducted by banks and universities in the past years were decisive, too.

Okisan General Manager Mr. Ekrem Özkara points out the increase in demand in Mobile DVR Systems. He says that 800-100 mobile DVR projects have been launched in school buses, public buses in many cities as the government made them mandatory in 2011 and predicts that this process will continue increasingly in the coming years, too. Another development on the product base has been in the fire sector. In 2011, the EN 54 standard which is known as the European standard in the fire detection systems was expanded so as to cover the sound system in order to meet the market demand for the integration of fire detection systems and emergency public address systems. Maintaining its leadership in the international standards in security products being widespread, Bosch was one of the first companies to support the new EN 54 standard in the sound system. (Source A&S Magazine)

BARRIERS

The problem of standards is giving hardship to all the players in the sector. It is one of the biggest obstacles before the better development of the sector. Even though Turkey is among a few countries that can grow in comparison with Europe, the regulations and standards in Turkey are not what they are expected to be.

Senkron Güvenlik General Manager Mr. Bülent Çobanoğlu states that "We have deficiencies about certification. There is no selection or superintendence in the participation of the companies in the sector although the number of the companies that join the sector is on the increase." Secondly, mentioning that there is no specialty customs for the security sector in Turkey,

Çobanoğlu says, “Unfortunately, we still pay SCT (Special Consumption Tax). A photograph camera in every man’s pocket is considered luxury, and so are the cameras that are used in closed circuits. However, these systems are not luxury but need. We would like the SCT to be cancelled and the VAT (Value Added Tax) to be decreased. Thereby, this will directly affect the end user and sales will increase.” He emphasizes that this process will also prevent illegalities. (Source A&S Magazine)

One last issue for US companies is the fact that the market is very price sensitive. US exporters’ product and services in some cases can be over the market price. Therefore American cutting edge technologies are more competitive in the Turkish market

Name: Yaprak Cakilcioglu
Position: Commercial Assistant
Email: Yaprak.Cakilcioglu@trade.gov
Phone: +90 312 417 24 37

TURKEY: GREEN BUILDING INDUSTRY

U.S. is one of the frontrunners with the acceptance and use of green building standards and guidelines. Though Turkey’s green buildings are more of a presence than ever, more inter-development is needed to enable production on a large scale. Therefore there is a great opportunity in Turkey for US architectural firms.

Varyap Meridian – When finished, planned to be the one of the biggest mixed-use LEED certified structure in Turkey

MARKET DEMAND

Turkey’s green building industry has recently been in a process of rapid development. Government policy is becoming more aligned with Turkey’s energy deficit and external pressures further encourage environmentally responsible development. Also, international investors and non-profits are importing an environmentally conscious ethos to some of Turkey’s high-profile developments. In many ways, green building in Turkey has reached an unprecedented peak. Unheard of several years ago, now major commercial developments advertise an awareness of environmental issues, or a design premised on sustainable principles. Malls and major office developments are engaging in green retrofit processes. For the eco-conscious tourist, the Turkish Ministry of Culture and Tourism has mobilized hotels and resorts with its Green Star program, based on established green building standards. These recent developments, however limited, signal the entrance of green building into Turkey’s mainstream building industry. Turkish Green Building Association has been established with intentions to be a Green Building Council (GBC) in October 2007. The association has been lobbying on green buildings since then.

MARKET DATA

Buildings and settlements are responsible for the 40% emission of the greenhouse gas – CO2. They are also responsible for the 12% of water usage, 65% of waste production and 71% of electricity usage. The extent of these percentages indicates a great potential to cut back the effects on environment. In this situation, it is ineluctable to understand the role of architects, engineers, urban planners and city managers.

As a political entity, Turkey first engaged with the environment in 1978 with the establishment of the Undersecretariat for the Environment. Five years later, the 1982 Constitution included the "right to live in a healthy, balanced environment," and in 1983, the first Environmental Law was passed. Several environmentally directed laws followed, including regulations on pollution and the Mass Housing Law of 1984. Then in 1992, responsibility for Turkey's environmental management was given to the new Ministry of the Environment, which still exists today. A key piece of legislation was the Environmental Impact Assessment law of 1992, requiring municipal approval of all public land development. Generally, however, development interests have trumped the environmental intent of this law. Recently, regulations for Turkey's accession into the EU have increased incentive on environmental reform, though little progress has been found. Another motivating factor for green building and environment came from the UN-HABITAT II forum, held in Istanbul in 1996. This international event was a watershed for ideas on improved urban habitat and building.

Turkey's energy dependence and the need for energy efficiency have also prompted regulatory and rhetorical changes. In 2008, the central government enforced insulation requirements for both new commercial and residential buildings. One hundred percent compliance would be expected to save billions of dollars and 70% of the country's heating energy. Though not directly related to the environment, per se, these measures to represent an advancement of the building industry.

Even though there are 21 LEED certified buildings in Turkey, there are 85 registered projects which are in construction phase or in the process of getting the certification. The list of LEED certified buildings in Turkey with their developers can be found from the web site: http://www.usgbc.org/LEED/Project/CertifiedProjectList.aspx (Please write Turkey under country). Turkish Green Building Association's Building Code and Certification Committee has been following the national and international progresses on this subject and has started its own studies in order to form a nationally appropriate certification system with the incorporation of experts.

BEST PROSPECTS

As the green building concept is fairly new in Turkey, there are not many local architects with LEED certificates. Moreover in projects with large scale, developers are more likely to prefer foreign architectural firms, even though there are good and capable Turkish architects. The reason for this is the perception in the Turkish market for the foreign architects, which is that their work is superior quality. Also one other reason is; in the projects with large scale, there is more funding available. , As a result, the funds that are reserved for the architecture is also bigger. Therefore hiring a foreign architect can be feasible over fairly cheaper local architects. This would mean US architects have more chance to be hired in the high-end projects such as high-rise or hospitality or mixed-use green projects. LED Street and building lighting systems, solarcell lighting, sunlighting, heat pumps, more efficient HVAC systems, fuel cells, efficient boilers, heat insulation systems and other energy efficiency systems are the other best prospects.

KEY SUPPLIERS AND PROSPECTIVE BUYERS

The recent development of green building in the Turkish commercial sector has been closely tied to the international architectural community. Indeed, much of the green building projects and ethos has been imported from top firms abroad. The Kaplankaya project, for example, is a nearly 5 million m2 eco-tourism resort in construction near Milas in southwestern Turkey. Renowned international architects such as Steven Holl, Lord Norman Foster, and Robert A.M. Stern will bring green design expertise on a level currently still gestating in Turkey. In Istanbul, Zaha Hadid and Ken Yeang each have a major urban project with green ambitions on the horizon as well. Two of Turkey's largest retail developers, Metro and the Dutch-based REDEVCO, have corporate-wide sustainability policies and construction companies like SOYAK, ZORLU, TEKFEN, VARYAP and ECZACIBASI are developing theirs. Also, Turkish-owned Kanyon Mall both won the 2006 Cityscape Architectural Review Award and employed the London-based firm ARUP, which specialized in advanced green engineering, as project engineers. More locally, in 2007 Erginoglu & Calislar Architects built an ecologically designed telecommunications company headquarters in the Tübitak Marmara Research Center Zone near Istanbul. These developments indicate that "green" design and operations are achieving cache for both building owners and potential buyers alike.

MARKET ENTRY

The best way to enter the market would be to first researching local architects to partner up with because all the Turkish developers' first question is if US architect have an office or a local partner in Turkey. The classic way of working would be the US architect doing the conceptual work and the local partner doing the detail designs such as the electrical or pluming drawings. However many developers still would like the main architect of the project to be physically present on site in the country of the project. The local architect office can also be help with the business development phase and get projects for the US firm. For energy efficiency type of building products, the best way would be to enter into the market through distributors, which should hold local stocks.

After completing a few projects in the Turkish market, the next step ideally would be to open an office with locally employed staff. This way, US architectural firms can be more competitive. The perception of the firm in the market would also be effected positively, as having an office in the country would show the Turkish developers that the US firm is serious about the Turkish market and plans to stay long periods. The potential project range would expand. US firm could follow the tenders more closely with its native Turkish speaker staff.

Being in the Turkish market also means networking with the globally working Turkish contractors, which may result working also in the region. As Turkey is a hub; from Turkey, the US firms can easily reach to the projects in the Middle East, North Africa, Caucasus and Balkan countries.

MARKET ISSUES & OBSTACLES

The main obstacle for US firms is their high fees because of their large overheads compared to their local competitors. There is already a fierce competition in the construction market among local architects. Therefore the fees that the Turkish developers are accustomed to are very low compared to the normal fees of US architects. This means when an US firm is bidding for a project in Turkey, it needs to considerably lower its usual price. However, many foreign architectural companies being active in the Turkish market indicates that they can still be feasible.

One other obstacle is the time constraints of the projects. US architects are used to working in long time frames. Whereas the Turkish developers want their project to be done in much shorter time spans, because they would like to start to earn profits as soon as possible. One of the other reasons is that the contractors are given short timeframe to bid at a tender. One way the Turkish architects overcome this short time obstacle is providing rough designs for the bidding and finishing the details afterwards.

Lastly, besides the few exceptions, green designs are paid by developers because it is the market trend right now, however not because they are strong believers of sustainability. Therefore if the trend ever changes, the uprising use of green buildings can lose acceleration.

U.S. firms can also meet major competition from European and Asian companies as the Turkish market is a large market attracting many foreign firms.

RESOURCES & CONTACTS

Turkish Green Building Council:

The Turkish Green Building Association aims to contribute to the building industry's development by means of the principles of sustainability. Turkish Green Building Association; which was established in 2007, under the leadership of the founding president Mr. Ali Nihat GOKYIGIT and the founding vice president Ms. Duygu ERTEN has now more than 100 active members.

Turkish Green Building Association conducts its activities with the belief that buildings and settlements designed and constructed with an ecological sensibility allow us to live and work in healthier places and lead healthier lives.

Turkish Green Building Association organizes educational programs, develops pilot projects with government and universities and conducts lobbying activities to increase public awareness about the necessity of green building while also encouraging the building industry to develop along principles of sustainability.

Systems evaluating the environmental impacts of buildings and their surroundings are effective tools when aiming for green transformation of construction industry. Turkish Green Building Association is currently working to fill this void by adapting an environmental certificate system for buildings specific to the geographical, climatic, political, social and technological context of Turkey.

Turkish Green Building Association has been granted Full Council Status with the World Green Building Council (WGBC) on June 2012 and continues to develop its substructure through an increasing participation both with other Green Building Councils (GBC's) in the world and with the local construction sector. For more information please visit: http://www.cedbik.org/default_eng.asp

Turkish Contractor Association (TCA):

The Turkish Contractors Association (TCA) is an independent, non-profit professional organization based in Ankara, Turkey. The association was founded in 1952 and represents the leading construction companies in Turkey. The business volume of its members encompasses nearly 70% of all domestic and 90% of all international contracting work done so far by Turkish construction companies.

From the beginning of the 1970's up to the present, Turkish contractors have completed almost 6000 projects in 89 countries. Their business volume abroad has reached approximately 188 Billion US Dollars.

In addition to offering contracting services at international standards both within and outside Turkey, nearly 75% of TCA members are also active in various fields of construction industry investments, manufacturing, engineering and consulting.

Besides the TCA, 94% of its member companies operate with the quality system certificates.

For more information please visit: http://www.tmb.org.tr/?language=eng

The Association of Real Estate Investment Companies:

GYODER, The Association of Real Estate Investment Companies, was established on 2nd August 1999 by the representatives of existing and founding Real Estate Investment Companies (REICs), to promote and represent the promising real estate industry that leads the economy as a locomotive, to encourage the development of the industry, to provide, improve and protect standards for quality, control and education within the sector. For more information please visit: http://www.gyoder.org.tr/EN/Default.aspx

Motorcycling is a relatively new phenomenon in Turkey. The total motorcycles, parts and accessories market was around $321.1 in 2012. Both high-end and low-end products seem to be in good demand. More than 63% of demand is met by imports. There are a few local manufacturers that produce under the license of foreign brands; however, imports are dominated by Chinese products. U.S. motorcycle imports account for 1.8% of the market and mainly consist of motorcycles with engines exceeding 800 cc.

U.S. suppliers, which currently have a very low market share both in the motorcycles sales and accessories markets, are strongly encouraged to work with a local distributor to both overcome the lengthy procedures for importation of motorcycles, and also get their products known in the local market.

The number of motorcycles registered in Turkey 2012: *Source: MOTED*

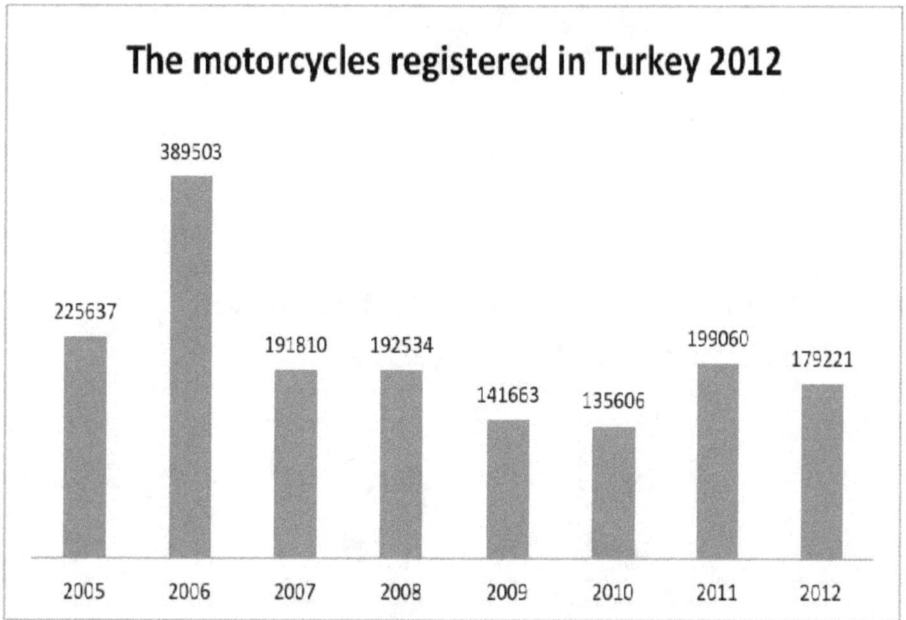

As seen from above table, sales of motorcycles boomed in 2006. The Government of Turkey (GOT) wanted to take advantage of this booming market and that year increased the Special Consumption Tax (OTV) on motorcycle sales from 8% to 22% for engine sizes of less than 250 cc and 37% for engines over 250cc i. However, this tax increase resulted in a dramatic decrease the following year (only 192K units). In 2008, due to the economic crisis, GOT took measures to assist their indigenous industry. They decreased the OTV from 22% to 11% engine sizes below

250 cc and decreased the OTV from 37% to 32% for those above 250 cc. However, while the tax decrease helped the industry to reduce inventory a little, but it wasn't sufficient to increase sales to expected levels as can be clearly seen in the above graph.

Very recently, on February 25, 2013, GOT has decreased OTV to 8%, announcing this move at the Eurasia Moto Bike Expo in Istanbul, where it was very well received. Experts expect a positive impact in the sales volumes. Two major associations of the market, MOTED and MOTODER, had been working hard to decrease the OTV for the last five years.

Italy has the highest per capita motorcycle ownership in Europe (181 per 1000 citizens), whereas Turkey is only at 39 per 1000 . Currently, the number of motorcycles in Turkey is 1. 93million.

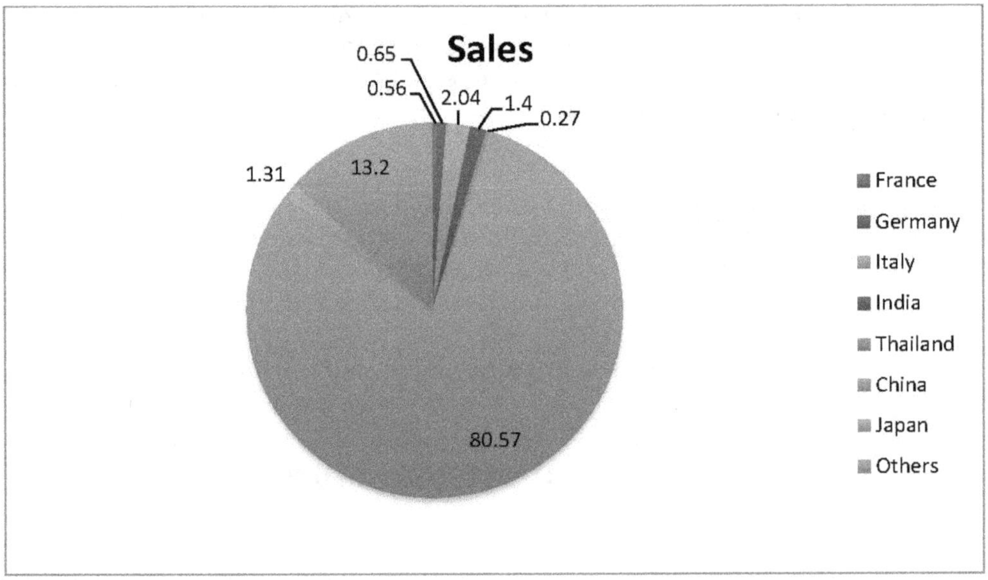

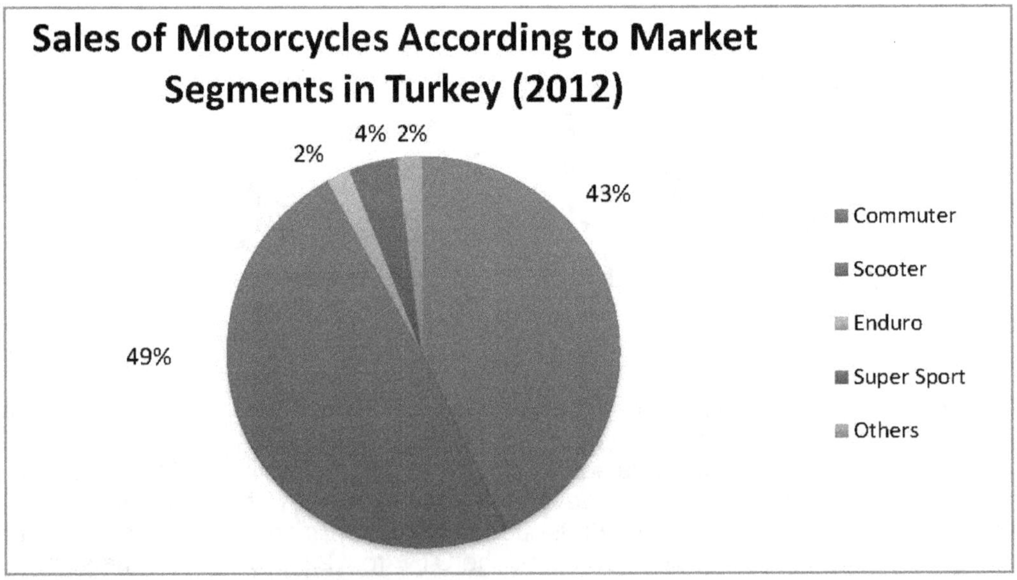

In 2004, there were 10 internationally known motorcycle brands present in Turkey. The additional imports from China have increased that number to 22. However, these brands are not taking market share away from other internationally known brands, but rather have increased the size of the overall market by supplying cheaper products.

Major suppliers of two-wheeled vehicle according to TUIK figures are broken down in the chart below (2012)

The motorcycle accessory market is broken down by country of origin in the chart below according TUIK (2012):

As can be seen from the charts above, China is the primary supplier both for motorcycles (49%), and for motorcycle accessories (80.57%).

As seen from the chart above, cheaper models, like scooters, have the largest market share.

There was an increase of 21% in scooter sales in 2012 compared to 2011. Clearly, scooters were the most preferred with 49% (21,293), followed by commuters, with 43% (25,226) shares.

Different brands sold in the Turkish market and their sales volumes are shown below:

Source: MOTED

According to these results, we see that Mondial retains its leadership in sales, with 33,068. Honda takes the 3rd place. As can be seen in above chart, a large number of brands are sold in the Turkish market, however, apart from some brands like Asya Motor, Kanuni, Kuba, Motoran, rest aren't very popular.

The total number of motorcycles sold in 2012 was 179,221.

- High end motorcycles – above 800 cc

- Low-end motorcycles or scooters for commercial use (deliveries). 42% of all imported motorcycles have engine sizes below 250 cc. Motorcycles between 500 and 800 cc were %7.9 and motorcycles with engines larger than 800 cc were 16.6% of the total imports.

Eurasia Moto Bike Expo 2014

Istanbul, Turkey
February 27-March 2, 2014
www.motoplus.org
Associations:
MOTED - Motorsiklet Endustrisi Dernegi (Motorcycle Industry Association)
Web: http://www.moted.net
Türkiye Motosiklet Federasyonu (Turkish Motorcycles Federation)
Web: http://www.tmf.org.tr
Senior Commercial Specialist: Berrin Erturk, Izmir, TURKEY
Email: Berrin.Erturk@trade.gov
Phone: + [90] (232) 441-2446
Fax: + [90] (232) 489-0267
Website: http://www.export.gov/turkey

FRANCHISING OPPORTUNITIES

Franchising is a well-known concept to Turkish investors and consumers, with many international brands that are already present in the market through master franchisees. Until now the concentration of these ventures has mainly been in the food sector. However, given Turkey□s strong economic growth over the last decade, there are great opportunities for U.S. franchisors of almost all types of goods and services. Furthermore, the availability of bank loans that facilitate business investment in franchising is making Turkey an increasingly attractive market for U.S. franchising companies. However, the availability of strong local brands and the preference of joint ventures by the Turkish investors stand out as major challenges.

MARKET DEMAND

Turkey□s geographic position between the Middle East, Southeastern Europe, the Caucasus and Central Asia gives it a unique character. Its dynamic economy, population of approximately 74 million, and young and ambitious entrepreneurs make the country an attractive market for franchisors around the world.

It has been more than twenty five years since franchising arrived in Turkey. The first brand to enter the Turkish market was McDonald□s in 1985 and the influx of foreign brands has continued since then. In order to structure the sector and create cooperation between the franchisor and franchisee communities, the Turkish National Franchising Association (UFRAD) was founded in 1991; UFRAD is now a member of the World Franchise Council and the European Franchise Federation. The Association has members of both local and foreign origin.

The demand for new franchising concepts in the market is primarily triggered by the following factors:

* Turkey has a vibrant economy with a highly developed entrepreneurial spirit. Turkish companies have understood the importance of expanding their market through popular brands and thus invest in activities that help brand creation. As a result of this demand for brand names, as well as global brands entering the Turkish market, there has been an increase in the presence of Turkish brands through franchising.

* Since the start of the economic recovery in 2004, Turks have enjoyed growing purchasing power, a power that is supported by the population□s average age of 29. This triggers demand for well-known, global brands and quality service. Below please refer to a demographic breakdown at five-year increments; this reflects the market potential for various age groups all the way from newborns, to teenagers and adults.

Age and sex distribution for the year 2010:

Over the years, the sector has grown mainly on the axis of restaurants and real estate franchises, but as mentioned above, demand is increasing for the following types of services as well:

* Children□s education

* Training and personal development

* Services: Facility management, janitorial, healthcare, elder-care, maintenance, personal beauty, hotels, IT maintenance services, car care, industrial cleaning services, services for pets, and education

MARKET DATA

There is no definitive figure for the size of the market. This is mainly due to the fact that franchising is a developing concept in this country and selling through dealers is also perceived as a franchise system. When this is taken into account, we note that there are approximately 1.400 brands in the market that generate an annual turnover of $35 billion; the turnover of car dealers and ready-to-wear companies is also included in this figure. 400 of these brands are noted to be of foreign origin whereas 1.000 of them are Turkish.

Some of the U.S. brands in the Turkish market are:

* Fast food: Arby□s, Burger King, Kentucky Fried Chicken, Mc Donald□s, Schlotsky□s,

* Pizza: Domino's Pizza, Little Caesars, Pizza Hut

* Sandwiches: Quizno□s Sub, Subway

* Coffee and cookies: Dunkin□ Donuts, Starbucks

* Automotive products and services: Ziebart

* Business services: Dale Carnegie Training, Regus Group, UPS, DHL, Fedex, Office 1 Superstore

* Children□s services: Gymboree

* English as a Foreign Language: ELS, Wall Street Institute

* Hotels: Hilton, Conrad, Sheraton, Hyatt, Ritz Carlton

* Janitorial & Cleaning Services: Jani King, Servicemaster, Truly Nolen

* Car Rental: AVIS

Competition for American companies stems from Turkish brands and foreign, non-U.S. ones. Turkish entrepreneurs have comfortably borrowed the pizza restaurant concept, opening and heavily marketing restaurants with very similar decoration, menus and take-away service. The main competitors of U.S. fast food companies are Turkish fast food chains that serve Turkish cuisine, such as fish, kebab, meatball or pide (Turkish pizza), in fast food fashion.

In response to the aggressive market building by U.S. coffee brands, such as Starbuck□s, Turkish coffee chains have started to pop-up. In fact, the coffee market is growing so rapidly that there are new stores being opened almost every day by both Turkish and international brands.

In the automotive services and car care sector, Turkish entrepreneurs have introduced concepts similar to U.S. ones. German brands like Sonax have also been influential in this area. The total vehicle stock in Turkey stands at approximately 15 million, with 700,000 new vehicles sold in this market on an annual basis.

Turkish companies are active in delivering educational services towards children as well. Providing childcare and educational services has been developing rapidly in the last few years. Especially, in big cities, like Istanbul, Ankara and Izmir, the number of career women is on the increase, which has automatically resulted in an increase for these kinds of services.

The distribution of the chain stores by sector is:

BEST PROSPECTS

The Turkish market is open to the following type of franchise investments:

*** Fast food/casual dining and coffee franchises:**

Many of the major U.S. franchisors in the fast food/casual dining and coffee concepts are already in the Turkish market. However, due to the size of the population and the improving economic conditions, demand from Turkish investors for contacts with U.S. franchisors remains strong. Improving economic conditions are producing large investments in commercial real estate and shopping mall projects. All of these projects are designed to include food courts, and Turkish companies are always looking for new U.S. brands to offer in these new venues.

*** Real-estate franchises:**

Construction of housing is expected to be a target for major investments in the coming years. The total housing stock in Turkey is 17 million units, about 4 million of them being only in Istanbul. Even when only legally-registered houses are taken into account, the number of new houses needed is 650.000 per year. Demand for housing is lower than pre- 2008 global financial crisis period but recovery is observed.

An important factor that is expected to trigger demand for housing projects is the mortgage law, passed in the Turkish Parliament in 2007. This measure is expected to dramatically increase the base number of people who can afford to buy a house.

Non-residential construction is another area of growth in this industry. There is a constant increase in shopping mall investments. Total number of shopping malls in Turkey reached 261 and this figure is expected to increase. Investments are concentrated in major cities.

*** Child-care/education franchises:**

Approximately 15 percent of the population is at the elementary school age. The number of mothers who return to work following maternity leave is increasing. This is a trend that is pushing the demand for quality child care and development centers.

*** Retailers/Textile/Ready-to-Wear Brands:**

Domestic and foreign department stores stocking primarily clothing items are growing in number and are spreading to various parts of the country through their franchisees. Stores that cater specifically to consumer groups with higher purchasing power are increasingly evident in the Turkish market.

*** Services:**

There is potential for many types of service enterprises in Turkey. There is demand for **maintenance or repair services,** stemming largely from the insurance industry. As the number of commercial offices and residences is on the increase, **facility management services** of high quality is needed. This service is also necessary in hospitals, as investment in new hospitals is a growing segment in Turkey due to the government□s decision to integrate the private sector into the healthcare system.

Tourism is currently one of the largest service sectors in the country, a sector that will continue to expand as investments rise with growing tourist figures. New hotels are under construction and they are looking for **'hotel management'** companies. Additionally, **spa** tourism is growing and U.S. companies in the spa business could develop a healthy market in Turkey. Finally, given the increase in purchasing power in the country, demand for **personal care services, like beauty centers, fitness centers and hair saloons,** is on the rise.

MARKET ENTRY

It is essential to enter the Turkish market with a „master franchisee□ that is already experienced in the sector in question, or has the financial capacity to make the right investments. Knowing the regulatory and business framework in Turkey is almost an impossible task for foreign companies without the support of a local business partner. In addition, rents for office/restaurant space are expensive in Turkey, necessitating a substantial amount of investment on the franchisee□s side. Retail office space rent in relatively central locations of the city starts at $45/m2 and go all the way up to $400/m2. In shopping malls, the rent range is between $30-65/m2 in Istanbul whereas it is in $19-35/m2 range in smaller cities.

The Commercial Service in Turkey has a number of programs and services available to assist the U.S. business community in establishing a presence in this market. In addition, the Commercial Service in Turkey employs experienced commercial specialists with industry sector expertise who can tailor your business approach to the right audience and help steer your company through the often less than transparent bureaucratic procedures that are common in Turkey. To find out more about what we do to help you, please visit our web site at www.buyusa.gov/turkey/en .

U.S. Commercial Service prepares a „Country Commercial Guide□ every year. You may find detailed information on „How to Do Business in Turkey□ at https://www.buyusa.gov/turkey/en/country_commercial_guide.html

MARKET ISSUES AND OBSTACLES

LEGAL ISSUES

There is no specially designed regulation for franchise agreements under Turkish Law. Therefore it is very important that U.S. franchisors prepare the franchise agreements they will have with their master franchisees under the guidance of a local law firm with experience in this area.

The Turkish Commercial Code and the Trademark Code protect registered trademarks in Turkey. Internationally known trademarks not registered in Turkey are protected under the general provisions of the Turkish Commercial Code regarding Unfair Competition, and the Paris Treaty, to which Turkey is a party.

In the case of the termination of an indefinite-term franchise agreement between the franchisor and the master franchisee, the termination notice of the agreement must provide the franchisee time to reorganize its business. Therefore, the application of the "six months period provision stated in the Turkish Code of Obligations for ordinary partnerships" to the Franchise Agreements would be reasonable for the franchisees as well as for the franchisors.

Another important point to mention regarding the termination of the franchise agreements is the status of competition after the termination of the agreement. Unless otherwise stated in the franchise agreement, the franchisee cannot be bound by a non-competition structure after the termination of the relationship.

When choosing the applicable law and competent courts, the parties should consider that there is no agreement between United States and Turkey for the recognition and enforcement of the judgments rendered by national courts; actual reciprocity exists only between some states of the USA and Turkey. On the other hand, as Turkey is a party to New York Convention on the Recognition and Enforcement of Foreign Arbitral Awards, the parties are entitled to have recourse to arbitration proceedings.

FINANCIAL ISSUES

A) Approximately 1,400 local and international brands are operated as franchisees or sub-franchisees in Turkey. As more and more franchisors have decided to assign master franchisees in the country, many of the major commercial banks have launched franchise support loans for franchisees that are entering the system for the first time or for those that are already franchisees, but want to upgrade their systems. The loans are generally targeted to franchisees that plan to operate food, maintenance, facility management, cosmetics or textile related operations. The content of these loans is usually:

* franchise fee loans

* franchise investment loans

* office space purchase loans

* fleet loans

B) Additionally, a U.S. Government Agency, the Overseas Private Investment Corporation (OPIC) is committed to helping U.S. business franchisors grow by providing long-term financing in emerging markets around the world and is able to provide financing to a variety of business entities involved in international franchise relationships: http://www.opic.gov/financing/loan-structures/franchise-loan

OPIC requires significant U.S. involvement in franchising transactions. This means that 25 percent of the project must be under the ownership of a U.S. small business, or have significant involvement of the U.S. franchisor in the project. "Significant involvement" can mean:

* the business concepts and systems employed by the franchisee were originally developed by the U.S. small-business franchisor;

* there is a long-term franchise agreement among the U.S. franchisor, the local in-country master franchisor, and the franchisee;

* local use of the U.S. franchisor□s trademark or brand-name; and

* U.S. franchisor has a long-term financial interest through receipt of franchise fees.

OPIC also expects the project to meet the general requirements outlined in the section on "Financing Details□□ on the website http://www.opic.gov/financing/financing-details

Loan terms for franchise loans generally range between 3-8 years, with an interest-only grace period not to exceed six months. Available loan amounts range from $100,000 up to $4 million. Loans over $1.5 million should generally involve multiple units.

STRONG LOCAL BRANDS AND JOINT VENTURE ALTERNATIVE

According to the figures of European Franchise Federation, Turkey is the leading country in Europe with the most number of brands (1.375).The market is dominated by Turkish franchise and dealer brands (1.058) and the foreign franchise and dealer brand number is at 413. Local entrepreneurs have established very strong brands especially in food and apparel sectors, successfully competing with their international counterparts. Therefore, it is not as easy to enter the Turkish market as in other countries in the region. Brand awareness is an important factor to consider while entering Turkey. A not very well known brand in U.S. has lower chances of success in Turkey because local investors usually prefer to invest in world famous brands. Another challenge in Turkey is the preference of forming a joint venture with the foreign partner. Turkish investor would like to share the risk of opening a business. Therefore the alternative of forming a joint venture usually comes up during franchising discussions. The franchisor should be able to inform the investor in detail about advantages of franchising to overcome this problem. Additionally, competitive advantages of the concept should be clearly mentioned. If the concept is not original enough, Turkish entrepreneurs tend to consider options different than franchising.

Key Contacts

UFRAD – NATIONAL FRANCHISING ASSOCIATION
Address: Besyol Mah. Inonu Cad. A Blok No:40 Kat:7
Sefakoy Kucukcekmece
Istanbul, Turkey
Phone #: [90] (212) 599-1784
Fax #: [90] (212) 425-5759
Website: http://www.ufrad.org.tr

ICT MARKET OPPORTUNITIES

Software Market The software market in Turkey is projected at $933 million in 2012 and is forecast to reach $1.5 bn in 2016, with an expected growth rate of 13%. However, much will depend on the success in bringing down illegal software use, which at 65% is nearly twice the global average.

BarriersThe CE mark is an issue for American firms who have not invested in this important compliance requirement. Since Turkey has adapted full acceptance of the regulations due to its European Union Customs Union membership, IT products need to meet the European Union directives on low voltage and electromagnetic compatibility. IT products need a CE mark to be imported into Turkey. The European Union (EU) Waste from Electrical and

Electronic Equipment Directive (WEEE) and Restriction of Hazardous Substances Directive (RoHS), is also an issue.

This report, prepared by the U.S. Embassy's Commercial Service in Ankara, provides an overview of the market and follow-up steps for American exporters to make sales in this dynamic market. With an estimated average growth rate of 9% for the past 3 years, with an expected growth rate similar for 2013, Turkey ranks as one of the fastest growing markets in the world. With a population of 75 million and half of the population being under 30 years of age, the market is ideal for targeting ICT services and products.

BEST PRODUCTS/SERVICES

IT Cyber Security

Consumer Electronics

Notebook PC's

Audio Visual Equipment

Wireless equipment / services

3G and 4G related technologies/services

Telecomm services

Content and media

Fiber Optic Solutions

Smart Phones

3G/4G related technologies and services, online services, content and media services, E-business, personalized services, music/video downloads, games, multi-play, and other mobile entertainment services will be best prospects.

ICT MARKET OVERVIEW

Turkey's Information and Communication Technologies (ICT) market size reached $34 billion in 2011, with a breakdown of $25 billion in Telecommunications and $9 billion in Information Technologies. (ref. Interpro). The Turkish ICT sector continues to be one of the key growth sectors in Turkey with an estimated growth of 8-10% for 2012, despite the ongoing economic global crisis.

INTERNET IN TURKEY

(ref: www.btk.gov.tr -BTK (Turkish Telecom Authority) / (www.agentschapnl.nl)

According to the April 2011 BTK (Informatics Council of Turkey) survey , "Household Information Technology Usage", 42.9 % of households have internet access throughout Turkey.

There are over 16.68 million internet subscribers as of first quarter 2012.

There has been an increase in internet subscriptions of 18.2% compared to the last trimester. The growth rate of the number of total internet subscribers has been rapidly growing and stands at 81.2%.

In the last quarter 2012, the number of xDSL subscribers was 6.7 million subscribers with a 0.6% decline compared to the previous quarter.

The OECD recently called for more initiatives to increase public use of ICT, with research from Eurostat showing that Turkey is among the countries in which internet access is low. The research found that only 39% of Turks had computers at home and that Turkey was below the EU average in terms of computers per household and internet access. (www.agentschapnl.nl)

Although other operators in Turkey are providing ADSL services, they are reliant on the incumbent Turk Telekom's ADSL infrastructure (service provided by another Turk Telekom company-TTNET). (www.agentschapnl.nl)

TTNet has the biggest share in the internet adsl market. Superonline, Dogan Telekom, Vodafone Net and Turknet follow. Breakdown is as follows:

Internet Operators Market Share	%
TTNet	84,13
Superonline	6,42
Dogan Telekom	3,80
Vodafone Net	1,85
Turknet	1,56

IT MARKET

A significant increase is expected in PC usage as the Ministry of Education plans to increase the number of computers and internet connections. The National Fatih Project is one such development project to provide schools with 2 million tablets, thousands of smart boards and high speed internet connection, project is worth an estimated $5 billion. Schools in remote areas are to be connected to the net via satellite with the cooperation of the Turkish satellite company Turksat.

The Turkish IT services market is expected to grow at a 14% over 2012-2016. The Turkish IT market is projected to achieve an compound annual growth rate (CAGR) of 16% during 2012-2016. Computer penetration is expected to pass 50% by 2016. Turkish spending on all categories of IT services is projected at US$1.5 bn in 2013. Banks and Telco's are expected to be among the lead organizations spending on new IT platforms (www.agentschapnl.nl).

There has, however, been a recent shift in the driving forces behind the IT industry in Turkey. Although until recently the the industry was focused on desktop and notebook sales, the consumer electronics market has significantly caught up and increased its share of the market. The consumer electronics market in Turkey is estimated at $3 billion. While the rest of the world averaged an increase of 10% in the consumer electronics market in 2011, the Turkish market averaged 30% growth..

Traditionally significant PC sales were confined to Istanbul, Ankara and Izmir, but now PC sales have received new momentum as the focus of demand has shifted towards the Anatolian region; this is expected to continue as the rate of PC sales rises. The PC sales have ripple effects increasing the sales of other items such as ADSL subscriptions, modems, software and other IT products and services.

COMPUTER SALES

Turkey's computer hardware sales are projected at $6.1 bn in 2013 and are forecasted to reach around $10.6 bn in 2016. The market is forecast to remain in positive growth territory in 2012, with revenue forecast to grow at a 17% CAGR in 2012-2016.

SOFTWARE MARKET

The software market in Turkey is projected at $933 million in 2012 and is forecast to reach $1.5 bn in 2016, with an expected growth rate of 13%. However, much will depend on the success in bringing down illegal software use, which at 65% is nearly twice the global average.

TELECOMM MARKET

In the telecommunications market, as of March 2012, there are 65.8 million mobile subscribers, corresponding to 88% penetration rate. In the first quarter of 2012, 64% of mobile subscribers are prepaid subscribers; and the rate of invoice subscribers have increased from 32.7% to 36.4% last year. The number of total subscribers of GMPCS (Global Mobile Personal Communications by Satellite) mobile phone service is 5,326.

As the first-trimester of 2012 ends,; Turkcell has 52.50%, Vodafone has 27.83% and Avea has 19.67% share of the mobile telecom market.

As per the report of the Informatics Council, in the first quarter 2012, the number of calls were 14,023,844; and total call time was 19,538,608 minutes. In the first quarter 2012, total mobile traffic volume has been 39.08 billion. When traffic data in the first quarter 2011 are compared with the previous trimester, it shows that total traffic grew by 1.5%; compared with the same period last year and that the annual growth rate is 15.1%. (www.btk.gov.tr)

The breakdown of subscribers are as follows: Turk Telekom has 14.83 million fixed-line telephone subscribers as of the first quarter 2012, a decrease from previous high of 17 million fixed line subscribers. This suggests a significant loss of market share to gsm operators, 6.5 million ADSL lines and 13 million GSM mobile subscribers via AVEA.

Turk Telekom owns 99.9% of TTnet, Argela, Innova, Sebit, Sobee ve AssisTT. Turk Telecom also owns 81% of AVEA, one of the three GSM mobile operators in Turkey. And they have a minority share of ALB telecom in Albania. 55% of the shares of Turk Telekom belong to Ojer Telecom Inc. and 30% belongs to the Turkish Treasury. The remaining 15% is floated on the Istanbul Stock Exchange (IMKB). The value of Turk Telekom was over $15 billion in 2011.

The total number of GSM cellular service subscribers reached almost 65 million with an approximate penetration rate of almost 89%. The total telecom equipment and services market grew to $20 billion and is expected to expand in 2012 as the GSM sector remains the driving force as subscribers are expected to use more and more 3G services. The total number of 3G subscribers reached 35 million. Fixed line subscribers are almost 15 million, reaching almost 100% of the households.

The three GSM cellular operators, Turkcell, Vodafone and AVEA and the fixed line operator Turk Telekom invested in equipment and services at a total value of $3 billion to expand their services. Turkcell has almost 36 million subscribers (56.6% of total GSM cellular subscribers), Vodafone has 15 million (24.5% of subscribers) and AVEA has 12 million (almost 19% of subscribers). Turk Telekom, Turkcell, Vodafone and Avea have all increased their revenues. Turk Telekom's total net sales revenues was 22.4 billion TL (12.4 billion dollars) in 2012. Other operators' revenues were 5.66 billion TL ($3.1 billion) in 2011 and total industry revenues reached 28 billion TL ($15.5 billion).

In 2011, Turk Telekom's investments increased by 24.77%, Turkcell's by 14.75% and Vodafone's by 23.34% compared to 2010. Avea's investments were decreased by 4.64% compared to the previous year. In the first quarter of 2012, total investment amount of the four large operators have been approximately 760 million TL ($422 million).

Turk Telekom seems to be the most profitable operator of the industry. Turk Telekom's EBIDTA (Earnings Before Interest, Taxes, Depreciation and Amortization) margin is 51.1%. It is followed by Turkcell with 29.3%, Vodafone with 17.0% and Avea with 9.91%.

While mobile call traffic is increasing every year, fixed call traffic is decreasing. Talk time in 2010 was 149.5 billion minutes, and increased to 168.9 billion minutes in 2011. 147.1 billion minutes out of a total of the 168.9 billion minutes consisted of mobile traffic.

36,980 people are employed in this industry. The number of Turk Telekom employees is 24,148, the number of employees of mobile operators is 8,377 and the number of employees of other operators is 4,455. In other words, Turk Telekom has the 65.30% of industry employees, mobile industry has 22.65% and other industries have 12.05%. (Ref: ICT Magazine)

Subscriber penetration for fixed lines is 23.5% and is not expected to increase due to hard competition from GSM cellular operators. With the introduction of 3G, IPTV, online services, content and media services, E-business, personalized services, music download, games, multi-play, video services, other mobile entertainment and soon 4G, the services segment has been developing rapidly, creating new business areas and revenues.

Turk Telekom will continue to be the major buyer of fixed-line telecommunications equipment and technology. Turk Telekom's main revenue growth came from ADSL revenues (29%) and from mobile revenues (14%) through AVEA. Turk Telekom introduced a new technology which provides fixed line services through the GSM mobile phones that have Wi-Fi capability. Consumers can now use both fixed line services and mobile GSM services through same mobile phone by uploading special software. Turk Telekom will also introduce 3N technology through fixed Internet and other ISPs by using its Wi-Fi capabilities spread around the country. 3N technology will provide mobile internet services.

Over 40 private long distance telephone companies have been also operating over the last 5 years, mostly using VoIP via an interconnection agreement with Turk Telekom. Some of these companies have established or continue to establish their own networks.

BTK (Turkish Telecom Authority) has registered over 60 million GSM cellular phone handsets in Turkey. BTK estimates that Turkey imports approximately 10 million mobile handsets every year. Many subscribers continuously change their cell phones with new models sustaining consistent growth in the handset market. Apple's Iphone has been extremely successful in the market in the past two years.

GSM cell phone sets suitable for video downloading and TV broadcasting equipped with wide band Internet access will be the driving force for growth in this sector. These new technologies will be the basis for the enhanced 3G and 4G operations.

In Turkey, Northern Telecom, Alcatel, Siemens, Ericsson and NEC supply majority of fixed lines switches, trans-multiplexers, and other telephony equipment. U.S. companies can be competitive in software programs required for customer databases, emergency call services, corporate management and intelligent network operation centers. Motorola, Nokia, Ericsson and Siemens are the main GSM switch and base station suppliers. U.S. companies can be competitive in new software products required by GSM cellular operators to provide new services to their clients and better corporate and client management.

The government's E-Government projects still continue to move forward, although most of the projects have been completed. The Turkish ICT market is far from being saturated and still has significant growth potential as the technology driven young population continues to invest in computers, consumer electronics, software and ICT services. The ICT market has grown every year and even in times of global crisis the growth has only dropped slightly, a good indicator that the ICT industry remains an attractive industry in Turkey. (UNDP, Harnessing ICT For Development In Turkey).

This attractive consumer electronics trend has lured many international and national electronic retail supermarkets to establish themselves in the market. German Mediamarkt, British Electro World, Turkish Teknosa, Vatanbilgisayar and Gold Bilgisayar have been competing for a number of years in Turkey.

SMART PHONES

According to "Our Mobile Planet Data", the smart phone usage rate in Turkey is 14% in 2011. (http://kisalt.com/2s2)

When growth figures for smart phones are taken into account at between 1.4 and 1.7, it shows that the actual usage rate is more like 20-24%. (www.sorula.com)

The number of smart phone sales was over 3 million in 2011. (www.sondakika.com)

The smart phone market is expected to grow by 50% in 2012; and 35% of all mobile phones will be smart phones.

There will be 22 million smart phones at the end of 2012, 35 million smart phones in 2013; and by 2014, 45-50 million smart phones are expected to be in the Turkish market. (Ref: General Manager of KVK, Özcan Ermiş)

Following is the market size estimate for the IT Sector (excluding the telecommunication sector)

Unit: USD thousands

	2009	2010	2011 (estimated)	2012 (estimated)
Total Market Size	5,600	6,160	6,776	7,454
Total Local Production	2,300	2,530	2,783	3,061
Total Exports	1,200	1,320	1,452	1,597
Total Imports	4,500	4,950	5,445	5,990
Imports from the U.S.	1,950	2,145	2,360	2,596
Exchange Rate: 1 USD	TL 1.54	TL 1.49	TL 1.54	TL 1.54

Following is the market size estimate for the Telecommunication Sector (excluding IT): Unit: USD thousands

	2009	2010	2011 (estimated)	2012 (estimated)
Total Market Size	19,300	21,000	23,100	25,310
Total Local Production	12,800	14,000	15,400	16,940
Total Exports	2,900	3,500	3,850	4,335
Total Imports	9,400	10,500	11,550	12,705
Imports from the U.S.	490	560	6,160	6,778
Exchange Rate: 1 USD	TL 1.54	TL 1.49	TL 1.54	TL 1.54

Total Market Size = (Total Local Production + Total Imports) – (Total Exports) Data Sources: Government of Turkey statistics bureau, Interpro Medya www.interpromedya.com.tr , http://www.x-rates.com/cgi-bin/hlookup.cgi

The young population of Turkey continues to drive the sales of pc's, cell phones, consumer electronics and cellular voice and data services. The audio visual market is expected to rise further as smart buildings are constructed with audio visual and control room installations and supporting entertainment consumer goods and services such as IPTV.

Fiber Optic solutions expected to gradually gain market access as infrastructure investments are made by Turk Telecom and TTNet and other ISP's.

The cyber security segment is expected to grow as corporate and government ICT security systems remain to attract significant funding. Security of coporate data as well as identity theft, network security against attackers, viruses, trojans and storage of network activities are among the top priorities with particular emphasis on providing legally sustainable evidence used in courts of law.

The Turkish Government has increased its expenditures in hardware and software in battling cyber threats. In order to implement these defenses the Departments of Justice, Interior, the Turkish National Police, and the Turkish military will continue to update their cyber security technologies.

The Turkish Government plans to invest $5 billion IT Projects – the bulk of this figure coming from the FATIH Project. The FATIH Project is a project with the goal of having every school under the Ministry of Education set up an IT lab and get connected to the internet – an ambitious project expected to reach 570,000 classrooms over the next five years.

The project also encompasses e-learning platforms and smart usage of IT technologies in the education field. The education sector, including IT investments belonging to the Ministry of Education and universities, has a lead share with approximately 43% of the GOT (Government of Turkey) IT investments.

TDZ (TECHNOLOGY DEVELOPMENT ZONES -TECHNO CITIES)

Recently established, Technology Development Zones ("TDZ") are affiliated with major universities (and are usually located on campuses-also called Techno City) to increase technology development and cooperation. Software developers benefit from significant tax and investment incentives provided by the government in these zones. The Turkish government has implemented new legal frameworks to encourage R&D and IT spending, which supports the growth of the sector. Income earned as a result of R&D activities by companies located in TDZs is exempt from tax. Additional incentives include contributions to the social security premiums of R&D staff. These TDZs are open to foreign investors who have the same benefits of their local counterparts. As Turkey has many competent young and dynamic computer engineers and software developers , TDZs have proven themselves to successful ventures.

IT SECURITY DEVELOPMENTS IN TURKEY

Corporate and government IT security systems are a particular focus in the Turkish market. Corporate data security as well as identity theft, network security against attackers, viruses, trojans and storage of network activities are among the top priorities with particular emphasis on providing legally sustainable evidence used in courts of law. The Turkish Government has increased its expenditures in hardware, software and education in battling cyber threats. In order to implement these defenses the Departments of Justice, Interior, the Turkish National Police, and the Turkish military have all updated their information security technologies. All governmental and military institutions have been training their personnel up to international standards and have been inviting expert professionals from abroad to provide further training. Resources indicate that the Turkish government and private sector institutions are looking at new technologies to enhance their IT security systems.

One such project, representing a significant improvement in the Turkish Government's efforts to centralize information and information security has been spear-headed by the Turkish Department of Justice. It has implemented 'UYAP – National Judiciary Informatics System' which is in line with the National Plan for the Adoption of the Acquis (NPAA) to achieve objectives stated in the 'EU' Accession Partnership. Modernization of justice and penal reform are included as fundamental priorities in the Accession Partnership and in the NPAA.

UYAP has been carried out to establish an electronic network covering all Courts, Offices of Public Prosecutors, and Law Enforcement Offices together with the Central Organization of the Ministry of Justice in order to realize these aims. This presents strong medium-term opportunities for U.S. IT firms, however European competition will be stiff.

UYAP is a relatively new project and is in progress, providing many opportunities for those companies with specific solutions for such large enterprise systems. The project includes video &

audio recording, and video conferencing systems in criminal courts, e-signature, and e-litigation solutions as well as SMS integrated information inquisition systems.

Along with UYAP, and the NPAA, Turkish authorities have been investing in digital investigation, surveillance, and forensics laboratories. These laboratories carry voice biometrics, Automated Finger Identification Systems (AFIS), data recovery, video processing, critical infrastructure protection, document examination, lawful interception, cryptology, intelligence, threat assessment, intelligence support systems, network intelligence, cyber crime investigations, anti-money laundering, national security solutions and more. Providing these technologies, as well as training operating personnel, create a promising market for U.S technology providers. This year the Turkish National Police together with the Istanbul Governorship announced plans to invest approximately 10 million USD into building an accredited laboratory in Istanbul, which will also dedicate itself to training regional police forces in the CIS and the Middle East. Although not officially confirmed, approximately 60 million USD is expected to be invested in Ankara in a similar project by the Turkish National Police. It is important to mention that Hacettepe University in Ankara, one of the most prominent state universities in Turkey, has just made the necessary investment to form a research and development facility for digital forensic sciences. Given that there are 15 major cities in which the national police has established crime laboratories, it is expected that the government spending on digital IT investigations will increase.

Due to Turkey's position as a founding NATO member, Turkey has been a trusted partner in implementing and manufacturing information security solutions. The Turkish government financed 'Tubitak UEKAE – The Turkish Institute of Electronics and Cryptology' -perhaps the best example of one of the top manufacturers of cryptology devices used by NATO members. Tubitak works closely with U.S. companies and is a prime customer of such technologies enjoying strong partnerships with international firms.

Another such institution is the Turkish International Cooperation and Development Agency (TIKA), an organization used by the Turkish Government to share know-how and technologies in the region. TIKA is the Turkish Government's technical assistance agency. TIKA has coordination offices in 20 countries and operates across Africa, Asia and Europe, delivering development assistance to partner countries through its projects and activities.'

Turkey continues to play a crucial role in the region on cyber security. For example, Turkey has been very active in the implementation of a Cyber Crimes Unit within the Turkish National Police and has also been an example in the region by pushing for a Cyber Crimes Law, which awaits for approval at the Turkish Parliament.

Authorities in digital investigations, and forensic sciences as well as training partners for CIS and Middle Eastern authorities include the Gendarmerie Criminal Department governed by the Ministry of Defense, the Council of Forensic Sciences governed by the Department of Justice of Turkey, and National Police Criminal Laboratories governed by the Interior Ministry, all of which are members of the European Network of Forensic Science Institutes (ENFSI), and are accredited internationally. In short Turkey represents an excellent platform for U.S. IT Security firms to expand to other markets in the region.

Recent regulations from the Turkish Government include law 5651 (currently in the Parliament awaiting acceptance) which designs a concrete framework of regulations regarding evidence gathering and convicting cyber-criminals. According to government sources, the law seeks to protect personal and corporate data against unlawful collection, usage and sharing of sensitive data. The Turkish National Police Cyber Crimes Unit based in Ankara is the main unit responsible for protecting citizens and corporations and implementing the law in cyber crimes.

Turkey is expected to move to internet protocol technologies to better gather evidence and convict criminals. The technology will need to upgrade from IPv4 to IPv6 and solutions relating to this upgrade will be required by the Turkish Government.

BEST PROSPECTS IN IT SECURITY

Enterprise Resource Planning software with embedded security applications.

Testing software and hardware. Virtual attack testing software and hardware is required by companies to simulate live attacks to better train and equip themselves in case of attacks. Also, system testers are needed to asses capacity and quality control of the integral IT system.

Training for employees to better understand attacks and threats and what can be done to avoid system weaknesses. Synergy training to create defense shields consisting of technology-human actions-training are required in the industry.

Monitoring software and hardware. In order to stop sensitive information leakage and to be able to collect evidence for court cases, monitoring software and hardware are in demand.

Encrypted data storage and back-up systems. Correct data storage and back-ups are an integral part of IT security and mission critical applications.

BARRIERS

The CE mark is an issue for American firms who have not invested in this important compliance requirement. Since Turkey has adapted full acceptance of the regulations due to its European Union Customs Union membership, IT products need to meet the European Union directives on low voltage and electromagnetic compatibility. IT products need a CE mark to be imported into Turkey. The European Union (EU) Waste from Electrical and Electronic Equipment Directive (WEEE) and Restriction of Hazardous Substances Directive (RoHS), is also an issue.

Apart from electro-mechanical standards, IT producers must ensure that all electronics be compatible with the radio-frequency levels of the Turkish national standards on frequencies.

Products manufactured prior to 1 January 2000 cannot be imported. The regulation from 1999 not allowing the importation of second hand IT products stands today. Used IT equipment is not allowed into Turkey 'unless the IT equipment is an integral part of a manufacturing machine' (for example the computer attached to an used embroidery machine is allowed).

U.S.

ITC hardware and software manufacturers will find that due to time commitment, cost, and complexity of the regulatory and commercial environment, it is essential to have local representation.

Although many people in larger urban commercial centers understand English, this may be a serious barrier in rural areas. It is therefore imperative that marketing information and user guides be written to the consumers' own language. Language barriers do pose a challenge for U.S. companies, hence a Turkish partner, distributor and/or agent is strongly advised.

U.S.

partners and products perceived well and favorably amongst business circles and consumers. To win over the local customer, a Turkish language web site would be extremely useful. Having a local representative or partner could help in translating your advertising so as to catch the eye and interest of the Turkish consumer.

For companies seeking to gauge market receptivity, exhibitions and conferences are excellent product launch vehicles. Reconfiguring the user interface and software would not be necessary in initial market fact finding stages and once market interest is determined and confirmed, the U.S. company and its local partner can look at packaging the hardware and software to meet the needs of the Turkish consumer.

Software translations may not be needed for professionals; however translations for software products for the general consumer are necessary. Recent Turkish regulations state that Turkish manuals and Turkish labeling on products should be inserted into product packaging hence arriving 'ready to sell' at Turkish customs. Previously the importer or the distributor would add these manuals and labels to the products after shipment was received and cleared through customs.

Market Opportunity Events: EMEA Intelligence, Istanbul (www.emeaintelligence.com) Turkey continues to act as the regional meeting point for information technology based security, intelligence, and surveillance providers and technologies. A key business development event is 'EMEA Intelligence: International Intelligence & Surveillance Technologies Conference and Exhibition' which will take place in Istanbul. EMEA

Intelligence 2011 was an officially certified US Department of Commerce trade event and the same certification is expected to be given for 2012. EMEA Intelligence is currently the only US Department of Commerce certified trade event in Turkey.

The same company previously organized a similar successful event with a focus on forensic sciences. Facts: Fifty-eight international companies, 79 international speakers, over 1000 professional visitors and government agencies from 20 countries, including USA, UK, Russia, Israel, Eastern Europe, Turkey, CIS Countries, Middle East Countries and more will attend.

Cebit Bilisim Eurasia, Istanbul (www.cebitbilisim.com) The leading ICT industry exhibition in Eurasia gathering local and international companies, governmental bodies, NGO's and academicians.

An ideal platform for information sharing with forums & summit topics covering the full spectrum of business technologies, and making business with special delegation programs and matchmaking activities. Facts for last year's event: 22 countries represented, 67,000 professional visitors, 985 exhibitors.

SOURCES OF INFORMATION:

Turkish Ministry of Transportation www.ubak.gov.tr

Turkish Ministry of Industry and Trade www.sanayi.gov.tr

Turk Card www.turkcards.com

Ongur Law www.arzuongurergan.av.tr/en-EN/index.html (www.buyusa.gov/turkey/en/business_service_providers.html?bsp_cat=80120000&bsp_id=150)

Zaman Newspaper http://www.zaman.com.tr

Turkish Prime Ministry http://rega.basbakanlik.gov.tr

Turkish International Development and Cooperation Organization www.tika.gov.tr

Emea Intelligence Trade Event www.emeaintelligence.com

Cebit Bilisim Eurasia, Istanbul, Turkey. IT and Telecom solutions trade fair. Details : www.cebitbilisim.com

EMEA Intelligence, Istanbul, Turkey Cyber Security solutions, trade event and seminar Details: www.emeaintelligence.com

Interpro Medya

http://www.interpromedya.com.tr/en/index.htm

TUBISAD (Informatics Association)

http://www.tubisad.org.tr/eng/Pages/default.aspx

MEDICAL EQUIPMENT MARKET

(Unit: USD millions)	2011	2012	2013 (estimated)	2014 (estimated)
Total Market Size	2,403	2,603	2,790	2,990
Total Local Production	360	390	418	508
Total Exports	192	156	139	179
Total Imports	2,234	2,369	2,511	2,661
Imports from the U.S.	335	355	377	400
Exchange Rate: 1 USD	TL 1.88	TL 1.85	TL 1.90	TL 1.90

Total Market Size = (Total Local Production + Total Imports) – (Total Exports)

Data Sources: Industry feedback, Turkish Ministry of Industry reports

Turkey has a population of 75 million people and is a growing market for medical technologies and healthcare services. Although, the Ministry of Health (MoH) (www.saglik.gov.tr) is the largest provider of healthcare and the only public provider of preventive healthcare services in Turkey, there is a rapidly growing presence of private sector in the system. Additionally, the MoH is the policy setter and national regulator. In fiscal year 2013, TL17 Billion (approximately $10 billion) was allocated to the MoH budget which translates to 4.4% of the country's total budget, an increase from 2.2% in 2002. In the same period, per capita health spending grew from $330 to $780. Considering the average OECD country per capita healthcare spending was $2386in 2012, as well as Turkey's growing income and government programs, there is significant growth potential in this market.

Turkish medical equipment market is approximately $3 billion and has been growing at the rate of 5-10% every year since 2002. 90% of the products used are imported; however, there is strong push by Turkish Government to strengthen and grow local manufacturing. In the coming years, percentage of imported products in the market may go down; however, Turkey and region will continue to be an attractive market for advanced and innovative American products.

MARKET OVERVIEW

Turkey has a 2-level approach to the delivery of public healthcare services. First-level treatment is delivered by family practitioners who are appointed to population groups of 3,000 people living in the same area. For illnesses requiring further treatment, patients are referred by family practitioners to second-level treatment facilities, which are 'state' and 'university' hospitals.

There are 1,453 hospitals and 194,000 hospital beds operating in Turkey. 840 of these hospitals are built and operated by the MoH and are known as 'state hospitals'. These hospitals constitute 57% of the current hospital stock and 62% of current hospital bed capacity in Turkey. There are 503 'private hospitals' and 65 'university hospitals'.

Doctors working in state hospitals are appointed by the MoH. All people living in Turkey can benefit from being treated in these hospitals. If they are 'universal healthcare insurance" holders, all of their expenses are reimbursed by the Social Security Institute (SGK) (www.sgk.gov.tr). In order to be universal healthcare insurance holder, you have to be paying monthly premiums to SGK throughout your working life. Children who are dependents of holders of this insurance also benefit from its healthcare benefits. Today, 95% of the population is covered under this insurance plan. University hospitals are attached to medical schools. In addition to acting as training and education centers for the medical industry, university hospitals function as the state hospitals for healthcare consumers. Private hospitals are also regulated by the MoH; however, investment, management and delivery of medical services in these facilities are the responsibility of their investors. Please refer to the below table to see the distribution of hospitals and hospital bed capacity by ownership.

	2002	2011	Growth %							
Type	# of hospitals	%	# of hospital beds	%	# of hospitals	%	# of hospital beds	%	# of hospitals	# of hospital beds
Ministry of Health (MoH)	774	67%	107,394	65%	840	58%	121,297	62%	8.5%	12%
University	50	4%	26,341	16%	65	4%	34,802	18%	30%	32%
Private	271	23%	12,387	8%	503	35%	31,648	16%	85%	155%
Other	61	6%	18,349	12%	45	3%	6,757	4%	-26%	-63%
Total	1,156		164,471		1,453		194,504		26%	19%

Source: Turkish Ministry of Health

As the table reflects, in the last decade, number of hospitals and number of hospitals beds grew. Major growth is seen in the relevant numbers of the private hospitals. This is due to the fact that Government of Turkey's strategy to make participation of private sector in healthcare investments more attractive. Private hospitals used to serve patients who either were private insurance holders, who are 2.3% of the population translating to 1.7 million people, or paid out of pocket. SGK made agreements with private hospitals that were interested to serve universal insurance holders at the reimbursement rates established by SGK. This, automatically, increased the patients population of private industry and boosted investment.

There is an emerging group of hospitals that will be built and managed by the Public-Private-Partnership (PPP) model. The MoH, which had been the sole builder of state hospitals, has recently been contracting out the construction and management of 29 healthcare campuses around Turkey. Each campus will house 2,000 to 4,000 beds divided among general and specialized hospitals, laboratories, and accompanying recreational areas. International tenders are being opened for the contracting of each of these hospitals to consortiums composed of construction companies, architectural designers, operators, and medical technologies companies. The winning consortium of each project will finance the construction and will operate the campus for 25 years against guaranteed annual lease payments to be made by the MoH. Some tenders have already been finalized. When construction of all these campuses is finished, 45,000 beds will have been replaced. You may get more information on these projects at http://www.kamuozel.gov.tr/koo/?q=en/main-page

There are two government bodies that are involved in reimbursing healthcare expenses incurred by healthcare institutions, The Social Security Institute (SGK) and the Ministry of Health (MoH).

SGK reimburses expenses incurred by using the treatment type and medical device listed in the Healthcare Implementation Communique (SUT). The SUT is revised every few years to include new medical technologies, equipment, techniques, and an updated reimbursement price list. In order for medical equipment to be listed in SUT, it has to be registered in the National Databank managed by the MoH. Products listed in the National Databank are assessed by SGK for their reimbursability and if approved, they can be reimbursed and can also be proposed in public procurement tenders.

Clinical laboratory services are also prices in the SUT list and for every clinical test delivered, there is a reimbursement price set. In Turkey, every inpatient serving hospital has to have an in-house clinical laboratory which means that there are at least 1,450 clinical laboratories established in the country. Besides these laboratories, there are laboratories private outpatient clinics whose number, at the time this report is written, is not known. Ministry of Health has started an initiative to license every laboratory following assessment of its quality standards, which will determine the number of qualified laboratories in Turkey.

In Turkey, hospitals do not buy the laboratory devices but their reagents. Hospitals commit to a certain number of reagents they will use throughout the term of their agreements with manufacturers. The top 5 tests that are made in hospitals in Turkey in general and their share are as follows:

1. Clinical biochemistry tests

2. Immunoassay tests

3. Blood count tests

4. Infectious disease tests

5. Full urine tests

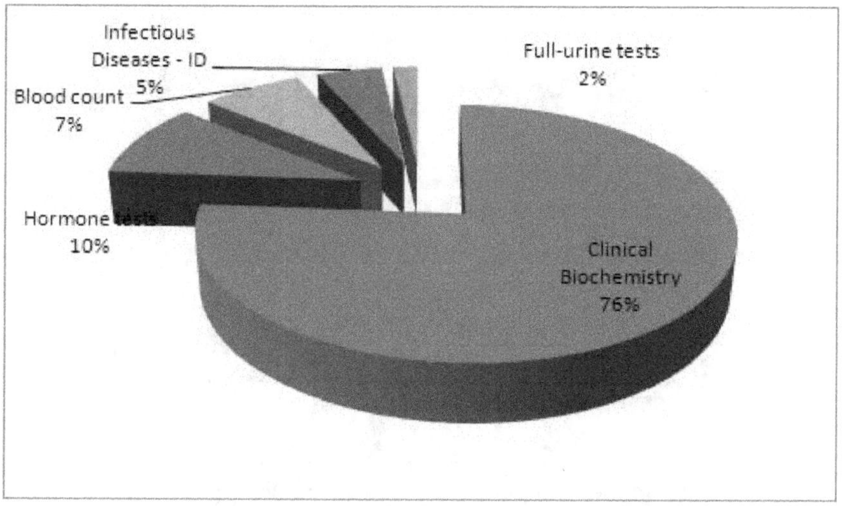

Source: Turkish Institute of Status through Global Trade Atlas

There are many players in the market; thus, it is quite a saturated market for these five tests. They have a steady growth of 5% every year and this is expected to stay so in the coming years as well.

Tests that are commonly made and follow the first five tests listed above are:

• Coagulation tests

• Microbiology tests

• Molecular tests for measuring viral loads - PCR tests

- E-health Transformation in Turkey

Turkey has been leading a rather aggressive approach since 2005 towards establishing an electronic system to manage patients' records, reimburse healthcare expenses, manage prescriptions flow, and use tele-medicine for offering healthcare services to remote parts of the country. The Ministry of Health's

E-Health Department cooperates with industry to develop various software to reach a position where all elements of Turkish healthcare system will be integrated in the central system whose map can be seen in the chart below.

Currently, healthcare records of all patients who visit first-level healthcare facilities are kept electronically and prescriptions are issued likewise. MEDULA system, co-developed SGK and the industry, makes it possible for pharmacies to communicate with SGK real-time for the reimbursement of the prescription amount.

Tele-medicine service has been started by establishing alliances between rural hospitals and central hospitals for the evaluations of radiological and laboratory outputs.

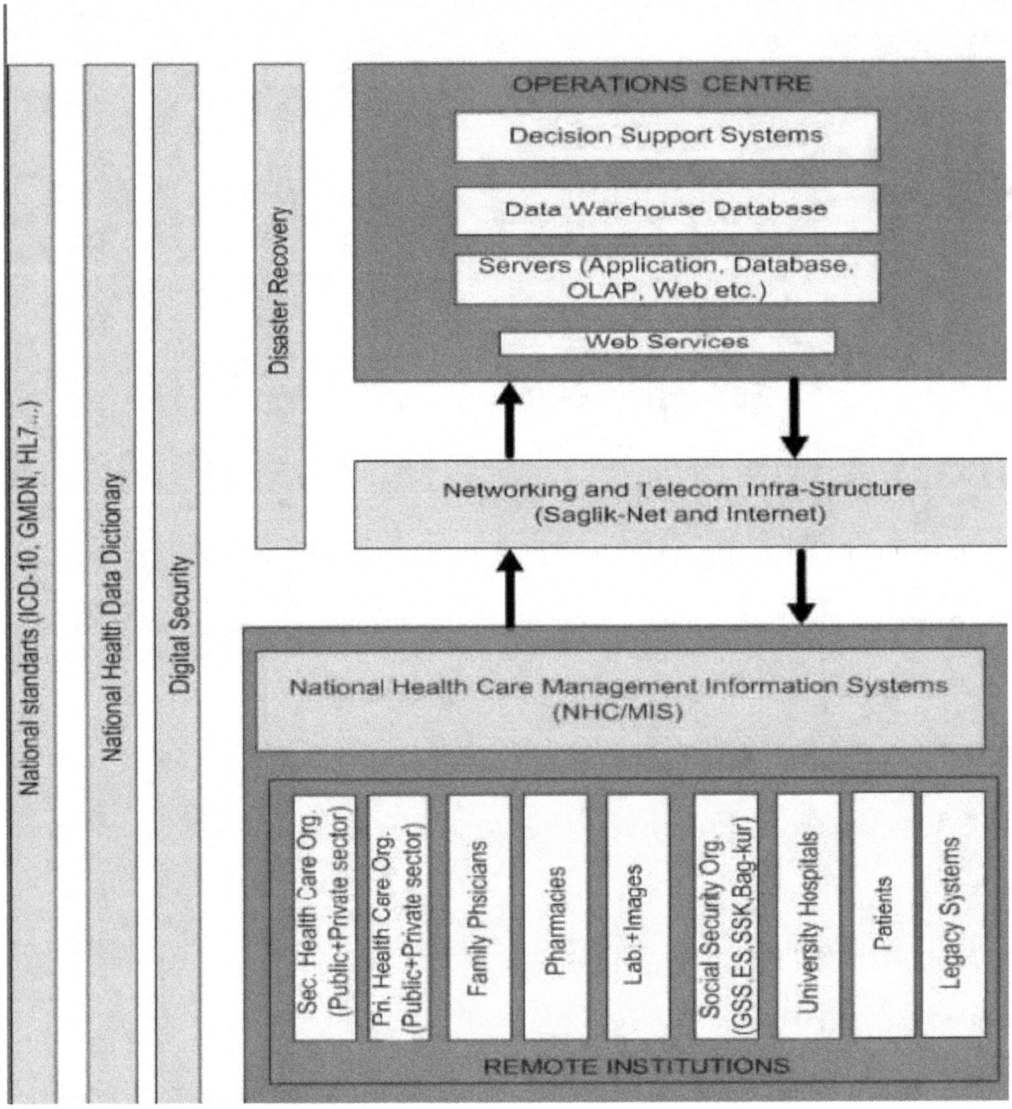

- **Medical Tourism Initiative**

Turkey has become a major healthcare center for patients from countries that are neighboring Turkey and from Europe. The Turkish Government will soon announce a project which will support the construction of healthcare free zones where international patients will receive high-quality healthcare treatment at economical prices. Number of international patients that visited Turkey between the years 2008 and 2012:

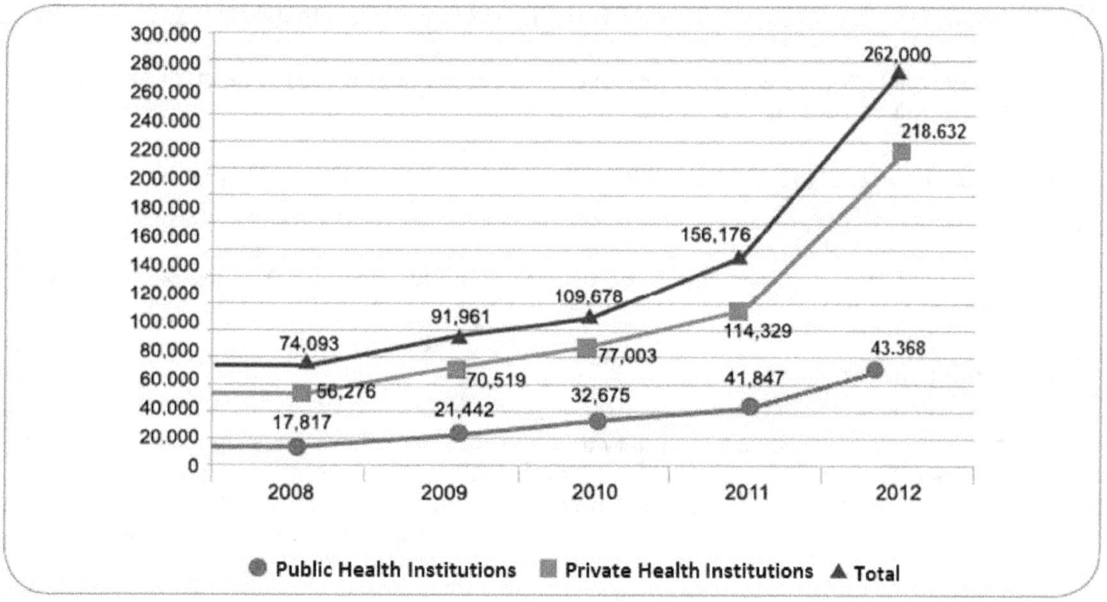

Source: Ministry of Health, Department of Health Tourism

Numbers of international patients targeted by the Ministry of Health by 2023 by year are:

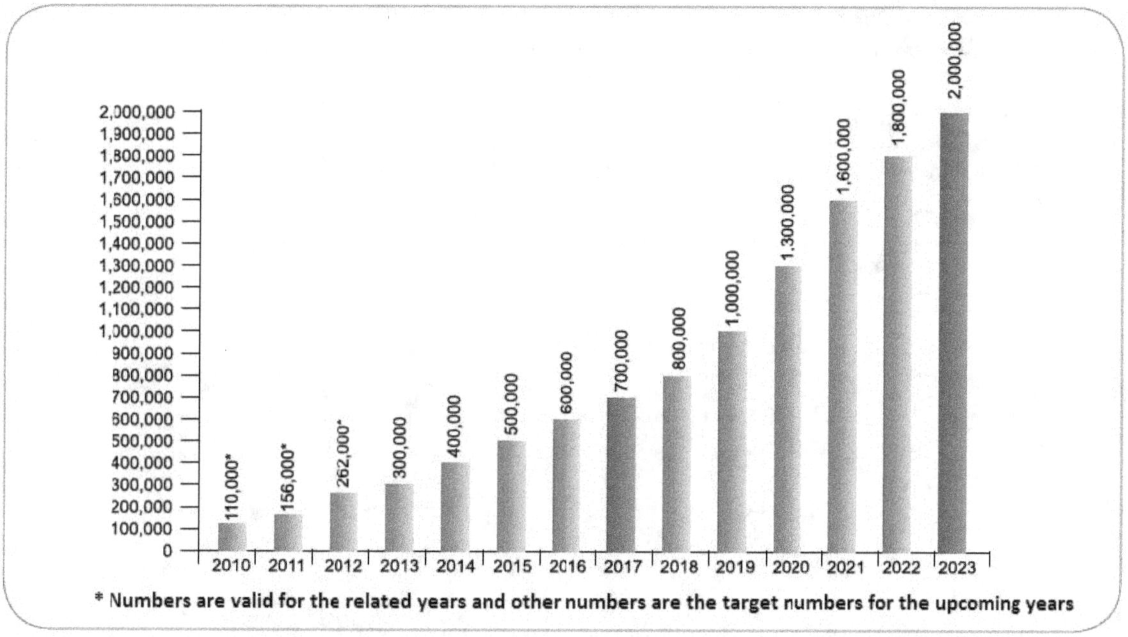

Source: Ministry of Health, Department of Health Tourism

MARKET OPPORTUNITIES

When discussed with industry, following developments are expected to occur in the market in the coming years:

- Closing of some of the old hospitals and their replacement with 'health campuses' made by PPP model. A total of 45,000 new hospital beds that will be installed in the health campuses will replace beds in older hospitals. Besides beds, hospitals in these health campuses will be procuring new medical devices.

- Replacing some of the medical devices, especially imaging and ICU unit devices, with new devices

- Managing chronic illnesses like heart diseases, blood pressure, obesity, and diabetes more effectively

- Detecting cancer at early stage

In the two graphs below, you may see the growth in the number of ICU units and imaging devices between the years 2002 and 2011, both of which displayed fast and above average growth. According to industry, some of these units will have to be replaced as some of them are out of date and some of them are not of high quality: thus creating major maintenance expenses.

Figure 6.8. Total Number of Intensive Care Unit Beds by Years and Sectors, Turkey

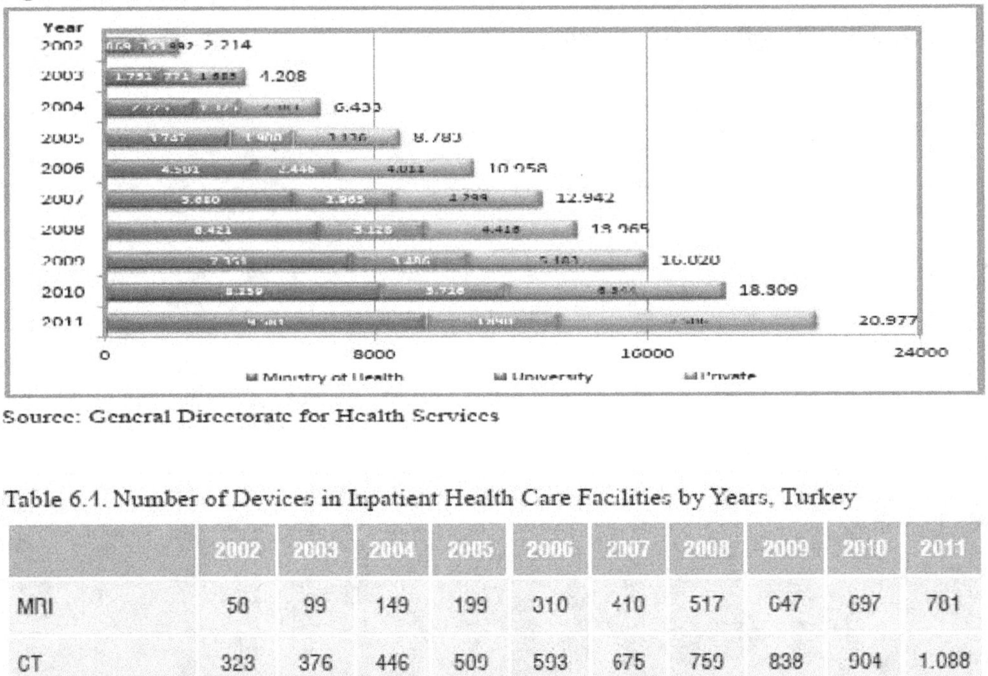

Source: General Directorate for Health Services

Table 6.4. Number of Devices in Inpatient Health Care Facilities by Years, Turkey

	2002	2003	2004	2005	2006	2007	2008	2009	2010	2011
MRI	50	99	149	199	310	410	517	647	697	701
CT	323	376	446	509	593	675	759	838	904	1.088
ECHO	259	338	391	453	518	598	689	791	881	1.181
Ultrasound	1.005	1.164	1.309	1.493	1.699	1.900	2.117	2.283	2.436	3.775
Doppler Ultrasonography	681	743	805	845	920	1.006	1.095	1.251	1.397	2.091

Source: General Directorate for Health Services

MoH keeps statistics of the highest prevailing health problems in Turkey. This statistics is compiled on an annual basis following the analyses of diagnoses reported by doctors in Turkey in that year. In the table below, you may see the problems that were diagnosed by doctors in 2010 from highest to lowest. Medical devices that can deliver recovery to patients using innovative technologies but at affordable pricing levels would have potential for success in the Turkish market.

Table 3.8 Distribution of 15 and 15+ Aged Individuals' Morbidity/ Health Problems Diagnosed by Physician, by Sex and Residence, (%), 2010

Diseases/Health problems	Rural			Urban			Turkey		
	Male	Female	Total	Male	Female	Total	Male	Female	Total
Back Musculoskeletal System Disorders (Lumbago, Back Hernia etc.)	10,1	18,2	14,4	8,9	15,6	12,3	9,3	16,5	12,9
High Blood Pressure (Hypertension)	10,3	19,9	15,3	7,7	15,3	11,5	8,4	16,8	12,7
Rheumatismal Joint Disease (Rheumatoid Arthritis)	7,7	16,5	12,3	4,5	11,6	8,0	5,4	13,1	9,3
Stomach Ulcer (Gastric Ulcer)	8,4	12,1	10,4	6,0	10,2	8,1	6,7	10,8	8,8
Osteoarthritis (Osteoarthritis, Arthrosis, Joint Degeneration)	5,6	13,1	9,5	3,5	9,0	6,7	4,1	10,0	7,5
Anemia (Iron Deficiency Anemia)	1,8	11,1	6,6	1,6	12,7	7,2	1,7	12,2	7,0
Sinusitis (Inflammation of Sinus)	5,0	7,8	6,5	5,5	8,2	6,9	5,4	8,1	6,7
Neck Musculoskeletal System Disorders (Neck Pain, Neck Hernia, etc.)	3.7	8.5	6.2	2.9	9.0	6.0	3.1	8.9	6.1
Diabetes	4,4	7,5	6,0	4,6	7,6	6,1	4,5	7,5	6,0
Migraine and Severe Headache	2,5	9,0	5,8	2,4	8,6	5,5	2,4	8,7	5,6
Allergy, Such as Rhinitis, Eye Inflammation, Dermatitis, Food Allergy or Other (Allergic Asthma Excluded)	3.5	5.3	4.5	4.0	6.0	5.4	3.9	6.3	5.1
Asthma (Allergic Asthma Included)	4.2	5.7	5.0	3.3	6.2	4.8	3.6	6.0	4.8
Coronary Heart Disease (Angina Pectoris, Chest Pain, Spasm)	5.2	5.3	5.3	3.6	3.7	3.7	4.2	4.2	4.2
Chronic Obstructive Pulmonary Disease (Emphysema, Chronic Bronchitis)	4,9	5,0	4,9	3,6	3,0	3,6	4,2	4,2	4,2
Thyroid Disease	1,2	5,3	3,3	0,9	5,6	3,3	1,0	5,5	3,3
Chronic Depression	1,3	2,8	2,1	1,2	4,1	2,7	1,2	3,7	2,5
Urinary Incontinence, Problems in Controlling the Bladder	2.1	3.7	2.9	1.1	2.6	1.8	1.3	2.9	2.2
Chronic Heart Failure	2,3	2,3	2,3	1,1	1,8	1,5	1,5	2,0	1,7
Other Psychological Health Problems	1,4	2,2	1,8	1,2	2,0	1,6	1,3	2,1	1,7
Hepatitis	2,2	1,3	1,7	1,6	1,1	1,4	1,8	1,2	1,5
Permanent Injury or Defect Caused By An Accident	2,7	0,6	1,6	1,8	0,7	1,3	2,1	0,7	1,4
Myocardial Infarction (Heart Attack)	2,4	1,1	1,7	1,3	0,6	1,0	1,7	0,8	1,2
Stroke (Cerebral Hemorrhage, Cerebral Thrombosis)	1,6	1,6	1,6	1,0	0,8	0,9	1,2	1,0	1,1
Duodenal Ulcer	1,1	1,3	1,2	0,9	1,1	1,0	1,0	1,2	1,1
Chronic Anxiety	0.3	0.7	0.5	0.2	0.9	0.5	0.3	0.8	0.5
Cirrhosis of the Liver, Liver Dysfunction	0,6	0,9	0,7	0,4	0,4	0,4	0,5	0,5	0,5
Cancer (Malign, Malignant, Leukemia, Lymphoma Included)	0,2	0,3	0,3	0,5	0,5	0,5	0,4	0,5	0,5

Source: TURKSTAT Health Interview Survey 2010

BEST PROSPECTS

• Advanced pre-screening, imaging and diagnostics devices

• Advanced point-of-care devices

• Advanced surgical devices using laporascopic and robotics technology

• Cancer treatment devices

• Clinical chemistry and laboratory devices

o Molecular tests

o Genetics tests

o Hormone tests

o Chromotography tests

o DNA tests

• Dental devices

• E-health and M-health systems

o Remote patient monitoring devices

• Implants used in orthopedics and trauma

• Telemedicine systems

MARKET ACCESS

U.S. companies that want to market their products in Turkey should either open their own offices in Turkey or assign a distributor who will import, market and distribute their products in Turkey. For SMEs, it may be better if they are to work with a distributor initially before opening their own offices as this will give them a chance to understand market dynamics.

Unless there is a specific need for multiple distributors, for most medical equipment and devices, one distributor, managing a reseller channel to market the products it represents, is enough to cover the whole country of Turkey.

Turkey has Customs Union Agreement with the European Union (EU) which led to Turkey's almost completely adapting most of its medical equipment directives to those of the EU. This necessitates that Turkey requires CE Mark certification for medical devices and it means that U.S. manufacturers, that can currently export to a country in EU, would probably have already met all the requirements for exporting to Turkey, too. As Turkey's official language is Turkish, language of labels on medical devices and their manuals have to be in Turkish. Along with the translations of the product labels, the user manuals and CE certification, the importers are required to provide EAN 13 (Global Synchronization 1/ EAN) or HIBCC (Health Industry Business Coding Council) codes for the products they register. It is the responsibility of manufacturers to deliver products with the required codes. For this reason, importers or distributors need to notify manufacturers about the subject requirement and obtain accurate codes.

Once a U.S. company assigns a Turkish company to distribute its products in Turkey and completes necessary certification and documentation for exporting to Turkey, its distributor has to register the products in the MoH managed National Databank. Following this, if the U.S. company wants to be in the SGK managed reimbursement system (SUT), it has to agree on the reimbursement price established by SGK for that product group. If that product group is not listed in SUT, U.S. company and its distributor have to present the product and its technology to SGK to convince them for the product to be included in SUT. If U.S. company does not want to be part of SUT, it would lose its chance to sell to the large public sector but only to private sector.

The Commercial Service in Turkey has a number of programs and services available to assist the U.S. business community in establishing a presence in this market, e.g., the International Partner Search, the Gold Key Service, and the International Company Profile. Please visit the following website for our further information: http://www.export.gov/Turkey

KEY SUPPLIERS

Most of the global medical technologies companies are either represented in Turkey through their distributors or they have their own offices. Turkish importers attend a lot of international expos and follow the developments in the industry.

Companies from the U.S., Germany, France, Italy, the UK and Japan are dominant in the market. There are suppliers from China who have gained market share especially in the medical disposables area.

Turkish market has potential for medical technologies companies that have unique and newly commercialized technologies that will advance application of medicine in Turkey.

PROSPECTIVE BUYERS

There are 3 customer groups of medical equipment in Turkey:

- **Private hospitals:** Each hospital operator chain buys through its own purchasing department. They

ask for quotes and decide in line with their criteria for that specific purchase. It is very critical that distributors/manufacturers promote their products witch the clinicians in these organizations as well as their purchasing departments.

- **University hospitals:** Each university hospital that is part of medical schools has its own purchasing department. They open tenders for these purchases. Payment terms of university hospitals are somewhat longer which sometimes become problematic for smaller size distributors.

- **Public hospitals:** Until January 2013, each public hospital had the authority to administer its own tender and procure per its own needs. However, as of January 2013, a new regulation is in place which groups public hospitals into 90 profit centers. There are about 800 public hospitals which have been grouped under these centers. Each center has been assigned a CEO who will manage the purchasing of all the hospitals in his/her group centrally. They will collect the needs of hospitals for at least the next one year and will administer tenders for the procurement. This restructuring is expected to consolidate the players in the market as volume of purchase in each tender will be higher and not every company will be able to finance this much of volume. This development is also expected to impact prices in the market as with larger volumes to procure, tendering authorities will be expecting lower prices per unit of equipment.

Turkish Ministry of Health has started contracting the construction and operational management of 29 medical campuses to private sector by Public-Private-Partnership model. Each medical campus will have 1,000 to 3,500 beds. Clinical laboratory services will be outsourced to private sector which is not the practice in many of the public hospitals. As much as this project is getting the attention of equipment and reagents manufacturers, international clinical laboratory operators have also started displaying interest in forming consortiums with Turkish companies to compete for these contracts.

MARKET ISSUES AND OBSTACLES

There are no specific market access issues or trade barriers that would inhibit U.S. medical technologies manufacturers from exporting to Turkey. Turkey has customs union agreement with the European Union (EU) which provides that products manufactured in the EU are exempt from customs tax when exported to Turkey. As U.S. is not part of this agreement and Turkey does not have free trade agreement with the U.S., some of the U.S. medical devices are levied customs tax ranging from 3% to 5%.

RESOURCES & KEY CONTACTS

Ministry of Health
Ilac ve Tibbi Cihaz Kurumu (General Directorate of Pharmaceuticals and Medical Device)
Address: Sogutozu Mahallesi 2176. Sokak
No:5 06520
Cankaya, Ankara
Phone #: +90 (312) 218-3000
Website: http://www.titck.saglik.gov.tr/Default.aspx?sayfa=anasayfa&lang=en

---

TURKEY: CARBON CREDIT INDUSTRY

As of today, Turkey is not eligible for carbon compliance markets such as CDM, JI or IET. However, the Ministry of Environment announced in 2009 that Turkey was ready to participate in a post-2012 Kyoto Protocol compliance system. This system has not yet been defined. To date, carbon projects in Turkey are being developed to generate Verified Emissions Credits (VERs) sold on the voluntary market. When developed using the Golden Standard (GS) methodology, it is expected that VERs may be convertible to Certified Emissions Reductions (CERs) under a compliance market.

MARKET DEMAND

Turkey is an Annex I country which is the category for developing and emerging countries. Annex I countries are potential carbon credit buyers. While it's considered Annex I by the United Nations

Framework Convention on Climate Change, the main global forum for fighting climate change, Turkey was granted a special designation under the 1997 Kyoto Protocol as an "advanced developing country" when it finally ratified the treaty in 2009. Turkey has however not set any emission reduction target; hence, it is not listed as an Annex B country, which is the category for developed and emerging countries of Annex I that adopted greenhouse gas (GHG) emission reduction targets under the Kyoto Protocol and cannot participate to the Clean Development Mechanism (CDM) nor to the EU Emissions Trading Scheme (EU-ETS). Under these circumstances, the non-Kyoto market, which involves Voluntary Emission Reductions (VERs), is emerging in the country. As of today, VERs cannot be converted to Carbon Emission Reductions (CERs, traded within the CDM framework) nor to EURs (traded within the EU-ETS system) to cover legal reduction requirements. There is no official statement from the Turkish Government about the voluntary carbon market yet. However, the voluntary carbon market in Turkey evolves quickly, creating new economic and environmental opportunities for investors, businesses, banks, NGOs and individuals. The VER market plays a unique role in increasing awareness over climate change, its threats and solutions in the public and business world.

Market Data VCM Project Profile in Turkey

Voluntary Carbon Market (VCM) Profile of Turkey	
Number of Registered VCM Projects up to date (limited to the publicly available registries)	**201**
Estimated Annual Emission Reduction (all applied projects)	**~15 million CO_2 eq. tons**

Source: Gold Standard, VCS, January 2012

Types, Number and Percentage of VCM Projects in Turkey, as of July 2011

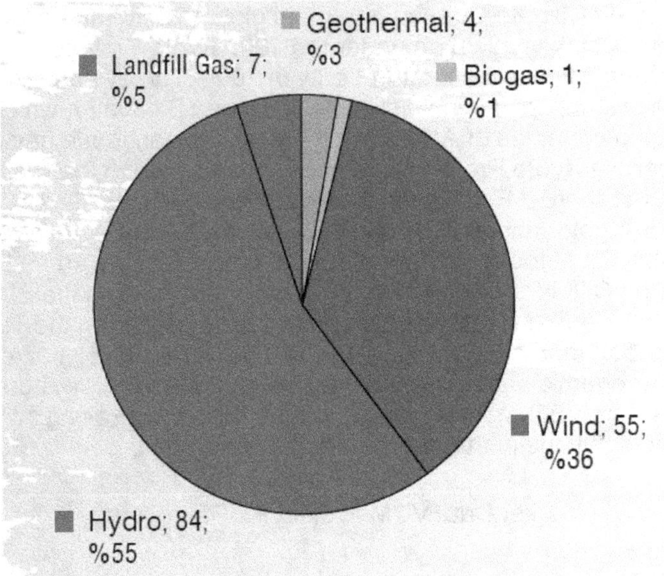

Source: Ministry of Environment and Urbanization, July 2011

Carbon Credit Potential in Turkey Page 3 of 6

VER Project in Turkey, as of July 3, 2008

Project Year	Project Developer / Carbon Consultant	Project Name	Capacity (MW)	Project Type	Carbon Certification Methodology	Status	State /Province	tCO_2equ. avoided per year	Sale price/ tCO_2equ.	Investment cost (€)
2007	Anemon Enerji Elektrik Üretim A.Þ.	Anemon Intepe	30.4	Wind	GS	Registered	Çanakkale			
	FutureCamp GmbH	Yuntdag	42.5	Wind	GS	Validated	Izmir	100 738		
	FutureCamp GmbH	Tuzla	7.5	Geothermal	GS	Validated	Canakkale	32 000		
	Future Camp GmbH	Catalca	60	Wind	GS	Validated	Catalca District			
2007	MareManastýr Rüzgar Enerji Santrali San.veTic.AÞ	Mare Manastır	39	Wind	GS	Registered	Izmir			
2007	Demirer Holding, "Dogal Enerji Uretim A.S." / One Carbon International BV	Sayalar	30.4	Wind	GS	Registered	Manisa	85 035	5€	41 million€
	One Carbon International BV	Kozdere Run-off River		Small, Low-Impact Hydro	GS	Listed	N/A			
	One Carbon International BV	Çayaðazý Run-off River		Small, Low-Impact Hydro	GS	Listed	N/A			
	One Carbon International BV	Burgaz	14.9	Wind	GS	Listed	Çanakkale			
2007	ITC / One Carbon International B.V.		11.2	Biogas	GS	Not yet listed	Ankara	620 000		35 million€
2008	ISTAC	Odayeri and Komurcuoda	21	Biogas	GS	Under construction	Istanbul		3-5€	
Under development	ITC / One Carbon International B.V.		11.2	Biogas	GS	Under development	Adana	620 000		20-25 million €
		Sebenoba	30	Wind	VCS	Listed				
		Karakurt	10.8	Wind	VCS	Validated				
		Balikesir Samli	90	Wind			Balikesir	162 000		
2006	Future Camp GmbH	Balikesir "BARES II"	30	Wind	VER+	Validated	Balikesir	72 000	5-6€	
		Soma	172	Wind						
2007	Deniz A.S. / ?	Uevecik	10.8	Wind			Manisa / Akhisar			

Source: AFD

Number of license applications for the production of electricity from renewable energy projects received by EMRA between 2001 and 2008, and capacities

	Number of applications*	Total capacity
Wind power	889**	83 000 MW
Hydropower	648	13 700 MW
Geothermal power	6	37 MW
Biomass	1	4 MW
Biogas	8	17 MW
Photovoltaïc	1	10 MW
Landfill gas	6	48 MW

* Includes applications at all stages of the review process, from newly received applications to those for which a license has been issued. ** Note that applications for wind power farms are overlapping, several of them being submitted for the same locations. MENR expects that only 10% of these applications be realized due to their geographic overlapping, investors/developers' inadequate financial resources, limiting capacity of electric transformers and lack of grid connections.

Source: AFD

In the Ministry of Environment And Urbanization's National Climate Change Action Plan that was released July 2011, it states that: "Circular on the Registry of Projects for Greenhouse Gas Mitigation by the Ministry of Environment and Urbanization was prepared to ensure a more effective functioning of voluntary carbon markets and to provide guidance to project developers. This circular took effect following its publication in the Official Gazette No. 27665 on 07.08.2010. By registering these projects, the main objective is to increase the credibility of carbon certificates that are developed in Turkey."

Sector-based Breakdown of Greenhouse Gas Emissions between 1990 and 2009

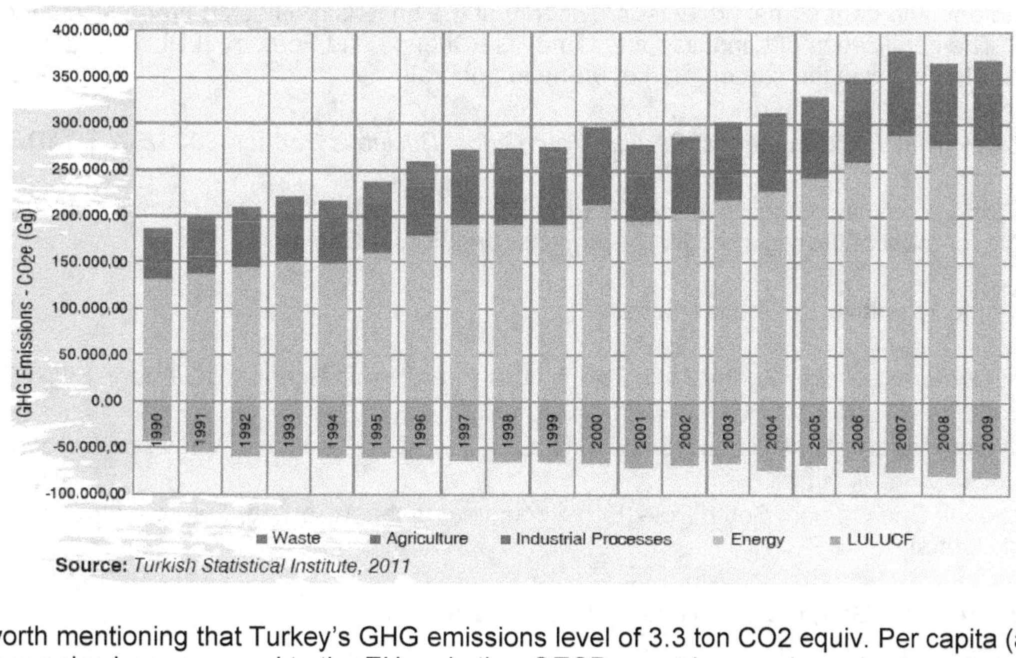

Source: *Turkish Statistical Institute, 2011*

It is worth mentioning that Turkey's GHG emissions level of 3.3 ton CO2 equiv. Per capita (as of 2003) remains low compared to the EU and other OECD countries, as shown in above Table.

BEST PROSPECTS

The voluntary market does not only enable companies in the non-Kyoto markets to gain experience with carbon inventories, emission reductions and carbon markets; it also raises awareness among consumers and market participants as well as creates incentives for emissions reduction projects in the unregulated sectors of countries outside of the Kyoto system (like U.S. or Turkey).

Because of the overall lack of monitoring, overseeing and regulation in voluntary markets, project developers enjoy the flexibility of implementing small or dispersed projects that would normally be unrealizable projects in regulated markets. The voluntary market furthermore creates a general consumer expectation regarding companies for CSR activities in a sustainable development framework by supporting emission reducing projects. Companies also benefit from the positive effects in terms of public relations and corporate identity.

KEY SUPPLIERS AND PROSPECTIVE BUYERS

As of July 3rd, 2008, only 4 wind projects were registered (3 of them under the Gold Standard methodology and one under the VCS methodology) and 4 projects were validated (2 wind and one geothermal project under GS and one wind project using the VER+ methodology). In addition, about 25 VER projects were in the pipeline in Turkey on 2008. They include not only wind farm projects but also small hydropower and methane projects.

According to data from March 2011, of all the projects that are developed in Turkey (151 projects), 84 projects are on hydroelectricity, 55 are on wind, 4 are on geothermal, 7 are on landfill gas and 1 is on biomass.

With regard to VERs, potential projects in Turkey mostly include wind power farms and methane projects, as well as some small-hydropower projects carefully chosen to have low impact on the environment, and geothermal projects, provided that the brine is re-injected properly into the ground. The certification of Land Use and Land Use Change and Forestry (LULUCF) projects is highly controversial in the carbon market arena in general.

Major carbon consultants active in the VER markets in Turkey include One Carbon (which accounts for most of the registered VER projects) and Future Camp.

Some of the key players of the market are:

Project Owners: Demirer Enerji, Zorlu Enerji, Dost Enerji, Polat Enerji, ADO Enerji, Bilgin Enerji

Project Developers: Local: Mavi Consultants, GAIA, En-Çev, Turkuaz Energy and Carbon

International: One Carbon, South Pole, Eco-Securities, Pioneer Carbon, Future Camp, 3 C, Carbon Neutral

Project Funders: Garanti Bank, Turkish Development Bank

Standards Organizations: Gold Standard, Voluntary Carbon Standard (VCS)

Supporting International NGOs: World Wildlife Fund (WWF), Greenpeace, Renewable Energy and Energy

Efficiency Partnerships (REEEP)

Local Institutions: Turkish Scientific and Technical Research Council (TUBITAK), Ministry of Environment

and Forestry, Regional Environment Center (REC) Turkey

Interested Parties: US Export Import Bank (US Exim), Worldbank, US Trade and Development Agency

(USTDA), International Finance Corporation (IFC), United Nations Development Program (UNDP) Turkey,

Turkish Industry and Business Association (TUSIAD), United Nations Environment Program (UNEP)

Validators & Verifiers: TUV SUD, TUV Rheinland, SGS

In Turkey, the **buyer-side** is missing.

MARKET ENTRY

Legislation about building capacity for monitoring, reporting and verification of emissions data (MRV system) will enter into force in 2012 and the implementing will take place in 2016. Turkish Government released an action plan for Climate Change on July 2011. When MRV law takes effect, it will allow the government to track about half of Turkey's emissions using rules similar to those in the European Union's Emissions Trading Scheme (EUETS), the world's largest carbon cap and emissions-trading program, or "cap and trade." The scheme sets a limit on global warming emissions and allows utilities and other emitters to trade pollution permits among themselves. Turkey's carbon-regulation program could be linked to Europe's—when it opens. For now the timeline and form of the scheme are still very much up in the air. Under Turkey's 2011 National Climate Change Action plan, the government must create cap-and-trade "infrastructure" by 2015—but it's not clear how binding this mandate is and what is expected to happen beyond MRV. Turkey is a developing economy and country, so the amount of energy that Turkey uses increases rapidly every year. When Turkey's GHG emissions are projected, a peaking point is not seen until 2030.

To enter the market initially a local partner can be used. After knowing the market better, ideally the next step would be to open an office in Turkey.

MARKET ISSUES & OBSTACLES

GHG reduction potential in Turkey is relatively high. However, not all of this potential can be commercialized in the voluntary carbon markets because of its characteristics. Turkish banks "may" consider VER revenues in the cash flow. However, they do not take such revenues into consideration as collateral because of their unforeseeable nature. Banks are expressing an interest in the voluntary carbon market. However, their lack of knowledge on the concept of sustainable finance, climate change and impacts on the financial institutions, as well as carbon market mechanisms make it difficult for them to envisage a credit line based on carbon credits.

Financial gains from voluntary market transactions are not high, but they are steady. For example Demirer Energy initially covers about 2 percent of its investment costs and then obtains about the same amount each year for 20 years.

Some other deficiencies in Turkey are regarding the lack of a national registry for such projects and an ambiguity about what needs to be done in the post-Kyoto period.

RESOURCES & CONTACTS

The main institutional bodies in charge of energy policy and management are:

The Ministry of Energy and Natural Resources (MENR) which prepares energy policy, plans and programmes, coordinates the relevant public institutions related to energy issues and ensures the implementation of its energy related programmes. http://www.enerji.gov.tr/index.php?dil=en

Renewable Energy Directorate (RED or YGM in Turkish) is working under EIE.

http://www.yegm.gov.tr/english/index-e.html

BUSINESS TRAVEL

IMPORTANT INFORMATION FRO TRAVELERS

BUSINESS CUSTOMS

The Turkish people feel close to their traditions and culture. However, having ties with western countries, Turkish people in major cities have adopted a western way of life. A foreigner visiting any one of the large cities in Turkey will find himself or herself in an atmosphere similar to that of a contemporary western city. There are no local customs, beyond the bounds of normal courtesy, that a visiting businessman should feel compelled to observe. In general, a personal relationship is an important basis for a successful business relationship in Turkey. It is usually important to allow time for friendly conversation before commencing with a business agenda. Business cards are almost always exchanged, and visitors are usually offered a glass of tea or a cup of Turkish coffee.

TRAVEL ADVISORY AND VISAS

U.S. citizens are required to obtain visas before entering Turkey. U.S. citizens traveling to Turkey as tourists may obtain their visas either from Turkish Consular Offices abroad, or at the border crossing point--for a stay up to three months. For visits of longer duration, or for those intending to study or to obtain employment in Turkey, the appropriate visa must be obtained in advance. A fee will be collected, notwithstanding the type of visa issued.

Street crime is not a major concern in Turkey. However, as in other large metropolitan areas throughout the world, there is some crime against tourists, particularly in Istanbul, including pickpocketing, purse snatching and mugging. In the past three years, dozens of Americans, Canadian and European tourists were robbed by English-or French-speaking foreigners, who identified themselves as Tunisian, Moroccan, Kuwaiti, or Romanian. These persons befriended the tourists and then drugged them using teas, juice, alcohol, or food. The two most common drugs are Nembutal (tm), known on the street as sari bombasi (the yellow bomb) and benzodiazepine.

Since the 1970's, urban and rural acts of terrorism throughout Turkey have caused loss of life and injury to government officials and civilians, including some foreign tourists. These incidents have occurred both in eastern Turkey and in urban areas. In the past year, Turkish police and military authorities have conducted very successful operations against the Kurdistan Workers' Party (PKK) in southeastern Turkey and various leftist and fundamentalist groups throughout Turkey. While these groups have not been eliminated altogether, their operational capabilities have greatly diminished. Although sporadic incidents involving terrorist groups continue to occur, the general security situation throughout Turkey is stable at this time.

Visitors to any part of southeastern Turkey are advised to travel only during daylight hours and on major highways. The Turkish Jandarma (Gendarmerie) and police forces monitor checkpoints on roads throughout the southeastern region. Travelers are cautioned not to accept letters, parcels or other items from strangers for delivery either in or outside Turkey. The PKK has attempted to use foreigners to deliver messages and packages in or outside of Turkey. If discovered, individuals could be arrested for aiding and abetting the PKK-a serious charge. Additional information is available on the U.S. Embassy web page at www.usemb-ankara.org.tr and on the State Department web www.travel.state.gov or http://travel.state.gov/turkey.html.

Unauthorized purchase or removal from Turkey of antiquities or other important cultural artifacts is strictly forbidden. U.S. visitors may obtain updated information on travel and security in Turkey from the U.S. Embassy in Ankara or Consulates in Istanbul and Adana, or posted on the Embassy's home page: www.usemb-ankara.org.tr.

TURKISH HOLIDAYS

January 1	New Year's Day
February 21-25	Kurban Bayrami (Sacrifice Holiday) begins 13:00 on Feb. 21)
April 23	National Sovereignty and Children's Day
May 19	Ataturk Memorial, Youth and Sports Day
August 30	Victory Day
October 28-29	Turkish Independence Day (Begins 13:00 on October 28)
December 4-7	Seker Bayrami (Ramazan) begins 13:00 on Dec. 4

BUSINESS INFRASTRUCTURE

TRANSPORTATION

The national flag carrier, Turkish Airlines (THY), together with its subsidiaries, dominates air passenger service and flies non-stop daily to most major European, Middle Eastern, Asian cities and U.S. gateways including Tokyo, London, Frankfurt, Paris, New York, Chicago and Miami. Delta Airlines flies non-stop from Istanbul to New York with direct onward service to Atlanta. Major European airlines have also frequent non-stop flights to Turkey. American Airlines and THY have a code-share arrangement with THY serving American's hubs in New York, Chicago, and Miami. Rail transportation is also available between most of the major cities. Comprehensive networks of long distance buses, which are inexpensive, operate between the major cities. Car rental is relatively expensive although gasoline (benzene) is cheaper than in Europe, and fuel stations are numerous. Public transportation is available in the cities. However, businessmen are advised to use taxis, as taxis are relatively inexpensive.

LANGUAGE

The official language spoken by more than 90 percent of the population is Turkish. Most educated Turks have a command of at least one foreign language, with sufficient fluency to carry out business transactions. Most company executives were educated in western countries. English is the dominant language for international business. Other frequently spoken languages are German and French.

COMMUNICATION:

The telephone system in Turkey's major cities is good. Email and faxes are widely used in international business.

LODGING

Medium to luxury-type hotels, including international hotels such as the Hilton, Sheraton, Hyatt, Holiday Inn, Conrad and Swissotel, are available in major cities. Apartment rents in Istanbul are expensive. Rents in Ankara and Izmir are more reasonable. The rental of a good quality apartment in a popular area of a city, with payment usually made in a foreign currency. Generally, 6 months to one year's rent is expected in advance.

HEALTH

Medical facilities are available, but may be limited outside urban areas. Cutting edge medical care does not exist in Turkey. Neither do the accepted practices of frequent soapy handwashing or covering of the mouth when coughing or sneezing and then washing hands.

Food and water borne diseases are prevalent throughout Turkey. Anyone coming to Turkey should have comprehensive medical insurance. Useful information on medical emergencies abroad, including overseas insurance programs, is provided in the Department of State's Bureau of Consular Affairs brochure, Medical Information for American Traveling Abroad, available via the Bureau of Consular Affairs home page (write in web page) or autofax: (202) 647-3000.

Vaccines: Vaccines necessary for Turkey are all childhood immunizations, Typhoid, Hepatitis B, Hepatitis A (or Immune Globulin as an alternative). Visitors who will visit rural areas, or go on hiking, or trekking trips in the country may wish to get Rabies vaccine although this is not required.

Information on vaccinations and other health precautions can be obtained from the Center for Diseases Control and Prevention's (CDC) hotline for international travelers at 1-877-FYI-TRIP (1-877-394-8747), fax 1-800-CDC-FAXX (1-800-232-3299), or via CDC's Internet site at http://www.cdc.gov.

FOOD

Turkish cuisine is characterized by the freshness of its ingredients and most American business travelers have no trouble finding a good meal. All major hotels have at least one restaurant serving continental cuisine. Several European and ethnic restaurants are also available in major cities. Prices at these places are usually moderate-to-expensive. Good food is available not only at expensive restaurants but also at moderately priced establishments. One also has the choice of fast food restaurants such as McDonald's, Wendy's, Kentucky Fried Chicken, Burger King and their Turkish equivalents such as Kebap 49. A variety of fresh fruits and vegetables are available throughout the year.

TEMPORARY ENTRY OF GOODS

Travelers entering Turkey on a temporary basis and carrying items such as laptop computers and accessories, display and exhibit materials are permitted to bring these items into Turkey duty free. Customs officials register the items to the traveler's passport and subsequently cancel them as the traveler exits the country with the same items. Catalogs, brochures, pamphlets, and similar advertising materials are exempt from customs duty. For additional information about temporary entry, please see VI. Trade Regulations and Standards, Temporary Entry section.

INFORMATION ON TYPICAL PRODUCT PRICING STRUCTURES

Pricing strategies in Turkey reflect the dynamics of the market place and are influenced by various market forces that include demand and supply. While there is not one typical pricing scheme, a model pricing structure based on general merchandise follows:

Imported merchandise CIF	100.00

+ Import Duty (a) @ 5 pct	105.00
+ VAT (KDV) (b) @ 18 pct	123.90= cost to distributor
+ Distributor markup (c) @ 25 pct	154.88= cost to retailer
+ Retailer markup (c) @ 25 pct	193.60 = cost to consumer

(a) Duties: Turkey applies EU's common external tariffs to third countries including the U.S. Overall duty rates have been declining over time and are now averaging approximately five percent.
(b) VAT tax varies depending on product: "luxury" items, 26 percent; general, 18 percent; food, 1 percent; automobiles (exceeding 1600 cc), 40 percent.
(c) Markups are hypothetical, but reflect observed prices. Distributor / retailer markups are not limited by law, only demand and competition.

SUPPLEMENTS

IMPORTANT CONTACTS

CHAMBER OF COMMERCE

ACIPAYAM CHAMBER OF COMMERCE
Address : D.Ü.Ç YOLU ÜZERİ SARGIN APT. KAT : 1 NO:2-4
Province : DENİZLİ / ACIPAYAM
Phone 1 : +90 258-5183409
Phone 2 :
Fax : +90 258-5184903
WEB : http://acipayamticaretodasi.org.tr/
E-Mail :
PRESIDENT OF BOARD OF DIRECTOR : MEHMET SÜRÜCÜOĞLU
PRESIDENT OF ASSEMBLY : AYHAN SARGIN
SECRETARY GENERAL : BAHTİYAR ASLAN

ADANA CHAMBER OF COMMERCE
Address : ABİDİNPAŞA CAD. NO:42/A
Province : ADANA / -
Phone 1 : +90 322-3513911-
Phone 2 : +90 322-3515506-
Fax : +90 322-3518009
WEB : http://www.adana-to.org.tr
E-Mail : yazi@adana-to.org.tr
PRESIDENT OF BOARD OF DIRECTOR : ATİLA MENEVŞE
PRESIDENT OF ASSEMBLY : TARKAN KULAK
SECRETARY GENERAL : AHMET NEVRUZ

ALIAGA CHAMBER OF COMMERCE
Address : KAZIM DİRİK MAH. 262.SOK. NO:29
Province : İZMİR / ALİAĞA
Phone 1 : +90 232-6164151-
Phone 2 :
Fax : +90 232-6166772
WEB : http://www.alto.org.tr/
E-Mail : bilgi@alto.org.tr
PRESIDENT OF BOARD OF DIRECTOR : ADNAN SAKA
PRESIDENT OF ASSEMBLY : MEVLÜT ENDER ÖZER
SECRETARY GENERAL : TAKDİR YARIŞ

ANKARA CHAMBER OF COMMERCE
Address : ATO SARAYI ESKİŞEHİR YOLU SÖĞÜTÖZÜ MAHALLESİ 2.CAD.NO:5 06530
Province : ANKARA / -
Phone 1 : +90 312-2857950
Phone 2 :
Fax : +90 312-2863446-
WEB : http://www.atonet.org.tr/
E-Mail : info@atonet.com
PRESIDENT OF BOARD OF DIRECTOR : SALİH BEZCİ
PRESIDENT OF ASSEMBLY : OSMAN NURETTİN GÜRGÜR
SECRETARY GENERAL : AHMET KUTUP GÜRAN

AYDIN CHAMBER OF COMMERCE
Address : ÜRGEN PAŞA CAD.NO:13
Province : AYDIN / -
Phone 1 : +90 256-2132202
Phone 2 :
Fax : +90 256-2128254-
WEB : http://www.atob.org.tr/
E-Mail : aydin.info@atob.org.tr
PRESIDENT OF BOARD OF DIRECTOR : HAKAN ÜLKEN
PRESIDENT OF ASSEMBLY : ABDULLAH SEFA YÜKSEL
SECRETARY GENERAL : İLKNUR KABASAKAL

AYVALIK CHAMBER OF COMMERCE
Address : FEVZİ PAŞA MAH.GÜMRÜK CADDESİ ESKİ PTT SOKAK NO:10 10400
Province : BALIKESİR / AYVALIK
Phone 1 : +90 266-3121517-
Phone 2 :
Fax : +90 266-3122283
WEB : http://www.ayvalikto.org.tr/
E-Mail : ayvalikto@tobb.org.tr
PRESIDENT OF BOARD OF DIRECTOR : BENHAN İBRAHİM KANTARCI
PRESIDENT OF ASSEMBLY : AHMET ŞEFİK SÜNER
SECRETARY GENERAL : AHMET BAÇ

BABADAG CHAMBER OF COMMERCE
Address : HÜKÜMET CADDESİ NO:1
Province : DENİZLİ / BABADAĞ
Phone 1 : +90 258-4812026
Phone 2 :
Fax : +90 258-4812026
WEB :
E-Mail :
PRESIDENT OF BOARD OF DIRECTOR : ASIM AKTEPE
PRESIDENT OF ASSEMBLY : İSMAİL KASAPLAR
SECRETARY GENERAL : SENA TARAKÇI

BALIKESIR CHAMBER OF COMMERCE
Address : BASIN SOK.NO.10/2-3
Province : BALIKESİR / -
Phone 1 : +90 266-2446868
Phone 2 :
Fax : +90 266-2446781

WEB : http://www.bato.org.tr/
E-Mail : info@bato.org.tr
PRESIDENT OF BOARD OF DIRECTOR : FAHRİ ERMİŞLER
PRESIDENT OF ASSEMBLY : MUSTAFA KEREM KIRIMLI
SECRETARY GENERAL : SERKAN ACAR

BANDIRMA CHAMBER OF COMMERCE
Address : MEHMET AKİF ERSOY CADDESİ NO:29 K:2
Province : BALIKESİR / BANDIRMA
Phone 1 : +90 266-7151800-
Phone 2 : +90 7151802-7151
Fax : +90 266-7151806
WEB : http://www.bandirmato.org.tr
E-Mail : bandirmaticoda@superonline.com
PRESIDENT OF BOARD OF DIRECTOR : MEHMET KILKIŞLI
PRESIDENT OF ASSEMBLY : BAHADIR ÇENBERCİ
SECRETARY GENERAL : SERAP ÖZDEMİR

BAYINDIR CHAMBER OF COMMERCE
Address : ATATÜRK CADDESİ NO:46
Province : İZMİR / BAYINDIR
Phone 1 : +90 232-5813504
Phone 2 :
Fax : +90 232-5817215
WEB : http://www.bayindirto.tobb.org.tr
E-Mail :
PRESIDENT OF BOARD OF DIRECTOR : ADNAN İNANIR
PRESIDENT OF ASSEMBLY : YAVUZ ŞENDİL
SECRETARY GENERAL : ÖZGÜR ARIK

BERGAMA CHAMBER OF COMMERCE
Address : BANKALAR CAD.NO:47/2
Province : İZMİR / BERGAMA
Phone 1 : +90 232-6331078-
Phone 2 :
Fax : +90 232-6320594
WEB : http://www.berto.org.tr/
E-Mail : bergamato@tobb.org.tr
PRESIDENT OF BOARD OF DIRECTOR : FİKRET ÜRPER
PRESIDENT OF ASSEMBLY : EROL IŞILDAK
SECRETARY GENERAL : GÜLAY KOÇ

BEYPAZARI CHAMBER OF COMMERCE
Address : GAZİ GÜNDÜZALP İŞ MERK. K:1 NO:61 06730
Province : ANKARA / BEYPAZARI
Phone 1 : +90 0312-7628989
Phone 2 :
Fax : +90 0312-7628988
WEB : http://www.beypazarito.tobb.org.tr/
E-Mail : beypazarito@tobb.org.tr
PRESIDENT OF BOARD OF DIRECTOR : HAMDİ NECDET ÇALIŞKAN
PRESIDENT OF ASSEMBLY : ALİ NİYAZİ ERCAN
SECRETARY GENERAL : MEHMET YURDAKUL

BEYSEHIR CHAMBER OF COMMERCE
Address : EVSAT MAH.ŞEHİT MAHMUT AKSIN SOK. NO:2/204
Province : KONYA / BEYŞEHİR
Phone 1 : +90 332-5122134
Phone 2 :
Fax : +90 332-5127021
WEB : http://www.beysehirto.org.tr/
E-Mail : beysehirto@tobb.org.tr
PRESIDENT OF BOARD OF DIRECTOR : SALİH GÜL
PRESIDENT OF ASSEMBLY : ALİ BİLİR
SECRETARY GENERAL : MEHMET TÜLEK

BODRUM CHAMBER OF COMMERCE
Address : YOKUŞBAŞI MAH.KIBRIS ŞEHİTLERİ CAD. KOCADERE MEVKİİ
Province : MUĞLA / BODRUM
Phone 1 : +90 252-3161412
Phone 2 : +90 252-3138405
Fax : +90 252-3131694
WEB : http://www.bodto.org.tr/
E-Mail : bilgi@bodto.org.tr
PRESIDENT OF BOARD OF DIRECTOR : MAHMUT SERDAR KOCADON
PRESIDENT OF ASSEMBLY : İLHAN ERSAN
SECRETARY GENERAL : PROF.DR.FUAT ÖNDER

BULDAN CHAMBER OF COMMERCE
Address : HÜKÜMET CAD.NO:20
Province : DENİZLİ / BULDAN
Phone 1 : +90 258-4313009
Phone 2 :
Fax : +90 258-4315585
WEB : http://www.buldanticaretodasi.org.tr
E-Mail :
PRESIDENT OF BOARD OF DIRECTOR : HALİL BAŞTÜRKMEN
PRESIDENT OF ASSEMBLY : NAZİF ÇAKAR
SECRETARY GENERAL : AYHAN EMİRDAĞ

BUNYAN CHAMBER OF COMMERCE
Address : DERVİŞAĞA MAH. HALI FUARI CAD. NO:2
Province : KAYSERİ / BÜNYAN
Phone 1 : +90 352-7121147
Phone 2 :
Fax : +90 352-7121147
WEB : http://www.bunyanto.org.tr
E-Mail : bunyanto@tobb.org.tr
PRESIDENT OF BOARD OF DIRECTOR : NAİM YAVUZ
PRESIDENT OF ASSEMBLY : AHMET HAMDİ GÖKÇE

SECRETARY GENERAL : AHMET REŞAT ALTAY

BURHANIYE CHAMBER OF COMMERCE
Address : KOCACAMİ MAH.HÜRRİYET CAD. NO:58/2
Province : BALIKESİR / BURHANİYE
Phone 1 : +90 266-4221044
Phone 2 :
Fax : +90 266-4127328
WEB : http://www.burhaniyeto.org.tr/
E-Mail :
PRESIDENT OF BOARD OF DIRECTOR : HÜSEYİN SARIBAŞ
PRESIDENT OF ASSEMBLY : MUSTAFA AYSEL
SECRETARY GENERAL : ERSEL PAZARBAŞI

CEYHAN CHAMBER OF COMMERCE
Address : HÜKÜMET CAD.NO:77
Province : ADANA / CEYHAN
Phone 1 : +90 322-6131073-
Phone 2 :
Fax : +90 322-6132044
WEB : http://www.ceyhanto.org.tr/
E-Mail :
PRESIDENT OF BOARD OF DIRECTOR : ŞEREF CAN
PRESIDENT OF ASSEMBLY : MEHMET ALİ TOPTAŞ
SECRETARY GENERAL : ZAFER ÖZ

CUMRA CHAMBER OF COMMERCE
Address : İZZETBEY MAH.SEDEF SOK.NO:6/1
Province : KONYA / ÇUMRA
Phone 1 : +90 332-4471066
Phone 2 :
Fax : +90 332-4476928
WEB : http://www.cumrato.org/
E-Mail :
PRESIDENT OF BOARD OF DIRECTOR : METİN KURAL
PRESIDENT OF ASSEMBLY : MEHMET ALİ AYKUT
SECRETARY GENERAL : AHMET TEMİZ

DENIZLI CHAMBER OF COMMERCE
Address : SARAYLAR MAH.SALTAK CAD. NO:5
Province : DENİZLİ / -
Phone 1 : +90 258-2611939-
Phone 2 :
Fax : +90 258-2651705-
WEB : http://www.dto.org.tr/
E-Mail : info@dto.org.tr
PRESIDENT OF BOARD OF DIRECTOR : NECDET ÖZER
PRESIDENT OF ASSEMBLY : HABİB YILDIZ
SECRETARY GENERAL : ALİ RIZA TEKİN

DEVELI CHAMBER OF COMMERCE
Address : İBRAHİMAĞA MAH.İNÖNÜ CAD. NO:10/A
Province : KAYSERİ / DEVELİ
Phone 1 : +90 352-6216181-
Phone 2 :
Fax : +90 352-6219590
WEB : http://www.develito.org.tr/
E-Mail : develito@develito.org.tr, develito@tobb.org.tr
PRESIDENT OF BOARD OF DIRECTOR : MUSTAFA MAŞLAK
PRESIDENT OF ASSEMBLY : UĞUR ÖZYALÇIN
SECRETARY GENERAL : AHMET SÜHA BÜLBÜL

DİDİM CHAMBER OF COMMERCE
Address : YENİMAHALLE 19 MAYIS CADDESİ NO:19
Province : AYDIN / DİDİM
Phone 1 : +90 256-8112563
Phone 2 :
Fax : +90 256-8113558
WEB : http://www.didimto.org.tr/
E-Mail : didimticaretodasi@hotmail.com
PRESIDENT OF BOARD OF DIRECTOR : ŞABAN ÜSTÜNDAĞ
PRESIDENT OF ASSEMBLY : HİLMİ YILDIRIM
SECRETARY GENERAL : MUSTAFA ERĞAN

DOGANHISAR CHAMBER OF COMMERCE
Address : ŞIH MAHALLESİ FATİH SOKAK NO :17
Province : KONYA / DOĞANHİSAR
Phone 1 : +90 332-5561140
Phone 2 :
Fax : +90 332-5562549
WEB : http://www.doganhisarto.org.tr/
E-Mail : doganhisarto@tobb.org.tr
PRESIDENT OF BOARD OF DIRECTOR : ABDULLAH SAMİ ACAR
PRESIDENT OF ASSEMBLY : MESUT ÜSTÜNKOL
SECRETARY GENERAL : ŞENER TOKLU

EDREMIT CHAMBER OF COMMERCE
Address : MENDERES BULVARI NO:85 10300
Province : BALIKESİR / EDREMİT
Phone 1 : +90 266-3731061-
Phone 2 :
Fax : +90 266-3733963
WEB : http://www.edremit-to.org.tr/
E-Mail : edrticodasi@ttnet.net.tr
PRESIDENT OF BOARD OF DIRECTOR : İSMAİL AYNUR
PRESIDENT OF ASSEMBLY : NECATİ UYTUN
SECRETARY GENERAL : RECEP AKGÜN

ERDEK CHAMBER OF COMMERCE

Address : YALI MAHALLESİ-MÜZE SOKAK NO:11 10500
Province : BALIKESİR / ERDEK
Phone 1 : +90 266-8351090
Phone 2 :
Fax : +90 266-8356292
WEB : http://www.erdekto.tobb.org.tr/index.htm
E-Mail : ahmetdiler_eto@hotmail.com
PRESIDENT OF BOARD OF DIRECTOR : FAİKA ÖZLEM SARI
PRESIDENT OF ASSEMBLY : HALUK CAN TURAN
SECRETARY GENERAL : HATİCE DİLEK LAP

ESKISEHIR CHAMBER OF COMMERCE
Address : 2 EYLÜL CAD.NO:38/6 26010
Province : ESKİŞEHİR / -
Phone 1 : +90 222-2307230-
Phone 2 :
Fax : +90 222-2307233
WEB : http://www.etonet.org.tr/
E-Mail : bilgi@etonet.org.tr, servis@etonet.org.tr
PRESIDENT OF BOARD OF DIRECTOR : METİN GÜLER
PRESIDENT OF ASSEMBLY : AHMET İSKENDER BAYAR
SECRETARY GENERAL : ALİ VAROL

GAZIANTEP CHAMBER OF COMMERCE
Address : İNCİLİPINAR MAH. 16 NOLU SOKAK ŞEHİT KAMİL
Province : GAZİANTEP / -
Phone 1 : +90 342-2203030-
Phone 2 :
Fax : +90 342-2311041
WEB : http://www.gto.org.tr/
E-Mail : gto@gto.org.tr
PRESIDENT OF BOARD OF DIRECTOR : EYÜP BARTIK
PRESIDENT OF ASSEMBLY : ALİ YENER
SECRETARY GENERAL : İBRAHİM HALİL GÖÇER

GEBZE CHAMBER OF COMMERCE
Address : GÜZELLER MAHALLESİ-KAVAK CADDESİ NO:3
Province : KOCAELİ / GEBZE
Phone 1 : +90 262-6442234
Phone 2 :
Fax : +90 262-6466076
WEB : http://www.gebzeto.org.tr/
E-Mail : bilgi@gebzeto.org.tr
PRESIDENT OF BOARD OF DIRECTOR : NAİL ÇİLER
PRESIDENT OF ASSEMBLY : NEJAT HASAN KARAAĞAÇLI
SECRETARY GENERAL : MUSTAFA YAŞAR SEKİN

GONEN CHAMBER OF COMMERCE
Address : ALTAY MAH.10 NOLU SOKAK NO:7
Province : BALIKESİR / GÖNEN
Phone 1 : +90 266-7621091-
Phone 2 :
Fax : +90 266-7625899
WEB : http://www.gonento.tobb.org.tr/
E-Mail : gonento@tobb.org.tr
PRESIDENT OF BOARD OF DIRECTOR : HASAN ÖZÇAĞLAYAN
PRESIDENT OF ASSEMBLY : ALİ ÖZER
SECRETARY GENERAL : ALPER ÇETİNKAYA

HAYMANA CHAMBER OF COMMERCE
Address : SEYRAN MAH.ANKARA CAD. KILINÇ İŞ MERKEZİ NO:13/5
Province : ANKARA / HAYMANA
Phone 1 : +90 312-6581562
Phone 2 : +90 312-6582450
Fax : +90 312-6581562
WEB :
E-Mail :
PRESIDENT OF BOARD OF DIRECTOR : ERCAN ÖZKAN
PRESIDENT OF ASSEMBLY : MEVLÜT ÖZER
SECRETARY GENERAL : ALİ BİÇER

ILGIN CHAMBER OF COMMERCE
Address : CAMİATİK MAH.MUHSİN YAZICIOĞLU CAD. TİCARET İŞ MERKEZİ K:2 42600
Province : KONYA / ILGIN
Phone 1 : +90 332-8816138-
Phone 2 : +90 8816159
Fax : +90 332-8827383
WEB : http://www.ilginto.org.tr/
E-Mail :
PRESIDENT OF BOARD OF DIRECTOR : VEHBİ ÖZLEN
PRESIDENT OF ASSEMBLY : MUSTAFA PALA
SECRETARY GENERAL : BÜLENT ŞÜKRÜ TEKTEK

ISLAHIYE CHAMBER OF COMMERCE
Address : ÇAMLICA MAHALLESİ İSTASYON CADDESİ 278000
Province : GAZİANTEP / İSLAHİYE
Phone 1 : +90 342-8621126
Phone 2 :
Fax : +90 342-8631465
WEB : http://www.islahiyeto.org.tr
E-Mail : islahiyeto@tobb.org.tr
PRESIDENT OF BOARD OF DIRECTOR : SELAHATTİN TÜRKMEN
PRESIDENT OF ASSEMBLY : OSMAN YILDIRIM
SECRETARY GENERAL : HAŞİM ERDOĞAN

ISTANBUL CHAMBER OF COMMERCE
Address : REŞADİYE CADDESİ NO:7 EMİNÖNÜ
Province : İSTANBUL / -

Phone 1 : +90 212-4556000
Phone 2 :
Fax : +90 212-5131565-
WEB : http://www.ito.org.tr
E-Mail : ito@ito.org.tr
PRESIDENT OF BOARD OF DIRECTOR : İBRAHİM ÇAĞLAR
PRESIDENT OF ASSEMBLY : ŞEKİB AVDAGİÇ
SECRETARY GENERAL : ÖMER BAL

IZMIR CHAMBER OF COMMERCE
Address : ATATÜRK CAD.NO:126 PASAPORT-ALSANCAK
Province : İZMİR / -
Phone 1 : +90 4449292
Phone 2 :
Fax : +90 232-4984698
WEB : http://www.izto.org.tr/
E-Mail : info@izto.org.tr
PRESIDENT OF BOARD OF DIRECTOR : EKREM DEMİRTAŞ
PRESIDENT OF ASSEMBLY : REBİİ AKDURAK
SECRETARY GENERAL : DUYGU MUTLUEL

KADIRLI CHAMBER OF COMMERCE
Address : SAVRUN MAH.TURGUT ÖZAL CAD. NO:39
Province : OSMANİYE / KADİRLİ
Phone 1 : +90 0328-7181175
Phone 2 : +90 7182430
Fax : +90 328-7175504
WEB : http://www.kadirlito.tobb.org.tr
E-Mail : kadirlito@tobb.org.tr
PRESIDENT OF BOARD OF DIRECTOR : HASAN KASTAL
PRESIDENT OF ASSEMBLY : MEHMETHAN YÜKSEL
SECRETARY GENERAL : ŞİNASİ DEMİRALAY

KAYSERI CHAMBER OF COMMERCE
Address : KİÇİKAPI TENNURİ SOK. NO:6
Province : KAYSERİ / -
Phone 1 : +90 352-2224528-
Phone 2 : +90 2224444
Fax : +90 352-2321069-
WEB : http://www.kayserito.org.tr
E-Mail : kaytic@kayserito.org.tr
PRESIDENT OF BOARD OF DIRECTOR : MAHMUT HİÇYILMAZ
PRESIDENT OF ASSEMBLY : MEHMET FİLİZ
SECRETARY GENERAL : MURAT YERLİKHAN

KOCAELİ CHAMBER OF COMMERCE
Address : KARABAŞ MAH. ÖMER TÜRKÇAKAL BULVARI NO:2 İZMİT/KOCAELİ
Province : KOCAELİ / -
Phone 1 : +90 262-3223010
Phone 2 :
Fax : +90 262-3216918-
WEB : http://www.koto.org.tr/
E-Mail : koto@koto.org.tr
PRESIDENT OF BOARD OF DIRECTOR : MURAT ÖZDAĞ
PRESIDENT OF ASSEMBLY : BÜLENT KARAGÖZ
SECRETARY GENERAL : YAŞAR OKTAY BALTALI

KONYA CHAMBER OF COMMERCE
Address : VATAN CAD. NO:1 SELÇUKLU
Province : KONYA / -
Phone 1 : +90 332- 2215252
Phone 2 :
Fax : +90 332-3530546
WEB : http://www.kto.org.tr/
E-Mail : kto@kto.org.tr
PRESIDENT OF BOARD OF DIRECTOR : SELÇUK ÖZTÜRK
PRESIDENT OF ASSEMBLY : AHMET ARICI
SECRETARY GENERAL : MUSTAFA ÖDEMİŞ

KOZAN CHAMBER OF COMMERCE
Address : CUMHURİYET MAH. EMNİYET SOK. NO: 4
Province : ADANA / KOZAN
Phone 1 : +90 322-5158466-
Phone 2 :
Fax : +90 322-5158466
WEB : http://www.kozanto.tobb.org.tr/
E-Mail : kozanticodasi@mynet.com
PRESIDENT OF BOARD OF DIRECTOR : HİLMİ BAYSAL
PRESIDENT OF ASSEMBLY : YAŞAR ÇELEN
SECRETARY GENERAL : TANER KAVUKLU

KÖRFEZ CHAMBER OF COMMERCE
Address : HACI OSMAN MAH. HIZIRREİS CAD. NO.130 41780
Province : KOCAELİ / KÖRFEZ
Phone 1 : +90 262-5284800
Phone 2 : +90 533-9680115-
Fax : +90 262-5288322
WEB : http://www.korfezto.org.tr
E-Mail :
PRESIDENT OF BOARD OF DIRECTOR : MUSTAFA EFE
PRESIDENT OF ASSEMBLY : GÜNGÖR AYHAN
SECRETARY GENERAL : KENAN MİNTAŞ

KUSADASI CHAMBER OF COMMERCE
Address : İKİÇEŞMELİK MAH.SÜLEYMAN DEMİREL BULVARI NO:31
Province : AYDIN / KUŞADASI
Phone 1 : +90 256-6125763-
Phone 2 :
Fax : +90 256-6145393
WEB : http://www.kuto.org.tr/
E-Mail : kusadasito@tobb.org.tr

PRESIDENT OF BOARD OF DIRECTOR : SERDAR AKDOĞAN
PRESIDENT OF ASSEMBLY : MAHMUT ÖZTAŞ
SECRETARY GENERAL : BURHAN SEZER

MARMARİS CHAMBER OF COMMERCE
Address : MERKEZ MAHALLESİ 350.SOKAK NO:5 48700 ARMUTALAN
Province : MUĞLA / MARMARİS
Phone 1 : +90 252-4170469-
Phone 2 :
Fax : +90 252-4170483
WEB : http://www.mto.org.tr/
E-Mail : mto@mto.org.tr
PRESIDENT OF BOARD OF DIRECTOR : MEHMET BAYSAL
PRESIDENT OF ASSEMBLY : AHMET ALİ KANSU
SECRETARY GENERAL : TAŞKIN BAYKARA

MENEMEN CHAMBER OF COMMERCE
Address : ERTUĞRUL CADDESİ NO-15 35660
Province : İZMİR / MENEMEN
Phone 1 : +90 232-8321021-
Phone 2 : +90 232-8321029
Fax : +90 0232-8321634
WEB : http://www.menemento.tobb.org.tr
E-Mail :
PRESIDENT OF BOARD OF DIRECTOR : YILMAZ GÜRAL
PRESIDENT OF ASSEMBLY : ALİ AZGIN
SECRETARY GENERAL : GÖNÜL ORUN

NAZILLI CHAMBER OF COMMERCE
Address : KARAÇAY MAH.REŞİT GALİP CAD.NO:1
Province : AYDIN / NAZİLLİ
Phone 1 : +90 256-3131678
Phone 2 :
Fax : +90 256-3156251
WEB : http://www.naztic.org.tr/
E-Mail : naztic@naztic.org.tr
PRESIDENT OF BOARD OF DIRECTOR : NURİ ARSLAN
PRESIDENT OF ASSEMBLY : GÜRDAL YÜZÜGÜLER
SECRETARY GENERAL : ERAY RÜŞTÜ TAKA

NIZIP CHAMBER OF COMMERCE
Address : İSTASYON MAHALLESİ İSTASYON CAD.NO: 2
Province : GAZİANTEP / NİZİP
Phone 1 : +90 342-5171011-
Phone 2 :
Fax : +90 342-5121036
WEB : http://www.nto.org.tr/
E-Mail : info@nto.org.tr, nto@nizip.com
PRESIDENT OF BOARD OF DIRECTOR : MEHMET ÖZYURT
PRESIDENT OF ASSEMBLY : MUSTAFA DOKTOROĞLU
SECRETARY GENERAL : SERPİL GÜNDOĞDU

ODEMIS CHAMBER OF COMMERCE
Address : ÜÇ EYLÜL MAH.ORDU CAD.NO:1 35760
Province : İZMİR / ÖDEMİŞ
Phone 1 : +90 232-5431168-
Phone 2 :
Fax : +90 232-5441630
WEB : http://www.odemisto.org.tr/
E-Mail : odemisto@tobb.org.tr
PRESIDENT OF BOARD OF DIRECTOR : KASIM SEVİN
PRESIDENT OF ASSEMBLY : ALİM KORKMAZ
SECRETARY GENERAL : MEHMET SOYER

POLATLI CHAMBER OF COMMERCE
Address : KARAPINAR CAD.ŞEN SOK.NO.2/3
Province : ANKARA / POLATLI
Phone 1 : +90 312-6231084
Phone 2 :
Fax : +90 312-6229552
WEB : http://www.pto.org.tr/
E-Mail : iletisim@pto.org.tr
PRESIDENT OF BOARD OF DIRECTOR : ULVİ SAKARYA
PRESIDENT OF ASSEMBLY : YAŞAR MURAT ÇELİK
SECRETARY GENERAL : LEMAN SİBEL ÖZEKEN

SARAYKOY CHAMBER OF COMMERCE
Address : BELEDİYE İŞHANI NO:109
Province : DENİZLİ / SARAYKÖY
Phone 1 : +90 258-4151061
Phone 2 :
Fax : +90 258-4151061
WEB : http://www.saraykoyticaretodasi.org.tr/
E-Mail : saraykoyto@tobb.org.tr
PRESIDENT OF BOARD OF DIRECTOR : ORHAN DİKİCİ
PRESIDENT OF ASSEMBLY : ERHAN KILINÇ
SECRETARY GENERAL : AHMET DUMAN

SELCUK CHAMBER OF COMMERCE
Address : ATATÜRK MAH. 1064.SOK. NO:1
Province : İZMİR / SELÇUK
Phone 1 : +90 232-8927008-
Phone 2 :
Fax : +90 232-8927009
WEB : http://www.selcukticaretodasi.org.tr/
E-Mail : info@selcukticaretodasi.org.tr
PRESIDENT OF BOARD OF DIRECTOR : KORAY YOLCU
PRESIDENT OF ASSEMBLY : YUSUF DERELİ
SECRETARY GENERAL : FİLİZ ACARGİL

SEREFLIKOCHISAR CHAMBER OF COMMERCE
Address : İSTİKLAL MAHALLESİ ANKARA CADDESİ NO.188
Province : ANKARA / Ş.KOÇHİSAR
Phone 1 : +90 312-6871152
Phone 2 :
Fax : +90 312-6877272
WEB : http://www.sereflikochisarto.org.tr/
E-Mail :
PRESIDENT OF BOARD OF DIRECTOR : YASİN TEKİN
PRESIDENT OF ASSEMBLY : MAHMUT REŞAT ÜNSAL
SECRETARY GENERAL : FİKRET ONAT

SOKE CHAMBER OF COMMERCE
Address : KONAK MAH.YILDIRIM SOK.NO:22 KAT:2
Province : AYDIN / SÖKE
Phone 1 : +90 256-5182980
Phone 2 :
Fax : +90 256-5182331
WEB : http://www.sto.org.tr/
E-Mail :
PRESIDENT OF BOARD OF DIRECTOR : REŞAT ANYA
PRESIDENT OF ASSEMBLY : BEHLÜL ER
SECRETARY GENERAL : YUSUF ASAR

SUSURLUK CHAMBER OF COMMERCE
Address : HAN MAHALLESİ ŞEHİT FİKRET GÜNEY CAD. NO.6
Province : BALIKESİR / SUSURLUK
Phone 1 : +90 266-8654672
Phone 2 :
Fax : +90 266-8654673
WEB : http://www.susurlukto.org.tr
E-Mail :
PRESIDENT OF BOARD OF DIRECTOR : İLKER KURT
PRESIDENT OF ASSEMBLY : MEHMET ÇETİN
SECRETARY GENERAL : YÜCEL SARI

TAVAS CHAMBER OF COMMERCE
Address : BELEDİYE MEYDANI BELEDİYE "C" BLOK K:3 20500
Province : DENİZLİ / TAVAS
Phone 1 : +90 258-6131294
Phone 2 :
Fax : +90 258-6131294
WEB :
E-Mail : tavasto@tobb.org.tr
PRESIDENT OF BOARD OF DIRECTOR : SAFFET İNAMLIK
PRESIDENT OF ASSEMBLY : KEMAL BÜYÜKELYAS
SECRETARY GENERAL : EMİN SANDIKCI

TIRE CHAMBER OF COMMERCE
Address : KURTULUŞ MAH.İSMAİL TAŞLI CAD. NO:25 35900
Province : İZMİR / TİRE
Phone 1 : +90 232-5121079
Phone 2 : +90 5123673
Fax : +90 232-5125811
WEB : http://www.tireto.tobb.org.tr/
E-Mail : tireto@tobb.org.tr
PRESIDENT OF BOARD OF DIRECTOR : HÜSEYİN ÇAPKINOĞLU
PRESIDENT OF ASSEMBLY : İBRAHİM ŞENTÜRK
SECRETARY GENERAL : AYDIN TAŞAN

TORBALI CHAMBER OF COMMERCE
Address : TEPEKÖY MAH.KAZIMDİRİK CAD.NO:21/1 K:1
Province : İZMİR / TORBALI
Phone 1 : +90 232-8561334
Phone 2 :
Fax : +90 232-8568405
WEB : http://www.torbalito.tobb.org.tr/
E-Mail : torbalito@tobb.org.tr
PRESIDENT OF BOARD OF DIRECTOR : ABDULVAHAP OLGUN
PRESIDENT OF ASSEMBLY : ERKAN AKSOY
SECRETARY GENERAL : BAHADIR YILMAZER

YAHYALI CHAMBER OF COMMERCE
Address : CAMİKEBİR MAH.HACIHIDIROĞLU SOKAK NO:4 K:1-2
Province : KAYSERİ / YAHYALI
Phone 1 : +90 352-6113013
Phone 2 :
Fax : +90 352-6118968
WEB : http://yahyalito.org.tr
E-Mail : yahyalito@tobb.org.tr
PRESIDENT OF BOARD OF DIRECTOR : MUSTAFA TÜTÜNCÜ
PRESIDENT OF ASSEMBLY : ADNAN AYDIN
SECRETARY GENERAL : İBRAHİM PARLAK

CHAMBERS OF INDUSTRY

ADANA CHAMBER OF INDUSTRY
Address : TURHAN CEMAL BERİKER BULVARI NO:156 01130 SEYHAN-
Province : ADANA / -
Phone 1 : +90 322-4366363
Phone 2 :
Fax : +90 322-4361636
WEB : http://www.adaso.org.tr
E-Mail : adaso@adaso.org.tr
PRESIDENT OF BOARD OF DIRECTOR : ZEKİ KIVANÇ
PRESIDENT OF ASSEMBLY : HÜSEYİN NURİ ÇOMU
SECRETARY GENERAL : GAZİ YILMAZ

ANKARA CHAMBER OF INDUSTRY

Address : ATATÜRK BULVARI NO: 193 KAVAKLIDERE
Province : ANKARA / -
Phone 1 : +90 312-4171200
Phone 2 : +90 4735555
Fax : +90 312-4175205-
WEB : http://www.aso.org.tr
E-Mail : aso@aso.org.tr
PRESIDENT OF BOARD OF DIRECTOR : MEHMET NURETTİN ÖZDEBİR
PRESIDENT OF ASSEMBLY : ŞERAFETTİN CECELİ
SECRETARY GENERAL : YAVUZ CABBAR

AYDIN CHAMBER OF INDUSTRY
Address : ESKİ SANAYİ SİTESİ ALTI ATA MAH. 610.SOKAK 60.YIL İLKOKULU ARKASI SAİME CAMBAZOĞLU PARKI
Province : AYDIN / -
Phone 1 : +90 0256-2310404
Phone 2 :
Fax : +90 0256-2310405
WEB : http://www.ayso.org.tr/
E-Mail : info@ayso.org.tr
PRESIDENT OF BOARD OF DIRECTOR : MEHMET YUNUS ŞAHİN
PRESIDENT OF ASSEMBLY : ERCAN ÇERÇİOĞLU
SECRETARY GENERAL : KEREM ÖDEN

BALIKESIR CHAMBER OF INDUSTRY
Address : ORGANİZE SANAYİ BÖLGESİ 7.CAD. NO:3/C
Province : BALIKESİR / -
Phone 1 : +90 266-2811180
Phone 2 :
Fax : +90 266-2811189
WEB : http://www.bso.org.tr/
E-Mail : bso@bso.org.tr, balikesirso@tobb.org.tr
PRESIDENT OF BOARD OF DIRECTOR : İSMAİL UĞUR
PRESIDENT OF ASSEMBLY : HAKAN ÖZDAMAR
SECRETARY GENERAL : İBRAHİM BARBAROSHAN AYNAOĞLU

DENIZLI CHAMBER OF INDUSTRY
Address : ATATÜRK BULVARI NO:94/2-3
Province : DENİZLİ / -
Phone 1 : +90 258-2655599-
Phone 2 : +90 258-2655667
Fax : +90 258-2638125-
WEB : http://www.dso.org.tr/
E-Mail : dso@dso.org.tr
PRESIDENT OF BOARD OF DIRECTOR : MÜJDAT KEÇECİ
PRESIDENT OF ASSEMBLY : MEHMET TOSUNOĞLU
SECRETARY GENERAL : ZEREN GERELİOĞLU

EGE BOLGESI CHAMBER OF INDUSTRY
Address : CUMHURIYET BULV. NO:63 PASAPORT 35210
Province : İZMİR / -
Phone 1 : +90 232-4552905
Phone 2 :
Fax : +90 232-4894567
WEB : http://www.ebso.org.tr
E-Mail : mustafa.kalyoncu@ebso.org.tr
PRESIDENT OF BOARD OF DIRECTOR : ENDER YORGANCILAR
PRESIDENT OF ASSEMBLY : SALİH ESEN
SECRETARY GENERAL : MUSTAFA KALYONCU

ESKISEHIR CHAMBER OF INDUSTRY
Address : ORGANİZE SANAYİ BOLGESİ MÜMTAZ ZEYTİNOĞLU BULVARI 26110
Province : ESKİŞEHİR / -
Phone 1 : +90 222-2360360-
Phone 2 : +90 222-2360380
Fax : +90 222-2360041
WEB : http://www.eso.org.tr/
E-Mail : eso@eso.org.tr, info@eso.org.tr
PRESIDENT OF BOARD OF DIRECTOR : SAVAŞ MEHMET ÖZAYDEMİR
PRESIDENT OF ASSEMBLY : İSMAİL KUNDURACI
SECRETARY GENERAL : Y. EMRE HEPER

GAZIANTEP CHAMBER OF INDUSTRY
Address : İSTASYON CADDESİ TİCARET SARAYI K:4
Province : GAZİANTEP / -
Phone 1 : +90 342-2210900-
Phone 2 :
Fax : +90 342-2301682
WEB : http://www.gso.org.tr/
E-Mail : gso@gso.org.tr
PRESIDENT OF BOARD OF DIRECTOR : ADİL SANİ KONUKOĞLU
PRESIDENT OF ASSEMBLY : MUSTAFA TOPÇUOĞLU
SECRETARY GENERAL : KÜRŞAT GÖNCÜ

ISTANBUL CHAMBER OF INDUSTRY
Address : MESRUTİYET CAD. NO:62 TEPEBAŞI
Province : İSTANBUL / -
Phone 1 : +90 212-2522900(
Phone 2 : +90 212-2922200
Fax : +90 212-2495084-
WEB : http://www.iso.org.tr/
E-Mail : info@iso.org.tr
PRESIDENT OF BOARD OF DIRECTOR : ERDAL BAHÇIVAN
PRESIDENT OF ASSEMBLY : ZEYNEP BODUR OKYAY
SECRETARY GENERAL : MELEK US

KAYSERI CHAMBER OF INDUSTRY
Address : YENİ PERVANE MAH. KOCASİNAN BLV.NO:161
Province : KAYSERİ / -
Phone 1 : +90 352-2451050
Phone 2 :
Fax : +90 352-2451040-
WEB : http://www.kayso.org.tr/
E-Mail : info@kayso.org.tr
PRESIDENT OF BOARD OF DIRECTOR : MUSTAFA BOYDAK
PRESIDENT OF ASSEMBLY : NUREDDİN OKANDAN
SECRETARY GENERAL : NİHAT MOLU

KOCAELI CHAMBER OF INDUSTRY
Address : FUAR İÇİ 41040 İZMİT
Province : KOCAELİ / -
Phone 1 : +90 262-3158000-
Phone 2 :
Fax : +90 262-3219070
WEB : http://www.kosano.org.tr/
E-Mail : kso@kosano.org.tr
PRESIDENT OF BOARD OF DIRECTOR : AYHAN ZEYTİNOĞLU
PRESIDENT OF ASSEMBLY : HASAN TAHSİN TUĞRUL
SECRETARY GENERAL : MEMET BARIŞ TURABİ

KONYA CHAMBER OF INDUSTRY
Address : 1.ORGANİZE SANAYİ BÖLGESİ İSTİKAMET CAD. SELÇUKLU
Province : KONYA / -
Phone 1 : +90 332-2510670(
Phone 2 :
Fax : +90 332-2489351
WEB : http://www.kso.org.tr/
E-Mail : kso@kso.org.tr
PRESIDENT OF BOARD OF DIRECTOR : MEMİŞ KÜTÜKCÜ
PRESIDENT OF ASSEMBLY : TAHİR ŞAHİN
SECRETARY GENERAL : MUSTAFA SEDAT TAŞKAZAN

CHAMBERS OF COMMERCE AND INDUSTRY

ADIYAMAN CHAMBER OF COMMERCE AND INDUSTRY
Address : HOCAÖMER MAH.YAHYA KEMAL CAD. NO:14
Province : ADIYAMAN / -
Phone 1 : +90 416-2164646
Phone 2 : +90 416-2136375
Fax : +90 416-2149741
WEB : http://www.adiyamantso.org.tr
E-Mail : atso@adiyamantso.org.tr
PRESIDENT OF BOARD OF DIRECTOR : MUSTAFA USLU
PRESIDENT OF ASSEMBLY : MEHMET HANİFİ BEREKET
SECRETARY GENERAL : NAİM HARPUTLUOĞLU

AFSIN CHAMBER OF COMMERCE AND INDUSTRY
Address : ATATÜRK CAD.GEDİK SOK.SEVENLER PASAJI NO:17/A
Province : K.MARAŞ / AFŞİN
Phone 1 : +90 344-5118462-
Phone 2 :
Fax : +90 344-5114325
WEB : http://www.afsintso.org.tr
E-Mail : afsintso@hotmail.com
PRESIDENT OF BOARD OF DIRECTOR : BEKİR SITKI CAN
PRESIDENT OF ASSEMBLY : YUNUS KARABULUT
SECRETARY GENERAL : AYFER ASLAN

AFYONKARAHİSAR CHAMBER OF COMMERCE AND INDUSTRY
Address : DÖRTYOL MAH.TURGUT ÖZAL CAD. NO:69 (İZMİR KARAYOLU)
Province : AFYONKARAHİSAR / -
Phone 1 : +90 272-2135657
Phone 2 :
Fax : +90 272-2135660
WEB : http://www.afyontso.org.tr/
E-Mail : info@afyonkarahisartso.org.tr
PRESIDENT OF BOARD OF DIRECTOR : HÜSNÜ SERTESER
PRESIDENT OF ASSEMBLY : MEHMET ÇARKGİL
SECRETARY GENERAL : SÜLEYMAN UĞUR ÜNSOY

AGRI CHAMBER OF COMMERCE AND INDUSTRY
Address : ERZURUM CADDESİ AĞRI TİCARET VE SANAYİ ODASI HİZMET BİNASI 04100
Province : AĞRI / -
Phone 1 : +90 472-2151210
Phone 2 :
Fax : +90 472-2156463
WEB : http://www.agritso.org.tr
E-Mail :
PRESIDENT OF BOARD OF DIRECTOR : SAİM ALPASLAN
PRESIDENT OF ASSEMBLY : CEMAL YILDIRIM
SECRETARY GENERAL : FERDİ BAYCAN ÖGEL

AKCAKOCA CHAMBER OF COMMERCE AND INDUSTRY
Address : YALI MAH. BAHADIR YALÇIN CAD. NO:21
Province : DÜZCE / AKÇAKOCA
Phone 1 : +90 380-6114143

Phone 2 : +90 6114144
Fax : +90 380-6115944
WEB : http://www.akcakocatso.org.tr/
E-Mail : akcakocatso@tobb.org.tr
akcakocatso@hotmail.com
PRESIDENT OF BOARD OF DIRECTOR :
MEHMET NAZIM PAZVANT
PRESIDENT OF ASSEMBLY : HÜSNÜ KOÇ
SECRETARY GENERAL : KEMAL BAŞAR

AKHİSAR CHAMBER OF COMMERCE AND INDUSTRY
Address : TAHİR ÜN CAD.14 SOKAK NO:87 K:2
Province : MANİSA / AKHİSAR
Phone 1 : +90 236-4141563-
Phone 2 :
Fax : +90 236-4148044
WEB : http://www.akhisartso.org.tr
E-Mail : akhisartso@tobb.org.tr
PRESIDENT OF BOARD OF DIRECTOR :
ABDURRAHMAN YILMAZ
PRESIDENT OF ASSEMBLY : ŞENOL ÜRKÜP
SECRETARY GENERAL : ALİ ÖZKERVANCI

AKSARAY CHAMBER OF COMMERCE AND INDUSTRY
Address : HACILAR HARMANI MAH.5.BULVAR NO: 53/1 (TERMİNAL YOLU ÜZERİ)
Province : AKSARAY / -
Phone 1 : +90 382-4444756
Phone 2 : +90 2131049
Fax : +90 382-2139910
WEB : http://www.aksaraytso.org.tr
E-Mail : aksaraytso@gmail.com
PRESIDENT OF BOARD OF DIRECTOR :
AHMET KOÇAŞ
PRESIDENT OF ASSEMBLY : FATİH TEKİN
SECRETARY GENERAL : MUSTAFA MURAT YILMAZ

AKSEHIR CHAMBER OF COMMERCE AND INDUSTRY
Address : HÜKÜMET CAD.NO.12
Province : KONYA / AKŞEHİR
Phone 1 : +90 332-8133827
Phone 2 : +90 332-8133124
Fax : +90 332-8139708
WEB : http://www.aktso.org.tr
E-Mail :
PRESIDENT OF BOARD OF DIRECTOR :
ERDAL ÇİFTCİ
PRESIDENT OF ASSEMBLY : YUSUF İZZETTİN YAYLA
SECRETARY GENERAL : OSMAN ÇORUMLU

AKYAZI CHAMBER OF COMMERCE AND INDUSTRY
Address : ÖMERCİKLER MAH.BANKALAR CADDESİ NO:5
Province : SAKARYA / AKYAZI
Phone 1 : +90 264-4188485
Phone 2 :
Fax : +90 264-4181548-
WEB : http://akyazitso.tobb.org.tr/
E-Mail : akatso@superonline.com.tr
PRESIDENT OF BOARD OF DIRECTOR :
ZAFER ŞİNASİ BAYRAKTAR
PRESIDENT OF ASSEMBLY : MUZAFFER BAŞER
SECRETARY GENERAL : YALÇIN KARAÇAYIR

ALACA CHAMBER OF COMMERCE AND INDUSTRY
Address : BELEDİYE İŞHANI KAT:1 NO.101
Province : ÇORUM / ALACA
Phone 1 : +90 364-4115042
Phone 2 :
Fax : +90 364-4116486
WEB : http://alacatso.tobb.org.tr/
E-Mail : alacatso@tobb.org.tr
PRESIDENT OF BOARD OF DIRECTOR :
GÜNSER ŞİRİN
PRESIDENT OF ASSEMBLY : MEHMET ÖZARSLAN
SECRETARY GENERAL : FATİH ARSLAN

ALANYA CHAMBER OF COMMERCE AND INDUSTRY
Address : ATATÜRK CAD.NO:33 07400
Province : ANTALYA / ALANYA
Phone 1 : +90 242-5121697-
Phone 2 :
Fax : +90 242-5136907
WEB : http://www.altso.org.tr
E-Mail : altso@altso.org.tr
PRESIDENT OF BOARD OF DIRECTOR :
MEHMET ŞAHİN
PRESIDENT OF ASSEMBLY : METİN ATALAY
SECRETARY GENERAL : ERHAN AKMAN

ALAPLI CHAMBER OF COMMERCE AND INDUSTRY
Address : MERKEZ MAH. MEHMET AKİF ERSOY CAD. NO:26
Province : ZONGULDAK / ALAPLI
Phone 1 : +90 372-3786910
Phone 2 :
Fax : +90 372-3786903
WEB : http://www.alaplitso.tobb.org.tr
E-Mail :
PRESIDENT OF BOARD OF DIRECTOR :
RECEP OCAK
PRESIDENT OF ASSEMBLY : HASAN ÖZTÜRK
SECRETARY GENERAL : TANER ARSLAN

ALASEHİR CHAMBER OF COMMERCE AND INDUSTRY
Address : SOĞUKSU MAH.MEKTEP CAD.NO.58 45600
Province : MANİSA / ALAŞEHİR

Phone 1 : +90 236-6531061
Phone 2 :
Fax : +90 236-6543810
WEB : http://www.alasehirtso.com/
E-Mail : alasehirtso@tobb.org.tr
PRESIDENT OF BOARD OF DIRECTOR : MUSTAFA SEYHAN
PRESIDENT OF ASSEMBLY : HALDUN UYAR
SECRETARY GENERAL : BİROL ŞEN

AMASYA CHAMBER OF COMMERCE AND INDUSTRY
Address : ZİYAPAŞA BULVARI NO:31/1 05100
Province : AMASYA / -
Phone 1 : +90 358-2181079
Phone 2 : +90 358-2128235-
Fax : +90 358-2182397
WEB : http://www.amasyatso.org.tr/
E-Mail : amasyatso@tobb.org.tr
PRESIDENT OF BOARD OF DIRECTOR : MURAT KIRLANGIÇ
PRESIDENT OF ASSEMBLY : HASAN HÜSEYİN ERGEN
SECRETARY GENERAL : HASAN CİNBAZ

ANAMUR CHAMBER OF COMMERCE AND INDUSTRY
Address : GÖKTAŞ MAHALLESİ DR.ALPAY SOKAK
Province : MERSİN / ANAMUR
Phone 1 : +90 324-8141050
Phone 2 :
Fax : +90 324-8143085
WEB : http://www.anamurtso.org
E-Mail :
PRESIDENT OF BOARD OF DIRECTOR : FERİDUN TORUNOĞLU
PRESIDENT OF ASSEMBLY : ABDÜLKERİM ÇİLİNGİR
SECRETARY GENERAL : MUHAMMET ŞİMŞEK

ANTAKYA CHAMBER OF COMMERCE AND INDUSTRY
Address : CUMHURİYET MAH.ADNAN MENDERES CD.SEÇMEN APT. NO:24/2 EROL BİLECİK ENDÜSTRİ MESLEK LİSESİ KARŞISI
Province : HATAY / -
Phone 1 : +90 326-2165800
Phone 2 :
Fax : +90 326-2162405
WEB : http://www.antakyatso.org.tr/
E-Mail : antakyatso@tobb.org.tr
PRESIDENT OF BOARD OF DIRECTOR : HİKMET ÇİNÇİN
PRESIDENT OF ASSEMBLY : SELAHATTİN ESKİOCAK
SECRETARY GENERAL : SERDAR YILMAZ SARAÇ

ANTALYA CHAMBER OF COMMERCE AND INDUSTRY
Address : ÇEVRE YOLU ÜZERİ GÖKSU MAH.GAZİ BULVARI NO:531
Province : ANTALYA / -
Phone 1 : +90 242-3143737
Phone 2 :
Fax : +90 242-3143738-
WEB : http://www.atso.org.tr
E-Mail : info@atso.org.tr
PRESIDENT OF BOARD OF DIRECTOR : ÇETİN OSMAN BUDAK
PRESIDENT OF ASSEMBLY : İZZET BAYAR
SECRETARY GENERAL : VİLDAN DEMER

ARDAHAN CHAMBER OF COMMERCE AND INDUSTRY
Address : KARAGÖL MAH.KONGRE CAD. NO:64 KAT:4 MERKEZ
Province : ARDAHAN / -
Phone 1 : +90 478-2113036
Phone 2 :
Fax : +90 478-2112970
WEB : http://www.ardahantso.org.tr/
E-Mail :
PRESIDENT OF BOARD OF DIRECTOR : ÇETİN DEMİRCİ
PRESIDENT OF ASSEMBLY : SEBAHATTİN GÜNDOĞDU
SECRETARY GENERAL : İBRAHİM TIRPANCI

ARDEŞEN CHAMBER OF COMMERCE AND INDUSTRY
Address : ATATÜRK CADDESİ NO:86 K:3 53400
Province : RİZE / ARDEŞEN
Phone 1 : +90 464-7153524
Phone 2 :
Fax : +90 464-7155665
WEB : http://www.ardesentso.org.tr/
E-Mail :
PRESIDENT OF BOARD OF DIRECTOR : RECEP EKSİLMEZ
PRESIDENT OF ASSEMBLY : BÜLENT ESKİÇIRAK
SECRETARY GENERAL : ZEYNEP DALBASTI AYATA

ARHAVI CHAMBER OF COMMERCE AND INDUSTRY
Address : MUSAZADE MAH.CUMHURİYET MEYDANI CORDAN APT.K:2
Province : ARTVİN / ARHAVİ
Phone 1 : +90 466-3122335
Phone 2 : +90 466-3125541
Fax : +90 466-3122335
WEB : http://www.arhavitso.org.tr
E-Mail : arhavitso@tobb.org.tr
PRESIDENT OF BOARD OF DIRECTOR : ATIF KESİM
PRESIDENT OF ASSEMBLY : SERKAN ERGİN

SECRETARY GENERAL : NAZIM KARADENİZ

ARTVİN CHAMBER OF COMMERCE AND INDUSTRY
Address : ÇARŞI MAH.CUMHURİYET CAD. NO:5/2
Province : ARTVİN / -
Phone 1 : +90 466-2121061
Phone 2 :
Fax : +90 466-2125207
WEB : http://www.artvintso.tr/
E-Mail : artvintso@tobb.org.tr
PRESIDENT OF BOARD OF DIRECTOR : KURTUL ÖZEL
PRESIDENT OF ASSEMBLY : NACİ AKIN
SECRETARY GENERAL : ÖZTÜRK KALKAN

BABAESKI CHAMBER OF COMMERCE AND INDUSTRY
Address : BELEDİYE HAL DÜKKANLARI B-BLOK K:2
Province : KIRKLARELİ / BABAESKİ
Phone 1 : +90 288-5122031
Phone 2 :
Fax : +90 288-5125743
WEB :
E-Mail :
PRESIDENT OF BOARD OF DIRECTOR : SEBAHATTİN ÖNER
PRESIDENT OF ASSEMBLY : HASAN GÜRE
SECRETARY GENERAL : CENK DÖNMEZ

BAFRA CHAMBER OF COMMERCE AND INDUSTRY
Address : TEKEL CAD. NO:55
Province : SAMSUN / BAFRA
Phone 1 : +90 362-5425848
Phone 2 : +90 362-5431075
Fax : +90 362-5431075
WEB : http://www.bafratso.org.tr/
E-Mail : info@bafratso.org.tr
PRESIDENT OF BOARD OF DIRECTOR : GÖKSEL BAŞAR
PRESIDENT OF ASSEMBLY : NUR AYDINER MERAL
SECRETARY GENERAL : SUAT LEKESİZ

BARTIN CHAMBER OF COMMERCE AND INDUSTRY
Address : YUKARI ÇARŞI CAD. NO.20 KAT.3
Province : BARTIN / -
Phone 1 : +90 378-2271046-
Phone 2 :
Fax : +90 378-2282066
WEB : http://www.bartintso.org.tr/
E-Mail : info@bartintso.org
PRESIDENT OF BOARD OF DIRECTOR : CİHAT ÇAKIR
PRESIDENT OF ASSEMBLY : HALİL ÇELEN
SECRETARY GENERAL : MUSTAFA SOYAL

BATMAN CHAMBER OF COMMERCE AND INDUSTRY
Address : AKYÜREK MAH.32.CADDE NO:11
Province : BATMAN / -
Phone 1 : +90 488-2131245
Phone 2 :
Fax : +90 488-2137406
WEB : http://www.batso.org.tr/
E-Mail : info@batso.org.tr
PRESIDENT OF BOARD OF DIRECTOR : ABDULKADİR DEMİR
PRESIDENT OF ASSEMBLY : MEHMET EMİN ÇELİK
SECRETARY GENERAL : ŞEYHMUS İŞCAN

BAYBURT CHAMBER OF COMMERCE AND INDUSTRY
Address : ŞEYHHAYRAN MAH.DEDEKORKUT CADDESİ NO:46/3
Province : BAYBURT / -
Phone 1 : +90 458-2117013
Phone 2 :
Fax : +90 458-2116042
WEB : http://www.bayburttso.org.tr
E-Mail : bayburttso@hotmail.com
PRESIDENT OF BOARD OF DIRECTOR : İBRAHİM YUMAK
PRESIDENT OF ASSEMBLY : SÜLEYMAN SEYHAN
SECRETARY GENERAL : GÖKHAN ÖNDER KARAOĞLU

BIGA CHAMBER OF COMMERCE AND INDUSTRY
Address : HAMİDİYE MAH.İNÖNÜ CAD.NO:6
Province : ÇANAKKALE / BİGA
Phone 1 : +90 286-3164888
Phone 2 :
Fax : +90 286-3163238
WEB : http://www.bigatso.tobb.org.tr/
E-Mail : bigatso@tobb.org.tr
PRESIDENT OF BOARD OF DIRECTOR : ŞADAN DOĞAN
PRESIDENT OF ASSEMBLY : EŞREF TEMİZ
SECRETARY GENERAL : MUSTAFA MUTLU

BILECIK CHAMBER OF COMMERCE AND INDUSTRY
Address : 1.ORGANİZE SANAYİ BÖLGESİ
Province : BİLECİK / -
Phone 1 : +90 228-2160011-
Phone 2 :
Fax : +90 228-2160013
WEB : http://bileciktso.org/
E-Mail : bileciktso@tobb.org.tr
PRESIDENT OF BOARD OF DIRECTOR : FEVZİ UZUN
PRESIDENT OF ASSEMBLY : ALİ ERCAN
SECRETARY GENERAL : FUAT GÜLER

BINGOL CHAMBER OF COMMERCE AND INDUSTRY
Address : KÜLTÜR CADDESİ TİCARET VE ESNAF SARAYI K:1
Province : BİNGÖL / -
Phone 1 : +90 426-2133163
Phone 2 :
Fax : +90 426-2137594
WEB : http://www.bintso.org.tr/
E-Mail : bingolticsan@superonline.com
PRESIDENT OF BOARD OF DIRECTOR : ERKAN ÇALBAY
PRESIDENT OF ASSEMBLY : MEHMET ALİ BUĞRAHAN
SECRETARY GENERAL : HAKAN BAŞBOZKURT

BIRECIK CHAMBER OF COMMERCE AND INDUSTRY
Address : MEYDAN MAH.HASTANE CAD.NO:20/A
Province : Ş.URFA / BİRECİK
Phone 1 : +90 414-6521165
Phone 2 :
Fax : +90 414-6527825
WEB :
E-Mail : btsob@netbulmail.com
PRESIDENT OF BOARD OF DIRECTOR : MÜSLÜM ACAR
PRESIDENT OF ASSEMBLY : HÜSEYİN YAŞAR
SECRETARY GENERAL : NAZİRE NAZAN CENGİZ

BITLIS CHAMBER OF COMMERCE AND INDUSTRY
Address : BANKALAR CAD.NO:45
Province : BİTLİS / -
Phone 1 : +90 434-2267115
Phone 2 : +90 434-2265175
Fax : +90 434-2266695
WEB : http://www.bitlistso.org.tr/
E-Mail :
PRESIDENT OF BOARD OF DIRECTOR : DAVUT TEZCAN
PRESIDENT OF ASSEMBLY : ŞAHİN UZAR
SECRETARY GENERAL : BURHAN TOPYÜZ

BOGAZLIYAN CHAMBER OF COMMERCE AND INDUSTRY
Address : KAYSERİ CAD.CUMHURİYET MEYDANI NO:5 K:1
Province : YOZGAT / BOĞAZLIYAN
Phone 1 : +90 354-6454785
Phone 2 :
Fax : +90 354-6452718
WEB :
E-Mail :
PRESIDENT OF BOARD OF DIRECTOR : ÖCAL ÖCALAN
PRESIDENT OF ASSEMBLY : ABDULLAH GÜNGÖR
SECRETARY GENERAL : MUSTAFA ÇAĞRI KILIÇ

BOLU CHAMBER OF COMMERCE AND INDUSTRY
Address : BORAZANLAR MAH. D-100 KARAYOLU CAD. NO:42 MERKEZ
Province : BOLU / -
Phone 1 : +90 374-2151218-
Phone 2 : +90 2151692
Fax : +90 374-2151694
WEB : http://www.bolutso.org.tr/
E-Mail : info@bolutso.org.tr
PRESIDENT OF BOARD OF DIRECTOR : TÜRKER ATEŞ
PRESIDENT OF ASSEMBLY : GÖKHAN YAMAN
SECRETARY GENERAL : İSMAİL GÖREN

BOLVADIN CHAMBER OF COMMERCE AND INDUSTRY
Address : ESKİ HÜKÜMET MEYDANI KULE İŞ HANI K:1 D:9
Province : AFYONKARAHİSAR / BOLVADİN
Phone 1 : +90 272-6125010
Phone 2 :
Fax : +90 272-6114019
WEB : http://www.bolvadintso.com/
E-Mail :
PRESIDENT OF BOARD OF DIRECTOR : MURAT TABAK
PRESIDENT OF ASSEMBLY : ABDULKADİR ÖZKAL
SECRETARY GENERAL : İSMAİL ÖZDİLEK

BOR CHAMBER OF COMMERCE AND INDUSTRY
Address : NİĞDE CAD.KEÇECİLER İŞ HANI K:1
Province : NİĞDE / BOR
Phone 1 : +90 388-3117185
Phone 2 :
Fax : +90 388-3117185
WEB : http://www.bortso.tobb.org.tr/index.htm
E-Mail : bortso@tobb.org.tr
PRESIDENT OF BOARD OF DIRECTOR : NURETTİN ERİÇ
PRESIDENT OF ASSEMBLY : NİHAT TARIM
SECRETARY GENERAL : ŞANVER KARAÇAY

BORCKA CHAMBER OF COMMERCE AND INDUSTRY
Address : KARS CADDESİ
Province : ARTVİN / BORÇKA
Phone 1 : +90 466-4151117
Phone 2 :
Fax : +90 466-4153777

WEB : http://www.borckatso.tobb.org.tr/
E-Mail : borckatso@tobb.org.tr
PRESIDENT OF BOARD OF DIRECTOR : EŞREF MERTTÜRK
PRESIDENT OF ASSEMBLY : MUHAMMET ÇAKMAK
SECRETARY GENERAL : HALİL ÖZTÜRK

BOYABAT CHAMBER OF COMMERCE AND INDUSTRY
Address : YUSUF KEMAL İNCE DAYI CADDESİ NO:3
Province : SİNOP / BOYABAT
Phone 1 : +90 368-3151203
Phone 2 :
Fax : +90 368-3156795
WEB : http://www.boyabattso.org.tr/
E-Mail :
PRESIDENT OF BOARD OF DIRECTOR : NUH TANDOĞAN
PRESIDENT OF ASSEMBLY : ZEKİ MOR
SECRETARY GENERAL : İRFAN ERŞAHİN

BOZÜYÜK CHAMBER OF COMMERCE AND INDUSTRY
Address : BELEDİYE İŞHANI KAT:3 NO:307-308
Province : BİLECİK / BOZÜYÜK
Phone 1 : +90 228-3142921-
Phone 2 :
Fax : +90 228-3142920
WEB : http://www.bozuyuktso.org.tr/
E-Mail : bozuyuk@bozuyuktso.org.tr
PRESIDENT OF BOARD OF DIRECTOR : BUĞRA LEVENT
PRESIDENT OF ASSEMBLY : MEHMET DOĞAN TUNÇ
SECRETARY GENERAL : BEDRİ ÖZTÜRK

BUCAK CHAMBER OF COMMERCE AND INDUSTRY
Address : OĞUZHAN MAH.OKULLAR CADDESİ NO:13
Province : BURDUR / BUCAK
Phone 1 : +90 248-3251101
Phone 2 :
Fax : +90 248-3256919
WEB : http://www.bucaktso.org.tr/
E-Mail : bucaktso@tobb.org.tr
PRESIDENT OF BOARD OF DIRECTOR : HASAN YALÇIN MEÇİKOĞLU
PRESIDENT OF ASSEMBLY : MALİK SARI
SECRETARY GENERAL : NEJMİ ÖREN

BULANCAK CHAMBER OF COMMERCE AND INDUSTRY
Address : İHSANİYE MAH.FATİH CAD. NO : 83 KAT : 1 28300
Province : GİRESUN / BULANCAK
Phone 1 : +90 454-3142829
Phone 2 :
Fax : +90 454-3181648
WEB : http://www.bulancak-tso.org.tr/
E-Mail : bulancak@bulancak-tso.org.tr, bulancaktso@tobb.org.tr
PRESIDENT OF BOARD OF DIRECTOR : ALİ FATOĞLU
PRESIDENT OF ASSEMBLY : NURETTİN ZERE
SECRETARY GENERAL : TUNAY GÜNDOĞAR

BURDUR CHAMBER OF COMMERCE AND INDUSTRY
Address : YENİ MAH.ŞEHİT TEĞMEN HALİL DEMİRÖRS CAD. NO:2
Province : BURDUR / -
Phone 1 : +90 248-2346205
Phone 2 : +90 2333317
Fax : +90 248-2336734
WEB : http://www.burdurtso.com/
E-Mail : burdur_tso@hotmail.com
PRESIDENT OF BOARD OF DIRECTOR : YUSUF KEYİK
PRESIDENT OF ASSEMBLY : FEYZİ OKTAY
SECRETARY GENERAL : SEDAT ÖZ

BURSA CHAMBER OF COMMERCE AND INDUSTRY
Address : ORGANİZE SANAYİ BÖLGESİ MAVİ CADDE 2.SOK.NO:2
Province : BURSA / -
Phone 1 : +90 224-2751600
Phone 2 :
Fax : +90 224-2751609
WEB : http://www.btso.org.tr/
E-Mail : btso@btso.org.tr
PRESIDENT OF BOARD OF DIRECTOR : İBRAHİM BURKAY
PRESIDENT OF ASSEMBLY : REMZİ TOPUK
SECRETARY GENERAL : HÜSEYİN GÜLER

CANAKKALE CHAMBER OF COMMERCE AND INDUSTRY
Address : ORGANİZE SANAYİ BÖLGESİ BURSA YOLU 7.KM. 1.CADDE NO:1
Province : ÇANAKKALE / -
Phone 1 : +90 286-2171014
Phone 2 : +90 286-2173046
Fax : +90 286-2130595
WEB : http://www.canakkaletso.org.tr/
E-Mail : oda@canakkaletso.org.tr
PRESIDENT OF BOARD OF DIRECTOR : BÜLEND ENGİN
PRESIDENT OF ASSEMBLY : OSMAN OKYAY
SECRETARY GENERAL : HALİME SEMA SANDAL

CANKIRI CHAMBER OF COMMERCE AND INDUSTRY
Address : KEÇECİLER CAD.NO:11
Province : ÇANKIRI / -
Phone 1 : +90 376-2131053

Phone 2 : +90 376-2133075
Fax : +90 376-2133114
WEB : http://www.catso.org.tr/
E-Mail : tic.san@catso.org.tr
PRESIDENT OF BOARD OF DIRECTOR : HAYRETTİN ÇELİKTEN
PRESIDENT OF ASSEMBLY : CAFER ÖZKAN
SECRETARY GENERAL : HÜLYA ATEŞ

CARSAMBA CHAMBER OF COMMERCE AND INDUSTRY
Address : ÇAY MAHALLESİ KÜÇÜK HAMAM SOK. NO:6/A
Province : SAMSUN / ÇARŞAMBA
Phone 1 : +90 362-8331360
Phone 2 : +90 362-8339281
Fax : +90 362-8339280
WEB : http://www.carsambatso.org.tr
E-Mail : bilgi@carsambatso.org.tr, carsambatso@hotmail.com
PRESIDENT OF BOARD OF DIRECTOR : AHMET YILMAZ
PRESIDENT OF ASSEMBLY : MUHARREM YARALI
SECRETARY GENERAL : GÜLTEKİN SÜRÜL

CAY CHAMBER OF COMMERCE AND INDUSTRY
Address : CUMHURİYET CADDESİ-BELEDİYE PASAJI K:1
Province : AFYONKARAHİSAR / ÇAY
Phone 1 : +90 272-6312087-
Phone 2 :
Fax : +90 272-6326801
WEB : http://www.caytso.org.tr
E-Mail : caytso_03@hotmail.com
PRESIDENT OF BOARD OF DIRECTOR : SALİH KAYGISIZ
PRESIDENT OF ASSEMBLY : ABDİL ERDOĞAN
SECRETARY GENERAL : MEHMET EFE UÇAN

CAYELI CHAMBER OF COMMERCE AND INDUSTRY
Address : ÇAYELİ BELEDİYESİ YENİ SİTESİ K:4
Province : RİZE / ÇAYELİ
Phone 1 : +90 464-5327510
Phone 2 :
Fax : +90 464-5321470
WEB : http://www.cayelitso.org.tr
E-Mail : cayeli_tso@hotmail.com
PRESIDENT OF BOARD OF DIRECTOR : GÜNGÖR SARI
PRESIDENT OF ASSEMBLY : VAHİT YILDIRIM
SECRETARY GENERAL : OSMAN DOĞRU

CİZRE CHAMBER OF COMMERCE AND INDUSTRY
Address : BELEDİYE CADDESİ NO: 28
Province : ŞIRNAK / CİZRE
Phone 1 : +90 486-6167254
Phone 2 :
Fax : +90 486-6167253
WEB : http://www.cizretso.tobb.org.tr
E-Mail : ctso98@hotmail.com
PRESIDENT OF BOARD OF DIRECTOR : SÜLEYMAN CAĞLI
PRESIDENT OF ASSEMBLY : ABDULLAH MÜŞTAK
SECRETARY GENERAL : MEHMET CASIM BOYACI

CORLU CHAMBER OF COMMERCE AND INDUSTRY
Address : CAMİATİK MAH.KANTARCI SOK.NO:14
Province : TEKİRDAĞ / ÇORLU
Phone 1 : +90 282-6511096
Phone 2 : +90 282-6527978
Fax : +90 282-6513510
WEB : http://www.corlutso.org.tr/
E-Mail : corlutso@yahoo.com
PRESIDENT OF BOARD OF DIRECTOR : ENİS SÜLÜN
PRESIDENT OF ASSEMBLY : METİN AKGÜN
SECRETARY GENERAL : İBRAHİM KARAĞÖZ

CORUM CHAMBER OF COMMERCE AND INDUSTRY
Address : GAZİ CAD. NO:18 19200
Province : ÇORUM / -
Phone 1 : +90 364-2244450
Phone 2 :
Fax : +90 364-2133205
WEB : http://www.ctso.org.tr/
E-Mail : sanod@ttnet.net.tr
PRESIDENT OF BOARD OF DIRECTOR : ÇETİN BAŞARANHINCAL
PRESIDENT OF ASSEMBLY : EROL KARADAŞ
SECRETARY GENERAL : MURAT ZEYBEL

ÇAYCUMA CHAMBER OF COMMERCE AND INDUSTRY
Address : ATATÜRK BULVARI NO.12
Province : ZONGULDAK / ÇAYCUMA
Phone 1 : +90 372-6151073
Phone 2 : +90 6157111
Fax : +90 372-6157326
WEB : http://www.caycumatso.tobb.org.tr/
E-Mail : caycumatso@tobb.org.tr
PRESIDENT OF BOARD OF DIRECTOR : RİFAT SARSIK
PRESIDENT OF ASSEMBLY : ERDOĞAN GÜNEY
SECRETARY GENERAL : ALPER PÜREN

ÇERKEZKÖY CHAMBER OF COMMERCE AND INDUSTRY

Address : GAZİ OSMAN PAŞA MAH. FEVZİ PAŞA CAD. NO:5-1 59500
Province : TEKİRDAĞ / ÇERKEZKÖY
Phone 1 : +90 282-7268888-
Phone 2 : +90 7268769
Fax : +90 282-7268889
WEB : http://www.cerkezkoytso.org.tr/
E-Mail : cer.tic.san.od@superonline.com
PRESIDENT OF BOARD OF DIRECTOR : SÜLEYMAN KOZUVA
PRESIDENT OF ASSEMBLY : TAHA ÜLKER
SECRETARY GENERAL : HAKAN GEL

DEMIRCI CHAMBER OF COMMERCE AND INDUSTRY
Address : HÜKÜMET CADDESİ NO:52
Province : MANİSA / DEMİRCİ
Phone 1 : +90 236-4621071
Phone 2 :
Fax : +90 236-4623868
WEB : http://www.demircitso.org.tr
E-Mail :
PRESIDENT OF BOARD OF DIRECTOR : MEHMET AKKILIÇ
PRESIDENT OF ASSEMBLY : GÖKHAN YILDIZEL
SECRETARY GENERAL : ŞENAY TİMURTAŞ SÖNMEZ

DEVREK CHAMBER OF COMMERCE AND INDUSTRY
Address : ESKİ MAH.SAZLIK ÇAYI MEVKİİ NO:2 67800
Province : ZONGULDAK / DEVREK
Phone 1 : +90 372-5563991
Phone 2 :
Fax : +90 372-5568166
WEB : http://www.devrektso.tobb.org.tr/
E-Mail : devrektso@tobb.org.tr
PRESIDENT OF BOARD OF DIRECTOR : ZEKAYİ BÜKRÜ
PRESIDENT OF ASSEMBLY : İLKİN TAŞÇI
SECRETARY GENERAL : CİHAT YABAN

DINAR CHAMBER OF COMMERCE AND INDUSTRY
Address : ÜÇLERCE MAH.ÜÇLERCE YOKUŞU
Province : AFYONKARAHİSAR / DİNAR
Phone 1 : +90 272-3536064
Phone 2 :
Fax : +90 272-3536546
WEB : http://www.dinartso.org.tr
E-Mail : dinartso@ttnet.net.tr
PRESIDENT OF BOARD OF DIRECTOR : AHMET HAKAN UYAN
PRESIDENT OF ASSEMBLY : AHMET ACAR
SECRETARY GENERAL : TANSU KURT

DIYARBAKIR CHAMBER OF COMMERCE AND INDUSTRY
Address : ALİ EMİRİ CAD.TİCARET MERKEZİ K:2-3
Province : DİYARBAKIR / -
Phone 1 : +90 412-2281718
Phone 2 : +90 412-2281719
Fax : +90 412-2244512
WEB : http://www.dtso.org.tr
E-Mail : dtso@turk.nets.com, ditso@ditso.org
PRESIDENT OF BOARD OF DIRECTOR : AHMET SAYAR
PRESIDENT OF ASSEMBLY : CELALETTİN BİRTANE
SECRETARY GENERAL : FERDANİ GÖKDERE

DOGUBAYAZIT CHAMBER OF COMMERCE AND INDUSTRY
Address : RIFKI BAŞKAYA CAD. TİCARET HİZMET BİNASI
Province : AĞRI / DOĞUBAYAZIT
Phone 1 : +90 472-3127853
Phone 2 :
Fax : +90 472-3125021
WEB : http://www.dogubayazittso.tobb.org.tr
E-Mail :
PRESIDENT OF BOARD OF DIRECTOR : ALİ EFE
PRESIDENT OF ASSEMBLY : ARİFE GÜL
SECRETARY GENERAL : NERİMAN MEMİŞ

DORTYOL CHAMBER OF COMMERCE AND INDUSTRY
Address : NUMUNE EVLER MAH. ABDİ İPEKÇİ CAD. NO:8
Province : HATAY / DÖRTYOL
Phone 1 : +90 326-7121041-
Phone 2 : +90 7130002-7127
Fax : +90 326-7121864
WEB : http://www.dortyoltso.org.tr
E-Mail : info@dortyoltso.org
PRESIDENT OF BOARD OF DIRECTOR : CEMAL TALAY
PRESIDENT OF ASSEMBLY : MEHMET EROL ERHAN
SECRETARY GENERAL : AHMET KARAPÜR

DUZCE CHAMBER OF COMMERCE AND INDUSTRY
Address : KÜLTÜR MAH.SÜLEYMAN KUYUMCU CAD. K:3 NO:11 81010
Province : DÜZCE / -
Phone 1 : +90 380-5242550
Phone 2 :
Fax : +90 380-5142855-
WEB : http://www.duzcetso.org.tr/
E-Mail : info@duzcetso.org.tr
PRESIDENT OF BOARD OF DIRECTOR : FAHRİ ÇAKIR
PRESIDENT OF ASSEMBLY : ERTAN TAŞLI
SECRETARY GENERAL : TUNCAY YÜKSEL

EDIRNE CHAMBER OF COMMERCE AND INDUSTRY
Address : 1.MURAT MAH.TALATPAŞA CAD. NO:80
Province : EDİRNE / -
Phone 1 : +90 284-2251014-
Phone 2 :
Fax : +90 284-2129864
WEB : http://www.etso.org.tr/
E-Mail : etso@etso.org.tr
PRESIDENT OF BOARD OF DIRECTOR : RECEP ZIPKINKURT
PRESIDENT OF ASSEMBLY : MEHMET EREN
SECRETARY GENERAL : NEVZAT TAŞKIN

ELAZIG CHAMBER OF COMMERCE AND INDUSTRY
Address : ÇARŞI MAH. MİMAR SİNAN CAD. ODA-BORSA İŞHANI NO:32 KAT:3
Province : ELAZIĞ / -
Phone 1 : +90 424-2183500
Phone 2 : +90 4443594
Fax : +90 424-2189690
WEB : http://www.elazigtso.org.tr/
E-Mail : elazigtso@elazigtso.org.tr
PRESIDENT OF BOARD OF DIRECTOR : ALİ ŞEKERDAĞ
PRESIDENT OF ASSEMBLY : ABDULHAMİT KAYA
SECRETARY GENERAL : MUSTAFA MEHMET KARABULUT

ELBISTAN CHAMBER OF COMMERCE AND INDUSTRY
Address : GÜNEŞLİ MAH.KARABAĞ CAD.N0:12
Province : K.MARAŞ / ELBİSTAN
Phone 1 : +90 344-4120081-
Phone 2 : +90 4135545
Fax : +90 344-4135546
WEB : http://www.elbistantso.org.tr
E-Mail : elbistan.ticvesanoda@ttnet.net.tr
PRESIDENT OF BOARD OF DIRECTOR : MUSTAFA PAKSOY
PRESIDENT OF ASSEMBLY : MEMET ERDOĞAN
SECRETARY GENERAL : YÜKSEL GÖZÜDELİ

EMIRDAG CHAMBER OF COMMERCE AND INDUSTRY
Address : ÇİLLİ MAH.KONYA CAD.NO:13 K:3
Province : AFYONKARAHİSAR / EMİRDAĞ
Phone 1 : +90 272-4425199
Phone 2 :
Fax : +90 272-4424399
WEB : http://www.emirdagtso.org.tr
E-Mail : emirdagtso@e-kolay.net
PRESIDENT OF BOARD OF DIRECTOR : HALİL İBRAHİM AKTEPE
PRESIDENT OF ASSEMBLY : AHMET YİĞİTER
SECRETARY GENERAL : KORAY GÜRBÜZ

ERBAA CHAMBER OF COMMERCE AND INDUSTRY
Address : İSMETPAŞA MAH.HÜKÜMET CAD. NO:180
Province : TOKAT / ERBAA
Phone 1 : +90 356-7152820
Phone 2 :
Fax : +90 356-7156157
WEB :
E-Mail :
PRESIDENT OF BOARD OF DIRECTOR : GÖKALP COŞKUN
PRESIDENT OF ASSEMBLY : SEMİH SALİM BAÇ
SECRETARY GENERAL : AHMET TEMİZ

ERCIS CHAMBER OF COMMERCE AND INDUSTRY
Address : KIŞLA MAHALLESİ ESKİ GARAJ CADDESİ NO: 20
Province : VAN / ERCİŞ
Phone 1 : +90 432-3516231-
Phone 2 :
Fax : +90 432-3510717
WEB : http://www.ercistso.tobb.org.tr/
E-Mail : ercistso@tobb.org.tr
PRESIDENT OF BOARD OF DIRECTOR : İZZET YAĞAR
PRESIDENT OF ASSEMBLY : MUHLİS KARAMAN
SECRETARY GENERAL : AHMET GÖZÜTOK

ERDEMLI CHAMBER OF COMMERCE AND INDUSTRY
Address : MERKEZ MAH.İBRAHİM ÖNGEL SOKAK ETSO HİZMET BİNASI NO:17 K:1
Province : MERSİN / ERDEMLİ
Phone 1 : +90 324-5151055-
Phone 2 :
Fax : +90 324-5160498
WEB : http://www.erdemlitso.org.tr
E-Mail :
PRESIDENT OF BOARD OF DIRECTOR : ORHAN SARI
PRESIDENT OF ASSEMBLY : NİHAT TANER
SECRETARY GENERAL : AYSEL AKSOY

EREGLI(KONYA) CHAMBER OF COMMERCE AND INDUSTRY
Address : SELÇUKLU MAH.HAMAM SOK.NO.9 PK.42 320
Province : KONYA / KON.EREĞLİ
Phone 1 : +90 332-7131073-
Phone 2 : +90 7132578
Fax : +90 332-7131802
WEB : http://www.ertso.org.tr
E-Mail :
PRESIDENT OF BOARD OF DIRECTOR : ENVER BOZKURT

PRESIDENT OF ASSEMBLY : MEHMET KOÇ
SECRETARY GENERAL : MURAT KARPUZCU

EREGLI/KDZ. CHAMBER OF COMMERCE AND INDUSTRY
Address : MÜFTÜ MAHALLESİ-MEYDANBAŞI CAD. ÇAMLIK SOKAK
Province : ZONGULDAK / KRDZ.EREĞLİ
Phone 1 : +90 372-3161161-
Phone 2 : +90 372-3234421
Fax : +90 372-3168897
WEB : http://www.ereglitso.org.tr
E-Mail : bilgi@ereglitso.org.tr
PRESIDENT OF BOARD OF DIRECTOR : YAŞAR TETİKER
PRESIDENT OF ASSEMBLY : FARUK YAZICI
SECRETARY GENERAL : GÜNDÜZ ACAR

ERZIN CHAMBER OF COMMERCE AND INDUSTRY
Address : KARAMUSTAFALI MAH.KARAMUSTAFALI CAD MİLENYUM APR.KAT.2
Province : HATAY / ERZİN
Phone 1 : +90 326-6814283
Phone 2 :
Fax : +90 326-6818530
WEB : http://www.erzintso.org.tr
E-Mail :
PRESIDENT OF BOARD OF DIRECTOR : BEKİR SOYLU
PRESIDENT OF ASSEMBLY : KADİR ÖZMEN
SECRETARY GENERAL : RAZİYE GÖKCEN

ERZINCAN CHAMBER OF COMMERCE AND INDUSTRY
Address : FEVZİPAŞA CADDESİ NO:19
Province : ERZİNCAN / -
Phone 1 : +90 446-2142105-
Phone 2 :
Fax : +90 446-2233693
WEB : http://www.erzincantso.org
E-Mail : erzincantso@tobb.org.tr
PRESIDENT OF BOARD OF DIRECTOR : SELÇUK POLAT
PRESIDENT OF ASSEMBLY : SÜLEYMAN SARAK
SECRETARY GENERAL : ABDÜSSAMED DOĞANÇAY

ERZURUM CHAMBER OF COMMERCE AND INDUSTRY
Address : CEMAL GÜRSEL CADDESİ NO: 1 HAVUZBAŞI
Province : ERZURUM / -
Phone 1 : +90 442-2333389
Phone 2 :
Fax : +90 442-2331256
WEB : http://erzurumtso.tobb.org.tr/
E-Mail : erzurumtso@tobb.org.tr
PRESIDENT OF BOARD OF DIRECTOR : LÜTFÜ YÜCELİK
PRESIDENT OF ASSEMBLY : SAİM ÖZAKALIN
SECRETARY GENERAL : HARUN DELİBAŞ

FATSA CHAMBER OF COMMERCE AND INDUSTRY
Address : EVKAF MAH.KUMRU KORGAN YOLU CAD. NO:28
Province : ORDU / FATSA
Phone 1 : +90 452-4231023
Phone 2 : +90 4239511-4239
Fax : +90 452-4235798
WEB : http://fatsatso.tobb.org.tr/
E-Mail : fatsatso@tobb.org.tr
PRESIDENT OF BOARD OF DIRECTOR : TAYFUN KARATAŞ
PRESIDENT OF ASSEMBLY : FAHRİ TANRIKULU
SECRETARY GENERAL : HAMDİ KARAMUSTAFA

FETHİYE CHAMBER OF COMMERCE AND INDUSTRY
Address : TAŞKAYA MAH.144.SOKAK NO:119/1
Province : MUĞLA / FETHİYE
Phone 1 : +90 252-6141115-
Phone 2 : +90 6126756
Fax : +90 252-6145791
WEB : http://www.fto.org.tr/
E-Mail : fethiyeto@tobb.org.tr
PRESIDENT OF BOARD OF DIRECTOR : AKİF ARICAN
PRESIDENT OF ASSEMBLY : OSMAN ÇIRALI
SECRETARY GENERAL : FÜSUN ŞAHİN

GEDIZ CHAMBER OF COMMERCE AND INDUSTRY
Address : ÖZYURT MAH.132.SOKAK NO:6
Province : KÜTAHYA / GEDİZ
Phone 1 : +90 274-4127036-
Phone 2 :
Fax : +90 274-4127036
WEB : http://geditzso.tobb.org.tr/
E-Mail : gediztso@kobinet.org.tr
PRESIDENT OF BOARD OF DIRECTOR : MESUT NACİ CEBECİOĞLU
PRESIDENT OF ASSEMBLY : MUHİTTİN KOCADAĞ
SECRETARY GENERAL : CAVİT CENGİZ

GELIBOLU CHAMBER OF COMMERCE AND INDUSTRY
Address : TUĞSAVUL CAD. NO: 108
Province : ÇANAKKALE / GELİBOLU
Phone 1 : +90 286-5661108
Phone 2 :
Fax : +90 286-5667313
WEB : http://www.gelibolutso.org.tr
E-Mail : bilgi@gelibolutso.com

PRESIDENT OF BOARD OF DIRECTOR : İBRAHİM ÖZEN
PRESIDENT OF ASSEMBLY : HÜSEYİN TUTUM
SECRETARY GENERAL : HÜSEYİN ÇAKMAK

GEMLIK CHAMBER OF COMMERCE AND INDUSTRY
Address : HAMİDİYE MAH.KUMSAL SOK.TİBEL OTELİ
Province : BURSA / GEMLİK
Phone 1 : +90 224-5131023
Phone 2 : +90 5131478
Fax : +90 224-5131566
WEB : http://www.gtso.org.tr/
E-Mail : bilgi@gtso.org.tr
PRESIDENT OF BOARD OF DIRECTOR : KEMAL AKIT
PRESIDENT OF ASSEMBLY : PAŞA AĞDEMİR
SECRETARY GENERAL : AGAH ARDA

GEREDE CHAMBER OF COMMERCE AND INDUSTRY
Address : YENİ CAMİ İŞ MERKEZİ K:2
Province : BOLU / GEREDE
Phone 1 : +90 374-3116711
Phone 2 :
Fax : +90 374-3117218
WEB : http://geredetso.tobb.org.tr/
E-Mail : geredetso@tobb.org.tr
PRESIDENT OF BOARD OF DIRECTOR : ERSİN KAŞKA
PRESIDENT OF ASSEMBLY : İBRAHİM SADİ ÖZALP
SECRETARY GENERAL : ŞERAFETTİN DAĞYILDIZI

GIRESUN CHAMBER OF COMMERCE AND INDUSTRY
Address : HACI MİKTAT MAH.İNCEDAYI SOK.NO:4 K:1 28200
Province : GİRESUN / -
Phone 1 : +90 454-2161127
Phone 2 : +90 454-2168801
Fax : +90 454-2162641
WEB : http://www.giresuntso.com/
E-Mail : giresun@giresun-tso.org.tr, giresuntso@tobb.org.tr
PRESIDENT OF BOARD OF DIRECTOR : HASAN ÇAKIRMELİKOĞLU
PRESIDENT OF ASSEMBLY : FİKRET GÜNAYDIN
SECRETARY GENERAL : ŞÜKRÜ CEBECİ

GORDES CHAMBER OF COMMERCE AND INDUSTRY
Address : BELEDİYE PASAJI NO:35
Province : MANİSA / GÖRDES
Phone 1 : +90 236-5471239
Phone 2 :
Fax : +90 236-5473170
WEB : http://gordestso.org.tr/
E-Mail :
PRESIDENT OF BOARD OF DIRECTOR : MEHMET HOŞAF
PRESIDENT OF ASSEMBLY : TURGUT YILDIZHAN
SECRETARY GENERAL : CENGİZ GÜNTAŞ

GUMUSHACIKOY CHAMBER OF COMMERCE AND INDUSTRY
Address : ÇAY MAH.ÇARŞI İÇİ YENİ MERZİFON CAD NO:2
Province : AMASYA / GÜMÜŞHACIKÖY
Phone 1 : +90 358-7171103
Phone 2 :
Fax : +90 358-7171103
WEB : http://gumushacikoytso.org/
E-Mail : gumushacikoytso@tobb.org.tr
PRESIDENT OF BOARD OF DIRECTOR : CAN KELEŞ
PRESIDENT OF ASSEMBLY : MUSA ALPASLAN
SECRETARY GENERAL : TAMER KISA

GUMUSHANE CHAMBER OF COMMERCE AND INDUSTRY
Address : ATATÜRK CADDESİ NO:55 KAT:2
Province : GÜMÜŞHANE / -
Phone 1 : +90 456-2131112
Phone 2 :
Fax : +90 456-2136059
WEB : http://gumushanetso.tobb.org.tr/
E-Mail :
PRESIDENT OF BOARD OF DIRECTOR : İSMAİL AKÇAY
PRESIDENT OF ASSEMBLY : SEBAHATTİN UÇAR
SECRETARY GENERAL : LÜTFİ KILIÇ

HAKKARI CHAMBER OF COMMERCE AND INDUSTRY
Address : KAYACAN CADDESİ HACI SAİT CAMİİ KARŞISI NO:16
Province : HAKKARİ / -
Phone 1 : +90 438-2112726
Phone 2 : +90 2118319
Fax : +90 438-2112726
WEB : http://www.hatso.org.tr
E-Mail : hakkaritso@tobb.org.tr
PRESIDENT OF BOARD OF DIRECTOR : SERVET TAŞ
PRESIDENT OF ASSEMBLY : NAZIM DEMİR
SECRETARY GENERAL : FİKRET KESKİN

HAVZA CHAMBER OF COMMERCE AND INDUSTRY
Address : BELEDİYE SARAYI ŞEHİR KULÜBÜ ÜSTÜ K:2
Province : SAMSUN / HAVZA

Phone 1 : +90 362-7142287-
Phone 2 : +90 0362-7147325
Fax : +90 362-7147326
WEB : http://www.havzatso.tobb.org.tr/
E-Mail :
PRESIDENT OF BOARD OF DIRECTOR : ERKAN ACAR
PRESIDENT OF ASSEMBLY : MUSTAFA BAŞARAN
SECRETARY GENERAL : ARİF ALTUN

HAYRABOLU CHAMBER OF COMMERCE AND INDUSTRY
Address : HİSAR MAH.TEKİRDAĞ CADDESİ NO:2 59400
Province : TEKİRDAĞ / HAYRABOLU
Phone 1 : +90 282-3151149
Phone 2 :
Fax : +90 282-3156705
WEB : http://www.hayrabolutso.com/
E-Mail : hayrabolutso@tobb.org.tr
PRESIDENT OF BOARD OF DIRECTOR : MEHMET BAŞOL
PRESIDENT OF ASSEMBLY : ÖMER ŞÜKRÜ COŞAR
SECRETARY GENERAL : YAVUZ YELKEN

HOPA CHAMBER OF COMMERCE AND INDUSTRY
Address : KULEDİBİ MAHALLESİ ÖZGÜRLÜK MEYDANI İŞ BANKASI ÜSTÜ KAT:2
Province : ARTVİN / HOPA
Phone 1 : +90 466-3514217-
Phone 2 :
Fax : +90 466-3516887
WEB : http://www.hopatso.org.tr
E-Mail :
PRESIDENT OF BOARD OF DIRECTOR : OSMAN AKYÜREK
PRESIDENT OF ASSEMBLY : METİN KARAMAN
SECRETARY GENERAL : ALİ UZUN

IGDIR CHAMBER OF COMMERCE AND INDUSTRY
Address : CUMHURİYET CAD.KASAPLAR SOK.NO:35
Province : IĞDIR / -
Phone 1 : +90 476-2278242
Phone 2 :
Fax : +90 476-2279625
WEB : http://www.igdirtso.org.tr
E-Mail : ticaretoda2@ttnet.net.tr
PRESIDENT OF BOARD OF DIRECTOR : KAMİL ARSLAN
PRESIDENT OF ASSEMBLY : OĞUZ NEFİS
SECRETARY GENERAL : GÖKÇEN TURAN

INEBOLU CHAMBER OF COMMERCE AND INDUSTRY
Address : KAŞİFBEY CAD.NO.28
Province : KASTAMONU / İNEBOLU
Phone 1 : +90 366-8114004
Phone 2 :
Fax : +90 366-8115202
WEB : http://www.inebolutso.org.tr
E-Mail :
PRESIDENT OF BOARD OF DIRECTOR : ŞAKİR İŞERİ
PRESIDENT OF ASSEMBLY : AHMET ÇEÇEN
SECRETARY GENERAL : MELEK DARENDE

INEGOL CHAMBER OF COMMERCE AND INDUSTRY
Address : SÜLEYMANİYE MAHALLESİ 108.SOKAK ORGANİZE SANAYİ BÖLGESİ 1.CADDE NO:24/A
Province : BURSA / İNEGÖL
Phone 1 : +90 224-7148260
Phone 2 :
Fax : +90 224-7149859
WEB : http://www.itso.org.tr/
E-Mail : itso@itso.org.tr
PRESIDENT OF BOARD OF DIRECTOR : METİN ANIL
PRESIDENT OF ASSEMBLY : SADIK GÜLERER
SECRETARY GENERAL : MUSTAFA ŞENTÜRK

ISKENDERUN CHAMBER OF COMMERCE AND INDUSTRY
Address : ATATÜRK BULVARI NO:51 31200
Province : HATAY / İSKENDERUN
Phone 1 : +90 0326-6145225
Phone 2 :
Fax : +90 0326-6145752
WEB : http://www.iskenderuntso.org.tr/
E-Mail : info@iskenderuntso.org
PRESIDENT OF BOARD OF DIRECTOR : LEVENT HAKKI YILMAZ
PRESIDENT OF ASSEMBLY : SERVET UGUTMEN
SECRETARY GENERAL : FİGEN GÜL DÖNMEZ

ISPARTA CHAMBER OF COMMERCE AND INDUSTRY
Address : MİMAR SİNAN CAD. NO.29/A 32100
Province : ISPARTA / -
Phone 1 : +90 246-2181613-
Phone 2 : +90 246-2327431
Fax : +90 246-2181016
WEB : http://www.itso.org/
E-Mail : itso@itso.org
PRESIDENT OF BOARD OF DIRECTOR : ŞÜKRÜ BAŞDEĞİRMEN
PRESIDENT OF ASSEMBLY : OSMAN DOĞAN ŞAHLAN
SECRETARY GENERAL : FATİH YAMAN

İZNİK CHAMBER OF COMMERCE AND INDUSTRY
Address : BEYLER MAH.KILIÇASLAN CAD.NO:115/3
Province : BURSA / İZNİK
Phone 1 : +90 224-7571576-
Phone 2 :
Fax : +90 224-7576507
WEB : http://www.izniktso.org.tr/
E-Mail :
PRESIDENT OF BOARD OF DIRECTOR : MAHMUT DEDE
PRESIDENT OF ASSEMBLY : SERKAN MANÇOLAR
SECRETARY GENERAL : NURAY YILDIRIM

KAHRAMANMARAS CHAMBER OF COMMERCE AND INDUSTRY
Address : EGEMENLİK MAH.İLAHİYAT CAD. GÜNEY ÇEVRE YOLU ÜZERİ
Province : K.MARAŞ / -
Phone 1 : +90 344-2353220
Phone 2 :
Fax : +90 344-2353230
WEB : http://www.kmtso.org.tr/
E-Mail : kmtso@kmtso.org.tr
PRESIDENT OF BOARD OF DIRECTOR : KEMAL KARAKÜÇÜK
PRESIDENT OF ASSEMBLY : MEHMET HANİFİ ÖKSÜZ
SECRETARY GENERAL : YILMAZ ÜLKER

KAMAN CHAMBER OF COMMERCE AND INDUSTRY
Address : CUMA MAHALLESİ SEBZE PAZARI SOK. NO:36 40300
Province : KIRŞEHİR / KAMAN
Phone 1 : +90 386-7122519
Phone 2 :
Fax : +90 386-7127106
WEB : http://www.kamantso.org.tr
E-Mail :
PRESIDENT OF BOARD OF DIRECTOR : ÜLKÜ AVŞAR
PRESIDENT OF ASSEMBLY : KENAN ALVAN
SECRETARY GENERAL : ERCAN GİZİROĞLU

KARABUK CHAMBER OF COMMERCE AND INDUSTRY
Address : HÜRRİYET CAD.NO.58/1
Province : KARABÜK / -
Phone 1 : +90 370-4241630
Phone 2 : +90 370-4122901
Fax : +90 370-4120484
WEB : http://www.karabuktso.org.tr/
E-Mail : tso@karabuktso.org.tr
PRESIDENT OF BOARD OF DIRECTOR : SEDAT NAMAL
PRESIDENT OF ASSEMBLY : TİMURÇİN SAYLAR
SECRETARY GENERAL : CEM BİÇEN

KARACABEY CHAMBER OF COMMERCE AND INDUSTRY
Address : SANAYİ SİTESİ KARŞISI 16700
Province : BURSA / KARACABEY
Phone 1 : +90 224-6718548-
Phone 2 : +90 6718550
Fax : +90 224-6718545
WEB : http://www.karacabeytso.com/
E-Mail : bilgi@karacabeytso.com
PRESIDENT OF BOARD OF DIRECTOR : NACİ GÜNCÜ
PRESIDENT OF ASSEMBLY : ASIM ÜNEN
SECRETARY GENERAL : ÖZGÜR CARLI

KARAHALLI CHAMBER OF COMMERCE AND INDUSTRY
Address : ÇARŞI İÇİ BELEDİYE İŞ HANI K:2
Province : UŞAK / KARAHALLI
Phone 1 : +90 276-5171163
Phone 2 :
Fax : +90 276-5173258
WEB :
E-Mail :
PRESIDENT OF BOARD OF DIRECTOR : ŞAKİR DURSUN
PRESIDENT OF ASSEMBLY : CELAL GÜL
SECRETARY GENERAL : ŞAHİP ACAR

KARAMAN CHAMBER OF COMMERCE AND INDUSTRY
Address : YUNUS KENT MAH. ALPARSLAN TÜRKEŞ BULVARI NO:2
Province : KARAMAN / -
Phone 1 : +90 338-2131021
Phone 2 :
Fax : +90 338-2130067
WEB : http://www.ktso.org.tr/
E-Mail : ktso@ktso.org.tr
PRESIDENT OF BOARD OF DIRECTOR : MUSTAFA TOKTAY
PRESIDENT OF ASSEMBLY : MUSTAFA GÖKHAN ALKAN
SECRETARY GENERAL : BEHİYE KIZILÖZ TUMAN

KARAPINAR CHAMBER OF COMMERCE AND INDUSTRY
Address : YENİ BELEDİYE İŞ HANI K:2 NO:51
Province : KONYA / KARAPINAR
Phone 1 : +90 332-7551276
Phone 2 :
Fax : +90 332-7552565
WEB : http://www.karapinartso.org.tr/
E-Mail :
PRESIDENT OF BOARD OF DIRECTOR : MUSTAFA KEMAL SÖZEN
PRESIDENT OF ASSEMBLY : METİN ZENGİN

SECRETARY GENERAL : ADEM SALİH İŞLEYEN

KARS CHAMBER OF COMMERCE AND INDUSTRY
Address : KARADAĞ CAD.NO:1
Province : KARS / -
Phone 1 : +90 474-2231072-
Phone 2 :
Fax : +90 474-2232497
WEB : http://karstso.org/
E-Mail : karstso@gmail.com
PRESIDENT OF BOARD OF DIRECTOR : FAHRİ ÖTEGEN
PRESIDENT OF ASSEMBLY : İDRİS ACAY
SECRETARY GENERAL : ALİEKBER TURAN

KASTAMONU CHAMBER OF COMMERCE AND INDUSTRY
Address : NASRULLAH MEYDANI
Province : KASTAMONU / -
Phone 1 : +90 366-2141074-
Phone 2 :
Fax : +90 366-2149467
WEB : http://kastamonutso.org/
E-Mail : katso37@hotmail.com
PRESIDENT OF BOARD OF DIRECTOR : SELÇUK ARSLAN
PRESIDENT OF ASSEMBLY : KADİR YÜKSEL TONBUL
SECRETARY GENERAL : MUSTAFA ELMAS

KELKIT CHAMBER OF COMMERCE AND INDUSTRY
Address : PAZAR YERİ NO:25/2
Province : GÜMÜŞHANE / KELKİT
Phone 1 : +90 456-3171548
Phone 2 :
Fax : +90 456-3171548
WEB :
E-Mail :
PRESIDENT OF BOARD OF DIRECTOR : CAFER HİRİK
PRESIDENT OF ASSEMBLY : MUSTAFA YENİÇERİ
SECRETARY GENERAL : BURCU ÖZLEM SUNUR

KESAN CHAMBER OF COMMERCE AND INDUSTRY
Address : YUKARI ZAFERİYE MAH. PAŞAYİĞİT CADDESİ NO:58
Province : EDİRNE / KEŞAN
Phone 1 : +90 284-7141137-
Phone 2 :
Fax : +90 284-7147608
WEB : http://www.kesantso.tobb.org.tr
E-Mail : kesantso@tobb.org.tr
PRESIDENT OF BOARD OF DIRECTOR : MUSTAFA HELVACIOĞLU
PRESIDENT OF ASSEMBLY : YÜKSEL ALİOĞLU
SECRETARY GENERAL : ERDEM BAŞAK

KIRIKHAN CHAMBER OF COMMERCE AND INDUSTRY
Address : CUMHURİYET MAH.İNÖNÜ BULVARI NO:1 K:3
Province : HATAY / KIRIKHAN
Phone 1 : +90 326-3441094
Phone 2 : +90 326-3451758
Fax : +90 326-3441094
WEB : http://www.kirikhantso.tobb.org.tr
E-Mail :
PRESIDENT OF BOARD OF DIRECTOR : HALİL İBRAHİM CESUR
PRESIDENT OF ASSEMBLY : MEHMET KURTOĞLU
SECRETARY GENERAL : BÜNYAMİN ÇELİK

KIRIKKALE CHAMBER OF COMMERCE AND INDUSTRY
Address : OSMAN TİRYAKİ CAD.NO.5
Province : KIRIKKALE / -
Phone 1 : +90 318-2249493-
Phone 2 :
Fax : +90 318-2187026
WEB : http://www.kirikkaletso.org.tr/
E-Mail : kktso@superonline.com
PRESIDENT OF BOARD OF DIRECTOR : EKREM GÖK
PRESIDENT OF ASSEMBLY : BEKİR ŞAHİN
SECRETARY GENERAL : AHMET ŞERBETÇİOĞLU

KIRKLARELI CHAMBER OF COMMERCE AND INDUSTRY
Address : KARAKAŞ MAH.KARAKAŞ BEY SOK.NO.8
Province : KIRKLARELİ / -
Phone 1 : +90 288-2144256
Phone 2 :
Fax : +90 288-2141109
WEB : http://www.kirklarelitso.org.tr/
E-Mail : ktso@kirklarelitso.org.tr
PRESIDENT OF BOARD OF DIRECTOR : ERTUĞRUL ZİYA ÇETİNTAŞ
PRESIDENT OF ASSEMBLY : ERDOĞAN SEMERCİ
SECRETARY GENERAL : SEDAT YILMAZ

KIRSEHIR CHAMBER OF COMMERCE AND INDUSTRY
Address : ATATÜRK CAD. ATA İŞ HANI NO:47/2
Province : KIRŞEHİR / -
Phone 1 : +90 386-2131186
Phone 2 :
Fax : +90 386-2136134
WEB : http://www.kirsehirtso.org/
E-Mail : kirsehirtso@tobb.org.tr

PRESIDENT OF BOARD OF DIRECTOR : SELAHATTİN EKİCİOĞLU
PRESIDENT OF ASSEMBLY : EŞREF AŞIK
SECRETARY GENERAL : MAHMUT MURAT YILDIRIM

KIZILTEPE CHAMBER OF COMMERCE AND INDUSTRY
Address : MARDİN CAD.KAT.2 NO:31/2
Province : MARDİN / KIZILTEPE
Phone 1 : +90 482-3121787-
Phone 2 : +90 3123273
Fax : +90 482-3134992
WEB : http://www.kiziltepetso.org.tr/
E-Mail :
PRESIDENT OF BOARD OF DIRECTOR : MAHMUT DÜNDAR
PRESIDENT OF ASSEMBLY : BEŞİR DÜNDAR
SECRETARY GENERAL : AHMET ASLAN

KİLİS CHAMBER OF COMMERCE AND INDUSTRY
Address : RIFAT KAZANCIOĞLU MAH. SAFTER NECİOĞLU BULVARI NO:74
Province : KİLİS / -
Phone 1 : +90 348-8131044-
Phone 2 :
Fax : +90 348-8137297
WEB : http://www.kilistso.tobb.org.tr/
E-Mail : kilistso@tobb.org.tr
PRESIDENT OF BOARD OF DIRECTOR : MEHMET ERDAL ÖNDEŞ
PRESIDENT OF ASSEMBLY : MEHMET ÖZÇİLOĞLU
SECRETARY GENERAL : MEHMET MURAT SAKAR

KUMLUCA CHAMBER OF COMMERCE AND INDUSTRY
Address : KARŞIYAKA MAH.ADNAN MENDERES BULVARI KARASİN SOKAK ANA SİTESİ C BLOK NO:23
Province : ANTALYA / KUMLUCA
Phone 1 : +90 242-8890707
Phone 2 :
Fax : +90 242-8890710
WEB : http://www.kumlucatso.org.tr
E-Mail : kutso@superonlıne.com
PRESIDENT OF BOARD OF DIRECTOR : MURAT HÜDAVENDİGAR GÜNAY
PRESIDENT OF ASSEMBLY : MEHMET ÇETİNTÜRK
SECRETARY GENERAL : MESUT BAKAR

KUTAHYA CHAMBER OF COMMERCE AND INDUSTRY
Address : 75.YIL MAHALLESİ DUMLUPINAR BULVARI NO:73/1
Province : KÜTAHYA / -
Phone 1 : +90 274-2283232
Phone 2 :
Fax : +90 274-2280440
WEB : http://www.kutso.org.tr/
E-Mail : kutso@kutso.org.tr
PRESIDENT OF BOARD OF DIRECTOR : NAFİ GÜRAL
PRESIDENT OF ASSEMBLY : İSMET ÖZOTRAÇ
SECRETARY GENERAL : SALİH NAFİ ALIÇ

LULEBURGAZ CHAMBER OF COMMERCE AND INDUSTRY
Address : KOCASİNAN MAH.İNÖNÜ CAD.NO:11/A
Province : KIRKLARELİ / LÜLEBURGAZ
Phone 1 : +90 288-4171121-
Phone 2 :
Fax : +90 288-4171989
WEB : http://www.ltso.org.tr/
E-Mail : luleburgaztso@tobb.org.tr
PRESIDENT OF BOARD OF DIRECTOR : AHMET ERGİN OKANDENİZ
PRESIDENT OF ASSEMBLY : ZAFER GİRGİN
SECRETARY GENERAL : KERİM OYTUN YAY

MALATYA CHAMBER OF COMMERCE AND INDUSTRY
Address : İNÖNÜ CADDESİ PTT YANI NO:1 44100
Province : MALATYA / -
Phone 1 : +90 422-4448944-
Phone 2 : +90 3237770
Fax : +90 422-3237776
WEB : http://www.malatyatso.org.tr/
E-Mail : tso@malatyatso.org.tr
PRESIDENT OF BOARD OF DIRECTOR : HASAN HÜSEYİN ERKOÇ
PRESIDENT OF ASSEMBLY : SAMİ PAYZA
SECRETARY GENERAL : ABDULLAH DURAN

MALKARA CHAMBER OF COMMERCE AND INDUSTRY
Address : GAZİBEY MAH.TEVFİKBEY CAD.NO:9 K.3
Province : TEKİRDAĞ / MALKARA
Phone 1 : +90 282-4271121
Phone 2 : +90 4273464
Fax : +90 282-4272821
WEB : http://www.malkaratso.org.tr/
E-Mail : malkara@malkaratso.org.tr
PRESIDENT OF BOARD OF DIRECTOR : ÜMRAN BİLGİN
PRESIDENT OF ASSEMBLY : CENGİZ UYSAL
SECRETARY GENERAL : SİNAN BEŞER

MANAVGAT CHAMBER OF COMMERCE AND INDUSTRY
Address : AYDINEVLER MAH.5578 SOK.NO:1 P.K.302
Province : ANTALYA / MANAVGAT

Phone 1 : +90 242-7428380
Phone 2 : +90 242-7423802
Fax : +90 242-7428381
WEB : http://www.matso.org.tr/
E-Mail :
PRESIDENT OF BOARD OF DIRECTOR : AHMET BOZTAŞ
PRESIDENT OF ASSEMBLY : KERİM ERDEM
SECRETARY GENERAL : HATİCE ÖZDEN DAĞ

MANİSA CHAMBER OF COMMERCE AND INDUSTRY
Address : MERKEZ EFENDİ MAH.MİMAR SİNAN BULVARI NO:127 YUNUSEMRE
Province : MANİSA / -
Phone 1 : +90 236-2311045-
Phone 2 :
Fax : +90 236-2312845
WEB : http://www.manisatso.org.tr
E-Mail : info@mtso.org
PRESIDENT OF BOARD OF DIRECTOR : YAŞAR COŞKUN
PRESIDENT OF ASSEMBLY : HAYATİ DULMAN
SECRETARY GENERAL : TAMER BALATLI

MARDIN CHAMBER OF COMMERCE AND INDUSTRY
Address : 1.CAD.CUMHURİYET ALANI
Province : MARDİN / -
Phone 1 : +90 482-2121033
Phone 2 : +90 482-2121833
Fax : +90 482-2130314
WEB : http://www.mardintso.tobb.org.tr/
E-Mail :
PRESIDENT OF BOARD OF DIRECTOR : MEHMET ALİ TUTAŞI
PRESIDENT OF ASSEMBLY : NECMİ DEMİR
SECRETARY GENERAL : ÇETİN SASA

MERSIN CHAMBER OF COMMERCE AND INDUSTRY
Address : ÇANKAYA MAH.ATATÜRK CAD.MTSO HİZMET BİNASI K:3 33070
Province : MERSİN / -
Phone 1 : +90 324-2389500(
Phone 2 : +90 324-2389800
Fax : +90 324-2319697
WEB : http://www.mtso.org.tr/
E-Mail : info@mtso.org.tr
PRESIDENT OF BOARD OF DIRECTOR : ŞERAFETTİN AŞUT
PRESIDENT OF ASSEMBLY : MAHMUT ARSLAN
SECRETARY GENERAL : ABDULKADİR DÖLEK

MERZIFON CHAMBER OF COMMERCE AND INDUSTRY
Address : CUMHURİYET MEYDANI NO:7/A
Province : AMASYA / MERZİFON
Phone 1 : +90 358-5138096
Phone 2 :
Fax : +90 358-5140972
WEB : http://www.merzifontso.tobb.org.tr
E-Mail : mtso@e-kolay.net
PRESIDENT OF BOARD OF DIRECTOR : FATİH ALTINAY
PRESIDENT OF ASSEMBLY : MUSTAFA ATAK
SECRETARY GENERAL : SEMİH SAĞLAMER

MİLAS CHAMBER OF COMMERCE AND INDUSTRY
Address : HAYITLI MAH. ÇEVRE YOLU ÜZERİ
Province : MUĞLA / MİLAS
Phone 1 : +90 252-5121118-
Phone 2 : +90 5128275
Fax : +90 252-5128999
WEB : http://mitso.org.tr/
E-Mail : info@mitso.org.tr
PRESIDENT OF BOARD OF DIRECTOR : REŞİT ÖZER
PRESIDENT OF ASSEMBLY : MUSTAFA YÜKSEL
SECRETARY GENERAL : KAZIM SARIOĞLU

MUCUR CHAMBER OF COMMERCE AND INDUSTRY
Address : BELEDİYE İŞ HANI K:3
Province : KIRŞEHİR / MUCUR
Phone 1 : +90 386-8124245
Phone 2 :
Fax : +90 386-8124245
WEB :
E-Mail :
PRESIDENT OF BOARD OF DIRECTOR : FERHAT ÇAĞLAYAN
PRESIDENT OF ASSEMBLY : FUAT SELÇUK
SECRETARY GENERAL : HAYATİ KIYAK

MUĞLA CHAMBER OF COMMERCE AND INDUSTRY
Address : MUSLİHİTTİN MAH. ŞEHİT YARBAY ALİM YILMAZ CAD. NO:3
Province : MUĞLA / -
Phone 1 : +90 252-2141122
Phone 2 : +90 2123440-2123
Fax : +90 252-2147121
WEB : http://www.mutso.org.tr/
E-Mail : mutod@superonline.com
PRESIDENT OF BOARD OF DIRECTOR : BÜLENT KARAKUŞ
PRESIDENT OF ASSEMBLY : ŞÜKRÜ ALTINAY
SECRETARY GENERAL : MEHMET ÇÜÇEN

MUS CHAMBER OF COMMERCE AND INDUSTRY
Address : HÜRRİYET MAH.CENGİZ TOPEL CAD. ŞİMŞEKLER APARTMANI KAT :2
Province : MUŞ / -

Phone 1 : +90 436-2121195-
Phone 2 :
Fax : +90 436-2129993
WEB : http://mustso.org.tr/
E-Mail : 49mustso49@mynet.com
PRESIDENT OF BOARD OF DIRECTOR : FATİH CENGİZ
PRESIDENT OF ASSEMBLY : MURAT GÜRESMER
SECRETARY GENERAL : HANİFİ AYDAR

MUSTAFAKEMALPASA CHAMBER OF COMMERCE AND INDUSTRY
Address : ATATÜRK MAH. FEVZİPAŞA CAD. NO:200
Province : BURSA / M.KEMALPAŞA
Phone 1 : +90 224-6180525-
Phone 2 :
Fax : +90 224-6180528
WEB : http://www.mkptso.org.tr
E-Mail : mkptso@mkptso.org
PRESIDENT OF BOARD OF DIRECTOR : İBRAHİM DIRAKMAN
PRESIDENT OF ASSEMBLY : CEMAL BURHAN
SECRETARY GENERAL : BİROL DENİZLİ

MUT CHAMBER OF COMMERCE AND INDUSTRY
Address : MEYDAN MAH.KIYI SOK.BELEDİYE BLOK- LARI NO:2 K:2
Province : MERSİN / MUT
Phone 1 : +90 324-7742773
Phone 2 :
Fax : +90 324-7746499
WEB : http://www.muttso.org.tr/
E-Mail : muttso@ttnet.net.tr
PRESIDENT OF BOARD OF DIRECTOR : MEHMET GÜRSEL AYDIN
PRESIDENT OF ASSEMBLY : ŞAHİN SEZER
SECRETARY GENERAL : MUSTAFA DEVAM

NEVSEHIR CHAMBER OF COMMERCE AND INDUSTRY
Address : ATATÜRK BULVARI N0.57/1
Province : NEVŞEHİR / -
Phone 1 : +90 384-2131036-
Phone 2 :
Fax : +90 384-2132385
WEB : http://www.ntso.org.tr/
E-Mail : nevtsoda@kaynet.com.tr
PRESIDENT OF BOARD OF DIRECTOR : MEHMET ARİF PARMAKSIZ
PRESIDENT OF ASSEMBLY : SEYİT İNCE
SECRETARY GENERAL : İSMAİL HAKKI AYDOĞAN

NIGDE CHAMBER OF COMMERCE AND INDUSTRY
Address : BANKALAR CAD.N0:17
Province : NİĞDE / -
Phone 1 : +90 388-2335501
Phone 2 :
Fax : +90 388-2335500
WEB : http://www.nitso.org.tr/
E-Mail : nigdetso@tobb.org.tr
PRESIDENT OF BOARD OF DIRECTOR : ŞEVKET KATIRCIOĞLU
PRESIDENT OF ASSEMBLY : MEHMET AYDUĞAN
SECRETARY GENERAL : GÜLSEVİL OZAN

NIKSAR CHAMBER OF COMMERCE AND INDUSTRY
Address : CEPNİBEY MAH.ESKİ TOPTANCI SEBZE HALİ KÜMESİ NO: 41
Province : TOKAT / NİKSAR
Phone 1 : +90 356-5271104-
Phone 2 :
Fax : +90 356-5283151
WEB : http://www.niksartso.tobb.org.tr
E-Mail : niksartso@tobb.org.tr
PRESIDENT OF BOARD OF DIRECTOR :
PRESIDENT OF ASSEMBLY : VEDAT ÜLKER
SECRETARY GENERAL : MUTTALİP ALTUNAY

NUSAYBIN CHAMBER OF COMMERCE AND INDUSTRY
Address : YENİ TURAN MAH. MİTHAT PAŞA SOKAK DIŞ KAPI NO: 2 AKTAŞLAR APARTMANI KAT:1 NO:3
Province : MARDİN / NUSAYBİN
Phone 1 : +90 482-4151846
Phone 2 :
Fax : +90 482-4161208
WEB : http://nusaybintso.org.tr/
E-Mail :
PRESIDENT OF BOARD OF DIRECTOR : MAHSUM ÖZMEN
PRESIDENT OF ASSEMBLY : MUFİT ADNAN YUMUŞAK
SECRETARY GENERAL : ABDULKADİR GÜNEŞ

OF CHAMBER OF COMMERCE AND INDUSTRY
Address : SULAKLI MAH.YILDIZ SOKAK NO:2 K:3-4
Province : TRABZON / OF
Phone 1 : +90 0462-7717160
Phone 2 :
Fax : +90 0-462-771716
WEB : http://www.oftso.org.tr/
E-Mail : oftso@tobb.org.tr
PRESIDENT OF BOARD OF DIRECTOR : ERDAL SARAL
PRESIDENT OF ASSEMBLY : ZÜHAL AKYÜZLÜ
SECRETARY GENERAL : MURAT ZIRIH

OLTU CHAMBER OF COMMERCE AND INDUSTRY
Address : ZİYA BEY CAD.NO:1/A
Province : ERZURUM / OLTU
Phone 1 : +90 442-8163999
Phone 2 : +90 442-8163990
Fax : +90 442-8161355
WEB : http://www.oltutso.tobb.org.tr/
E-Mail :
PRESIDENT OF BOARD OF DIRECTOR : BAKİ KARACA
PRESIDENT OF ASSEMBLY : HAMZA ERDEM
SECRETARY GENERAL : GÜNGÖR DURGUN

ORDU CHAMBER OF COMMERCE AND INDUSTRY
Address : DÜZ MAH.STADYUM CAD.NO:2
Province : ORDU / -
Phone 1 : +90 452-2141077
Phone 2 : +90 452-2141935
Fax : +90 452-2141999
WEB : http://www.otso.org.tr/
E-Mail : ordutso@tobb.org.tr
PRESIDENT OF BOARD OF DIRECTOR : SERVET ŞAHİN
PRESIDENT OF ASSEMBLY : UFUK ÜNAL
SECRETARY GENERAL : İSMAİL HAKKI ÜÇER

ORHANGAZI CHAMBER OF COMMERCE AND INDUSTRY
Address : HÜRRİYET MAH. BURSA YALOVA YOLU ÜZERİ NO:38/1
Province : BURSA / ORHANGAZİ
Phone 1 : +90 224-5738169
Phone 2 :
Fax : +90 224-5738173
WEB : www.orhangazitso.org.tr/
E-Mail : bilgi@orhangazitso.org.tr
PRESIDENT OF BOARD OF DIRECTOR : ERGÜN EFENDİOĞLU
PRESIDENT OF ASSEMBLY : EROL HATIRLI
SECRETARY GENERAL : GÜROL EROL

OSMANIYE CHAMBER OF COMMERCE AND INDUSTRY
Address : RAUF BEY MAH.ADNAN MENDERES BULVARI 9546 SOK. NO: 70 MERKEZ
Province : OSMANİYE / -
Phone 1 : +90 328-8250068-
Phone 2 : +90 328-8250070
Fax : +90 328-8250570
WEB : http://www.osmaniyetso.org.tr/
E-Mail : otso80@ttnet.net.tr
PRESIDENT OF BOARD OF DIRECTOR : MURAT TEKE
PRESIDENT OF ASSEMBLY : ALİ SAÇIKARA
SECRETARY GENERAL : ABDURRAHMAN TÜRKOĞLU

PASINLER CHAMBER OF COMMERCE AND INDUSTRY
Address : KETHÜDA MAH.ULUCAMİ SOKAK NO:68-A
Province : ERZURUM / PASİNLER
Phone 1 : +90 442-6613147
Phone 2 :
Fax : +90 442-6613847
WEB : http://www.pasinlertso.tobb.org.tr/
E-Mail :
PRESIDENT OF BOARD OF DIRECTOR : HİKMET AYRANCI
PRESIDENT OF ASSEMBLY : AYDIN TAŞBAŞI
SECRETARY GENERAL : HALİME GÖŞKER

PAZAR CHAMBER OF COMMERCE AND INDUSTRY
Address : BELEDİYE İŞ HANI KAT:3
Province : RİZE / PAZAR
Phone 1 : +90 464-6127100
Phone 2 :
Fax : +90 464-6121069
WEB : http://www.ptso.org.tr/
E-Mail :
PRESIDENT OF BOARD OF DIRECTOR : MUSTAFA MEMOĞLU
PRESIDENT OF ASSEMBLY : RECEP ALİ ÇATAN
SECRETARY GENERAL : GÜLBAHAR ÇAKIROĞLU

REYHANLI CHAMBER OF COMMERCE AND INDUSTRY
Address : CUMHURİYET MAH.FEVZİ ÇAKMAK CAD. S.ALTUNLU İŞ HANI K:2
Province : HATAY / REYHANLI
Phone 1 : +90 326-4131770-
Phone 2 : +90 326-4130289
Fax : +90 326-4131035
WEB : http://www.reyhanlitso.org.tr/
E-Mail : info@reyhanlitso.org.tr
PRESIDENT OF BOARD OF DIRECTOR : NECMEDDİN ZAROĞLU
PRESIDENT OF ASSEMBLY : HAMİT ŞANVERDİ
SECRETARY GENERAL : ORHAN YÜKSEL

RIZE CHAMBER OF COMMERCE AND INDUSTRY
Address : ATATÜRK CADDESİ NO:359
Province : RİZE / -
Phone 1 : +90 464-2175566-
Phone 2 : +90 464-2148856
Fax : +90 464-2122200
WEB : http://www.rizetso.org.tr/
E-Mail : rizetso@ttnet.net.tr
PRESIDENT OF BOARD OF DIRECTOR : ŞABAN AZİZ KARAMEHMETOĞLU
PRESIDENT OF ASSEMBLY : ÖMER FARUK OFLUOĞLU

SECRETARY GENERAL : GAFUR KARALİ

SAFRANBOLU CHAMBER OF COMMERCE AND INDUSTRY
Address : YENİ BELEDİYE İŞ MERKEZİ K:5
Province : KARABÜK / SAFRANBOLU
Phone 1 : +90 370-7121670
Phone 2 : +90 370-7127392
Fax : +90 370-7123593
WEB : http://www.safranbolutso.org.tr/
E-Mail : safranbolutso@tobb.org.tr
PRESIDENT OF BOARD OF DIRECTOR : ALİ SAMİ ACAR
PRESIDENT OF ASSEMBLY : AHMET ŞAHİN
SECRETARY GENERAL : ÖMER TÜFEKÇİ

SAKARYA CHAMBER OF COMMERCE AND INDUSTRY
Address : SAKARYA MAH. ŞEHİT ONBAŞI ZEKERİYA GÖZYUMAN CAD. NO: 19 HANLI-ARİFİYE 54060
Province : SAKARYA / -
Phone 1 : +90 264-8883000
Phone 2 :
Fax : +90 264-2912424
WEB : http://www.satso.org.tr
E-Mail : info@adptso.org.tr
PRESIDENT OF BOARD OF DIRECTOR : MAHMUT KÖSEMUSUL
PRESIDENT OF ASSEMBLY : AHMET AKGÜN ALTUĞ
SECRETARY GENERAL : UĞUR TIN

SALIHLI CHAMBER OF COMMERCE AND INDUSTRY
Address : MİTHATPAŞA CAD.NO:112 K.1-2
Province : MANİSA / SALİHLİ
Phone 1 : +90 236-7145342
Phone 2 :
Fax : +90 236-7131590
WEB : http://www.salihlitso.org.tr
E-Mail : salihlitso@tobb.org.tr
PRESIDENT OF BOARD OF DIRECTOR : İBRAHİM YÜKSEL
PRESIDENT OF ASSEMBLY : SÜLEYMAN ORAL
SECRETARY GENERAL : LEVENT KILINÇASLAN

SAMSUN CHAMBER OF COMMERCE AND INDUSTRY
Address : HANÇERLİ MAH.BUĞDAY PAZARI ABBASAĞA SOK.NO:8
Province : SAMSUN / -
Phone 1 : +90 362-4323626
Phone 2 :
Fax : +90 362-4329055
WEB : http://www.samsuntso.org.tr/
E-Mail : samsuntso@samsuntso.org.tr
PRESIDENT OF BOARD OF DIRECTOR : SALİH ZEKİ MURZİOĞLU
PRESIDENT OF ASSEMBLY : MUHARREM DURMUŞOĞLU
SECRETARY GENERAL : SÜLEYMAN KARABÜK

SANDIKLI CHAMBER OF COMMERCE AND INDUSTRY
Address : ÇAY MAH.DEREBOYU CAD.NO:53
Province : AFYONKARAHİSAR / SANDIKLI
Phone 1 : +90 272-5125139-
Phone 2 :
Fax : +90 272-5126029
WEB : http://www.sandiklitso.tobb.org.tr
E-Mail : sandiklitso@x.com
PRESIDENT OF BOARD OF DIRECTOR : MUSTAFA ÖZER
PRESIDENT OF ASSEMBLY : İBRAHİM ÖZER
SECRETARY GENERAL : MUSTAFA OĞUZ

SANLIURFA CHAMBER OF COMMERCE AND INDUSTRY
Address : PAŞABAĞI MAH. ADALET CAD. NO:9
Province : Ş.URFA / -
Phone 1 : +90 414-3181800-
Phone 2 :
Fax : +90 414-3181811
WEB : http://www.sutso.org.tr/
E-Mail : sanliurfatso@tobb.org.tr
PRESIDENT OF BOARD OF DIRECTOR : EYYÜP SABRİ ERTEKİN
PRESIDENT OF ASSEMBLY : İBRAHİM İLETMİŞ
SECRETARY GENERAL : FARUK YAŞAR

SEFAATLI CHAMBER OF COMMERCE AND INDUSTRY
Address : SOKULLU SOK.
Province : YOZGAT / ŞEFAATLI
Phone 1 : +90 354-5641274
Phone 2 :
Fax : +90 354-5641274
WEB : http://www.sefaatlitso.tobb.org.tr/
E-Mail :
PRESIDENT OF BOARD OF DIRECTOR : ALİ ULUSOY
PRESIDENT OF ASSEMBLY : FERHAT COŞKUN
SECRETARY GENERAL : YASİN KARACA

SEYDISEHIR CHAMBER OF COMMERCE
Address : ULUKAPI MAH.701 SOKAK NO:9/1
Province : KONYA / SEYDİŞEHİR
Phone 1 : +90 332-5826788
Phone 2 :
Fax : +90 332-5820900
WEB : http://www.seydisehirtso.org.tr/
E-Mail : bilgi@seydisehirtso.org.tr

PRESIDENT OF BOARD OF DIRECTOR : CEMAL KÜÇÜK
PRESIDENT OF ASSEMBLY : REFİK ŞENARSLAN
SECRETARY GENERAL : ÖZTÜRK HAN KÜÇÜK

SIIRT CHAMBER OF COMMERCE AND INDUSTRY
Address : BAHÇELİEVLER MAHALLESİ A.GAFFAR OKK AN CD.NO:32
Province : SİİRT / -
Phone 1 : +90 484-2231203/
Phone 2 :
Fax : +90 484-2234097
WEB : http://www.siirttso.org.tr
E-Mail : info@siirttso.org.tr
PRESIDENT OF BOARD OF DIRECTOR : GÜVEN KUZU
PRESIDENT OF ASSEMBLY : NİHAT ÖZDEMİR
SECRETARY GENERAL : RAŞİT BAŞAR TANER

SILIFKE CHAMBER OF COMMERCE AND INDUSTRY
Address : CAMİKEBİR MAH. MEFKURE SOK. NO:2
Province : MERSİN / SİLİFKE
Phone 1 : +90 324-7141038
Phone 2 : +90 324-7144538-
Fax : +90 324-7144483
WEB : http://www.sitso.org.tr/
E-Mail : silifketicaretodasi@ttnet.net.tr
PRESIDENT OF BOARD OF DIRECTOR : NURETTİN KAYNAR
PRESIDENT OF ASSEMBLY : ALİ DOĞAN
SECRETARY GENERAL : RECEP YILDIRIM BAYDAR

SIMAV CHAMBER OF COMMERCE AND INDUSTRY
Address : ŞADIRVANLAR CADDESİ 6.SOKAK NO:9
Province : KÜTAHYA / SİMAV
Phone 1 : +90 274-5131046
Phone 2 : +90 5135654
Fax : +90 274-5135742
WEB : http://www.simavtso.org.tr/
E-Mail : simavtso@tobb.org.tr
PRESIDENT OF BOARD OF DIRECTOR : ŞEREF KAZCIOĞLU
PRESIDENT OF ASSEMBLY : HÜSEYİN RACİ HAZIROĞLU
SECRETARY GENERAL : MUSTAFA ŞENFERAH

SINOP CHAMBER OF COMMERCE AND INDUSTRY
Address : ATATÜRK CAD.DİZDAROĞLU SOK.NO:5
Province : SİNOP / -
Phone 1 : +90 368-2611806
Phone 2 : +90 368-2601077
Fax : +90 368-2602470
WEB : http://www.sinoptso.tobb.org.tr/
E-Mail :
PRESIDENT OF BOARD OF DIRECTOR : EROL DERİCİ
PRESIDENT OF ASSEMBLY : MUHARREM DEMİRCAN
SECRETARY GENERAL : TANER AYDEMİR

SIVAS CHAMBER OF COMMERCE AND INDUSTRY
Address : TURGUT ÖZAL CADDESİ-FEN LİSESİ YANI
Province : SİVAS / -
Phone 1 : +90 346-2211384-
Phone 2 : +90 346-2231958
Fax : +90 346-2212237
WEB : http://www.sivastso.org/
E-Mail : info@sivastso.org
PRESIDENT OF BOARD OF DIRECTOR : HACI OSMAN YILDIRIM
PRESIDENT OF ASSEMBLY : NECATİ ŞAHİN
SECRETARY GENERAL : MUTLU TÜRKOĞLU

SIVEREK CHAMBER OF COMMERCE AND INDUSTRY
Address : CUMHURİYET CAD.İSPAHİ PAZARI ÜZERİ KAT:2 NO:44-45
Province : Ş.URFA / SİVEREK
Phone 1 : +90 414-5521023
Phone 2 :
Fax : +90 414-5522351
WEB : http://www.siverektso.org.tr
E-Mail : siverektso@tobb.org.tr
PRESIDENT OF BOARD OF DIRECTOR : SALİH SERDAL BUCAK
PRESIDENT OF ASSEMBLY : ZÜBEYİR KILIÇ
SECRETARY GENERAL : FATIMA KARA

SOMA CHAMBER OF COMMERCE AND INDUSTRY
Address : KURTULUŞ MAH.İSTİKLAL CAD.3
Province : MANİSA / SOMA
Phone 1 : +90 236-6131156-
Phone 2 :
Fax : +90 236-6120515
WEB : http://www.somatso.org.tr/
E-Mail : somaticodasi@superonline.com
PRESIDENT OF BOARD OF DIRECTOR : HAKAN IŞIK
PRESIDENT OF ASSEMBLY : NECATİ DANACI
SECRETARY GENERAL : MEHMET ERGİN GENÇ

SORGUN CHAMBER OF COMMERCE AND INDUSTRY
Address : YENİ BELEDİYE TERMİNALİ K:2

Province : YOZGAT / SORGUN
Phone 1 : +90 354-4151676
Phone 2 :
Fax : +90 0354-415 96
WEB : http://sorguntso.org.tr/
E-Mail :
PRESIDENT OF BOARD OF DIRECTOR : ÜZEYİR ARSLAN
PRESIDENT OF ASSEMBLY : RİFAT KAPLAN
SECRETARY GENERAL : SAMİ ERDOĞAN

SULUOVA CHAMBER OF COMMERCE AND INDUSTRY
Address : ORTA MAH.ATATÜRK BULVARI DENİZ İŞ HANI K:2
Province : AMASYA / SULUOVA
Phone 1 : +90 358-4171299
Phone 2 :
Fax : +90 358-4176592
WEB : http://www.suluovatso.com/
E-Mail :
PRESIDENT OF BOARD OF DIRECTOR : TURGUT AKSU
PRESIDENT OF ASSEMBLY : KENAN AYAZ
SECRETARY GENERAL : YALÇIN ÇAKMAK

SUNGURLU CHAMBER OF COMMERCE AND INDUSTRY
Address : SUNGUROĞLU MAH. LİSE CAD. ÇUHACILAR İŞHANI KAT:5
Province : ÇORUM / SUNGURLU
Phone 1 : +90 364-3112010
Phone 2 : +90 3120383
Fax : +90 364-3112010
WEB : http://www.sungurlutso.com
E-Mail : sungurlutso@ttnet.net.tr
PRESIDENT OF BOARD OF DIRECTOR : ALAİTTİN AKEL
PRESIDENT OF ASSEMBLY : İSHAK YELMENOĞLU
SECRETARY GENERAL : MEHMET FENERCİOĞLU

ŞIRNAK CHAMBER OF COMMERCE AND INDUSTRY
Address : YENİ MAHALLE ULUDERE CADDESİ NO:12
Province : ŞIRNAK / -
Phone 1 : +90 486-2165905-
Phone 2 :
Fax : +90 486-2165907
WEB : http://www.sirnaktso.org
E-Mail : bilgi@sirnaktso.org.tr
PRESIDENT OF BOARD OF DIRECTOR : OSMAN GELİŞ
PRESIDENT OF ASSEMBLY : SIDDIK BASAN
SECRETARY GENERAL : CİHAT SAKIN

TARSUS CHAMBER OF COMMERCE AND INDUSTRY
Address : 82.EVLER MAH. ADANA BULVARI BORSA SARAYI KAT:3
Province : MERSİN / TARSUS
Phone 1 : +90 324-6135550-
Phone 2 : +90 6135552-6135
Fax : +90 324-6135554
WEB : http://www.tarsustso.org.tr
E-Mail : tarsustso@tarsustso.org
PRESIDENT OF BOARD OF DIRECTOR : HASAN RUHİ KOÇAK
PRESIDENT OF ASSEMBLY : ALİ KIRAÇ
SECRETARY GENERAL : ALİ UKAV

TASKOPRU CHAMBER OF COMMERCE AND INDUSTRY
Address : CUMHURİYET MEYDANI BELEDİYE İŞ MERKEZİ KAT:2 37400
Province : KASTAMONU / TAŞKÖPRÜ
Phone 1 : +90 366-4173339
Phone 2 :
Fax : +90 366-4171130
WEB : http://taskoprutso.tobb.org.tr
E-Mail :
PRESIDENT OF BOARD OF DIRECTOR : MURAT BALCIOĞLU
PRESIDENT OF ASSEMBLY : MUSTAFA FAZIL KÖKYAY
SECRETARY GENERAL : HAKAN ÖZSOY

TATVAN CHAMBER OF COMMERCE AND INDUSTRY
Address : CUMHURİYET CAD.NO:180
Province : BİTLİS / TATVAN
Phone 1 : +90 434-8271266
Phone 2 :
Fax : +90 434-8279899
WEB : http://www.tatso.org.tr/
E-Mail :
PRESIDENT OF BOARD OF DIRECTOR : BİLAL DAĞDAĞAN
PRESIDENT OF ASSEMBLY : İHSAN BAKIRHAN
SECRETARY GENERAL : RAHİME YILMAZ ACET

TAVSANLI CHAMBER OF COMMERCE AND INDUSTRY
Address : YENİ MAH.ARİFAĞA SOK.NO:2 43300
Province : KÜTAHYA / TAVŞANLI
Phone 1 : +90 274-6141381-
Phone 2 : +90 6154358
Fax : +90 274-6148647
WEB : http://www.ttso.org/
E-Mail : ttso@ttso.org
PRESIDENT OF BOARD OF DIRECTOR : DAVUT EFE
PRESIDENT OF ASSEMBLY : İLHAMİ AYDIN
SECRETARY GENERAL : HACER MÜCELLA KIR

TEKIRDAG CHAMBER OF COMMERCE AND INDUSTRY
Address : ERTUĞRUL MAH.MİMAR SİNAN CAD.NO:3 59100
Province : TEKİRDAĞ / -
Phone 1 : +90 282-2612171
Phone 2 : +90 282-2611092
Fax : +90 282-2630002
WEB : http://www.tekirdagtso.org.tr/
E-Mail : ttso@tekirdagtso.org.tr
PRESIDENT OF BOARD OF DIRECTOR : CENGİZ GÜNAY
PRESIDENT OF ASSEMBLY : MUSTAFA ÖZDEN
SECRETARY GENERAL : İRFAN EKİCİ

TERME CHAMBER OF COMMERCE AND INDUSTRY
Address : ÇAY MAH.ÇAĞLAYAN CAD.NO:17 KAT:2
Province : SAMSUN / TERME
Phone 1 : +90 362-8762158
Phone 2 : +90 362-8765953
Fax : +90 362-8762158
WEB : http://termetso.org.tr/
E-Mail : info@termetso.org.tr
PRESIDENT OF BOARD OF DIRECTOR : AHMET EKMEKÇİ
PRESIDENT OF ASSEMBLY : MEHMET KÖRPE
SECRETARY GENERAL : FATMA MALKOÇ AVCI

TOKAT CHAMBER OF COMMERCE AND INDUSTRY
Address : GAZİOSMANPAŞA BULVARI NO:4/2 60030
Province : TOKAT / -
Phone 1 : +90 356-2141033
Phone 2 : +90 356-2141736
Fax : +90 356-2145040
WEB : http://www.tokattso.org.tr/
E-Mail : info@tokattso.org.tr
PRESIDENT OF BOARD OF DIRECTOR : AHMET ARAT
PRESIDENT OF ASSEMBLY : AHMET ORHAN GÜRGÜNOĞLU
SECRETARY GENERAL : YUSUF ZİYA ERDEM

TOSYA CHAMBER OF COMMERCE AND INDUSTRY
Address : MODERN ÇARŞI NO:213
Province : KASTAMONU / TOSYA
Phone 1 : +90 366-3131017
Phone 2 :
Fax : +90 366-3136066
WEB : http://www.tosyatso.org.tr
E-Mail : tosyatso@ttnet.net.tr
PRESIDENT OF BOARD OF DIRECTOR : METİN EKŞİ
PRESIDENT OF ASSEMBLY : MUSTAFA CEVİZCİ
SECRETARY GENERAL : NECATİ ABACI

TRABZON CHAMBER OF COMMERCE AND INDUSTRY
Address : PAZARKAPI MAH.SAHİL CAD.NO:103 61200
Province : TRABZON / -
Phone 1 : +90 462-3268070(
Phone 2 : +90 3212071-3221
Fax : +90 462-3218877
WEB : http://www.ttso.org.tr/
E-Mail : ttso@ttso.org.tr
PRESIDENT OF BOARD OF DIRECTOR : MUSTAFA SUAT HACISALİHOĞLU
PRESIDENT OF ASSEMBLY : MUSTAFA ŞADAN EREN
SECRETARY GENERAL : HAKAN GÜRHAN

TUNCELI CHAMBER OF COMMERCE AND INDUSTRY
Address : MOĞULTAY MAH.CUMHURİYET CADDESİ NO:27/1
Province : TUNCELİ / -
Phone 1 : +90 428-2122929
Phone 2 : +90 428-2122351
Fax : +90 428-2122351
WEB : http://www.tuncelitso.org.tr/
E-Mail : tuncelitso@mynet.com
PRESIDENT OF BOARD OF DIRECTOR : YUSUF CENGİZ
PRESIDENT OF ASSEMBLY : ALİ GÜYÜLDAR
SECRETARY GENERAL : VELİ GÜNGÖRMÜŞ

TURGUTLU CHAMBER OF COMMERCE AND INDUSTRY
Address : ERGENEKON MAHALLESİ FATİH BULVARI NO:2/1
Province : MANİSA / TURGUTLU
Phone 1 : +90 236-3136325-
Phone 2 : +90 3141790-3141
Fax : +90 236-3137019
WEB : http://www.tutso.org.tr/
E-Mail : posta@tutso.org.tr
PRESIDENT OF BOARD OF DIRECTOR : FARUK AYDIN
PRESIDENT OF ASSEMBLY : YAVUZ SEMİZLER
SECRETARY GENERAL : NEVZAT AVCI

TURHAL CHAMBER OF COMMERCE AND INDUSTRY
Address : YAVUZ SELİM MAH.TANRIVERDİ SOKAK NO:16/1 60300
Province : TOKAT / TURHAL
Phone 1 : +90 356-2751214
Phone 2 :

Fax : +90 356-2762744
WEB : http://www.turhaltso.org.tr/
E-Mail : turhaltso@tobb.org.tr
PRESIDENT OF BOARD OF DIRECTOR : ÖMER ÇENESİZ
PRESIDENT OF ASSEMBLY : SAMİ DİNLER
SECRETARY GENERAL : ALPER SAYGILI

UNYE CHAMBER OF COMMERCE AND INDUSTRY
Address : LİSELER MAH.DEVLET SAHİL YOLU NO: 357
Province : ORDU / ÜNYE
Phone 1 : +90 452-3231066
Phone 2 : +90 452-3240114
Fax : +90 452-3248343
WEB : http://www.unyetso.org.tr/
E-Mail : unyetso@unyetso.org.tr
PRESIDENT OF BOARD OF DIRECTOR : DURMUŞ ZOR
PRESIDENT OF ASSEMBLY : CAFER OCAK
SECRETARY GENERAL : AYDIN EKMEKCİ

URGUP CHAMBER OF COMMERCE AND INDUSTRY
Address : KAZIM KARABEKİR 1.CADDE NO:26
Province : NEVŞEHİR / ÜRGÜP
Phone 1 : +90 384-3414133
Phone 2 :
Fax : +90 384-3414662
WEB : http://urguptso.tobb.org.tr/
E-Mail : urguptso@tobb.org.tr
PRESIDENT OF BOARD OF DIRECTOR : AHMET AYDIN
PRESIDENT OF ASSEMBLY : HİLMİ YAZICI
SECRETARY GENERAL : EMRULLAH BAŞER

USAK CHAMBER OF COMMERCE AND INDUSTRY
Address : İSLİCE MAH. 2. GÜMÜŞ SK. NO:11
Province : UŞAK / -
Phone 1 : +90 276-2151084
Phone 2 : +90 276-2272539
Fax : +90 276-2152093
WEB : http://www.usaktso.org.tr
E-Mail : info@usaktso.org
PRESIDENT OF BOARD OF DIRECTOR : MUSTAFA KUVVET
PRESIDENT OF ASSEMBLY : İSMAİL KARAMAN
SECRETARY GENERAL : CANER URHAN

UZUNKOPRU CHAMBER OF COMMERCE AND INDUSTRY
Address : CUMHURİYET MEY.NO.21/A 22200
Province : EDİRNE / UZUNKÖPRÜ
Phone 1 : +90 284-5131064
Phone 2 : +90 5135413
Fax : +90 284-5132280
WEB : http://www.uzunkoprutso.tobb.org.tr
E-Mail : uzunkoprutso@tobb.org.tr
PRESIDENT OF BOARD OF DIRECTOR : ERCAN İHTİYAR
PRESIDENT OF ASSEMBLY : İSMAİL ŞENBAŞ
SECRETARY GENERAL : LEVENT YENİCİ

VAN CHAMBER OF COMMERCE AND INDUSTRY
Address : ALİ PAŞA MAHALLESİ İSKELE CAD. NO: 83 /65200
Province : VAN / -
Phone 1 : +90 04322143989-
Phone 2 : +90 04322142281
Fax : +90 432-2164488
WEB : http://www.vatso.org.tr/
E-Mail : vatso@vatso.org.tr
PRESIDENT OF BOARD OF DIRECTOR : NECDET TAKVA
PRESIDENT OF ASSEMBLY : HÜSEYİN GÜNEŞ
SECRETARY GENERAL : RAMAZAN TEMİZER

VEZIRKOPRU CHAMBER OF COMMERCE AND INDUSTRY
Address : KÖPRÜLÜLER CAD.ATATÜRK İŞ MERK. K:2 NO:122 55900
Province : SAMSUN / VEZİRKÖPRÜ
Phone 1 : +90 362-6471051
Phone 2 :
Fax : +90 362-6471051
WEB : http://www.vezirkoprutso.org.tr
E-Mail :
PRESIDENT OF BOARD OF DIRECTOR : ABDÜLKADİR FİŞEKÇİ
PRESIDENT OF ASSEMBLY : BEKİR KARADAŞ
SECRETARY GENERAL : EDİP ŞÜKRÜ KOÇ

YALOVA CHAMBER OF COMMERCE AND INDUSTRY
Address : DERE SOKAK NO:14
Province : YALOVA / -
Phone 1 : +90 226-8141224
Phone 2 : +90 8134410
Fax : +90 226-8121782
WEB : http://www.ytso.org.tr/
E-Mail : yalovatso@tobb.org.tr, info@ytso.org.tr
PRESIDENT OF BOARD OF DIRECTOR : TAHSİN BECAN
PRESIDENT OF ASSEMBLY : CEMİL DEMİRYÜREK
SECRETARY GENERAL : TANER ERİŞ

YALVAC CHAMBER OF COMMERCE AND INDUSTRY
Address : PAZAR AŞAĞI MAH. HAL SOKAK NO:2/201
Province : ISPARTA / YALVAÇ
Phone 1 : +90 246-4413374
Phone 2 :
Fax : +90 246-4417622

WEB : http://www.yalvactso.org.tr/
E-Mail : info@yalvactso.org.tr
PRESIDENT OF BOARD OF DIRECTOR : RAMAZAN NURİ DİRİK
PRESIDENT OF ASSEMBLY : FEVZİ YÜNCÜ
SECRETARY GENERAL : MEHMET SESLİ

YENISEHIR CHAMBER OF COMMERCE AND INDUSTRY
Address : ÇAYIR MAH.TEKEL SOK.NO:3 K:2 16900
Province : BURSA / YENİŞEHİR
Phone 1 : +90 224-7730238
Phone 2 : +90 224-7735816
Fax : +90 224-7732440
WEB : http://www.yenisehirtso.org.tr/
E-Mail :
PRESIDENT OF BOARD OF DIRECTOR : ORHAN TORUN
PRESIDENT OF ASSEMBLY : SALİH HOŞGÖNÜL
SECRETARY GENERAL : MEHMET GÖKGÖZ

YERKOY CHAMBER OF COMMERCE AND INDUSTRY
Address : YENİ MAH.HÜKÜMET CAD.YENİ PASAJ K:3
Province : YOZGAT / YERKÖY
Phone 1 : +90 354-5161188
Phone 2 :
Fax : +90 354-5161299
WEB : http://yerkoytso.org/
E-Mail : yerticodasi@hotmail.com
PRESIDENT OF BOARD OF DIRECTOR : MEHMET KAYA
PRESIDENT OF ASSEMBLY : MEHMET ATALAY
SECRETARY GENERAL : AHMET BARIŞ

YOZGAT CHAMBER OF COMMERCE AND INDUSTRY
Address : BELEDİYE HAL CADDESİ NO:11
Province : YOZGAT / -
Phone 1 : +90 354-2121121
Phone 2 : +90 354-2179104
Fax : +90 354-2121829
WEB : http://www.yozgattso.org.tr/
E-Mail :
PRESIDENT OF BOARD OF DIRECTOR : METİN ÖZIŞIK
PRESIDENT OF ASSEMBLY : SİNAN ÇELİK
SECRETARY GENERAL : ZİYA SAYDAM

YUKSEKOVA CHAMBER OF COMMERCE AND INDUSTRY
Address : CENGİZ TOPEL CAD. ZAGROS İŞ MERKEZİ K:5 NO:503
Province : HAKKARİ / YUKSEKOVA
Phone 1 : +90 438-3512447
Phone 2 :
Fax : +90 438-3515881
WEB : http://www.yuksekovatso.org.tr
E-Mail :
PRESIDENT OF BOARD OF DIRECTOR : SALİH ÖZDEMİR
PRESIDENT OF ASSEMBLY : NEDİM SELÇUK
SECRETARY GENERAL : MELEK MENGEŞ

ZILE CHAMBER OF COMMERCE AND INDUSTRY
Address : İSMET İNÖNÜ CADDESİ NO:42
Province : TOKAT / ZİLE
Phone 1 : +90 356-3171086-
Phone 2 : +90 356-3178254
Fax : +90 356-3171178
WEB : http://www.ziletso.org.tr/
E-Mail : ziletso@tobb.org.tr
PRESIDENT OF BOARD OF DIRECTOR : ŞÜKRÜ SARGIN
PRESIDENT OF ASSEMBLY : SAMİ SOLMAZ
SECRETARY GENERAL : ERTUĞRUL OĞUZ ŞENGÖR

ZONGULDAK CHAMBER OF COMMERCE AND INDUSTRY
Address : YAYLA MAHALLESİ BAĞLIK CAD. NO:5
Province : ZONGULDAK / -
Phone 1 : +90 372-2511156
Phone 2 : +90 372-2511511
Fax : +90 372-2531614
WEB : http://www.ztso.org.tr/
E-Mail : bilgi@ztso.org.tr
PRESIDENT OF BOARD OF DIRECTOR : MEHMET SALİH DEMİR
PRESIDENT OF ASSEMBLY : ZAFER SAĞLAM
SECRETARY GENERAL : RENDA OKAY

COMMODITY EXCHANGES

ADANA COMMODITY EXCHANGE
Address : ATATÜRK CAD.BELEDİYE KARŞISI NO:2 01330 SEYHAN
Province : ADANA / -
Phone 1 : +90 322-4543631-
Phone 2 : +90 4537034
Fax : +90 322-4543632-
WEB : http://www.adanatb.org.tr
E-Mail : genelsekreterlik@adanatb.org.tr
PRESIDENT OF BOARD OF DIRECTOR : MUAMMER ÇALIŞKAN
PRESIDENT OF ASSEMBLY : ŞAHİN BİLGİÇ
SECRETARY GENERAL : MUSTAFA HIZLI

ADIYAMAN COMMODITY EXCHANGE
Address : GÖLBAŞI KARAYOLU ÜZERİ 6.KM
Province : ADIYAMAN / -
Phone 1 : +90 416-2231877-
Phone 2 :
Fax : +90 416-2231879
WEB : http://www.adiyamantb.gov.tr

E-Mail : ticaret.borsasi@superonline.com
PRESIDENT OF BOARD OF DIRECTOR : MAHMUT FIRAT
PRESIDENT OF ASSEMBLY : ÖZCAN ÖNCEBE
SECRETARY GENERAL : ALİ UĞUR ÇİLCAN

AFYONKARAHİSAR COMMODITY EXCHANGE
Address : SELÇUKLU MAH. İZMİR KARAYOLU 8. KM NO: 16-18
Province : AFYONKARAHİSAR / -
Phone 1 : +90 272-2525650-
Phone 2 : +90 272-2525652
Fax : +90 272-2525653-
WEB : http://www.afyonborsa.org.tr
E-Mail : gensek@afyonborsa.org.tr
PRESIDENT OF BOARD OF DIRECTOR : MEHMET MÜHSÜRLER
PRESIDENT OF ASSEMBLY : FAHRETTİN ZOBALI
SECRETARY GENERAL : HÜSEYİN EKER

AKHISAR COMMODITY EXCHANGE
Address : HÜRRİYET MAHALLESİ 450.SOK.NO.103 AKHİSAR-MANİSA PK.45200
Province : MANİSA / AKHİSAR
Phone 1 : +90 236-4141832-
Phone 2 : +90 236.4132554
Fax : +90 236-4125542
WEB : http://www.akhisartb.org.tr
E-Mail : bilgi@akhisartb.org.tr
PRESIDENT OF BOARD OF DIRECTOR : ALPER ALHAT
PRESIDENT OF ASSEMBLY : BAHATTİN ALKIN
SECRETARY GENERAL : GÖKBEN DİKİLİ ALTAŞ

AKSARAY COMMODITY EXCHANGE
Address : KARASU MEVKİ YENİ BUĞDAY PAZARI E-90 KARAYOLU ÜZERİ
Province : AKSARAY / -
Phone 1 : +90 382-2151099
Phone 2 :
Fax : +90 382-2157449
WEB :
E-Mail :
PRESIDENT OF BOARD OF DIRECTOR : HAMİT ÖZKÖK
PRESIDENT OF ASSEMBLY : NURETTİN YAPILCAN
SECRETARY GENERAL : RAMAZAN ETLİK

AKSEHIR COMMODITY EXCHANGE
Address : TİPİ MAH.YENİ BUĞDAY PAZARI NO:54 PK.32 42551
Province : KONYA / AKŞEHİR
Phone 1 : +90 332-8136305-
Phone 2 :
Fax : +90 332-8121501
WEB : http://www.aksehirtb.org.tr/
E-Mail : aksehirtb@tobb.org.tr
PRESIDENT OF BOARD OF DIRECTOR : YUSUF İZZETTİN YAYLA
PRESIDENT OF ASSEMBLY : MUSTAFA DOĞAN
SECRETARY GENERAL : HASAN SAYIN ARI

AKYAZI COMMODITY EXCHANGE
Address : FATİH MAHALLESİ YAHYALI CADDESİ 54400
Province : SAKARYA / AKYAZI
Phone 1 : +90 264-4186184-
Phone 2 : +90 4185517
Fax : +90 264-4186186
WEB : http://www.akyazitb.org.tr
E-Mail :
PRESIDENT OF BOARD OF DIRECTOR : ALİ ŞENER BAYRAKTAR
PRESIDENT OF ASSEMBLY : HÜSAMETTİN ŞEN
SECRETARY GENERAL : ADEM İSMAİLTEVFİKOĞLU

ALACA COMMODITY EXCHANGE
Address : ZİLE CAD.ZAHİRE PAZARI NO:17/A
Province : ÇORUM / ALACA
Phone 1 : +90 364-4112475
Phone 2 :
Fax : +90 364-4116189
WEB : www.alacatb.org.tr
E-Mail : alacatb@tobb.org.tr
PRESIDENT OF BOARD OF DIRECTOR : FAHRİ COŞKUN
PRESIDENT OF ASSEMBLY : NİHAT GÜNDER
SECRETARY GENERAL : FAİK YETGİN

ALASEHIR COMMODITY EXCHANGE
Address : OSMAN AKÇA TÜCCARLAR SİTESİ NO:2 45600
Province : MANİSA / ALAŞEHİR
Phone 1 : +90 236-6531366
Phone 2 :
Fax : +90 236-6540526
WEB :
E-Mail : alasehirtb@ttmail.net.tr
PRESIDENT OF BOARD OF DIRECTOR : HÜSEYİN SOYGÜR
PRESIDENT OF ASSEMBLY : YILMAZ YILDIRIM
SECRETARY GENERAL : HAKAN ALBAN

ANKARA COMMODITY EXCHANGE
Address : MACUN MAH.171.SOKAK NO:4 YENİMAHALLE
Province : ANKARA / -
Phone 1 : +90 312-3270000
Phone 2 :
Fax : +90 312-3240857
WEB : http://www.ankaratb.org.tr/
E-Mail : info@ankaratb.org.tr

PRESIDENT OF BOARD OF DIRECTOR : FAİK YAVUZ
PRESIDENT OF ASSEMBLY : EROL GEMALMAZ
SECRETARY GENERAL : EYÜP ŞENOL ÖMEROĞLU

ANTAKYA COMMODITY EXCHANGE
Address : SÜREYYA HALEFOĞLU CADDESİ BORSA İŞ HANI K:1
Province : HATAY / -
Phone 1 : +90 326-2144594-
Phone 2 : +90 2151586
Fax : +90 326-2125748
WEB : http://www.antakyatb.gov.tr/
E-Mail : info@antakyatb.gov.tr
PRESIDENT OF BOARD OF DIRECTOR : MEHMET ALİ KUSEYRİ
PRESIDENT OF ASSEMBLY : ERKAN MISTIKOĞLU
SECRETARY GENERAL : METİN KUSEYRİ

ANTALYA COMMODITY EXCHANGE
Address : CUMHURİYET CAD.BORSA İŞHANI KAT:2 07040
Province : ANTALYA / -
Phone 1 : +90 242-2442670-
Phone 2 : +90 2412828
Fax : +90 242-2411158
WEB : http://www.antalyaborsa.org.tr/
E-Mail : info@antalyaborsa.org.tr
PRESIDENT OF BOARD OF DIRECTOR : ALİ ÇANDIR
PRESIDENT OF ASSEMBLY : HÜSEYİN CAHİT KAYAN
SECRETARY GENERAL : TOLGAHAN ALAVANT

AYDIN COMMODITY EXCHANGE
Address : ATA MAHALLESİ DENİZLİ BULVARI NO:18 09010/AYDIN
Province : AYDIN / -
Phone 1 : +90 256-2116145-
Phone 2 : +90 256-211 63 1
Fax : +90 256-2116315
WEB : http://www.aydintb.gov.tr/
E-Mail : aydintb@tobb.org.tr
PRESIDENT OF BOARD OF DIRECTOR : ADNAN BOSNALI
PRESIDENT OF ASSEMBLY : AHMET BAHRİ ERDEL
SECRETARY GENERAL : ÇİMEN MUTLU

BABAESKİ COMMODITY EXCHANGE
Address : CUMHURİYET MAH.ESKİ EDİRNE ASFALTI CADDESİ NO:24
Province : KIRKLARELİ / BABAESKİ
Phone 1 : +90 288-5121756
Phone 2 : +90 5127556
Fax : +90 288-5125739
WEB : http://www.babaeskitb.tobb.org.tr/
E-Mail : babaeskitb@tobb.org.tr
PRESIDENT OF BOARD OF DIRECTOR : FAHRETTİN ÖZÜN
PRESIDENT OF ASSEMBLY : HİCRET ÖZCAN
SECRETARY GENERAL : İSMAİL DİMİTOKA

BAFRA COMMODITY EXCHANGE
Address : ALPARSLAN MAHALLESİ SİNOP/SAMSUN KARAYOLU ÜZERİ 55400
Province : SAMSUN / BAFRA
Phone 1 : +90 362-5443300-
Phone 2 : +90 BŞK.5443354
Fax : +90 362-5443353
WEB : http://www.bafratb.org.tr/
E-Mail : bafraborsa@ttnet.net.tr
PRESIDENT OF BOARD OF DIRECTOR : NAMIK KİBAROĞLU
PRESIDENT OF ASSEMBLY : MUSTAFA ACAR
SECRETARY GENERAL : BAYRAM TOSUN

BALIKESIR COMMODITY EXCHANGE
Address : TİCARET BORSASI SİTESİ ESKİ KEPSUT CAD. 3.KM 10040/BALIKESİR
Province : BALIKESİR / -
Phone 1 : +90 0266-2398700
Phone 2 :
Fax : +90 0266-2418288
WEB : http://balikesirtb.tobb.org.tr/
E-Mail : balborsa@ttnet.net.tr
PRESIDENT OF BOARD OF DIRECTOR : FARUK KULA
PRESIDENT OF ASSEMBLY : İBRAHİM AYTEKİN
SECRETARY GENERAL : İSMAİL ELGÜN

BANDIRMA COMMODITY EXCHANGE
Address : BALIKESİR ASFALTI 6.KM. PK.85
Province : BALIKESİR / BANDIRMA
Phone 1 : +90 266-7338465-
Phone 2 : +90 0266-7338435
Fax : +90 266-7338459
WEB : http://www.bantb.org.tr/
E-Mail : bantb@bantb.org.tr
PRESIDENT OF BOARD OF DIRECTOR : HALİT SEZGİN
PRESIDENT OF ASSEMBLY : İSMAİL TUNÇBİLEK
SECRETARY GENERAL : ERTUNÇ İŞBAY

BATMAN COMMODITY EXCHANGE
Address : HİLAL MAH. NERGİZ CAD. NO: 145 YENİ OTOGAR ARKASI
Province : BATMAN / -
Phone 1 : +90 488-2153792
Phone 2 : +90 212 50 76
Fax : +90 488-2146492
WEB : http://batmantb.org.tr
E-Mail : batmanborsa@hotmail.com

PRESIDENT OF BOARD OF DIRECTOR : ARİF GÜNEŞ
PRESIDENT OF ASSEMBLY : MEHMET BEŞİR ALTUNÇ
SECRETARY GENERAL : VEHBİ AKBULUT

BIGA COMMODITY EXCHANGE
Address : GÜMÜŞÇAY CAD.ZAHİRECİLER SİTESİ NO:23
Province : ÇANAKKALE / BİGA
Phone 1 : +90 286-3163339-
Phone 2 :
Fax : +90 286-3167780
WEB : http://www.bigatb.tobb.org.tr/
E-Mail : bigatb@tobb.org.tr
PRESIDENT OF BOARD OF DIRECTOR : MESUT OKYAY
PRESIDENT OF ASSEMBLY : FAHRETTİN DENİZ
SECRETARY GENERAL : HALİL EROL

BOĞAZLIYAN COMMODITY EXCHANGE
Address : KAYSERİ YOLU 3. KM.
Province : YOZGAT / BOĞAZLIYAN
Phone 1 : +90 354-6452882
Phone 2 :
Fax : +90 354-6452022
WEB : http://www.bogazliyantb.org.tr/
E-Mail :
PRESIDENT OF BOARD OF DIRECTOR : HARUN HALICI
PRESIDENT OF ASSEMBLY : TAYYAR AKSU
SECRETARY GENERAL : ALİ AYIK

BOLVADİN COMMODITY EXCHANGE
Address : LALASİNANPAŞA MAH. MODA SOKAK NO:5
Province : AFYONKARAHİSAR / BOLVADİN
Phone 1 : +90 272-6127220
Phone 2 :
Fax : +90 272-6127230
WEB : http://www.bolvadintb.org.tr/
E-Mail : bolvadinticaretborsasi@hotmail.com
PRESIDENT OF BOARD OF DIRECTOR : ABDÜLKADİR BOYAR
PRESIDENT OF ASSEMBLY : LATİF BAYRAM
SECRETARY GENERAL : FATİH ÇELİKER

BURDUR COMMODITY EXCHANGE
Address : ÖZGÜR MAH. OTOTAMİRCİLER 5.SOKAK NO:1-7
Province : BURDUR / -
Phone 1 : +90 248-2337991-
Phone 2 : +90 233 38 76
Fax : +90 248-2337567
WEB : http://www.burdurtb.tobb.org.tr/
E-Mail : burdurtb@tobb.org.tr
PRESIDENT OF BOARD OF DIRECTOR : YILMAZ BAŞAR
PRESIDENT OF ASSEMBLY : HİKMET ÇANGIR
SECRETARY GENERAL : HALİL GÖKER

BURSA COMMODITY EXCHANGE
Address : UZUNÇARŞI BORSA SOK.NO:3/1 16020
Province : BURSA / -
Phone 1 : +90 224-2211218-
Phone 2 :
Fax : +90 224-2213030
WEB : http://btb.org.tr/
E-Mail : bursaticaretborsasi@superonline.com
PRESIDENT OF BOARD OF DIRECTOR : ÖZER MATLI
PRESIDENT OF ASSEMBLY : MEHMET AYDIN
SECRETARY GENERAL : FEHMİ YILDIZ

CANAKKALE COMMODITY EXCHANGE
Address : BURSA YOLU 2.KM.
Province : ÇANAKKALE / -
Phone 1 : +90 286-2124770-
Phone 2 :
Fax : +90 286-2124769
WEB : http://www.canakkaleticaretborsasi.org.tr/
E-Mail : ticaretborsasi@ttnet.net.tr
PRESIDENT OF BOARD OF DIRECTOR : SEFER KAYA ÜZEN
PRESIDENT OF ASSEMBLY : ABDULLAH DENİZ
SECRETARY GENERAL : SEVCAN ELVER

CANKIRI COMMODITY EXCHANGE
Address : KASTAMONU YOLU ÜZERİ SÜT FABRİKASI KARŞISI NO:1
Province : ÇANKIRI / -
Phone 1 : +90 376-2138880
Phone 2 : +90 2138881
Fax : +90 376-2122653
WEB : http://www.cankiritb.org.tr
E-Mail :
PRESIDENT OF BOARD OF DIRECTOR : OĞUZ AK
PRESIDENT OF ASSEMBLY : HÜSNÜ ÜNAL
SECRETARY GENERAL : ÖZLEM KOCA

CARSAMBA COMMODITY EXCHANGE
Address : ÇAY MAH.KÜÇÜK HAMAM SOK.NO:6
Province : SAMSUN / ÇARŞAMBA
Phone 1 : +90 362-8331396-
Phone 2 : +90 8322426
Fax : +90 362-8322864
WEB : http://www.carsambatb.org.tr
E-Mail :
PRESIDENT OF BOARD OF DIRECTOR : KAZIM GÜROL YILMAZ
PRESIDENT OF ASSEMBLY : NURETTİN ÖZTEKİN
SECRETARY GENERAL : EFTAL YETİMOĞLU

CEYHAN COMMODITY EXCHANGE
Address : TÜRLÜBAŞ MAH.35.SOK.N0:6

Province : ADANA / CEYHAN
Phone 1 : +90 322-6133019-
Phone 2 :
Fax : +90 322-6139128
WEB : http://www.ceyhantb.tobb.org.tr
E-Mail : ceyhanborsa@hotmail.com
PRESIDENT OF BOARD OF DIRECTOR : MEMİCİ GÜLEÇYÜZ
PRESIDENT OF ASSEMBLY : MUSTAFA AYDAR
SECRETARY GENERAL : MAHMUT ELMA

CİHANBEYLİ COMMODITY EXCHANGE
Address : ANKARA KONYA YOLU 5.KM.
Province : KONYA / CİHANBEYLİ
Phone 1 : +90 0332-6732223
Phone 2 :
Fax : +90 0332-6732210
WEB :
E-Mail :
PRESIDENT OF BOARD OF DIRECTOR : HACI KABAKCI
PRESIDENT OF ASSEMBLY : FARUK YILMAZ KANAT
SECRETARY GENERAL : ALİ ÇİVİ

CORLU COMMODITY EXCHANGE
Address : HIDIRAĞA MAH. SİNAN DEDE KÜME EVLER NO:2-A
Province : TEKİRDAĞ / ÇORLU
Phone 1 : +90 282-6511130-
Phone 2 : +90 6530717-6511
Fax : +90 282-6511073
WEB : http://www.corlutb.tobb.org.tr/
E-Mail : corluticborsasi@superonline.com
PRESIDENT OF BOARD OF DIRECTOR : YÜKSEL ERTAN
PRESIDENT OF ASSEMBLY : MUSTAFA YAVUZ AKIN
SECRETARY GENERAL : SELMA TOKSÖZ

CORUM COMMODITY EXCHANGE
Address : AKKENT MAH.T.C ÇORUM TİCARET BORSASI KOMPLEKSİ
Province : ÇORUM / -
Phone 1 : +90 364-2240950-
Phone 2 : +90 2242568-2247
Fax : +90 364-2124670
WEB : http://www.corumtb.org.tr
E-Mail : corumtb@tobb.org.tr
PRESIDENT OF BOARD OF DIRECTOR : ALİ BEKTAŞ
PRESIDENT OF ASSEMBLY : MUSTAFA BOYRAZ
SECRETARY GENERAL : FUNDA ERTEKİN

CUBUK COMMODITY EXCHANGE
Address : CUMHURİYET MAH. SANAYİ CAD. NO: 8
Province : ANKARA / ÇUBUK
Phone 1 : +90 312-8383581-
Phone 2 : +90 312-8372575
Fax : +90 312-8382805
WEB : http://www.cubuktb.org.tr/
E-Mail : cubuktb@tobb.org.tr
PRESIDENT OF BOARD OF DIRECTOR : VELİ DEMİR
PRESIDENT OF ASSEMBLY : AHMET DEMİR
SECRETARY GENERAL : MEHMET BAL

DENIZLI COMMODITY EXCHANGE
Address : KAYALIK CAD.ULUÇARŞI İŞHANI KAT.5
Province : DENİZLİ / -
Phone 1 : +90 258-2641990-
Phone 2 :
Fax : +90 258-2641770-
WEB : http://www.denizlitb.tobb.org.tr/
E-Mail : denizlitb@tobb.org.tr
PRESIDENT OF BOARD OF DIRECTOR : İBRAHİM TEFENLİLİ
PRESIDENT OF ASSEMBLY : İBRAHİM YAYAN
SECRETARY GENERAL : ALİ ŞAHİN

DIYARBAKIR COMMODITY EXCHANGE
Address : ŞANLIURFA YOLU 8.KM
Province : DİYARBAKIR / -
Phone 1 : +90 412-2550909-
Phone 2 : +90 2550922-26(5
Fax : +90 412-2550893-
WEB : http://www.ditib.org/
E-Mail : bilgi@ditib.org, diyarbakirtb@tobb.org.tr
PRESIDENT OF BOARD OF DIRECTOR : EBUBEKİR BAL
PRESIDENT OF ASSEMBLY : AHMET AY
SECRETARY GENERAL : KAMİRAN KARADAĞ

DÜZCE COMMODITY EXCHANGE
Address : D-100 KARAYOLU ÜZERİ İHSANİYE KÖYÜ
Province : DÜZCE / -
Phone 1 : +90 380-5365217
Phone 2 : +90 380-5365219
Fax : +90 380-5365218
WEB : http://www.duzcetb.org.tr/
E-Mail : duzcetb@superonline.com
PRESIDENT OF BOARD OF DIRECTOR : NURETTİN KARSLIOĞLU
PRESIDENT OF ASSEMBLY : RAHMİ SOLAK
SECRETARY GENERAL : DURSUN KARA

EDIRNE COMMODITY EXCHANGE
Address : BÜYÜKDÖLLÜK KÖYÜ YOLU ÜZERİ,TARIM AÇIK CEZAEVİ BİTİŞİĞİ P.K.:94 22020
Province : EDİRNE / -
Phone 1 : +90 284-2268500
Phone 2 :
Fax : +90 284-2268501
WEB : http://www.etb.org.tr/

E-Mail : etb@etb.org.tr
PRESIDENT OF BOARD OF DIRECTOR : ÖZAY ÖZTÜRK
PRESIDENT OF ASSEMBLY : FEDAİ ÇANIM
SECRETARY GENERAL : SERKAN KÖSEM

EDREMİT COMMODITY EXCHANGE
Address : MENDERES BULVARI NO:83
Province : BALIKESİR / EDREMİT
Phone 1 : +90 0266-3736566
Phone 2 :
Fax : +90 0266-3730701
WEB : http://www.edremittb.tobb.org.tr
E-Mail : edremitticaret@superonline.com
PRESIDENT OF BOARD OF DIRECTOR : ABDURRAHİM TARKAN DENİZER
PRESIDENT OF ASSEMBLY : ALİ RIZA TİMUR
SECRETARY GENERAL : SERVET YERLİ

ELAZIG COMMODITY EXCHANGE
Address : ÇARŞI MAH.MİMAR SİNAN CAD. NO:32/2
Province : ELAZIĞ / -
Phone 1 : +90 424-2386406-
Phone 2 : +90 424-2386405
Fax : +90 424-2184904
WEB : http://www.elazigtb.org.tr
E-Mail :
PRESIDENT OF BOARD OF DIRECTOR : MEHMET ALİ DUMANDAĞ
PRESIDENT OF ASSEMBLY : ABDULKERİM SİS
SECRETARY GENERAL : MURAT ÇİÇEK

EREGLI/KONYA COMMODITY EXCHANGE
Address : ZİYA GÖKALP MAH.REGÜLATÖR CAD. ER-SU MEYVE SUYU FAB.KARŞISI (YENİ BUĞDAY PAZARI)
Province : KONYA / KON.EREĞLİ
Phone 1 : +90 332-7347141-
Phone 2 :
Fax : +90 332-7345804
WEB : http://www.ereglitb.org
E-Mail :
PRESIDENT OF BOARD OF DIRECTOR : ZEKERİYA ÜNLÜ
PRESIDENT OF ASSEMBLY : DURMUŞ ALİ YÖNET
SECRETARY GENERAL : TUNCAY TUNÇ

ERZİNCAN COMMODITY EXCHANGE
Address : FEVZİPAŞA CAD.NO:19
Province : ERZİNCAN / -
Phone 1 : +90 0446-2147755
Phone 2 : +90 0446-2147757
Fax : +90 0446-2147758
WEB : http://www.erzincantb.org.tr/
E-Mail : erzincantb@tobb.org.tr
PRESIDENT OF BOARD OF DIRECTOR : NECMİ YAPINCA
PRESIDENT OF ASSEMBLY : SÜLEYMAN YILDIRIM
SECRETARY GENERAL : FUAT ÇAMURCU

ERZURUM COMMODITY EXCHANGE
Address : ALİ PAŞA MAH.MUSALLA CAD.NO:19
Province : ERZURUM / -
Phone 1 : +90 442-2420240-
Phone 2 : +90 442-2420242
Fax : +90 442-2420244
WEB : http://www.erzurumtb.org.tr/
E-Mail : erzurumtb@veezy.com
PRESIDENT OF BOARD OF DIRECTOR : İSMAİL HAKKI HINISLIOĞLU
PRESIDENT OF ASSEMBLY : MEHMET AKGÜN
SECRETARY GENERAL : VEYSEL GARANİ BİLİCİ

ESKISEHIR COMMODITY EXCHANGE
Address : GUNDOĞDU MAH. BORSA CAD. NO:21
Province : ESKİŞEHİR / -
Phone 1 : +90 222-2372783
Phone 2 : +90 222-2372786
Fax : +90 222-2379450
WEB : http://www.esktb.org.tr/
E-Mail : etb@turkport.net
PRESIDENT OF BOARD OF DIRECTOR : ÖMER ZEYDAN
PRESIDENT OF ASSEMBLY : HASAN ÖZTÜRK
SECRETARY GENERAL : ADNAN YILMAZ

FATSA COMMODITY EXCHANGE
Address : M.KEMAL PAŞA MAH.ATA CAD.NO:6
Province : ORDU / FATSA
Phone 1 : +90 452-4235355
Phone 2 :
Fax : +90 452-4233432
WEB : http://www.fatsatb.org.tr
E-Mail : fatsatb@tobb.org.tr
PRESIDENT OF BOARD OF DIRECTOR : ALİ FEYZİ
PRESIDENT OF ASSEMBLY : HÜSEYİN AYDIN
SECRETARY GENERAL : OSMAN CARLI

GAZIANTEP COMMODITY EXCHANGE
Address : GATEM BÖLGESİ BORSA SARAYI 27170 ŞEHİTKAMİL
Province : GAZİANTEP / -
Phone 1 : +90 342-2380839-
Phone 2 : +90 2381673-2381
Fax : +90 342-2381675
WEB : http://www.gtb.org.tr/
E-Mail : gtb@gtb.org.tr
PRESIDENT OF BOARD OF DIRECTOR : AHMET TİRYAKİOĞLU
PRESIDENT OF ASSEMBLY : SELAMİ MEMİŞ
SECRETARY GENERAL : ÖZGÜR BAYRAM

GEMLIK COMMODITY EXCHANGE
Address : DR.ZİYA KAYA MAHALLESİ CUMHURİYET CADDESİ NO:2
Province : BURSA / GEMLİK
Phone 1 : +90 224-5134373-
Phone 2 : +90 5140881
Fax : +90 224-5140882
WEB : http://www.gemliktb.tobb.org.tr/
E-Mail : gemliktb@tobb.org.tr
PRESIDENT OF BOARD OF DIRECTOR : ÖZDEN ÇAKIR
PRESIDENT OF ASSEMBLY : MUSTAFA DOĞAN
SECRETARY GENERAL : MELİH KARBAY

GIRESUN COMMODITY EXCHANGE
Address : HACI MİKTAT MAH.İNCEDAYI SOK. NO:4/2 28200
Province : GİRESUN / -
Phone 1 : +90 454-2161023-
Phone 2 :
Fax : +90 454-2123158
WEB : http://www.giresuntb.org.tr
E-Mail : info@giresuntb.org.tr
PRESIDENT OF BOARD OF DIRECTOR : MUSTAFA DEMİRCİ
PRESIDENT OF ASSEMBLY : HARUN AYDIN
SECRETARY GENERAL : EREN NİZAM

GÖNEN COMMODITY EXCHANGE
Address : KURTULUŞ MAH.HÜSEYİN TÜMER CAD. NO:94
Province : BALIKESİR / GÖNEN
Phone 1 : +90 0266-7621742
Phone 2 :
Fax : +90 0266-7621764
WEB : http://www.gonentb.tobb.org.tr/
E-Mail : gonentb@tobb.org.tr
PRESIDENT OF BOARD OF DIRECTOR : İBRAHİM MUTLU
PRESIDENT OF ASSEMBLY : MUSTAFA AVCI
SECRETARY GENERAL : TANER KEŞANLI

HAYMANA COMMODITY EXCHANGE
Address : SEYRAN MAH.YENİCE YOLU ÜZERİ 1.KM HAYMANA
Province : ANKARA / HAYMANA
Phone 1 : +90 312-6581866-
Phone 2 :
Fax : +90 312-6581866
WEB : http://www.haymanaborsasi.org.tr
E-Mail :
PRESIDENT OF BOARD OF DIRECTOR : SERVET ÖZER
PRESIDENT OF ASSEMBLY : ERDAL ÖZER
SECRETARY GENERAL : LOKMAN SARI

HAYRABOLU COMMODITY EXCHANGE
Address : KAHYA MAH.TEKİRDAĞ CADDESİ NO:56
Province : TEKİRDAĞ / HAYRABOLU
Phone 1 : +90 282-3151178-
Phone 2 :
Fax : +90 282-3151179
WEB : http://www.hayrabolutb.tobb.org.tr/
E-Mail : hayrabolutb@tobb.org.tr
PRESIDENT OF BOARD OF DIRECTOR : SÜREYYA ÇİFTÇİOĞLU
PRESIDENT OF ASSEMBLY : AHMET AKGÜN
SECRETARY GENERAL : SAİM DEMİRBAŞ

IGDIR COMMODITY EXCHANGE
Address : CUMHURİYET MAH.ZÜBEYDE HANIM BULVARI (AKBANK YANI) EMİN EKİNCİ İŞ MERKEZİ KAT:3
Province : IĞDIR / -
Phone 1 : +90 476-2279177
Phone 2 :
Fax : +90 476-2279177
WEB :
E-Mail :
PRESIDENT OF BOARD OF DIRECTOR : SERHAT KUMTEPE
PRESIDENT OF ASSEMBLY : EKREM AYDIN
SECRETARY GENERAL : SİBEL GÜNEŞ

ILGIN COMMODITY EXCHANGE
Address : UÇARI MAHALLESİ YENİ BUĞDAY PAZARI 42600
Province : KONYA / ILGIN
Phone 1 : +90 332-8810426-
Phone 2 :
Fax : +90 332-8827411
WEB : http://www.ilgintb.org.tr/
E-Mail :
PRESIDENT OF BOARD OF DIRECTOR : LÜTFİ KOÇ
PRESIDENT OF ASSEMBLY : DERMAN ESER
SECRETARY GENERAL : MUSTAFA ERTOK

IPSALA COMMODITY EXCHANGE
Address : ENEZ CAD.KABRİSTAN SOK.NO:105 NO:60
Province : EDİRNE / İPSALA
Phone 1 : +90 284-6161809-
Phone 2 :
Fax : +90 284-6161178
WEB : http://www.ipsalatb.org.tr/
E-Mail :
PRESIDENT OF BOARD OF DIRECTOR : İBRAHİM GİRGİN
PRESIDENT OF ASSEMBLY : NECATİ GÖRÜR
SECRETARY GENERAL : CÜNEYT ALTINBAŞ

ISKENDERUN COMMODITY EXCHANGE
Address : CUMHURİYET MEYDANI 40.SOK.NO:7 PK.130
Province : HATAY / İSKENDERUN
Phone 1 : +90 326-6171185-
Phone 2 :

Fax : +90 326-6142830
WEB : http://www.iskenderuntb.org.tr/
E-Mail : iskenderuntb@linuxmail.org
PRESIDENT OF BOARD OF DIRECTOR : SÜLEYMAN ÖZER
PRESIDENT OF ASSEMBLY : İBRAHİM KIRICI
SECRETARY GENERAL : AHMET ENGİN VAYISOĞLU

ISPARTA COMMODITY EXCHANGE
Address : KUTLUBEY MAHALLESİ-ÇINAR SOKAK NO:13
Province : ISPARTA / -
Phone 1 : +90 246-2328360-
Phone 2 : +90 2326674
Fax : +90 246-2326740
WEB : http://www.ispartatb.org.tr/
E-Mail : ispartatb@ispartatb.org.tr
PRESIDENT OF BOARD OF DIRECTOR : AHMET ADAR
PRESIDENT OF ASSEMBLY : NURİ SELÇUK
SECRETARY GENERAL : ALİ KOYAK

ISTANBUL COMMODITY EXCHANGE
Address : ZAHİRE BORSASI SOK.NO:7 34420 BAHÇEKAPI
Province : İSTANBUL / -
Phone 1 : +90 212-5118440
Phone 2 : +90 5118441
Fax : +90 212-5222677
WEB : http://www.istib.gov.tr
E-Mail : gensek@istanbulticaretborsasi.org.tr
PRESIDENT OF BOARD OF DIRECTOR : ÇAMUR ALİ KOPUZ
PRESIDENT OF ASSEMBLY : BÜLENT KASAP
SECRETARY GENERAL : ALİ YAVUZ YİĞİT

IZMIR COMMODITY EXCHANGE
Address : GAZİ BULVARI NO:2 35210
Province : İZMİR / -
Phone 1 : +90 232-4251370-
Phone 2 :
Fax : +90 232-4842954
WEB : http://www.itb.org.tr/
E-Mail : muamelat@itb.org.tr
PRESIDENT OF BOARD OF DIRECTOR : IŞINSU KESTELLİ
PRESIDENT OF ASSEMBLY : ŞÜKRÜ BARIŞ KOCAGÖZ
SECRETARY GENERAL :

KADİRLİ COMMODITY EXCHANGE
Address : K.KARA BULVARI KIZILAY İŞ HANI NO:14 K:2
Province : OSMANİYE / KADİRLİ
Phone 1 : +90 328-7174300-
Phone 2 :
Fax : +90 328-7177890
WEB : http://www.kadirlitb.tobb.org.tr/
E-Mail : kadirlitb@posta.tobb.org.tr
PRESIDENT OF BOARD OF DIRECTOR : YALÇIN TATLI
PRESIDENT OF ASSEMBLY : SEYFETTİN ÖZTOK
SECRETARY GENERAL : HÜSEYİN ALICI

KAHRAMANMARAS COMMODITY EXCHANGE
Address : BORSA CADDESİ-TRABZON BULVARI NO:9
Province : K.MARAŞ / -
Phone 1 : +90 344-2259440-
Phone 2 :
Fax : +90 344-2259439-
WEB : http://kmtb.org.tr/
E-Mail : borsa@kmarasborsa.org.tr
PRESIDENT OF BOARD OF DIRECTOR : AHMET DURAN BALSUYU
PRESIDENT OF ASSEMBLY : MEHMET TAŞ
SECRETARY GENERAL : AHMET BALBABA

KARACABEY COMMODITY EXCHANGE
Address : BANDIRMA YOLU ÜZERİ 1.KM 16700-KARACABEY
Province : BURSA / KARACABEY
Phone 1 : +90 224-6761376-
Phone 2 : +90 224-6769197
Fax : +90 224-6769125
WEB : http://www.karacabeytb.org.tr/
E-Mail : iletisim@karacabeytb.com
PRESIDENT OF BOARD OF DIRECTOR : MURAD BERTAN
PRESIDENT OF ASSEMBLY : HALİT ELBİR
SECRETARY GENERAL : İBRAHİM TEMEL

KARAMAN COMMODITY EXCHANGE
Address : HASAN ÖZKAYMAK BUĞDAY PAZARI NO:2 70100
Province : KARAMAN / -
Phone 1 : +90 338-2133769
Phone 2 : +90 338-2136183
Fax : +90 338-2135892
WEB : http://www.karamantb.org.tr/
E-Mail : karamantb@tobb.org.tr
PRESIDENT OF BOARD OF DIRECTOR : EKREM BAŞTUĞ
PRESIDENT OF ASSEMBLY : EKREM ÇAVAŞ
SECRETARY GENERAL : MEHMET METİN DEMİR

KARAPINAR COMMODITY EXCHANGE
Address : BUĞDAY PAZARI NO:55
Province : KONYA / KARAPINAR
Phone 1 : +90 332-7557680
Phone 2 :
Fax : +90 332-7557681
WEB : http://www.krptb.org.tr/
E-Mail :
PRESIDENT OF BOARD OF DIRECTOR : NAZIM SEZER
PRESIDENT OF ASSEMBLY : NAİM BOZU

SECRETARY GENERAL : HALİL TÜYSÜZ

KARS COMMODITY EXCHANGE
Address : İSTASYON MAH.İSTASYON CAD. NO:240
Province : KARS / -
Phone 1 : +90 474-2120767
Phone 2 :
Fax : +90 474-2231073
WEB : http://www.karstb.org.tr/
E-Mail :
PRESIDENT OF BOARD OF DIRECTOR : İSMET ÇELİK
PRESIDENT OF ASSEMBLY : MUHLİS ACAY
SECRETARY GENERAL : ADEM MOCO

KASTAMONU COMMODITY EXCHANGE
Address : SİNANBEY SOKAK NO:1
Province : KASTAMONU / -
Phone 1 : +90 366-2144440
Phone 2 :
Fax : +90 366-2145655
WEB : http://www.kastamonutb.org.tr
E-Mail :
PRESIDENT OF BOARD OF DIRECTOR : SEDAT İŞERİ
PRESIDENT OF ASSEMBLY : ÖMER FARUK YANIK
SECRETARY GENERAL : EMRE UZER

KAYSERI COMMODITY EXCHANGE
Address : SANAYİ MAHALLESİ KOCASİNAN BULVARI NO:70
Province : KAYSERİ / -
Phone 1 : +90 352-3366888
Phone 2 :
Fax : +90 352-3360373
WEB : http://www.kayseritb.org.tr/
E-Mail : info@kayseritb.org.tr
PRESIDENT OF BOARD OF DIRECTOR : ŞABAN ÜNLÜ
PRESIDENT OF ASSEMBLY : RECEP BAĞLAMIŞ
SECRETARY GENERAL : FATİH MERDOĞLU

KESAN COMMODITY EXCHANGE
Address : ZAHİRECİLER SİTESİ SOSYAL TESİSLERİ P.K.13
Province : EDİRNE / KEŞAN
Phone 1 : +90 284-7141087
Phone 2 : +90 7141301
Fax : +90 284-7144293
WEB : http://www.kesantb.tobb.org.tr
E-Mail : kesantb@tobb.org.tr
PRESIDENT OF BOARD OF DIRECTOR : YUSUF YÖRÜK
PRESIDENT OF ASSEMBLY : NECMİ KAYMAZ
SECRETARY GENERAL : EMİNE KAYMAK

KIRIKKALE COMMODITY EXCHANGE
Address : YENİDOĞAN MAHALLESİ OSMAN TİRYAKİ CAD.NO:4/5
Province : KIRIKKALE / -
Phone 1 : +90 318/2248904
Phone 2 :
Fax : +90 318-2248905
WEB : http://www.kirikkaletb.org.tr/
E-Mail : info@kirikkaletb.org.tr
PRESIDENT OF BOARD OF DIRECTOR : HARUN SÜMER
PRESIDENT OF ASSEMBLY : BÜLENT GÜRBÜZTÜRK
SECRETARY GENERAL : HARUN KAHRAMAN

KIRKLARELI COMMODITY EXCHANGE
Address : İSTANBUL YOLU ÜZERİ 1.KM
Province : KIRKLARELİ / -
Phone 1 : +90 288-2141013
Phone 2 :
Fax : +90 288-2144750
WEB : http://www.kirklarelitb.org.tr/
E-Mail : ktb@kirklarelitb.org.tr
PRESIDENT OF BOARD OF DIRECTOR : TURHAN ALTINTEL
PRESIDENT OF ASSEMBLY : SALİH ÖZLEK
SECRETARY GENERAL : DERYA URASLI

KIRŞEHİR COMMODITY EXCHANGE
Address : CANLI HAYVAN PAZAR YERİ-TARIM TİCARET MERKEZİ ORGANİZE SANAYİ BÖLGESİ YOLU ÜZERİ
Province : KIRŞEHİR / -
Phone 1 : +90 386-2528249
Phone 2 :
Fax : +90 386-2528251
WEB : http://kirsehirtb.org.tr/
E-Mail : kirtb@e-kolay.net
PRESIDENT OF BOARD OF DIRECTOR : NEŞET YAVUZ
PRESIDENT OF ASSEMBLY : SÜLEYMAN KAYA
SECRETARY GENERAL : BATTAL ÇELİK

KIZILTEPE COMMODITY EXCHANGE
Address : ATATÜRK BULVARI 529.SOK. DÜNDARLAR İŞ MERKEZİ TOPRAK BLOK KAT:4
Province : MARDİN / KIZILTEPE
Phone 1 : +90 482-3127175
Phone 2 :
Fax : +90 482-3133132
WEB : http://www.kiziltepetb.org.tr/
E-Mail :
PRESIDENT OF BOARD OF DIRECTOR : MEHMET ŞAHİN
PRESIDENT OF ASSEMBLY : NEZİR YILDIZ
SECRETARY GENERAL : ABDULKADİR ŞAHİN

KONYA COMMODITY EXCHANGE

Address : ADANA-ANKARA ÇEVRE YOLU 42050
Province : KONYA / -
Phone 1 : +90 332-3421444-
Phone 2 : +90 3421444(9HAT
Fax : +90 332-3421456
WEB : http://www.ktb.org.tr/
E-Mail : bilgi@ktb.org.tr
PRESIDENT OF BOARD OF DIRECTOR : MUHAMMET UĞUR KALELİ
PRESIDENT OF ASSEMBLY : HÜSEYİN ÇEVİK
SECRETARY GENERAL : HÜSEYİN ERGUN

KOZAN COMMODITY EXCHANGE
Address : CUMHURİYET MAHALLESİ-YILDIZ SOKAK ÇANDIKLI İŞ HANI K:3 NO:2 KOZAN
Province : ADANA / KOZAN
Phone 1 : +90 322-5166146
Phone 2 :
Fax : +90 322-5166147
WEB : http://www.kozantb.tobb.org.tr/
E-Mail : kozantb@tobb.org.tr
PRESIDENT OF BOARD OF DIRECTOR : MEHMET YAĞAN
PRESIDENT OF ASSEMBLY : TURGAY BOZKURT
SECRETARY GENERAL : ABDULLAH KILINÇ

KUMLUCA COMMODITY EXCHANGE
Address : YENİ MAH.AHMET ALİ AĞA BULVARI NO:2 KAT:2
Province : ANTALYA / KUMLUCA
Phone 1 : +90 242-8873333
Phone 2 :
Fax : +90 242- 8873130
WEB : http://www.kumlucatb.tobb.org.tr
E-Mail :
PRESIDENT OF BOARD OF DIRECTOR : FATİH DURDAŞ
PRESIDENT OF ASSEMBLY : EKREM KARAKAYA
SECRETARY GENERAL : EŞREF AYDIN

KÜTAHYA COMMODITY EXCHANGE
Address : CUMHURİYET CAD. POSTANE KARŞISI OYAKBANK ÜSTÜ KAT: 3 DAİRE: 6-7
Province : KÜTAHYA / -
Phone 1 : +90 274-2233043-
Phone 2 :
Fax : +90 274-2233064
WEB : http://www.kutbo.org.tr/
E-Mail : kutbo@kutbo.org.tr
PRESIDENT OF BOARD OF DIRECTOR : AHMET ALTINKAYA
PRESIDENT OF ASSEMBLY : ALİ BERBER
SECRETARY GENERAL : YASEMİN YOL

LULEBURGAZ COMMODITY EXCHANGE
Address : DURAK MAH.İNÖNÜ 1. CADDE NO:1
Province : KIRKLARELİ / LÜLEBURGAZ
Phone 1 : +90 288-4201450
Phone 2 : +90 4201370
Fax : +90 288-4201833
WEB : http://www.ltb.org.tr
E-Mail : ltb@ltb.org.tr
PRESIDENT OF BOARD OF DIRECTOR : KENAN VAR
PRESIDENT OF ASSEMBLY : YAŞAR CİHAN
SECRETARY GENERAL : MURAT KAVAL

MALATYA COMMODITY EXCHANGE
Address : YENI ŞİRE PAZARI KAT:2
Province : MALATYA / -
Phone 1 : +90 422-3255757
Phone 2 :
Fax : +90 422-3225039
WEB : http://malatyatb.tobb.org.tr/
E-Mail : malatyatb@tobb.org.tr
PRESIDENT OF BOARD OF DIRECTOR : GÜRSEL ÖZBEY
PRESIDENT OF ASSEMBLY : MEHMET AKİF BAŞTÜRK
SECRETARY GENERAL : ABDULVAHAP BULGURLU

MALKARA COMMODITY EXCHANGE
Address : GAZİBEY MAH.YENİ SANAYİ SİTESİ YANI
Province : TEKİRDAĞ / MALKARA
Phone 1 : +90 282-4271035/
Phone 2 : +90 4278372
Fax : +90 282-4270665
WEB : http://www.malkaratb.tobb.org.tr/Â
E-Mail : malkaratb@tobb.org.tr
PRESIDENT OF BOARD OF DIRECTOR : ATİLA AYAZ
PRESIDENT OF ASSEMBLY : ADNAN SUNGUR
SECRETARY GENERAL : FATİH YILMAZ

MANISA COMMODITY EXCHANGE
Address : EGE MAHALLESİ BORSA CADDESİ NO:20
Province : MANİSA / -
Phone 1 : +90 236-2310078
Phone 2 :
Fax : +90 236-2311532-
WEB : http://www.manisatb.tobb.org.tr/
E-Mail : info@manisatb.tobb.org.tr
PRESIDENT OF BOARD OF DIRECTOR : SADIK ÖZKASAP
PRESIDENT OF ASSEMBLY : ERGUN TÜREK
SECRETARY GENERAL : MUTLU KARAKAŞ

MERSIN COMMODITY EXCHANGE
Address : ÜÇ OCAK MAH.İSMET İNÖNÜ BULVARI (MERSİN-ADANA KARAYOLU ÜZERİ)YENİ HAL KAVŞAĞI MEV.LİMAN D GİRİŞİ YANI
Province : MERSİN / -

Phone 1 : +90 324-2385900
Phone 2 :
Fax : +90 324-2336022-
WEB : http://www.mersintb.org/
E-Mail : mersinborsa@superonline.com
PRESIDENT OF BOARD OF DIRECTOR : ÖMER ABDULLAH ÖZDEMİR
PRESIDENT OF ASSEMBLY : HÜSEYİN ARSLAN
SECRETARY GENERAL : İSMAİL SARI

MUĞLA COMMODITY EXCHANGE
Address : MUĞLA-AYDIN KARAYOLU 11.KM NO: 3 BAYIR
Province : MUĞLA / -
Phone 1 : +90 252-2124006-
Phone 2 : +90 252-2124008
Fax : +90 252-2124010
WEB : http://www.muglaticaretborsasi.org.tr/
E-Mail : info@muglaticaretborsasi.org.tr
PRESIDENT OF BOARD OF DIRECTOR : HASAN GÖKMEN
PRESIDENT OF ASSEMBLY : MEHMET MERPEZ
SECRETARY GENERAL : SADETTİN ÖZER

MUSTAFAKEMALPAŞA COMMODITY EXCHANGE
Address : FEVZİDEDE MAHALLESİ MEZBAHA CADDESİ NO:18
Province : BURSA / M.KEMALPAŞA
Phone 1 : +90 224-6140088
Phone 2 :
Fax : +90 224-6138705
WEB : http://www.mkptb.org.tr
E-Mail : mkptbo@ixir.com
PRESIDENT OF BOARD OF DIRECTOR : ALİ MURAT DÜVENCİ
PRESIDENT OF ASSEMBLY : NECATİ GÜNİNDİ
SECRETARY GENERAL : OKAN ÇAKIR

NAZILLI COMMODITY EXCHANGE
Address : CUMHURİYET MAH.228.SOK.NO:33
Province : AYDIN / NAZİLLİ
Phone 1 : +90 256-3131418
Phone 2 :
Fax : +90 256-3132288
WEB : http://www.nazillitb.org.tr/
E-Mail : info@nazillitb.org.tr
PRESIDENT OF BOARD OF DIRECTOR : ZİYA AKSÜT
PRESIDENT OF ASSEMBLY : NEVZAT İZGÜ
SECRETARY GENERAL : NİLÜFER AŞIKOĞLU

NEVŞEHİR COMMODITY EXCHANGE
Address : AKSARAY CADDESİ NO:14
Province : NEVŞEHİR / -
Phone 1 : +90 384-2128103
Phone 2 :
Fax : +90 384-2128102
WEB : http://www.ntb.org.tr
E-Mail :
PRESIDENT OF BOARD OF DIRECTOR : İBRAHİM SALAŞ
PRESIDENT OF ASSEMBLY : AYDIN KARAYILAN
SECRETARY GENERAL : UĞUR AYDOĞAN

NİĞDE COMMODITY EXCHANGE
Address : BANKALAR CADDESİ NO:17 KAT :3 51100
Province : NİĞDE / -
Phone 1 : +90 0388-2327336
Phone 2 :
Fax : +90 0388-2121760
WEB : http://www.nigdetb.org.tr
E-Mail : nigdetb@tobb.org.tr
PRESIDENT OF BOARD OF DIRECTOR : ZAFER UYANIK
PRESIDENT OF ASSEMBLY : ZEKERİYA YERLİKAYA
SECRETARY GENERAL : SACİT KOÇ

NİZİP COMMODITY EXCHANGE
Address : İSTASYON MAH. E-90 KARAYOLU ÜZERİ BORSA HİZMET BİNASI
Province : GAZİANTEP / NİZİP
Phone 1 : +90 342-5181690-
Phone 2 :
Fax : +90 342-5181692
WEB : http://www.nizipticaretborsasi.org.tr
E-Mail : niziptb@tobb.org.tr
PRESIDENT OF BOARD OF DIRECTOR : İBRAHİM SARI
PRESIDENT OF ASSEMBLY : MAHMUT ŞAHİN
SECRETARY GENERAL : M.ERAY ÖLÇAL

NUSAYBİN COMMODITY EXCHANGE
Address : YENİ TURAN MAHALLESİ MİTHATPAŞA SOKAK B-BLOK NO:2-1 KAT:2 NO:4 AKTAŞLAR APT.
Province : MARDİN / NUSAYBİN
Phone 1 : +90 482-4154071
Phone 2 :
Fax : +90 482-4152605
WEB : http://www.nusaybintb.org.tr
E-Mail :
PRESIDENT OF BOARD OF DIRECTOR : NECDET AKTAŞ
PRESIDENT OF ASSEMBLY : UMİT YUMUŞAK
SECRETARY GENERAL : MEHMET EMİN DOĞAN

ODEMIS COMMODITY EXCHANGE
Address : SARAÇOĞLU CAD.ATASOY İŞHANI NO:3/210-211 35750
Province : İZMİR / ÖDEMİŞ
Phone 1 : +90 232-5451378-
Phone 2 :

Fax : +90 232-5452438-
WEB : http://www.otb.org.tr/
E-Mail : odemistb@tobb.org.tr
PRESIDENT OF BOARD OF DIRECTOR : ABDÜLLATİF AKA
PRESIDENT OF ASSEMBLY : TURGUT AKIN
SECRETARY GENERAL : ALİ ÖZ

ORDU COMMODITY EXCHANGE
Address : SÜLEYMAN FELEK CAD.NO:101 ALTINORDU
Province : ORDU / -
Phone 1 : +90 452-2252029-
Phone 2 : +90 452-2252032-
Fax : +90 452-2252034-
WEB : http://www.ordutb.org.tr/
E-Mail : ordutb@tobb.org.tr
PRESIDENT OF BOARD OF DIRECTOR : ZİVER KAHRAMAN
PRESIDENT OF ASSEMBLY : SALİH GÜNEY
SECRETARY GENERAL : BİROL ÖZTÜRK

OSMANIYE COMMODITY EXCHANGE
Address : İSTİKLAL MAH.M.ŞEHİT MEHMET EROĞLU CAD.NO:58
Province : OSMANİYE / -
Phone 1 : +90 328-8141133
Phone 2 : +90 8133043
Fax : +90 328-8145735
WEB : http://www.osmaniyetb.org.tr/
E-Mail :
PRESIDENT OF BOARD OF DIRECTOR : SAİT ÇENET
PRESIDENT OF ASSEMBLY : SEYFETTİN ŞEHİDOĞLU
SECRETARY GENERAL : SÜLEYMAN BÖRKLÜ

POLATLI COMMODITY EXCHANGE
Address : TİCARET BORSASI SİTESİ
Province : ANKARA / POLATLI
Phone 1 : +90 312-6255006-
Phone 2 : +90 6255060
Fax : +90 312-6255025
WEB : http://www.polatliborsa.org.tr/
E-Mail : webmaster@polatliborsa.org.tr, admin@polatliborsa.org.tr
PRESIDENT OF BOARD OF DIRECTOR : YAHYA TOPLU
PRESIDENT OF ASSEMBLY : KADİR ÖZGÖNÜL
SECRETARY GENERAL : AHMET YILMAZ

REYHANLI COMMODITY EXCHANGE
Address : FEVZİ ÇAKMAK CAD. SÜLEYMAN ALTUNLU İŞHANI KAT-3
Province : HATAY / REYHANLI
Phone 1 : +90 326-4135120-
Phone 2 :
Fax : +90 326-4131428
WEB : http://www.reyhanlitb.org/
E-Mail : reyhanlitb@gmail.com
PRESIDENT OF BOARD OF DIRECTOR : BÜLENT KARACA
PRESIDENT OF ASSEMBLY : İSMET ÇALIM
SECRETARY GENERAL : UFUK TOKDEMİR

RİZE COMMODITY EXCHANGE
Address : İSLAMPAŞA MAH.MENDERES BULVARI NO: 522
Province : RİZE / -
Phone 1 : +90 464-2174313-
Phone 2 : +90 2130660-2147
Fax : +90 464-2173994
WEB : http://www.rtb.org.tr/
E-Mail : ribor@ttnet.net.tr
PRESIDENT OF BOARD OF DIRECTOR : MEHMET ERDOĞAN
PRESIDENT OF ASSEMBLY : RESUL OKUMUŞ
SECRETARY GENERAL : İSMAİL KOCAMAN

SAKARYA COMMODITY EXCHANGE
Address : TEKELER MAH.ÇEVRE YOLU ÜZERİ
Province : SAKARYA / -
Phone 1 : +90 264-2784230(
Phone 2 : +90 2784235
Fax : +90 264-2784232
WEB : http://www.stb.org.tr/
E-Mail : sakarya@stb.org.tr
PRESIDENT OF BOARD OF DIRECTOR : CEVDET METE
PRESIDENT OF ASSEMBLY : RECEP PULAT
SECRETARY GENERAL : YASEMİN ARIKAN

SALIHLI COMMODITY EXCHANGE
Address : GAZİLER MAHALLESİ TÜCCARLAR SİTESİ
Province : MANİSA / SALİHLİ
Phone 1 : +90 236-7141181
Phone 2 : +90 7130643
Fax : +90 236-7130643
WEB : http://www.salihlitb.org.tr
E-Mail : salihlitb@superonline.com
PRESIDENT OF BOARD OF DIRECTOR : YETİŞ AKSOY
PRESIDENT OF ASSEMBLY : HALİL ÇÖYGÜN
SECRETARY GENERAL : TURAN YALÇIN

SAMSUN COMMODITY EXCHANGE
Address : KIRAN MAHALLESİ GIDA BORSASI G BLOK NO:1 YEŞİLKENT
Province : SAMSUN / -
Phone 1 : +90 362-4355075-
Phone 2 :
Fax : +90 362-4314737
WEB : http://www.samsuntb.org.tr
E-Mail :
PRESIDENT OF BOARD OF DIRECTOR : SİNAN ÇAKIR
PRESIDENT OF ASSEMBLY : AHMET TAKIŞ
SECRETARY GENERAL : AHMET ALİYAZICI

SANDIKLI COMMODITY EXCHANGE
Address : YENİ ZAHİRE PAZARI NO:70
Province : AFYONKARAHİSAR / SANDIKLI
Phone 1 : +90 0272-5120080
Phone 2 :
Fax : +90 0272-5120085
WEB : http://www.sandiklitb.org.tr/
E-Mail : sandikliborsa@e-kolaymail.com
PRESIDENT OF BOARD OF DIRECTOR : HİDAYET ŞAHİN
PRESIDENT OF ASSEMBLY : REŞİT MUTLU
SECRETARY GENERAL : MEHMET ŞENGÜN

SANLIURFA COMMODITY EXCHANGE
Address : CUMHURİYET CAD.YENİHAL CİVARI BORSA BİNASI NO:38/3
Province : Ş.URFA / -
Phone 1 : +90 414-3151066-
Phone 2 : +90 414-3159450
Fax : +90 414-3151069
WEB : http://www.sutb.org.tr
E-Mail : sanliurfatb@tobb.org.tr
PRESIDENT OF BOARD OF DIRECTOR : MEHMET KAYA
PRESIDENT OF ASSEMBLY : ÖMER EYYÜPOĞLU
SECRETARY GENERAL : MEHMET DURMUŞ

SIVAS COMMODITY EXCHANGE
Address : CELAL BAYAR CAD.DEMİRCİLERARDI MAH. NO:3
Province : SİVAS / -
Phone 1 : +90 346-2222509-
Phone 2 :
Fax : +90 346-221 33 3
WEB : http://www.sivastb.org.tr/
E-Mail :
PRESIDENT OF BOARD OF DIRECTOR : ABDULKADİR HASTAOĞLU
PRESIDENT OF ASSEMBLY : İHSAN AKSOY
SECRETARY GENERAL : SEMA GÖRCÜN

SOKE COMMODITY EXCHANGE
Address : MİLAS ÇEVRE YOLU ÜZERİ,D.S.İ YANI P.K.35 09200
Province : AYDIN / SÖKE
Phone 1 : +90 256-5181625-
Phone 2 :
Fax : +90 256-5122905
WEB : http://www.soketb.org.tr/
E-Mail : info@soketb.org.tr
PRESIDENT OF BOARD OF DIRECTOR : SALİH DENİZ GÜNAL
PRESIDENT OF ASSEMBLY : AHMET NEJAT SAĞEL
SECRETARY GENERAL : YALÇIN ATEŞ

SUNGURLU COMMODITY EXCHANGE
Address : YENİ BUĞDAY PAZARI 19300
Province : ÇORUM / SUNGURLU
Phone 1 : +90 364-3115620-
Phone 2 :
Fax : +90 364-3117711
WEB : http://www.sungurlutb.org.tr/
E-Mail : sungurlutb@mynet.com
PRESIDENT OF BOARD OF DIRECTOR : HALİM KARAÇİL
PRESIDENT OF ASSEMBLY : NAZIM BULCUN
SECRETARY GENERAL : LEVENT AKKAŞ

SUSURLUK COMMODITY EXCHANGE
Address : HAN MAH.ŞEHİT FİKRET GÜNEY CAD. NO:6
Province : BALIKESİR / SUSURLUK
Phone 1 : +90 0266-8655457
Phone 2 :
Fax : +90 0266-8655469
WEB : http://www.susurluktb.tobb.org.tr
E-Mail :
PRESIDENT OF BOARD OF DIRECTOR : SEFER GÖÇER
PRESIDENT OF ASSEMBLY : HÜSEYİN AVCIOĞLU TUNALI
SECRETARY GENERAL : YÜCEL KILIÇ

TARSUS COMMODITY EXCHANGE
Address : ŞAHİN MAH. 3294 SOKAK NO:1
Province : MERSİN / TARSUS
Phone 1 : +90 324-6243686
Phone 2 : +90 6241668
Fax : +90 324-6244075
WEB : http://tarsustb.tobb.org.tr/
E-Mail :
PRESIDENT OF BOARD OF DIRECTOR : MURAT KAYA
PRESIDENT OF ASSEMBLY : TEVFİK BAŞARIR
SECRETARY GENERAL : HASAN ŞANLI

TEKIRDAG COMMODITY EXCHANGE
Address : HAYRABOLU -MURATLI ÇEVRE YOLU ÜZERİ ZAHİRECİLER SİTESİ YANI P.K.59400
Province : TEKİRDAĞ / -
Phone 1 : +90 282-2611060
Phone 2 :
Fax : +90 282-2611309
WEB : http://www.tdag-ticbor.org.tr/
E-Mail : borsa@tdag-ticbor.org.tr
PRESIDENT OF BOARD OF DIRECTOR : OSMAN SARI
PRESIDENT OF ASSEMBLY : BAHATTİN ATICILAR
SECRETARY GENERAL : ERCAN İZGİ

TERME COMMODITY EXCHANGE
Address : YENİMAHALLE IRMAK CAD.NO:1 K:2
Province : SAMSUN / TERME
Phone 1 : +90 362-8768151-

Phone 2 :
Fax : +90 0362-8768152
WEB : http://www.termetb.org.tr
E-Mail : termeticborsa@ttmail.com
PRESIDENT OF BOARD OF DIRECTOR : HALUK TRABZON
PRESIDENT OF ASSEMBLY : BÜLENT BERK
SECRETARY GENERAL : EMRE KIZIL

TOKAT COMMODITY EXCHANGE
Address : G.O.P. BULVARI, SEMERKANT MAH. YAZICIK SOK. NO:8
Province : TOKAT / -
Phone 1 : +90 356-2123159
Phone 2 :
Fax : +90 356-2127183
WEB : http://www.tokattb.org.tr
E-Mail : info@tokattb.org.tr
PRESIDENT OF BOARD OF DIRECTOR : LÜTFİ BORA
PRESIDENT OF ASSEMBLY : NUREDDİN SÖYLER
SECRETARY GENERAL : MURAT YILMAZ

TRABZON COMMODITY EXCHANGE
Address : PAZARKAPI MAH.SAHİL CAD. MOLOZ MEVKİİ NO:103
Province : TRABZON / -
Phone 1 : +90 462-3264505
Phone 2 : +90 462-3211017
Fax : +90 462-3260966
WEB : http://www.tb.org.tr/
E-Mail : info@tb.org.tr
PRESIDENT OF BOARD OF DIRECTOR : ŞÜKRÜ GÜNGÖR KÖLEOĞLU
PRESIDENT OF ASSEMBLY : MEHMET CİRAV
SECRETARY GENERAL : ŞÜKRÜ ERÜZ

TURGUTLU COMMODITY EXCHANGE
Address : TARIM ÜRÜNLERİ VE GIDA ÇARŞISI 45410
Province : MANİSA / TURGUTLU
Phone 1 : +90 236-3131784-
Phone 2 :
Fax : +90 236-3136975
WEB : http://www.turgutlutb.org.tr
E-Mail : turgutlutb@tobb.org.tr
PRESIDENT OF BOARD OF DIRECTOR : YILMAZ ORCAN
PRESIDENT OF ASSEMBLY : ERCAN HIZAL
SECRETARY GENERAL : HASAN ERVARDAR

UNYE COMMODITY EXCHANGE
Address : BELEDİYE CAD.NO:21 52300
Province : ORDU / ÜNYE
Phone 1 : +90 452-3231707-
Phone 2 :
Fax : +90 452-3234828
WEB : http://www.unyetb.org.tr
E-Mail :
PRESIDENT OF BOARD OF DIRECTOR : MUSTAFA USLU
PRESIDENT OF ASSEMBLY : AHMET DURAK
SECRETARY GENERAL : MEHMET GÜR

UŞAK COMMODITY EXCHANGE
Address : HALİL KAYA GEDİK BULVARI ATATÜRK MAH. 1. YAPI SOK. NO: 1
Province : UŞAK / -
Phone 1 : +90 276-2279795
Phone 2 :
Fax : +90 276-2275452
WEB : http://www.usaktb.org.tr
E-Mail :
PRESIDENT OF BOARD OF DIRECTOR : MUSTAFA SEZER
PRESIDENT OF ASSEMBLY : MUHTEREM BALTA
SECRETARY GENERAL : PINAR KARAYOL

UZUNKOPRU COMMODITY EXCHANGE
Address : ZAHİRECİLER SİTESİ
Province : EDİRNE / UZUNKÖPRÜ
Phone 1 : +90 284-5131018-
Phone 2 : +90 5134987
Fax : +90 284-5131852
WEB : http://www.uzunkoprutb.tobb.org.tr
E-Mail : ticborsa@arnil.net.tr
PRESIDENT OF BOARD OF DIRECTOR : EGEMEN ASLAN
PRESIDENT OF ASSEMBLY : AHMET GÜR
SECRETARY GENERAL : MEHMET KARAMOLLA

VAN COMMODITY EXCHANGE
Address : VAN-ERCİŞ KARAYOLU ÜZERİ POLATOĞLU MAH.BEDİÜZZAMAN CAD.
Province : VAN / -
Phone 1 : +90 432-2154530-
Phone 2 :
Fax : +90 432-2154533
WEB : http://www.vatbo.org.tr
E-Mail : bilgi@vatbo.org.tr
PRESIDENT OF BOARD OF DIRECTOR : SELMAN TOPRAK
PRESIDENT OF ASSEMBLY : NAYİF SÜER
SECRETARY GENERAL : TARKAN GÜVEN

YENISEHIR COMMODITY EXCHANGE
Address : ÇAYIR MAH.SANAYİ CAD.TAHAL YANI NO:29 16900
Province : BURSA / YENİŞEHİR
Phone 1 : +90 224-7734399-
Phone 2 :
Fax : +90 224-7731242
WEB : http://www.yenisehirtb.org.tr/
E-Mail :
PRESIDENT OF BOARD OF DIRECTOR : SAİM BOLACA
PRESIDENT OF ASSEMBLY : MEHMET ŞEN

SECRETARY GENERAL : MURAT ÖZLÜ

YERKOY COMMODITY EXCHANGE
Address : HAŞİM KILIÇ MAH.BÜNYAMİN GAYRETLİ SOKAK A/2
Province : YOZGAT / YERKÖY
Phone 1 : +90 354-5161398
Phone 2 : +90 516 22 46
Fax : +90 354- 516 67
WEB : http://yerkoytb.com
E-Mail :
PRESIDENT OF BOARD OF DIRECTOR : DERVİŞ ESATBEYOĞLU
PRESIDENT OF ASSEMBLY : CEMALETTİN KÖMÜRCÜOĞLU
SECRETARY GENERAL : MUTTALİP SALMANLI

YOZGAT COMMODITY EXCHANGE
Address : SAKARYA CADDESİ ETİBANK YANI AÇIKGÖZ APT.NO:5 K:3-4-5
Province : YOZGAT / -
Phone 1 : +90 354-2129677-
Phone 2 : +90 2177788
Fax : +90 354-2170164
WEB : http://yozgattb.tobb.org.tr/
E-Mail :
PRESIDENT OF BOARD OF DIRECTOR : MEHMET ERKEKLİ
PRESIDENT OF ASSEMBLY : MEHMET TÜRKEKUL
SECRETARY GENERAL : ÖZDEN ARSLAN

ZİLE COMMODITY EXCHANGE
Address : CEDİT MAHALLESİ İSTASYON CAD. NO:8/2
Province : TOKAT / ZİLE
Phone 1 : +90 356-3172255
Phone 2 :
Fax : +90 356-3175775
WEB : http://www.ziletb.org.tr/
E-Mail : ziletb@tobb.org.tr
PRESIDENT OF BOARD OF DIRECTOR : MEHMET YENİ
PRESIDENT OF ASSEMBLY : ALİ ÖRNEK
SECRETARY GENERAL : ÖMER FARUK ÖNKUZU

CHAMBERS OF MARITIME TRADE

İMEAK CHAMBER OF MARITIME TRADE
Address : MECLİSİ MEBUSAN CAD.NO:22 SALIPAZARI
Province : İSTANBUL / -
Phone 1 : +90 212-2520130
Phone 2 : +90 212-2520137
Fax : +90 212-2937935
WEB : http://www.denizticaretodasi.org.tr/
E-Mail : iletisim@denizticaretodasi.org.tr/
PRESIDENT OF BOARD OF DIRECTOR : METİN KALKAVAN
PRESIDENT OF ASSEMBLY : CENGİZ KAPTANOĞLU
SECRETARY GENERAL : MEHMET MURAT TUNCER

MERSIN CHAMBER OF MARITIME TRADE
Address : PİRİREİS MAH.İSMET İNÖNÜ BULVARI NO:13 33100
Province : MERSİN / -
Phone 1 : +90 324-3277000(
Phone 2 :
Fax : +90 324-3295230
WEB : http://www.mdto.org
E-Mail : mersin@superonline.com
PRESIDENT OF BOARD OF DIRECTOR : MUSTAFA CİHAT LOKMANOĞLU
PRESIDENT OF ASSEMBLY : JAN TAŞÇI
SECRETARY GENERAL : KORER ÖZBENLİ

CORPORATIONS IN VATIOUS COUNTRIES

Abbreviation	Country	Full term in nation	Full term in English	Notes
AE	Greece	Anonimi Etairia	Anonymous society (Anonymous corporation)	Similar to S.A.
AB	Sweden	Aktiebolag	Stock company	When used within the company's name, it is turned into the definite form (i.e aktiebolaget).
AD	Bulgaria	Aktsionerno drujestvo	Joint Stock Company (JSCO)	
AD	Republic of Macedonia	Akcionersko društvo	Stock corporation	
A.D	Serbia and Montenegro	Akcionarsko društvo	Stock corporation	

AG	Austria	Aktiengesellschaft	Stock corporation	Equivalent to Public Limited Company (PLC) or incorporated company, min. capital 70.000 EUR
AG	Germany	Aktiengesellschaft	Stock corporation	Equivalent to PLC or incorporated company, min. capital 50.000 EUR
AG	Switzerland	Aktiengesellschaft	Stock corporation	Equivalent to PLC or incorporated company, min. capital 100.000 CHF
d.d.	Croatia	Dionicko društvo	Stock corporation	Equivalent to PLC or incorporated company
A/S	Denmark and Norway	Aktieselskab, aksjeselskap	Stock corporation	
a. s.	Czech Republic	Akciová spolecnost	Stock company	Can be both private or public. The minimum share capital is 2 million CZK (20 million CZK for IPOs). Organs: General Assembly, Board of Directors and Supervisory Board.
a. s.	Slovakia	Akciová spolocnost	Stock company	Assimilable to Public Limited Company, plc. The minimum share capital is 1 million SKK (approx. 25 000 EUR). Organs: General Assembly, Board and Control Council.
BAT	Ukraine	Vidkryte Aktsionerne Tovarystvo	ie i obr /> Open Joint-Stock Company	Similar to Public Limited Company (PLC) or (Public) Corporation)
Ltd or	Hong Kong, China	Limited, '' (in Traditional Chinese)	Can denote either a Private or Public Limited Company (liability limited by share capital)	Similar to a UK LTD/PLC. Under the Hong Kong Companies Ordinance (Chapter 32) the name of a Hong Kong incorporated company may be registered in either the English or Chinese language, or both.
Ltd or 'Cyf' (Welsh)	England & Wales	Limited, or 'Cyfyngedig' Welsh language equivalent	Private Limited Company (liability limited by share capital)	
Plc or 'Ccc' (Welsh)	England & Wales	Public Limited Company, or 'Cwmni Cyfyngedig Cyhoeddus' Welsh language equivalent	Public Limited Company (liability limited by share capital)	Requires authorised minimum share capital of GBP £50,000; of which it must have allotted shares to the value of at least GBP £50,000 and a minimum of 25% must be fully paid up prior to starting business.

Unltd or Ultd	England & Wales	Unlimited, or 'Anghyfyngedig' Welsh language equivalent	Private Unlimited Company (with share capital)	Unlimited Company; as word implies, members or shareholders of the company have no limit placed on their liability for the company's financial obligations in the event of it becoming insolvent, however, it is not a requirement under the Companies Act of GB for an Unlimited Company to state either Unltd, Ultd or Unlimited after its company name. It is nevertheless, a company (a legal entity like its peers Ltd and Plc) registered and formed (incorporated) under the Companies Act of Great Britain and subject to the Companies Act. The advantage of an unlimited company is that they are exempted from filing accounts with the Registrar of Companies for public disclosure (unless, during the accounting period covered, the company is a qualified subsidiary or a parent of a limited company undertaking) subject to a few exceptions to this rule.
SE	European Union	Societas Europaea (Latin for 'European Company')	European (Public) Limited Company (liability limited by share capital)	The legal form of the European (Public) Company. Similar to a UK PLC or German AG company etc. An SE (Societas Europaea) may be created on registration in any one of the Member States of the European Union, and is subject to the European Company Statute - Council Regulation (EC) No 2157/2001 on the Statute for a European company (the 'Regulation'). An SE is able to relocate its registered office to any other Member State of the EUand without it being wound up.

Sdn Bhd	Malaysia	Sendirian Berhad	Private limited Company	Equivalent to Public Limited Company in the UK
Bhd	Malaysia	Berhad	Stock Corporation	Denotes publicly listed companies in Malaysia
Co.	USA.	Company	Stock Corporation or Non-stock corporation	In some USA States, it is permissible to use Company or Co. in place of Inc. or Corp. for a corporation. See the table under USA in the article Types of corporations. Allowed by many states but not all; however, individuals and partnerships may register a ficticious name with the word "Company" in it either with the county where they reside or with the state in such areas where the state registers ficticious names.
Corp.	USA	Corporation	Stock corporation or non-stock corporation	"Corporation", "Incorporated" and the abbreviations "Corp." and "Inc." are the only terms universally accepted by all 51 corporation chartering agencies in the USA.
Inc.	U.S.A.	Incorporated	Stock corporation">Stock corporation or non-stock corporation	"Corporation", "Incorporated" and the abbreviations "Corp." and "Inc." are the only terms universally accepted by all 51 corporation chartering agencies in the United States.
K.K.	Japan	Kabushiki kaisha	Business corporation	The predominant form of company in Japan, and the only type that can be publicly traded.
LTD	Australia	Limited	Public Limited Company	Equivalent to PLC Public Limited Company in the UK
LTD	New Zealand	Limited	Public or private Limited Company	All NZ limited liability companies must use LTD
Ltd	India	Limited	Public Limited Company (liability limited in share capital)	Equivalent to a UK PLC.
Pvt Ltd	India	Private Limited	Private Limited Company (liability limited in share capital)	Equivalent to a UK LTD.
Ltd.	Some USA.	Limited	Corporation	In some USA States, it is

	States.			permissible to use Ltd. instead of Inc. or Corp. for a corporation.
N.V.	Belgium and Netherlands	Naamloze Vennootschap	A limited liability company, liability limited by shares. In its articles or corporation it may forbid public trading of its shares. However, it is the only type of company in the Netherlands that may allow public trading of its shares.	
OAO	Russia	Otkrytoye aktsionernoye obshchestvo	Open Joint-Stock Company	Similar to Public Limited Company (PLC). There is also ZAO (zakrytoye aktsionernoye obshchestvo-Close Joint-Stock Company, or closely-held corporation, no more than fifty shareholders)
Oy(j)	Finland	(Julkinen) osakeyhtiö	(Public) Limited Company	
Rt.	Hungary	Részvénytársaság	Stock company	
S.A.	Spain	Sociedad Anónima	Stock Corporation	Minimum capital is 60.101,21€
S.A.	Brazil	Sociedade Anônima	Public Limited Company	
S.A.	Portugal	Sociedade Anónima	Public Limited Company	
S.A.	France	Société Anonyme	Public Limited Company	public corporation.
S.A.	Switzerlan	Société Anonyme Società Anonima	Public Limited Company	
S.p.A.	Italy	Società per Azioni	Stock corporation	Italian plc. As with Ltd., some USA states also permit this designation (in which case, it is synonymous with corporation). Currently, only the state of Connecticut permits this use.
S.A.	Romania	Societate pe Actiuni	Stock corporation	Romanian plc.
S.A.	Poland	"Spólka Akcyjna"	Stock corporation	
Co., ltd.	Thailand	Company Limited	Private limited company or limited	

			company	
PLC.	Thailand	Public Company Limited	Stock corporation	
P.T. / PT	Indonesia	Perseroan Terbatas	Limited Company	
P.T. Tbk. / PT Tbk	Indonesia	Perseroan Terbatas, Terbuka	Stock corporation	

Limited Liability Companies and Partnerships

Name	Country	Type
Denmark	Anpartsselskab. Similar to Limited Liability Company. Taxwise, it is a separate entity. The company capital must be at least DKK 125.000	
BM or B.M.	Israel	Be'eravon Mugbal- The hebrew term for Ltd.. Not used much in English, usually translated as Ltd..
BV	Netherlands	Besloten Vennootschap"", a private limited liability company, liability limited by shares. The most common form of enterprise. Similar to GmbH, LLC, Ltd., BVBA, SPRL.
BVBA	Belgium	Besloten Vennootschap met Beperkte Aansprakelijkheid, a private limited liability company, liability limited by shares. The most common form of enterprise. Similar to GmbH, LLC, Ltd., BV, SPRL.
CC	South Africa	Closed corporation
C.V.	Netherlands	"commanditaire vennootschap"; a partnership with one or more silent partners.
d.o.o.	Slovenia	Družba z omejeno odgovornostjo, "company with limited liability"
d.o.o.	Croatia	ogranicenom odgovornošcu" Društvo s ogranicenom odgovornošcu, "company with limited liability"
d.o.o.	Serbia and Montenegro	Društvo s ogranicenom odgovornošcu , "company with limited liability"
E.P.E.	Greece	Etairia Periorismenis Euthinis (taa esµ)
G.D.K.		, a variant of the American LLC introduced in 2006
	Germany, Austria and Switzerland	limited liability". Similar to Limited Liability Company (LLC). In Germany, min. capital €25,000, in Austria €35,000, in Switzerland CHF 20,000
Inc.	Australia	An
Kft.	Hungary	Korlátolt felelosségu társaság (Limited liability company)
LLC LC Ltd. Co.	U.S.A.	Limited liability company, similar to a corporation and a limited liability partnership. May be legally abbreviated in multiple ways. The most common abbreviation is LLC. Allowable abbreviations may vary by USA State. Note: Ltd. by itself is not a valid abbreviation for an LLC,

		because in some states, like Texas, Ltd. may mean a Corporation instead of an LLC.
LLP	U.S.A.	Limited liability partnership where each partner is fully liable for the debts of the partnership, not including acts of professional negligence or malpractice.
Ltd.	U.K. and others	Private company with liability limited by shares (not traded publicly) or by guarantee. Established under English law and used by countries with similar company laws. In Australia, a company with the suffix Ltd may be a company limited by guarantee (e.g. for charities, universities etc). Such companies may obtain dispensation from the Registrar of Companies to operate without the suffix to distinguish their activities from those of a commercial company.
NL	Australia	Mining company not entitled to call on the unpaid issue price of shares; no liability for shareholders, as distinct from limited liability
PLC	U.K. and Ireland	A public limited company, liability limited by shares which are traded publicly.
OOD /	Bulgaria	Limited liability company (drujestvo s ogranichena otgovornost,).
OOO	Russia	Obshchestvo s ogranichennoy otvetstvennostyu - (Limited Liability Company)
Pty. / Pte.	Various	a prefix used to distinguish a Proprietary Limited company (Pty. Ltd.), essentially the same as a UK private limited company (Ltd.) Used in Australia, South Africa and others. A Proprietary company generally (depending on jurisdiction) is one with less then 50 members (shareholders), and not exceeding a certain annual revenue. In Australia, proprietary companies are classified as either small or large depending on the number of employees and the quantum of gross assets and operating capital.
Pvt. Ltd.	India	Private Limited Company, can have up to 50 shareholders and min 2 shareholders . Shares are not traded on a stock exchange.
Sàrl or SARL or SàRL	France Switzerland	Société à responsabilité limitée
SDN BHD	Malaysia	Sendirian Berhad (Private Limited)
S.L.	Spain	Sociedad Limitada. Minimum capital is 3.012€
S.L.N.E.		Sociedad Limitada Nueva Empresa Similar to SL, it was introduced in 2003 to speed up the registration of a new company (it takes one day to register). Minimum capital is 3.012€
SPRL	Belgium	Société privée à responsabilité limitée, a private limited liability company, liability limited by shares.
Sp.z o.o.	Poland	Spólka z ograniczona odpowiedzialnoscia, limited liability
S.R.L.	Romania	Societate cu Raspundere Limitata
Srl or	Italy Switzerland	Società a responsibilità limitata

S.r.l or S.R.L.		
S.R.L.	Spain	Sociedad de Responsabilidad Limitada (equivalent to S.L.)
s.r.o.	Czech Republic	Spolecnost s rucení

GOVERNMENT AND BUSINESS CONTACTS

U.S. Mission Trade-related Personnel

Mr. John D. Breidenstine
Commercial Counselor
The Commercial Service (CS)
John.Breidenstine@mail.doc.gov
American Embassy
Ataturk Bulvari 110
06100 Kavaklidere, Ankara, Turkey
Tel: [90] (312) 455-5555 ext. 2467
Fax: [90] (312) 467-1366

Mr. Erik Hunt
Commercial Attaché
The Commercial Service (CS)
Erik.Hunt@mail.doc.gov
American Embassy
Ataturk Bulvari 110
06100 Kavaklidere, Ankara, Turkey
Tel: [90] (312) 455-5555 ext. 2568
Fax: [90] (312) 467-1366

Ms. Mary Boscia
Commercial Consul
The Commercial Service (CS)
Mary.Boscia@mail.doc.gov
American Consulate General
Mesrutiyet Caddesi No. 104-108
Tepebasi, Istanbul,Turkey
Tel: [90] (212) 251-1651
Fax: [90] (212) 252-2417

Ms. Berrin Erturk
Commercial Specialist
The Commercial Service (CS)
Berrin.Erturk@mail.doc.gov
Izmir Office
Izmir Chamber of Commerce
Ataturk Caddesi No. 126, 5th Fl.
35210 Pasaport, Izmir, Turkey
Tel: [90] (232) 441-2446
Fax: [90] (232) 489-0267

Ms. Abaseh Mirvali
Director, Caspian Finance Center
U.S. Trade and Development Agency (TDA)
Amirvali@tda.gov
American Embassy
Ataturk Bulvari 110
06100 Kavaklidere, Ankara, Turkey
Tel: [90] (312) 455-5555 ext. 2075
Fax: [90] (312) 466-6082

Mr. Peter Ballinger
Director, Caspian Finance Center
Overseas Private Investment Corporation (OPIC)
Pballinger@opic.gov
American Embassy
Ataturk Bulvari 110
06100 Kavaklidere, Ankara, Turkey
Tel: [90] (312) 455-5555 ext. 2075
Fax: [90] (312) 466-6082

Ms. Julie Panaro
Business Development Manager
Export-Import Bank of the United States
(Please see Washington-based U.S. Government Country Contacts)

Ms. Greta Holtz
Principal Officer and Consul
HoltzG@state.gov
American Consulate
Ataturk Caddesi
Vali Yolu, Bossa Apt. 1
01120 Adana, Turkey
Tel: [90] (322) 454-2145
Fax: [90] (322) 457-6591

Mr. Scot A. Marciel
Economic Counselor
Economic Section (ECON)
MarcielS@state.gov
American Embassy
Ataturk Bulvari 110
06100 Kavaklidere, Ankara, Turkey
Tel: [90] (312) 455-5555 ext. 2254
Fax: [90] (312) 468-6138

Ms. Susan P. Schayes
Agricultural Counselor
Agricultural Affairs Office
Agankara@fas.usda.gov
American Embassy
Ataturk Bulvari 110
06100 Kavaklidere, Ankara, Turkey
Tel: [90] (312) 455-5555 ext. 2406
Fax: [90] (312) 467-0056

Col. Dennis Danielson

Defense Attaché
Defense Attache Office (DAO)
daoankara@attglobal.net
American Embassy
Ataturk Bulvari 110
06100 Kavaklidere, Ankara, Turkey
Tel: [90] (312) 455-5555 ext. 2300
Fax: [90] (312) 467-4468

Major General Craig P. Rasmussen
Chief ODC (Formerly JUSMMAT)
ODC-Office of Defense Cooperation, Turkey
Ismet Inonu Bulvari No. 94
Balgat, Ankara, Turkey
Tel: [90] (312) 418-5296
Fax: [90] (312) 287-9978

Washington-Based U.S. Government Country Contacts

Mr. David S. De Falco, Esq.
U.S. Department of Commerce-Turkey Desk Officer
Office of Western Europe
David_de_falco@ita.doc.gov
U.S. Department of Commerce
14th and Constitution Avenue, NW
Washington, D.C. 20230
Tel: (202) 482-2178
Fax: (202) 482-2897

Ms. Kelly Cecil
U.S. Department of State- Desk officer for Turkey
CecilK@state.gov
Department of State
Office of Southern Europe
Room 5511
U.S. Department of State
2201 C Street NW
Washington, DC 20520
Tel: (202) 647-6114
Fax: (202) 647-5087

Mr. Daniel D. Stein
Regional Director for Russia, NIS, and Turkey
dstein@tda.gov
U.S. Trade and Development Agency (TDA)
Room 309. SA-16
Washington, D.C. 20523-1602
Tel: (703) 875-4357
Fax: (703) 875-4009

Mr. Andy Burst
Area Officer
bursta@fas.usda.gov
Department of Agriculture
14th and Independence Ave., SW
Washington, D.C. 20250-1000
Tel: (202) 690-4053
Fax: (202) 690-2909

Ms. Julie Panaro, Business Development Officer
Julie.panaro@exim.gov
Export-Import Bank of the United States
811 Vermont Avenue, NW
Washington, D.C. 29571
Tel: (202) 565-3402
Fax: (202) 565-3628

Mr. Abed R. Tarbush, Regional Manager
Atarbush@opic.gov
Overseas Private Investment Corporation
1100 New York Avenue, NW
Washington, D.C. 50527
Tel: (202) 336-8632
Fax: (202) 408-5145

U.S.-Based Multipliers

Mr. Lincoln McCurdy, President
atc@americanturkishcouncil.org
American-Turkish Council (ATC)
1010 Vermont Avenue, NW, Suite 1020
Washington, D.C. 20005-4905
Tel: (202) 783-0483
Fax: (202) 783-0511

TURKISH GOVERNMENT CONTACTS:

Agriculture and Rural Affairs

Tarim, Orman ve Koyisleri Bakanligi
(Ministry of Agriculture, Forestry and Rural Affairs)
Tarimsal Uretim Gelistirme Genel Mudurlugu
(General Directorate of Agricultural Production Development)
www.tarim.gov.tr
Milli Mudafaa Caddesi No. 20
Kizilay, Ankara, Turkey
Tel: [90] (312) 417 8400
Fax: [90] (312) 425 2016

Contact: Mr. Ahmet Bulbul, General Manager
Tel: [90] (312) 418 2059
Fax: [90] (312) 417 0026

Orman Bakanligi
(Ministry of Forestry)
Ataturk Bulvari No. 153
Bakanliklar, Ankara, Turkey
Tel: [90] (312) 417 6000
Fax: [90] (312) 418 7354

Contact: Mr. Harun Ozturk, Undersecretary
Tel: [90] (312) 425 1285
Fax: [90] (312) 417 0237

Toprak Mahsulleri Ofisi (TMO)
(Soil Products Office)
Milli Mudafaa Caddesi No. 18
06100 Kizilay, Ankara, Turkey
Tel: [90] (312) 417 4400
Fax: [90] (312) 417 5934

Contact: Mr. Mevlut Karakaya, General Manager
Tel: [90] (312) 418 2316
Fax: [90] (312) 417 5934

Koy Hizmetleri Genel Mudurlugu
(General Directorate of Rural Services)
Eskisehir Yolu 9 Km,
Ankara, Turkey
Tel: [90] (312) 287 3360
Fax: [90] (312) 287 7213

Contact: Mr. Huseyin Alioglu, General Manager
Tel: [90] (312) 287 7212
Fax: [90] (312) 287 7213

Turkiye Zirai Donatim Kurumu (TZDK)
(Turkish Agricultural Supply Department)
Fatih Caddesi No. 33
Diskapi, Ankara, Turkey
Tel: [90] (312) 317 0220
Fax: [90] (312) 347 0474

Contact: Mr. Mustafa Dogan, General Manager
Tel: [90] (312) 316 4416
Fax: [90] (312) 347 0474

Communications

Ulastirma Bakanligi
(Ministry of Communications and Transportation)
www.ubak.gov.tr
Bahcelievler Son Durak
Emek, Ankara, Turkey
Tel: [90] (312) 212-6730
Fax: [90] (312) 212-4930
Activity: Responsible for construction of harbors, airports, and railways. Ministry establishes telecommunications policy and monitors telecom privatization.

Contact: Mr. Tahir Dengiz, Deputy Undersecretary
Tel: [90] (312) 212-4631
Fax: [90] (312) 212-4187

Turkiye Radyo ve Televizyon Kurumu, Genel Mudurlugu (TRT)
(General Directorate of Turkish Radio and Television)
www.trt.net.tr
Turan Gunes Bulvari
06109 Oran, Ankara, Turkey
Tel: [90] (312) 490-4300
Fax: [90] (312) 490-1109
Activity: Television and radio broadcasting

Contact: Mr. Yucel Yener, Director General
Tel: [90] (312) 490-4491
Fax: [90] (312) 490-4494

Telekomunikasyon Kurumu
(Telecommunications Authority)
www.tk.gov.tr
Yesilirmak Sokak No. 16
06420 Maltepe, Ankara, Turkey
Tel: [90] (312) 550-5100
Fax: [90] (312) 550-5151

Contact: Mr. Fatih Mehmet Yurdal, President
Tel: [90] (312) 550-5050
Fax: [90] (312) 550-5151

Turk Telekom A.S. (TTAS)
(Turk Telecommunications, Inc.)
www.telekom.gov.tr
Samsun Yolu Kavsagi
06103 Aydinlikevler, Ankara, Turkey
Tel: [90] (312) 555-1000
Fax: [90] (312) 313-1919
Activity: Telecommunications arm of Turkish PTT, scheduled for privatization. TTAS has exclusive rights to operate landlines and telecommunications satellites serving Turkey, lease channels and transponders from satellites.

Contact: Mr. Ibrahim Hakki Alpturk, Director General and Member of the Board
Tel: [90] (312) 313-1121
Fax: [90] (312) 313-1919

Defense

Milli Savunma Bakanligi (MND), Dis Tedarik Dairesi Baskanligi
(Ministry of National Defense, Foreign Procurement Department)
www.msb.mil.tr
Mudafaa Caddesi, Bakanliklar
Ankara, Turkey
Tel: [90] (312) 418-9616
Fax: [90] (312) 417-7342
Activity: Procurement for the Turkish Armed Forces from foreign and domestic sources according to the programs and priorities determined by theTurkish General Staff.

Milli Savunma Bakanligi, NATO Enf. Daire Baskanligi
(Ministry of National Defense, NATO Infrastructure Department)
Bakanliklar, Ankara, Turkey
Tel: [90] (312) 418-9814; 402-4202

Fax: [90] (312) 418-3384

Contact: General Huseyin Ozdel, Head of NATO Infrastructure Dept.

Savunma Sanayii Mustesarligi (SSM)
(Undersecretariat for Defense Industries)
Inonu Bulvari, Kirazlidere Mevkii
06100 Bahcelievler, Ankara, Turkey
Tel: [90] (312) 417-2326
Fax: [90] (312) 417-3266
Activity: Defense equipment and systems procurement. Promotion of an indigenous Turkish defense industry.

Contact: Prof. Dr. D. Ali Ercan, Undersecretary
Tel: [90] (312) 417-3415
Fax: [90] (312) 417-1166

Jandarma Genel Komutanligi, Tedarik Daire Baskanligi-Dis Tedarik Sube Mudurlugu
(Turkish Gendarmerie Command, Foreign Procurement Department)
Ankara, Turkey
Tel: [90] (312) 456-2487
Fax: [90] (312) 418-9208

Emniyet Genel Mudurlugu
(General Directorate of Security Affairs)
www.egm.gov.tr
Icisleri Bakanligi Yani
Bakanliklar, Ankara, Turkey
Tel: [90] (312) 468-5600
Fax: [90] (312) 417-3039

Contact: Mr. Ertugrul Cakir, Asst. Director General
Tel: [90] (312) 419-5600
Fax: [90] (312) 425-6520

Education

Milli Egitim Bakanligi (MEB)
(Ministry of National Education)
www.meb.gov.tr
Bakanliklar, Ankara, Turkey
Tel: [90] (312) 419-1410
Fax: [90] (312) 417-7027
Activity: Responsible for establishing primary and secondary schools, setting education policy and establishing teaching standards.

Contact: Mr. Bener Cordan, Undersecretary
Tel: [90] (312) 425-5294
Fax: [90] (312) 417-0083

Contact: Mr. Ibrahim Barbaros, Deputy Undersecretary
Tel: [90] (312) 428-8573
Fax: [90] (312) 428-8635

Yuksek Ogretim Kurulu (YOK)
(Higher Education Council)
www.yok.gov.tr
Bilkent Universitesi
Ankara, Turkey
Tel: [90] (312) 298-7000
Fax: [90] (312) 266-4759
Activity: An autonomous public body with the authority and responsibility to administer the activities of all universities, schools, and institutions of higher education.

Contact: Prof. Dr. Kemal Guruz, President
Tel: [90] (312) 298-7066
Fax: [90] (312) 266-4819

Energy and Natural Resources

Enerji ve Tabii Kaynaklar Bakanligi (MEN)
(Ministry of Energy and Natural Resources)
www.enerji.gov.tr
Inonu Bulvari No. 27
06440 Bahcelievler, Ankara, Turkey
Tel: [90] (312) 212-6915
Fax: [90] (312) 223-6984
Activity: Responsible for electricity generation, transmission, and distribution. Also responsible for energy and petroleum affairs and natural resources development.

Contact: Dr. Yurdakul Yigitguden, Undersecretary
Tel: [90] (312) 222-4059; 223-0572
Fax: [90] (312) 223-4084

TEDAS - Turkiye Elektrik Dagitim A.S.
(Turkish Electricity Distribution Co., Inc.)
www.tedas.gov.tr
Inonu Bulvari No. 27
06440 Bahcelievler, Ankara, Turkey
Tel: [90] (312) 212-6915
Fax: [90] (312) 213-8873
Activity: Operating rights of electrical distribution network.

Contact: Mr. Oguz Guren, Chairman and Acting Director General
Tel: [90] (312) 213-9777
Fax: [90] (312) 213-8873

TEAS - Turkiye Elektrik Iletim Uretim A.S.
(Turkish Electricity Generation and Transmission Co., Inc.)
www.teas.gov.tr
Inonu Bulvari No. 27
06490 Bahcelievler, Ankara, Turkey
Tel: [90] (312) 212-6900
Fax: [90] (312) 222-9890
Activity: Electricity generation and transmission.

Contact: Mr. Omer Esirgemez, Chairman and Acting Director General
Tel: [90] (312) 222-9537
Fax: [90] (312) 222-9890

Turkiye Petrolleri Anonim Ortakligi (TPAO)
(General Directorate of the Turkish Petroleum Corp.)
www.tpao.gov.tr
Mustafa Kemal Mahallesi 2. Cadde No. 86
06520 Esentepe, Ankara, Turkey
Tel: [90] (312) 286-9100
Fax: [90] (312) 286-9000
Activity: Exploration, drilling and production of oil, natural gas and geothermal energy.

Contact: Mr. Erol Memioglu, Chairman and Director General
Tel: [90] (312) 286-8032
Fax: [90] (312) 286-4238

BOTAS-Boru Hatlari ile Petrol Tasima
(Petroleum Pipeline Corporation)
www.botas.gov.tr
Bilkent Plaza, A2 Blok
Bilkent, Ankara, Turkey
Tel: [90] (312) 297-2401
Fax: [90] (312) 266-0623
Activity: Construction and operation of oil and gas pipelines.

Contact: Mr. Gokhan Bildaci, Chairman and Director General

PETKIM-Petrokimya Holding A.S.
(General Directorate of Petrochemical Industries)
www.petkim.com.tr
P.O. Box 12
35801 Aliaga, Izmir, Turkey
Tel: [90] (232) 616-1240
Fax: [90] (232) 616-1248; 616-2490
Activity: Petrochemicals producer.

Contact: Mr. Turgut Bozkurt, Director General
Tel: [90] (232) 616-1450
Fax: [90] (232) 616-1248

Environment

Cevre Bakanligi (MOE)
Ministry of Environment
General Directorate of Environmental Impact, Assessment and Planning
www.cevre.gov.tr
Eskisehir Yolu – 8. Km.
Ankara, Turkey
Tel: [90] (312) 287-9963
Fax: [90] (312) 285-2910
Activity: Regulatory agency for the environment.

Contacts: Ms. Havva Alp, Director General
Tel: [90] (312) 285-3283
Fax: [90] (312) 285-2910

Ms. Gunay Cakirer, Undersecretary for Environmental Impact Assessment
Tel: [90] (312) 286-3165
Fax: [90] (312) 285-9663

Health

Saglik Bakanligi (MOH)
(Ministry of Health)
www.saglik.gov.tr
Saglik Bakanligi Arastirma ve Planlama Dairesi
06343 Sihhiye, Ankara, Turkey
Tel: [90] (312) 433-7777
Fax: [90] (312) 434-4602
Activity: Provider of hospital care and primary care, and the only provider of preventive health services, responsible for health policy and services. Administers provincial health services.

Contact: Mr. Cevat Soysal, Head of Research and Planning Department

Mining

Turkiye Demir ve Celik Isletmeleri, Genel Mudurlugu (TDCI)
General Directorate of Turkish Iron and Steel Works
www.tdci.gov.tr
Ziya Gokalp Caddesi
Kurtulus, Ankara, Turkey
Tel: [90] (312) 435-4900
Fax: [90] (312) 434-4705

Contact: Mr. Celal Doggez, Director General
Tel: [90] (312) 430-4070
Fax: [90] (312) 433-6830

Turkiye Komur Isletmeleri Kurumu, Genel Mudurlugu (TKI)
General Directorate of the Turkish Coal Enterprises
Hipodrom Caddesi
Ulus, Ankara, Turkey.
Tel: [90] (312) 384-1720
Fax: [90] (312) 384-1635

Contact: Mr. Yusuf Cebi, Director General
Tel: [90] (312) 384-1600
Fax: [90] (312) 384-1612

Turkiye Taskomuru Kurumu, Genel Mudurlugu

(TTK)
(General Directorate of the Turkish Hard Coal Enterprises)
Zonguldak, Turkey
Tel: [90] (372) 252-4000
Fax: [90] (372) 251-1900
Activity: Hard coal mining.

Contacts: Mr. Omer Yenel, Director General
Tel: [90] (372) 252-1934
Fax: [90] (372) 253-1661

Mr. Ismail Verimbas, Deputy Director General
Tel: [90] (372) 252-1145
Fax: [90] (372) 253-1661

Karadeniz Bakir Isletmeleri A.S. (KBI)
(Black Sea Copper Works Co.)
www.kbi.gov.tr
Ziya Gokalp Caddesi No. 17
06100 Ankara, Turkey.
Tel: [90] (312) 435-5400
Fax: [90] (312) 435-1689
Activity: Mining of copper ore and copper

Contact: Mr. Rifat Kont, Director General
Tel: [90] (312) 431-2012
Fax: [90] (312) 435-5211

Maden Tetkik ve Arama Enstitusu (MTA)
(Mineral Research and Exploration Institute)
www.mta.gov.tr
Eskisehir Yolu
Balgat, Ankara, Turkey
Tel: [90] (312) 287-9150
Fax: [90] (312) 287-9151
Activity: Research Institute

Contact: Mr. Ali Kemal Isiker, Director General
Tel: [90] (312) 287-9152
Fax: [90] (312) 287-9151

Public Works and Housing

Bayindirlik ve Iskan Bakanligi
(Ministry of Public Works and Settlement)
Vekaletler Caddesi No. 1
Bakanliklar, Ankara, Turkey
Tel: [90] (312) 417-9260
Fax: [90] (312) 418-0406

Iller Bankasi Genel Mudurlugu
(Municipalities Bank)
www.ilbank.gov.tr
Ataturk Bulvari No. 21
Opera, Ulus, Ankara, Turkey
Tel: [90] (312) 310-3141
Fax: [90] (312) 312-2989; 310-7459
Activity: Municipal financing authority.

Contact: Mr. Irfan Onal, Director General
Tel: [90] (312) 311-2672
Fax: [90] (312) 311-7317

T.C. Basbakanlik- Guneydogu Anadolu Projesi (GAP)
(Prime Ministry- Southeastern Anatolia Project)
www.gap.gov.tr
Regional Development Administration
Willy Brandt Sokak No. 5
06680 Cankaya, Ankara, Turkey
Tel: [90] (312) 440-4093
Fax: [90] (312) 440-4094
Activity: Development authority for the Southeastern Anatolia Project

Contact: Dr. I. H. Olcay Unver, President

Devlet Su Isleri Genel Mudurlugu (DSI)
(General Directorate of State Water Works)
www.dsi.gov.tr
Inonu Bulvari, 06100 Yucetepe
Tel: [90] (312) 417-8300
Fax: [90] (312) 418-3413
Activity: Responsible for construction of dams and hydroelectric power plants.

Contact: Prof. Dr. Dogan Altinbilek, Director General
Tel: [90] (312) 418-3409
Fax: [90] (312) 418-2498

Demiryollari, Limanlar ve Hava Meydanlari (DLH)
(General Directorate of Railways, Harbors, and Airports Construction)
www.dlh.gov.tr
Ulastirma Bakanligi
Bahcelievler, Ankara, Turkey
Tel: [90] (312) 212-4725
Fax: [90] (312) 212-3847
Activity: Infrastructure construction of new railways, harbors and airports

Contact: Mr. Hasan Isguzar, Acting Director General
Tel: [90] (312) 212-4691
Fax: [90] (312) 212-3847

Trade and Economy

Devlet Planlama Teskilati
(State Planning Organization) (SPO)
www.dpt.gov.tr
Necatibey Caddesi No. 108
06100 Bakanliklar, Ankara, Turkey.
Tel: [90] (312) 230-8720
Fax: [90] (312) 231-3498
Activity: Develops and administers the State's investment programs. It is the approval agency

for allocating government funds for projects and is responsible for the preparation of Turkey's Five Year Plans

Contacts: Prof. Dr. Akin Izmirlioglu, Undersecretary
Tel: [90] (312) 230-0145
Fax: [90] (312) 231-3681

Mr. Ahmet Celenkoglu, Head of Conjunctural Evaluations Dept
Tel: [90] (312) 232-1088
Fax: [90] (312) 232-1089

Mr. Cavit Dagdas, General Director of Annual Programs and Conjunctural Evaluations
Tel: [90] (312) 232-1085
Fax: [90] (312) 232-1089

Hazine Mustesarligi
(Undersecretariat of the Treasury)
www.treasury.gov.tr
Eskisehir Yolu, Inonu Bulvari
06510 Emek, Ankara, Turkey
Tel: [90] (312) 212-8800
Fax: [90] (312) 212-8778
Activity: Information source on foreign investment opportunities, procedures and incentives. The agency is the primary source of information on Turkey's banking regulations.

Contacts: Mr. Faik Oztrak, Undersecretary of Treasury
Tel: [90] (312) 212-8630
Fax: [90] (312) 212-2257

Mr. Aydin Karaoz, Deputy Undersecretary of Treasury
Tel: [90] (212) 212-8719
Fax: [90] (312) 212-1071

Ms. Berrin Bingol, Acting Director General Director General, Foreign Investment Department
Tel: [90] (312) 212-8914
Fax: [90] (312) 212-8916

Mr. Zafer Baltaci, Director General of Banking and Foreign Exchange
Tel: [90] (312) 212-8723
Fax: [90] (312) 212-8775

Mr. Arif Erden, Deputy Director General, Foreign Economic Relations
Tel: [90] (312) 213-0297
Fax: [90] (312) 212-8855

Dis Ticaret Mustesarligi, Ithalat Genel Mudurlugu
(Undersecretariat of Foreign Trade, General Directorate of Imports)
Eskisehir Karayolu, Inonu Bulvari
06510 Emek, Ankara, Turkey
Tel: [90] (312) 212 8724
Fax: [90] (312) 212 8765
Activity: Information on Turkish import regulations. This agency also establishes customs duties and surcharges

Contacts: Mr. Kursad Tuzmen, Undersecretary for Foreign Trade
Tel: [90] (312) 212-8742
Fax: [90] (312) 212-1622

Mr. Abdullah Koten, Deputy Undersecretary
Tel: [90] (312) 212-8753
Fax: [90] (312) 212-8738

Ms. Samiye Aydar, Deputy Director General for Imports
Tel: [90] (312) 212-8758
Fax: [90] (312) 212-8765

Basbakanlik Ozellestirme, Idaresi Baskanligi
(Prime Ministry, Privatization Administration)
www.oib.gov.tr
Huseyin Rahmi Gurpinar Sokak No. 2
06680 Cankaya, Ankara, Turkey
Tel: [90] (312) 441-1500
Fax: [90] (312) 441-1494
Activity: Privatization of state economic enterprises

Contacts: Mr. Ugur Bayar, President
Tel: [90] (312) 438-3480
Fax: [90] (312) 439-9916

Ms. Hande Ascili, Head of Turk Telekom Privatization Committee
Tel: [90] (312) 467-4287
Fax: [90] (312) 467-5259

Devlet Istatistik Enstitusu (DIE)
(State Institute of Statistics)
www.die.gov.tr
Necatibey Caddesi No. 114
06100 Ankara, Turkey
Tel: [90] (312) 417-6440
Fax: [90] (312) 417-0432
Activity: Federal statistics institute

Contact: Mr. Sefik Yildizeli, President
Tel: [90] (312) 418-8719
Fax: [90] (312) 425-3387; 418-1182

Turk Standartlari Enstitusu (TSE), Standart Hazirlama Baskanligi
(Turkish Institute of Standards, Standards Preparation Department)
www.tse.org.tr
Necatibey Caddesi No. 112
06100 Bakanliklar, Ankara, Turkey

Tel: [90] (312) 417-8330
Fax: [90] (312) 425-4399
Activity: Standards authority

Contacts: Mr. Bekir Ozturk, President
Tel: [90] (312) 425-4101
Fax: [90] (312) 417-2551

Mr. Mustafa Agus, President, Standards Preparation Dept.
Tel: [90] (312) 417-0020
Fax: [90] (312) 424-1216

Turk Patent Enstitusu Baskanligi
(Turkish Institute of Patents)
www.turkpatent.gov.tr
Izmir Caddesi No. 28
Kizilay, Ankara, Turkey
Tel: [90] (312) 232-5425
Fax: [90] (312) 230-0445
[90] (312) 232-5437
Activity: Patent and trademark agency

Contact: Mr. Mustafa Selim Sengun, President
Tel: [90] (312) 232-5415
Fax: [90] (312) 232-5437

TUBITAK-Turkiye Bilimsel ve Teknik Arastirma Kurumu
(The Scientific and Technical Research Council of Turkey)
www.tubitak.gov.tr
Ataturk Bulvari No. 221
06100 Kavaklidere, Ankara, Turkey
Tel: [90] (312) 468-5300
Fax: [90] (312) 427-7409
Activity: Research and development

Contact: Prof. Dr. Namik Kemal Pak, President
Tel: [90] (312) 467-7798
Fax: [90] (312) 427-2672

IGEME-Ihracati Gelistirme Merkezi
(Export Promotion Center)
www.igeme.org.tr
Mithatpasa Caddesi No. 60
Kizilay, Ankara, Turkey.
Tel: [90] (312) 417-2223
Fax: [90] (312) 417-2233
Activity: Turkish exports promotion organization. Publishes periodicals on Turkey's export products and producers. Prepares market research on specific industry sectors.

Contacts: Mr. Emin Haluk Ayhan, Secretary General and
Deputy Undersecretary for Foreign Trade
Tel: [90] (312) 212-8725
Fax: [90] (312) 212-8255

Ms. Beratiye Oncu, Assistant Secretary General
Tel: [90] (312) 425-0372
Fax: [90] (312) 425-7174

Transportation

Karayollari Genel Mudurlugu
(General Directorate of State Highways)
www.kgm.gov.tr
06350 Yucetepe Mahallesi, Ankara, Turkey
Tel: [90] (312) 415-7000
Fax: [90] (312) 417-4738
Activity: Highway construction

Contact: Mr. Dincer Yigit, Director General
Tel: [90] (312) 425-2343
Fax: [90] (312) 425-7308

Turk Hava Yollari Genel Mudurlugu (THY)
(General Directorate of Turkish Airlines)
www.turkishairlines.com.tr
Ataturk Havalimani,Yesilkoy
Istanbul, Turkey
Tel: [90] (212) 663-6300
Fax: [90] (212) 663-4744
Activity: National airline of Turkey. Scheduled for privatization in the near future

Contact: Mr. Yusuf Bolayirli, Director General
Tel: [90] (212) 663-6600 Ext. 01
Fax: [90] (212) 574-3420

Devlet Hava Meydanlari Isletmesi (DHMI)
(State Airports Administration)
www.dhmi.gov.tr
Bahcelerarasi Caddesi
06330 Etiler, Ankara, Turkey
Tel: [90] (312) 212-6120
Fax: [90] (312) 212-5222
Activity: Agency responsible for construction and airport operations

Contact: Mr. Mahmut Tekin, Director General
Tel: [90] (312) 215-2266
Fax: [90] (312) 212-5222

Devlet Demiryollari Genel Mudurlugu (TCDD)
(General Directorate of State Railways Administration)
www.tcdd.gov.tr
Istasyon, Ankara, Turkey
Tel: [90] (312) 309-0515
Fax: [90] (312) 311-7634
www.tcdd.gov.tr
Activity: National railway. Maintains track, stations, rolling stock and operations infrastructure

Contact: Mr. Vedat Bilgin, Director General
Tel: [90] (312) 311-3088

Fax: [90] (312) 310-3727

Travel and Tourism

Turizm Bakanligi
(Ministry of Tourism)
www.turizm.gov.tr
Inonu Bulvari No. 5
06100 Emek, Ankara, Turkey
Tel: [90] (312) 212-8300
Fax: [90] (312) 212-8590
Activity: Tourism promotion authority

Contacts: Mr. Savas Kuce, Undersecretary
Tel: [90] (312) 212-8355
Fax: [90] (312) 212-3199

Mr. M. Haluk Akar, Director General, General Directorate of Investments
Tel: [90] (312) 212-8385
Fax: [90] (312) 212-8397

Turkish Business/Trade Associations

DEIK-Dis Ekonomik Iliskiler Kurulu
(Foreign Economic Relations Board)
www.deik.ogr.tr
Istiklal Caddesi, 286/9
80050 Odakule, Beyoglu
Istanbul, Turkey
Tel: [90] (212) 243-4180
Fax: [90] (212) 243-4184
Activity: External economic relations promotion authority and source of commercial information. DEIK promotes U.S.-Turkish bilateral business relations.

Contacts: Ms. Cigdem Tuzun, Director
Ms. Basak Kusefoglu, Turkish-U.S. Business Council, Regional Coordinator

EGEV-Ege Ekonomisini Gelistirme Vakfi
(Foundation for the Development of the Aegean Region)
Email: egev@efes.net.tr
Cumhuriyet Bulvari, 1380 Sokak
Alyans Apt. No. 2/1, Kat 6, Daire 11
Alsancak, Izmir, Turkey.
Tel: [90] (232) 463-4878
Fax: [90] (232) 421-2259
Activity: Foundation having 85 members including city administrators, chambers of industry and commerce, businessmen's associations and regional universities. EGEV is a foreign investment promotion authority.

EGIAD-Ege Genc Isadamlari Dernegi
(Aegean Young Businessmen's Association)
www.egiad.org.tr
Mustafa Kemal Sahil Bulvari
Levent Marina, Cakalburnu
Izmir, Turkey
Tel: [90] (232) 278-3030
Fax: [90] (232) 278-3030
Activity: Business association in the Izmir region

Contact: Mr. Ziya Bese, Chairman

ESIAD-Ege Sanayicileri ve Isadamlari Dernegi
(Aegean Industrialists and Businessmen's Association)
(TUSIAD's Izmir extension)
E-mail: esiad@esiad.org.tr
www.esiad.org.tr
Sehit Fethi Bey Caddesi No. 55, Kat 8
35210 Izmir, Turkey
Tel: [90] (232) 483-8833
Fax: [90] (232) 483-3525
Activity: Industrialists and businessmen's organization established to promote business in the Aegean region

Contact: Mr. Deniz Taner, Chairman

TABA/AmCham - Turk-Amerikan Isadamlari Dernegi
(Turkish-American Businessmen's Association/ Turkish-American Chamber of Commerce)
E-mail: amcham@amcham.org
www.taba.org.tr
Barbaros Bulvari, Eser Apt. 48/16, Kat: 5
80700 Balmumcu
Istanbul, Turkey
Tel: [90] (212) 274-2824
Fax: [90] (212) 275-9316
Activity: Promote business ties between the United States and Turkey. Promote U.S.-Turkish business relations in the NIS and Central Asia.

Contact: Dr. Zeynel Abidin Erdem, Chairman

TUSIAD-Turk Sanayicileri ve Isadamlari Dernegi
(Turkish Industrialists' and Businessmen's Association)
www.tusiad.org.tr
Mesrutiyet Caddesi No. 74
80050 Tepebasi, Istanbul, Turkey
Tel: [90] (212) 249-5448; 249-0723
Fax: [90] (212) 249- 1350
Activity: Association of the largest business owners in Turkey, acts as a business lobby, and the association publishes an authoritative annual report on the Turkish economy

Contact: Mr. Tuncay Ozilhan, Chairman

Union of Chambers of Commerce, Industry, Maritime Commerce and Commodity Exchanges of Turkey (TOBB)
www.tobb.org.tr

Ataturk Bulvari No. 149
06640 Bakanliklar, Ankara, Turkey
Tel: [90] (312) 418-4327
Fax: [90] (312) 417-9711
Activity: Promotes investment and joint ventures on behalf of the member firms.

Contacts: Mr. Rifat Hisarciklioglu, Chairman
Ms. Fusun Karacasoy, Manager, Foreign Economic Relations Dept.

YASED-Yabanci Sermaye Koordinasyon Dernegi
(Association for Foreign Capital Coordination)
www.yased.org.tr
Barbaros Bulvari, Morbasan Sokak
Koza Is Merkezi B Blok/Kat 1
80700 Besiktas, Istanbul, Turkey
Tel: [90] (212) 272-5094
Fax: [90] (212) 274-6664
Activity: Promotes investment and foreign direct investment to Turkey.

Contact: Mr. Faruk Yoneyman, Chairman

Agriculture

Turkiye Ziraat Odalari Birligi
(Turkish Farmers Union)
Izmir Caddesi No. 24
06440 Yenisehir, Ankara, Turkey
Tel: [90] (312) 425-2313
Fax: [90] (312) 417-3068

SETBIR-Turkiye Sut, Et, Gida San. Ve Ureticileri Birligi
(Turkish Dairy, Meat, Food Industry and Producers Union)
Mebusevleri Mahallesi, Ayten Sok. No. 27/8
06580 Tandogan, Ankara, Turkey
Tel: [90] (312) 212-7902
Fax: [90] (312) 212-3662

Contact: Prof. Dr. Erkan Benli, Secretary General

BESD-BIR-Beyaz Et Sanayicileri ve Damizlikcilar Birligi
(White Meat Industrialists Association)
Cetin Emec Bulvari 8. Cadde No. 4/6
06460 Ovecler, Ankara, Turkey
Tel: [90] (312) 479-6246
Fax: [90] (312) 479-6247

Contact: Mr. Kemal Akman, Chairman

Un Sanayicileri Birligi
(Flour Millers Association)
Selanik Caddesi No. 82/30
Kizilay, Ankara, Turkey
Tel: [90] (312) 417-5357
Fax: [90] (312) 417-5358

Contact: Mr. Ilker Tanik, Secretary General

Yem Sanayicileri Birligi
(Turkish Feed Millers Association)
Cetin Emec Bulvari 8. Cad. 79. Sok. No. 3/1
06460 Ovecler, Ankara, Turkey
Tel: [90] (312) 479-9591
Fax: [90] (312) 479-0698

Contact: Ms. Ulku Karakus, President

Turkiye Tohum Endustrisi Birligi
(Turkish Seed Industry Association)
Tuna Caddesi No. 14/14
06420 Yenisehir, Ankara, Turkey
Tel: [90] (312) 432-0050
Fax: [90] (312) 432-2650

Contact: Mr. Ayhan Elci, Secretary General

Makarnacilar Dernegi
(Union of Pasta Producers)
Cinnah Caddesi No. 59/5
Cankaya, Ankara, Turkey
Tel: [90] (312) 441-5547
Fax: [90] (312) 438-3433

Contact: Mr. Ergin Erzurumlu, Secretary General

Advertising

Reklamcilar Dernegi
(Advertising Firms' Association)
Yildiz Cicegi Sokak No. 19
80630 Etiler, Istanbul, Turkey
Tel: [90] (212) 257-8873
Fax: [90] (212) 257-8870

Contact: Mr. Faruk Atasoy, President

Automotive

Ithal Otomobilleri Turkiye Mumessilleri Dernegi
(Imported Vehicles Turkey Representatives'Association)
E-mail: ithaloto@mail.koc.tr
www.iod.org.tr
Barbaros Bulvari Bahar Sokak No. 4
Baraz Ishani Kat 3, Daire 6
Balmumcu, Istanbul, Turkey
Tel: [90] (212) 288-6184
Fax: [90] (212) 266-4409

Contact: Mr. Fahir Gurkan, General Coordinator

ISOD-Otomotiv Sektoru Mensuplari Dernegi
(Automotive Sector Member's Association)
E-mail: isp@ispexport.com

Taksim Caddesi No. 119/5
Taksim, Istanbul, Turkey
Tel: [90] (212) 238-9312
Fax: [90] (212) 238-9316

Contact: Mr. Hakan Ozer, Chairman

OSD-Otomotiv Sanayii Dernegi
(Automotive Industry Association)
E-mail: osd@osd.org.tr
www.osd.org.tr
Atilla Sokak No. 10
81190 Altunizade, Istanbul, Turkey
Tel: [90] (216) 318-2994
Fax: [90] (216) 321-9497

Contact: Mr. Ercan Tezer, Secretary General

OYDER-Otomotiv Yetkili Saticilari Dernegi
(Vehicle Sellers' Association)
E-mail: oyder@superonline.com
www.oyder.tr.com
Fahrettin Kerim Gokay Caddesi
Okul Sokak Altunizade Sitesi B Blok K: 4 D: 20
Altunizade, Uskudar
Istanbul, Turkey
Tel: [90] (216) 327-9229
Fax: [90] (216) 327-0044

Contact: Mr. Hamza Dursun, Director

TAYSAD Tasit Araclari Yan Sanayi Dernegi
(Auto Parts Association)
E-mail: barbaros@taysad.org.tr
www.taysad.org.tr
TOSB-TAYSAD Organize Sanayi Bolgesi
Sekerpinar, Gebze
41490 Kocaeli, Turkey
Tel: [90] (262) 658-9818
Fax: [90] (262) 658-9839

Contact: Mr. Barbaros Demirci, Secretary General

Contracting and Construction

Turkiye Muteahhitler Birligi
(Turkish Contractors Association/The Union of International Contractors)
E-mail: mailbox@tca-uic.org.tr
www.tca-uic.org.tr
Ahmet Mithat Efendi Sokak No. 21
96550 Cankaya, Ankara, Turkey
Tel: [90] (312) 439-1712
Fax: [90] (312) 440-0253

Contact: Mr. Kadir Sever, President

Turkiye Prefabrike Betonarme Yapi Ureten Kurulus Mensuplari Birligi
(Prefabricated Concrete Construction Producers Union)
E-mail: prefab@ada.net.tr
www.prefab.prefab.org.tr
Farabi Sokak, Bag Apt. No. 39/10
Kavaklidere, Ankara, Turkey
Tel: [90] (312) 467-6195
Fax: [90] (312) 4676295

Contact: Mr. Gur Coskun, President

Toplu Konut Yapimcilari Dernegi
(Mass Housing Builders Association)
www.tokyad.org.tr
Perpa Ticaret Merkezi B-Blok, Kat 9 No. 1372
Okmeydani, Istanbul, Turkey
Tel: [90] (212) 210-9113
Fax: [90] (212) 210-9114

Contacts: Mr. Uzeyir Garih, President
Mr. Reha Medin, Secretary General

Defense Industry

SASAD-Savunma Sanayii Imalatcilari Dernegi
(Defense Industries Manufacturers' Association)
Paris Caddesi, Yazanlar Sokak 4/206
06680 Kavaklidere, Ankara, Turkey
Tel: [90] (312) 426-2255
Fax: [90] (312) 426-2256

Electronics

Elektronik Cihaz Imalatcilari Dernegi
(Electronic Equipment Manufacturers' Association)
Yildiz, Barbaros Bulvari
Sahir Kesebir Sokak 34
80700 Besiktas, Istanbul, Turkey
Tel: [90] (212) 266-0290
Fax: [90] (212) 272-4711

Elektronik Sanayicileri Dernegi
(Electronic Industrialists Association)
Bagdat Caddesi No. 477/4
81070 Suadiye, Istanbul, Turkey
Tel: [90] (216) 386-0909
Fax: [90] (216) 386-0910

Environment and Pollution Control

Cevre Teknolojisi Uygulayicilari Dernegi
(Association of Practitioners of Environmental Technology)
Irfan Bastug Caddesi,Yuva Apt. 3/10
80280 Gayrettepe, Istanbul, Turkey

Tel: [90] (212) 272-2904
Fax: [90] (212) 272-2904

Turkiye'nin Tabiatini Koruma Dernegi
(Association for Preservation of Turkey's Nature)
Kemeralti Caddesi, Vekilharc Sokak No. 16
Kadikoy, Istanbul, Turkey
Tel: [90] (216) 349-6602
Fax: [90] (216) 336-5212

Information Technology

TUBISAD-Turkiye Bilgi Islem Sanayicileri Dernegi
(Turkish Data-Processing Industrialists' Association)
Setat Is Merkezi 100/203, Kat 2
80260 Ferikoy, Istanbul, Turkey
Tel: [90] (212) 224-9593
Fax: [90] (212) 232-9262
Activity: Association of Turkish computer manufacturing, marketing, software and computer related service companies

Turkiye Bilisim Dernegi
Mesrutiyet Caddesi Yakut Apt. 48/18
06420 Kocatepe, Ankara, Turkey
Tel: [90] (312) 425-2912
Fax: [90] (312) 425-4817
Activity: Association for Turkish computer firms; publishes monthly computer periodical.

Insurance

Turkiye Sigorta Sirketleri Birligi
(Turkish Insurance Firms' Association)
Balmumcu, Morbasan Sokak
Koza Is Merkezi, B Blok, Kat 3
Besiktas, Istanbul, Turkey
Tel: [90] (212) 275-8976
Fax: [90] (212) 275-9855

Medical and Health Care

Tabibler Odasi
(Chamber of Medical Doctors)
Turkocagi Caddesi 17, Kat 3
Cagaloglu, Istanbul, Turkey
Tel: [90] (212) 522-1911
Fax: [90] (212) 522-7374

Dis Hekimleri Birligi
(Turkish Dental Association)
Mesrutiyet Caddesi 32/8
Yenisehir, Ankara, Turkey
Tel: [90] (312) 417-7492
Fax: [90] (312) 417-1922

Mining and Minerals

Turkiye Madenciler Dernegi
(Turkish Miners' Association)
Istiklal Caddesi No. 471/1
Beyoglu, Istanbul, Turkey
Tel: [90] (212) 245-1503
Fax: [90] (212) 244-8335

Genc Madenciler Dernegi
(Young Miners Association)
4. Levent, Cinar Sokak No. 19
80620 Besiktas, Istanbul, Turkey
Tel: [90] (212) 264-6922
Fax: [90] (212) 264-2996

Packaging and Packing

Ambalaj Sanayicileri Dernegi
(Packaging Industrialists' Association)
Kozyatagi, Inonu Caddesi
STFA Bloklari Blok 3, Kat 8, Daire 35
81090 Kadikoy, Istanbul, Turkey
Tel: [90] (212) 362-8155
Fax: [90] (212) 352-8156

Karton, Ambalaj Sanayicileri Dernegi
(Carton/Paper Packaging Industrialists' Association)
23 Temmuz Meydani No. 1, Kat 2
80300 Esentepe, Istanbul, Turkey
Tel: [90] (212) 267-4933
Fax: [90] (212) 267-1207

Paper and Pulp

Seluloz ve Kagit Sanayicileri Vakfi
(Paper and Paper Pulp Industrialists' Foundation)
Buyukdere Caddesi No. 81
Kurgu Is Hani Kat 8, Daire 15
80300 Mecidiyekoy, Istanbul, Turkey
Tel: [90] (212) 266-9524
Fax: [90] (212) 266-9524

Textiles

Turkiye Giyim Sanayicileri Dernegi
(Turkish Clothing Manufacturers' Association)
Yildiz Posta Caddesi
Dedeman Is Hani 48/8
80700 Gayrettepe, Istanbul, Turkey
Tel: [90] (212) 274-2525
Fax: [90] (212) 272-4060

Travel and Tourism

BETUYAB-Belek Turizm Yatirimcilar Birligi

(Union of Belek Tourism Investors)
E-mail: betuyab@superonline.com
Kuzgun Sokak No. 88/1
Asagiayranci, Ankara, Turkey
Tel: [90] (312) 441-5427
Fax: [90] (312) 441-5428
Activity: Hotel and resort development association in Belek

Contact: Mr. Mustafa Nazik, President

MARYAT-Marina Yatirimcilari ve IsletmecileriDernegi
(Association of Marina Investors and Operators)
Turizm Bakanligi Sektor Temsilciligi
Inonu Bulvari 5
Emek, Ankara, Turkey
Tel: [90] (242) 814-1490
Fax: [90] (242) 814-1552
Activity: Association representing the Ministry of Tourism in marina development and investment

TUROB-Turkiye Otelciler Birligi
(Union of Turkish Hotel Operators)
Mete Caddesi, Mete Palas 26/2
Taksim, Istanbul, Turkey
Tel: [90] (212) 249-5153
Fax: [90] (212) 252-1664
Activity: Hotel owners lobbying organization. Maintains information on hotel and resort projects.

Contact: Mr. Sinan Babila, President

TURSAB-Turkiye Seyahat Acentalari Dernegi
(Association of Turkish Travel Agencies)
www.tursab.org.tr
Fulya Asik Kerem Sokak No. 48/50
Dikilitas Mahallesi
Besiktas, Istanbul, Turkey
Tel: [90] (212) 259-8404
Fax: [90] (212) 259-0656
Activity: Supports travel agents and the tourism industry.

Contact: Mr. Basaran Ulusoy, President

TYD-Turizm Yatirimcilari Dernegi
(Tourism Investors Association)
E-mail: tyd@iris.com.tr
Cumhuriyet Caddesi, Celik Apt. 235, Kat 3
80230 Elmadag, Istanbul, Turkey
Tel: [90] (212) 279-0365
Fax: [90] (212) 279-8894

Activity: Turkish tourism investment.

Contacts: Mr. Tavit Koletavitoglu, President
Ms. Nedret Koruyan, General Coordinator

Chambers of Commerce in the Three Largest Cities in Turkey

Union of Chambers of Commerce, Industry, Maritime Commerce and Commodity Exchanges of Turkey (TOBB)
www.tobb.org.tr
Ataturk Bulvari No. 149
06640 Bakanliklar, Ankara, Turkey
Tel: [90] (312) 418-4327
Fax: [90] (312) 417-9711
Activity: Association of local chambers of commerce and industry

Contact: Mr. Rifat Hisarciklioglu, Chairman

Ankara Chamber of Commerce
www.atonet.com
E-mail: distic@atonet.com
Eskisehir Yolu, Sogutozu
Ankara, Turkey
Tel: [90] (312) 286-4036; 285-7950
Fax: [90] (312) 286-3446

Contact: Mr. Sinan Aydin Aygun, Chairman

Ankara Chamber of Industry
www.aso.org.tr
Ataturk Bulvari 193/4
Kavaklidere, Ankara, Turkey
Tel: [90] (312) 417-1200
Fax: [90] (312) 417-2060

Contact: Mr. Zafer Caglayan, Chairman

Istanbul Chamber of Commerce
www.ito.org.tr
Ragip Gumuspala Caddesi No. 84
34378 Eminonu, Istanbul, Turkey
Tel: [90] (212) 455-6000
Fax: [90] (212) 520-1526

Contacts: Mr. Mehmet Yildirim, Chairman
Ms. Fugen Camlidere, Asst. Secretary General

Istanbul Chamber of Industry
www.iso.org.tr
Mesrutiyet Caddesi 118
80050 Tepebasi, Istanbul, Turkey
Tel: [90] (212) 252-2900
Fax: [90] (212) 249-3963

Contact: Mr. Husamettin Kavi, Chairman

Deniz Ticaret Odasi
(Chamber of Maritime Commerce)
www.chamber-of-shipping.org.tr
Meclisi Mebusan Caddesi No. 22
80154 Salipazari

Istanbul, Turkey
Tel: [90] (212) 252-0130
Fax: [90] (212) 293-7935

Contact: Mr. Cengiz Kaptanoglu, Chairman

Izmir Chamber of Commerce
www.izto.org.tr
Ataturk Caddesi No. 126
35210 Pasaport, Izmir, Turkey
Tel: [90] (232) 441-7777
Fax: [90] (232) 483-7853

Contact: Mr. Ekrem Demirtas, Chairman

Aegean Chamber of Industry
www.ebso.com.tr
Cumhuriyet Bulvari No. 63
Izmir, Turkey
Tel: [90] (232) 441-0909
Fax: [90] (232) 446-5354; 445-2904

Contact: Mr. Atil Akkan, Chairman

Market Research Firms

IBS-International Business Services A.S.
E-mail: mail@ibsresearch.com
www.ibsresearch.com
Abdi Ipekci Caddesi, Kizilkaya Apt. 59/4
80200 Macka, Istanbul, Turkey
Tel: [90] (212) 252-2460
Fax: [90] (212) 252-2430

Contact: Mr. David Tonge, General Manager

Arthur Andersen & Co.
Resit Galip Caddesi, No. 53/3
06700 Gaziosmanpasa, Ankara, Turkey
Tel: [90] (312) 447-2111
Fax: [90] (312) 447-2773

Contact: Mr. Sedat Tasdemir, Manager

Deloitte & Touche Turkey
Denet Mali Danismanlik A.S.
Buyukdere Caddesi - Yapi Kredi Plaza B Blok Kat 5
80620 Levent, Istanbul, Turkey
Tel: [90] (212) 283-1585
Fax: [90] (212) 283-1937

Contact: Mr. Levent Yaveroglu, Chairman

Major Commercial Banks

Akbank T.A.S.
Sabanci Center, 4. Levent
80745 Istanbul, Turkey
Tel: [90] (212) 270-0044
Fax: [90] (212) 269-8255
www.akbank.com.tr

Citibank, N.A.
www.citibank.com
Buyukdere Cad. Maya Is Merkezi 100
80280 Esentepe, Istanbul, Turkey
Tel: [90] (212) 288-7700
Fax: [99] (212) 288-7768

Koc Bank
www.kocbank.com.tr
Ataturk Bulvari No. 78
Kizilay, Ankara, Turkey
Tel: [90] (312) 418-1804
Fax: [90] (312) 425-3237

Turkiye Is Bankasi A.S.
www.isbank.net.tr
Is Kuleleri, 4. Levent
Istanbul, Turkey
Tel: [90] (212) 316-0000
Fax: [90] (212) 316-0990

Yapi ve Kredi Bankasi A.S.
Yapi Kredi Plaza A Blok
Buyukdere Caddesi
80620 Levent, Istanbul, Turkey
Tel: [90] (212) 339-7000
Fax: [90] (212) 339-6000

T.C. Ziraat Bankasi
Gazi Mustafa Kemal Bulvari
Sihhiye, Ankara, Turkey
Tel: [90] (312) 310-3747; 310-3750
Fax: [90] (312) 310-1134

Turkiye Garanti Bankasi A.S.
www.garanti.com.tr
Buyukdere Caddesi No. 63
80670 Maslak, Istanbul, Turkey
Tel: [90] (212) 285-4040
Fax: [90] (212) 285-4040

Turk Ticaret Bankasi A.S.
www.turkbank.com.tr
Yildiz Posta Caddesi No. 2
80280 Gayrettepe, Istanbul, Turkey
Tel: [90] (212) 288-5900 / Ext. 4130
Fax: [90] (212) 288-6113

TURKISH EMBASSIES ABROAD

Afghanistan
Shan Mahmoud Chazi Khan Street 134, Kabul
Tel: (93) 20 072/20 540

Albania
Rruga Konferenca E. Pezes, 31, Tirana
Tel: (355 - 42) 22 449

Algeria
Villa Dar El - Quard Chemin de la Rochelle
Boulevard Colonel Bougara
Tel: (213 - 2) 6012 57
Fax: (213 - 2) 59 31 61

Argentina
Palermo Chico Juez Tedin 2728, Buenos Aires
Tel: (54- 1) 802 4146
Fax: (54- 1) 804 9488

Australia
60 Mugga Way, Red Hill
Canberra A.C.T. 2603
Tel: (61 -6) 295 02 27/
295 02 28
Fax: (61 -6) 239 65 92

Austria
Prinz Eugen Strasse 40
40 1040 Wien
Tel: (43 -222) 505 55 59 -
505 73 38
Fax: (43 -222) 505 36 60

Azerbaijan
Turkish Embassy
Hegani Kuseci 27 Baku
Tel: (7 -8922) 988 133 -
988 301
Telefax: (7 -8922) 651 004

Bahrain
Diplomatic Area, Sehl Center 1st floor
Manama Town 317
Tel: (973) 53 34 48
Fax: (973) 53 65 57

Bangladesh
House No. 7, Road No. 62
Gulshan Dhaka - 1212
Tel: (880 -2) 88 21 98

Belgium
4, Rue Montoyer 1040 Brussels
Tel: (32 -2) 513 40 95
513 60 48 - 513 61 42
fax: (32 -2) 514 07 48

Brazil
Ses Av Das Nacoes Lote 23
70. 452 Basilia DF
Tel: (55 -61) 242 18 50
Fax: (55 -61) 24 14 48

Bulgaria
Boulevard Mareshal F. Tolbukhine 23
1000 Sofia
Tel: (359 -2) 87 23 06

Canada
197 Wertemburg Street
Ottwa - Ontario
Tel: (1 -613) 232 15 77
Fax: (1 -613) 232 54 98

Chile
Nuncio Sotero Sanz 136
Providencia - Santiago
Tel: (56 -2) 231 89 52
Fax: (56 -2) 231 77 62

Cuba
Calle 20, 301 Esquina 3A Miramar
La Habana
Tel: (53 -7) 29 01 33

Czech Republic
Stresovice Pevnostini
3 160 00 Prague,
Tel: 422) 32 05 97

Denmark
Vestlagervej 16-18 2100
Copenhagen
Tel: (45 -1) 20 55 00
Fax: (45 -1) 18 00 33

Egypt
25, El Falaki Street Bab El Louk - Cairo
Tel: (593 -2) 354 83 64-356 33 18
Fax: (593 -2) 355 81 10

Finland
Topeliluksenkatu 3B
A 1-2 00260 Helsinki
Tel: (358 -0) 44 60 58
Fax: (358 -0) 44 23 79

France
16 Avenue de Lamballe
75016 Paris, France
Tel: (33- 1) 45245224-
42884754
Fax: (33 -1) 45204191
10, Rue Aguste Lamey 67000
Strasbourg
Tel: (33 -1) 88366910
Fax: (33 -1) 88379739

Germany
Ute Str. 47 5300 Bonn 2
Tel: (49 -228) 34 60 52-
53 54 55
Fax: (49 -228) 34 88 77

Turkisches Generalkonsulat
Johan - George Strassed 12
1000 Berlin 31
Tel: (49 -30) 892 50 33
Fax: (49 -30) 893 18 98

Turkisches Generalkonsulat
Cecilienalle 41
4000 Dusseldorf
Tel: (49 -211) 45 47 80
Fax: (49 -211) 454 78 22

Turkisches Generalkonsulat
Zeppelinalle 17 Frankfurt am Main 6000
Tel: (49 -69) 795 00 30
Fax: (49 -69) 70 90 32

Turkisches Generalkonsulat
Tesdorpf Str. 18,
2000 Hamburg 13
Tel: (49 -40) 44 30 41
Fax: (49 -40) 44 52 58

Turkisches Generalkonsulat
An der Chrirstuskirce 3,
3000 Hanover 1
Tel: (49 -511) 17708-17709
Fax: (49 -511) 17700

Turkisches Generalkonsulat
Menzinger St. 3 8000
Munchen 2
Tel: (49 -89) 1780310
Fax: (49 -89) 1785660

Turkisches Generalkonsulat
Kemer Strasse 19/B
7000 Stuttgart 1
Tel: (49 -711) 166670
Fax: (49 -711) 2622102

Greece
Rue Vassileos Gheorgiou
B Street 8
10674 Athens
Tel: (30 -1) 724 59 15
Fax: (30 -1) 733 17 78

Hungary
Uri Utca 45 Budapest 1014
Tel: (36 -1) 155 19 75 -
155 07 37
Fax: (36 -1) 175 38 53

India
50-N. Nyaya Marg Chanakyapuri
New Delhi 110021
Tel: (91- 11) 60 17 01
Tel: (91- 11) 60 16 67

Iran
Ave. Ferdowski, 314
11446 Tehran
Tel: (98 -21) 31 52 99-
31 53 51

Iraq
2/8 Wazsinyah
F.O. Box: 14001 Baghdad
Tel: (964 -1) 444 93 64

Ireland
11 Clide Road Ballsbridge
Dublin 4
Tel: (353 -1) 68 52 40
Fax: (353 -1) 68 50 14

Israel
34 Rehov Amos.
P.O. Box 22770
Tel Avivk 62495, Israel
Tel: (972 -3) 45 41 55
Fax: (972 -1) 45 41 56

Italy
Via Palestro,
28 Roma 00185
Tel: (39 -6) 494 15 47-446 99 32
Fax: (39 -6) 494 15 26

Consolato Generale di Turchia
Via San. Barnaba 30,
20122 Milano
Tel: (39 -2) 551 33 70
Fax: (39 -2) 540 03 89

Japan
33-6, 2- Chome Jinguame Shibuya-ku

Tokyo 150
Tel: (81 -3) 34 70 51 31
Fax: (81 -3) 34 70 51 36

Jordan
Jabal Amman 2nd Circle,
Abbas Mahmoud
Alagad St. 31 Jabal-Amma
Tel: (962 -6) 64 12 51-
64 12 52
Fax: (962 -6) 61 23 53

Kazakhstan
Turkish Embassy
Tolebi 29 480100 Alma Ata
Tel: (7- 3272) 618 927
Fax: (7- 3272) 506 208

Kenya
Gigiri Road off Limuru Road
P.O. Box 30785 Nairboi
Tel: (242 -2) 52 04 04
Fax: (242 -2) 52 12 37

Kuwait
Embassies Area
Istiglal Street Plot No. 16
Tel: (7 -3312) 227 882
Fax: (7 -3312) 268 835

Lebanon
Rabieh, Zone II Rue 3 Beyrouth
Tel: (961- 1) 40 65 75-6

Libya
Shara Zavia Dahmani
P.O. Box: 947
Tripoli
Tel: (218 -21) 377 17-377 32

Fax: (218 -21) 376 86

Luxembourg
20 Rue Marie-Adelaide L-2128
Tel: (352) 44 32 81
Fax: (352) 44 32 61

Malaysia
118 Jalan U-Thant
P.O. Box: 6238-55000

Kuala Lumpur
Tel: (60 -3) 457 22 25
Fax: (60 -3) 457 22 27

Mexico
Passeo de Las Palmas,
1525 Lomas
Barrilaco
Mexico D.F.C.P. 11000
Tel: (52 -5) 520 23 44
Fax: (52 -5) 540 31 85

Morrocco
7, Avenue de Fes - Rabat
Tel: (212 -7) 76 26 05
Fax: (212 -7) 70 49 80

The Netherlands
Jan Everstraat 2514 Bs
The Hague
Tel: (31 -70) 360 49 12
Fax: (31 -70) 361 79 69

Nigeria
3. Okunola Martins Close
S.W. Ikoyi Lagos
Tel: (234 -1) 68 30 30 -
68 26 46
Fax: (234 -1) 68 26 46

Norway
Halvdan Svartes
Gate 5 N-0244
Oslo 2
Tel: (47 -2) 44 99 20
Fax: (47 -2) 55 62 63

Oman
South Bowscher
239 St. 3939
Building 301 Al Khuwair Muscat
Tel: (968) 69 70 50
Fax: (968) 69 70 53

Pakistan
House No. 42 Street
No. 12, F-6/3
Islamabad
Tel: (92 -51) 09 39-21
00 43
Fax: (92 -51) 82 05 26

People's Republic of China
San Li Tun Dong Wu Jie
No. 9
100600 Beijing
Tel: (86 -1) 532 26 50-
532 27 12
Fax: (86 -1) 532 54 80

Philippines
2278 Magnolia Street Dasmarinas Village
Makat - Metro Manila

Tel: (63 -2) 8171550
Fax: (63 -2) 8176387

Poland
UL. Malczewskiego
32 Mokotow
02-622 Varsow
Tel: (48 -22) 44 32 01
Fax: (48 -22) 44 34 37

Portugal
Avenida das Descobertas, 22 Lisbonne
Tel: (351 -1) 301 42 75-6
Fax: (351 -1) 301 79 34

Qatar
P.O. Box 1977 Mohammed bin Thani St.
Bin Omran 37 Doha, Quatar
Fax: (974) 86 43 93

Romania
Calea Dorobantilor
72 Bucharest
Tel: (40 -0) 19 37 15-
11 05 56
Fax: (40 -0) 12 04 07

Russian Federation
Vadkovsky Perr.
7/37 Moscow
Tel: (7- 95) 972 6500
Fax: (7- 95) 972 6573

Saudi Arabia
P.O. Box 94390
Riyadh 11693
Tel: (966- 1) 482 01 01
Fax: (966 -1) 40 62 06

Senegal
Villa "La Come d'Or"
Ave. des Ambassadeurs
Comiche-Ouest, Fann
Residence Dakar
Tel: (221) 24 58 11

Singapore
20-B Nassim Road
Singapore 1025
Tel: (65) 732 76 46
Fax: (65) 738 17 86

Somalia
Via Degfar Road Km. 6
Mogadishu
Tel: (252- 1) 819 75

South Africa
1067 Church Street Hatfield 0181
Pretoria
Tel: (27-12) 342 6053

South Korea
726-116 Hannam-Dong Yongsan -ku
Seoul 140-212
Tel: (974) 7940255
Fax: (974) 7978546

Spain
Calle de Rafael Calvo
18-2 Ay-B
Madrid 28010
Tel: (34 -1) 319 80 64-
319 87 47
Fax: (34 -1) 380 66 02

Sudan
Street 29 House No. 31
New Extension Khartoum 1
Tel: (249- 11) 471 94

Sweden
Strandvagen 84 11527 Stockholm
Tel: (46- 8) 823 0840
Fax: (46- 8) 6635514

Switzerland
Lombachweg 33 3006 ern
Tel: (41 -31) 43 16 91
Fax: (41 -31) 44 88 19
Markus Strasse 10 8006 Zurich
Tel: (41 -1) 3638755
Fax: (41 -1) 3638288

Syria
Chare Ziad Ben Abi Sofian 56/58 B.9.3738
Damas
Tel: (963- 11) 33 14 11

Tajikistan
Turkish Embassy Hotel
Tajikistan 734066
Sohtemur 22 Dushanbe 011
Tel: (7- 3772) 275 321

Thailand
153/2 Soi Mahadlek Luang 1
Rajdamri Road
Bangkok 103330

Tel: (66-2) 251 29 87
Fax: (66-2) 253 21 21

The Netherlands
Turkish Embassy
Economic and Commercial Counsellor
Jannan Nassaustraat 25
2596 BM-The Hague
Tel: (31 -70) 328 13 76
Fax: (31 -70) 324 82 11

Tunisia
Ambassade de Turquie
Conseiller Economique et Commercial
50, Bis Rue Ibn Bassam
El Menzah - IV 1004 Tunis
Tel: (216- 1) 23 07 85 -
23 73 18
Fax: (216 -1) 766 988

Turkish Republic of Northern Cyrus (K.K.T.C)
Turkiye Buyukelciligi
Ikonomi ve Ticaret Musavirligi
Bedrettin Demirel Caddesi
Lefkose, K.K.T.C.
Tel: (392) 227 23 14
Fax: (392) 208 22 09

Turkmenistan
Turkish Embassy
Shevchhenko Str. 9 Ashkhabat
Tel: (7- 3632) 294 250
Fax: (7- 3632) 511 673

Ukraine
Tel: (7 -044) 291 8845
Fax: (7 -044) 291 5468 -
291 8884

United Arab Emirates (U.A.E.)
Khaleed Bin Abdulaziz Str.
Khalidia West of Finance Dept.
P.O. Box 3204 Abu Dhabi
Tel: (971 -2) 655 421
Fax: (971 -2) 662 691

United Kingdom
43, Belgrave Square London,
SWIX, 8 PA
Tel: (44 -71) 655 421
Fax: (44 -71) 235 80 93

United States of America (U.S.A.)
1714 Massachusetts
Avenue, N.W.
Washington, D.C. 20066
Tel: (1- 202) 659 82 00-
659 0032
Fax: (1- 202) 659 07 44

Turkish Center
821 United Nations Plaza 5 TH Floor
New York, NY 10017
Tel: (1 -212) 9340188 -
9340149

Uzbekistan
Turkish Embassy Gogol Kucesi 87
Tashkent
Tel: (7 -3712) 332 107
Fax: (7 -3712) 331 358

Vatican
Via Lovanio 24/1 00198 Rome
Tel: (39 -6) 854 91 66
Fax: (39 -6) 854 39 86

Venezuela
Calle Kernal Ataturk 6
Quinta Turquesa Valle Ambia Caracas
Tel: (58- 2) 920442
Fax: (58- 2) 920442

Yemen
P.O. Box 12450 Sana
Tel: (967 -2) 24 13 95
Fax: (967 -2) 24 13 95

Yugoslavia
Ul. Proleterskiti Brig. 1
11000 Belgrade, Yugoslavia
Tel: (38- 11) 33 54 31
Fax: (38- 11) 33 54 33

TURKISH FREE ZONE CONTACTS

T.R PRIME MINISTERY,
UNDERSECRETARIAT FOR FOREIGN TRADE,
GENERAL DIRECTORATE OF FREE ZONES,
06510 EMEK/ANKARA
TEL: (0312) 212 58 87-88 Director General
(0312) 212 89 09 Deputy Director General
(0312) 212 58 90 Head of Department
FAX: (0312) 212 89 06

E-MAIL: sbgm@ foreigntrade.gov.tr

FREE ZONE DIRECTORATES	FREE ZONE OPERATOR-FOUNDER/OPERATOR FIRMS
MERSİN FREE ZONE DIRECTORATE ZONE DIRECTOR: Erol TAŞYÜREK P.K. 15 MERSİN Tel : (0324) 238 75 90-94 Fax : (0324) 238 75 97	MERSİN FREE ZONE OPERATOR INC. -MESBAŞ P.K. 01 MERSİN Tel : (0324) 238 74 00 (10 LINE) Fax: (0324) 238 74 10
ANTALYA FREE ZONE DIRECTORATE ZONE DIRECTOR: Tuğrul YALÇINER P.K. 1 S.B.07070 Yeniliman ANTALYA Tel : (0242)259 01 88 Fax : (0242) 259 09 34	ANTALYA FREE ZONE OPERATOR INC. - ASBAŞ P.K. 002 07070 Yeniliman- ANTALYA Tel : (0242) 259 09 30-31 Fax: (0242) 259 09 32
AEGEAN FREE ZONE DIRECTORATE ZONE DIRECTOR: Cemali ÇETİN Akçay Cad.No:144/1 Gaziemir/İZMİR Tel : (0232) 251 02 44-251 35 94 Fax : (0232) 251 16 62	AEGEAN FREE ZONE FOUNDER-OPERATOR INC. - ESBAŞ Akçay Cad.No:144/1 Gaziemir/İZMİR Tel: (0232) 251 38 51-251 39 51 Fax: (0232) 251 08 42
İSTANBUL ATATURK AIRPORT FREE ZONE DIRECTORATE ZONE DIRECTOR: Mustafa GÜNEŞ Havalimanı 34830 Yeşilköy/İSTANBUL Tel : (0212) 560 78 60-63 Fax : (0212) 560 78 63	İSTANBUL ATATURK AIRPORT. FREE ZONE FOUNDER-OPERATOR INC. -İSBİ Havalimanı 34830 Yeşilköy/İSTANBUL Tel : (0212) 560 96 17 Santral: (0212) 661 54 57-58-59-60 Fax : (0212) 560 78 66
TRABZON FREE ZONE DIRECTORATE ZONE DIRECTOR: Hikmet AKYAZI Trabzon Limanı-TRABZON Tel : (0462) 326 42 33-34 Fax : (0462) 326 42 35	TRABZON FREE ZONE FOUNDER-OPERATOR INC. - TRANSBAŞ Trabzon Limanı TRABZON Tel: (0462) 326 38 00-6 Fax: (0462) 326 38 07
İSTANBUL LEATHER & INDUSTRY FREE ZONE DIRECTORATE ZONE DIRECTOR: Salih AHMETCANOĞLU Aydınlı-Orhanlı Mevkii 81464 Tuzla/İSTANBUL Tel : (0216) 394 18 87 Fax : (0216) 394 12 53	İSTANBUL LEATHER & INDUSTRY FREE ZONE FOUNDER-OPERATOR INC. - DESBAŞ Aydınlı-Orhanlı Mevkii 81464 Tuzla/İSTANBUL Tel: (0216) 394 18 87-88-89 Fax (0216) 394 12 68-
İSTANBUL STOCK EXCHANGE FREE ZONE DIRECTORATE DEPUTY ZONE DIRECTOR: Ayşenur TAKAZ 80860 İstinye/İSTANBUL Tel: (0212) 298 21 00 Fax : (0212) 298 25 00	İSTANBUL STOCK EXCHANGE FREE ZONE FOUNDER-OPERATOR INC. - 80860 İstinye/İSTANBUL Tel: (0212) 298 23 76, 298 23 46 Fax: (0212)298 25 00 (0212)298 25 37
EAST ANATOLIAN FREE ZONE DIRECTORATE DEPUTY ZONE DIRECTOR: Hasan DİYARBAKIR 23 Temmuz Fuar Alanı 25050 ERZURUM Tel: (0442) 235 28 51 Fax: (0442) 235 28 52	EAST ANATOLIAN FREE ZONE FOUNDER-OPERATOR INC. - DASBAŞ 23 Temmuz Fuar Alanı 25050 ERZURUM Tel: (0442) 235 22 44-46 Fax: (0442) 235 22 45
MARDİN FREE ZONE DIRECTORATE ZONE DIRECTOR: Yusuf YILDIZ Organize San.Böl. 47060 MARDİN	MARDİN FREE ZONE FOUNDER-OPERATOR INC - MASBAŞ- Organize San.Böl.47060 MARDİN

Tel : (0482) 215 20 70-215 16 94 Fax : (0482) 215 15 17	Tel: (0482) 215 19 82 Fax: (0482) 215 15 17
RİZE FREE ZONE DIRECTORATE ZONE DIRECTOR: Kemalettin YÜCEDAL Engindere Mah.Küçük San. Sitesi Yanı 53100 RİZE Tel : (0464) 226 09 52-53-55 Fax : (0464) 226 09 56	RİZE FREE ZONE FOUNDER-OPERATOR INC. – RİSBAŞ Engindere Mah. Küçük San.Sitesi Yanı 53100 RİZE Tel: (0464) 226 58 59 Fax :(0464) 226 09 57
İSTANBUL THRACE FREE ZONE DIRECTORATE ZONE DIRECTOR: Ender ÜNLÜ Karatoprak Mevkii Ferhatpaşa Mah.Nato Karşısı Çatalca/İSTANBUL Tel : (0212) 789 60 00 Fax : (0212) 789 48 86	İSTANBUL THRACE FREE ZONE FOUNDER-OPERATOR INC. – İSBAŞ Karatoprak Mevkii Ferhatpaşa Mah.Nato Karşısı Çatalca/İSTANBUL Tel: (0212) 789 14 50- (0212) 789 14 40 Fax : (0212) 789 29 33
İZMİR MENEMEN LEATHER FREE ZONE DIRECTORATE ZONE DIRECTOR: Hüseyin KALYONCU Maltepe Köyü Panaz Tepe Mevkii Menemen/İZMİR Tel : (0232) 842 66 27 Fax : (0232) 842 63 47	İZMİR MENEMEN LEATHER FREE ZONE FOUNDER OPERATOR INC. - İDESBAŞ Maltepe Köyü Panaz Tepe Mevkii Menemen/İZMİR Tel: (0232) 842 67 51-52 Fax:(0232) 842 63 49
SAMSUN FREE ZONE DIRECTORATE ZONE DIRECTOR: Halittin TOK Limaniçi 55100 SAMSUN Tel : (0362) 445 19 96 (0362) 445 17 46 (0362) 445 14 89 FAX : (0362) 445 11 08	SAMSUN FREE ZONE FOUNDER OPERATOR INC. - SASBAŞ Limaniçi 55100 SAMSUN TEL: (362) 445 18 18 FAX: (362) 445 08 45
KAYSERİ FREE ZONE DIRECTORATE BÖLGE MÜDÜRÜ: Ali TAŞDELEN Kayseri FREE ZONE DIRECTORATE Tel : (0352) 311 39 81 Fax : (0352) 311 39 82	KAYSERİ FREE ZONE FOUNDER OPERATOR INC. - KAYSER Ankara Yolu 15.Km. Ambarlı Mevkii KAYSERİ Tel : (0352) 311 39 88-89 Fax: (0352) 311 39 87
ADANA-YUMURTALIK FREE ZONE DIRECTORATE DEPUTY ZONE DIRECTOR:Muharrem PUSAT P.K.10 01920 Ceyhan/ADANA Tel (0322) 657 25 75-76-77 Fax : (0322) 657 25 85	ADANA YUMURTALIK FREE ZONE FOUNDER OPERATOR INC. - TAYSEB P.K. 10 01920 Ceyhan/ADANA Tel: (0322) 657 25 75 -76-77 Fax: (0322) 657 25 85
EUROPE FREE ZONE DIRECTORATE ZONE DIRECTOR: Kenan TAŞKENTLİ P.K. 350 59860 Çorlu / TEKİRDAĞ Tel (0282) 659 95 08 -09-10 Fax : (0282) 659 94 79	EUROPE FREE ZONE FOUNDER OPERATOR INC. P.K. 363 59860 Çorlu / TEKİRDAĞ Tel: (0282) 659 95 00 (13 Line) Fax: (0282) 659 94 72
GAZİANTEP FREE ZONE DIRECTORATE ZONE DIRECTOR: Mehmet Y.GÖKTÜRK 27120 Başpınar Mevkii Şehitkamil/GAZİANTEP Tel (0342)337 42 00-04 -05-06-07-08 Fax : (0342) 337 42 07	GAZİANTEP FREE ZONE FOUNDER OPERATOR INC. - GASBAŞ 27500 Aktoprak Mevkii/G.ANTEP Tel (0342) 337 33 26-27 Fax : (0342) 337 15 70

BASIC TITLES ON TURKEY

Title	ISBN
Turkey A "Spy" Guide - Strategic Information and Developments	1433050099
Turkey A Spy" Guide"	1438748760
Turkey Air Force Handbook	1438748779
Turkey Air Force Handbook	1433050102
Turkey Army Weapon Systems Handbook	1433060981
Turkey Army Weapon Systems Handbook	1433060981
Turkey Army Weapon Systems Handbook	1433060981
Turkey Army, National Security and Defense Policy Handbook	1438748787
Turkey Army, National Security and Defense Policy Handbook	1433050110
Turkey Banking & Financial Market Handbook	1438748795
Turkey Banking & Financial Market Handbook	1433050129
Turkey Business and Investment Opportunities Yearbook	1438748809
Turkey Business and Investment Opportunities Yearbook	1433050137
Turkey Business and Investment Opportunities Yearbook Volume 1 Strategic Information and Opportunities	1438778139
Turkey Business and Investment Opportunities Yearbook Volume 2 Leading Export-Import, Business, Investment Opportunities and Projects	1577519655
Turkey Business Intelligence Report - Practical Information, Opportunities, Contacts	1438748817
Turkey Business Intelligence Report - Practical Information, Opportunities, Contacts	1433050145
Turkey Business Law Handbook - Strategic Information and Basic Laws	1438748825
Turkey Business Law Handbook - Strategic Information and Basic Laws	143877124X
Turkey Business Law Handbook - Strategic Information and Basic Laws	143877124X
Turkey Business Law Handbook - Strategic Information and Basic Laws	1433050153
Turkey Business Law Handbook Volume 2 Investment and Trade Laws Volume 2 Investment and Trade Laws	1577518233
Turkey Clothing & Textile Industry Handbook	1438748833
Turkey Clothing & Textile Industry Handbook	1433050161
Turkey Company Laws and Regulations Handbook	143307074X
Turkey Constitution and Citizenship Laws Handbook - Strategic Information and Basic Laws	1438780052
Turkey Country Study Guide - Strategic Information and Developments	1438748841
Turkey Country Study Guide - Strategic Information and Developments	143305017X
Turkey Country Study Guide - Strategic Information and Developments Volume 1 Strategic Information and Developments	1438775784
Turkey Customs, Trade Regulations and Procedures Handbook	143874885X
Turkey Customs, Trade Regulations and Procedures Handbook	1433050188
Turkey Diplomatic Handbook - Strategic Information and Developments	1438748868
Turkey Diplomatic Handbook - Strategic Information and Developments	1433050196
Turkey Ecology & Nature Protection Handbook	143305020X
Turkey Ecology & Nature Protection Laws and Regulation Handbook	1433075148
Turkey Economic & Development Strategy Handbook	1438748876
Turkey Economic & Development Strategy Handbook	1433050218
Turkey Education System and Policy Handbook	1433068559
Turkey Energy Policy, Laws and Regulation Handbook	1433072904
Turkey Energy Policy, Laws and Regulations Handbook	1438748884
Turkey Energy Policy, Laws and Regulations Handbook	1433050226
Turkey Export-Import Trade and Business Directory	1438748892

Title	ISBN
Turkey Export-Import Trade and Business Directory	1433050234
Turkey Foreign Policy and Government Guide	1438748906
Turkey Foreign Policy and Government Guide	1433050242
Turkey Government and Business Contacts Handbook	1438748914
Turkey Government and Business Contacts Handbook	1433050250
Turkey Immigration Laws and Regulations Handbook - Strategic Information and Basic Laws	1438783655
Turkey Industrial and Business Directory	1433050269
Turkey Industrial and Business Directory: Vol 2 Industrial & Export Contacts	1433068567
Turkey Industrial and Business Directory: Vol 3 Turkish Companies Exporting to the United States	1433068575
Turkey Industrial and Business Directory: Vol 4 Turkish Companies Exporting to the EU	1433068583
Turkey Industrial and Business Directory: Vol 5 Turkish Companies Exporting to the Russia	1433068591
Turkey Insolvency (Bankruptcy) Laws and Regulations Handbook - Strategic Information and Basic Laws	9781433085710
Turkey Intelligence & Security Activities & Operations Handbook	1438748922
Turkey Intelligence & Security Activities & Operations Handbook	1433050277
Turkey Internet and E-Commerce Investment and Business Guide - Strategic and Practical Information: Regulations and Opportunities	1438748930
Turkey Internet and E-Commerce Investment and Business Guide - Strategic and Practical Information: Regulations and Opportunities	1433050285
Turkey Investment and Business Guide - Strategic and Practical Information	1438748949
Turkey Investment and Business Guide - Strategic and Practical Information	1438768966
Turkey Investment and Business Guide - Strategic and Practical Information	1438768966
Turkey Investment and Business Guide - Strategic and Practical Information	1433050293
Turkey Investment and Business Guide Volume 2 Business, Investment Opportunities and Incentives	1577519280
Turkey Investment and Trade Laws and Regulations Handbook	1433076756
Turkey Justice System and National Police Handbook	1438748957
Turkey Justice System and National Police Handbook	1433050307
Turkey Labor Laws and Regulations Handbook - Strategic Information and Basic Laws	1438781857
Turkey Land Ownership and Agriculture Laws Handbook	1438760159
Turkey Medical & Pharmaceutical Industry Handbook	1438748965
Turkey Medical & Pharmaceutical Industry Handbook	1433050315
Turkey Mineral & Mining Sector Investment and Business Guide - Strategic and Practical Information	1438748973
Turkey Mineral & Mining Sector Investment and Business Guide - Strategic and Practical Information Volume 1 Energy Sector	1433050323
Turkey Mining Laws and Regulations Handbook	1433078376
Turkey National Intelligence Organization and Policy Handbook	1438748981
Turkey National Intelligence Organization and Policy Handbook	1433050331
Turkey Oil & Gas Sector Business & Investment Opportunities Yearbook	143874899X
Turkey Oil & Gas Sector Business & Investment Opportunities Yearbook	143305034X
Turkey Oil and Gas Exploration Laws and Regulation Handbook	143307902X
Turkey Oil and Gas Industry Business and Investment Opportunities Handbook	1438749007
Turkey Oil and Gas Industry Business and Investment Opportunities Handbook	1433050358
Turkey Privatization Programs and Regulations Handbook	1438749015

Title	ISBN
Turkey Privatization Programs and Regulations Handbook	1433050366
Turkey Recent Economic and Political Developments Yearbook	1433062615
Turkey Recent Economic and Political Developments Yearbook	1433062615
Turkey Recent Economic and Political Developments Yearbook	1433062615
Turkey Research & Development Policy Handbook	1433063018
Turkey Research & Development Policy Handbook	1433063018
Turkey Research & Development Policy Handbook	1433063018
Turkey Starting Business (Incorporating) in Turkey Guide	1433047217
Turkey Starting Business (Incorporating) in....Guide	1433068605
Turkey Taxation Laws and Regulations Handbook	1433081180
Turkey Telecom Laws and Regulations Handbook	1433082578
Turkey Telecommunication Industry Business Opportunities Handbook	1438749023
Turkey Telecommunication Industry Business Opportunities Handbook	1433050374
Turkey Transportation Policy and Regulations Handbook	1433068613
Turkey Wine Industry Investment and Business Opportunities Yearbook	1433068621
Turkey: How to Invest, Start and Run Profitable Business in Turkey Guide - Practical Information, Opportunities, Contacts	9781433084768

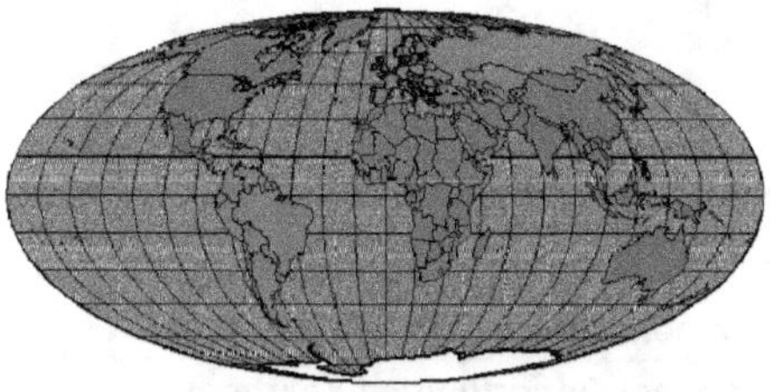

WORLD BUSINESS AND INVESTMENT OPPORTUNITIES LIBRARY

Price: $149.95 Each

World Business Information Catalog: http://www.ibpus.com

TITLE
1. Australia Business and Investment Opportunities Yearbook
2. Austria Business and Investment Opportunities Yearbook
3. Bangladesh Business and Investment Opportunities Yearbook
4. Belgium Business and Investment Opportunities Yearbook
5. Bolivia Business and Investment Opportunities Yearbook
6. Canada Business and Investment Opportunities Yearbook
7. Cayman Islands Business and Investment Opportunities Yearbook
8. Central African Republic Business and Investment Opportunities Yearbook
9. Chad Business and Investment Opportunities Yearbook
10. Chile Business and Investment Opportunities Yearbook
11. China Business and Investment Opportunities Yearbook
12. China Business and Investment Opportunities Yearbook
13. Colombia Business and Investment Opportunities Yearbook
14. Comoros Business and Investment Opportunities Yearbook
15. Congo Republic Business and Investment Opportunities Yearbook
16. Congo, Democratic Republic Business and Investment Opportunities Yearbook
17. Cook Islands Business and Investment Opportunities Yearbook
18. Costa Rica Business and Investment Opportunities Yearbook
19. Costa Rica Business and Investment Opportunities Yearbook
20. Cote d'Ivoire Business and Investment Opportunities Yearbook
21. Croatia Business and Investment Opportunities Yearbook
22. Cuba Business and Investment Opportunities Yearbook
23. Cuba Business and Investment Opportunities Yearbook
24. Cyprus Business and Investment Opportunities Yearbook
25. Czech Republic Business and Investment Opportunities Yearbook
26. Denmark Business and Investment Opportunities Yearbook
27. Djibouti Business and Investment Opportunities Yearbook
28. Dominica Business and Investment Opportunities Yearbook
29. Dominican Republic Business and Investment Opportunities Yearbook
30. Ecuador Business and Investment Opportunities Yearbook
31. Egypt Business and Investment Opportunities Yearbook
32. Egypt Business and Investment Opportunities Yearbook

**For additional analytical, business and investment opportunities information,
Please contact Global Investment & Business Center, USA
at (202) 546-2103. Fax: (202) 546-3275. E-mail: rusric@erols.com**

33.	Equatorial Guinea Business and Investment Opportunities Yearbook
34.	Eritrea Business and Investment Opportunities Yearbook
35.	Estonia Business and Investment Opportunities Yearbook
36.	Estonia Business and Investment Opportunities Yearbook
37.	Ethiopia Business and Investment Opportunities Yearbook
38.	Falkland Islands Business and Investment Opportunities Yearbook
39.	Faroes Business and Investment Opportunities Yearbook
40.	Fiji Business and Investment Opportunities Yearbook
41.	Finland Business and Investment Opportunities Yearbook
42.	Finland Business and Investment Opportunities Yearbook
43.	France Business and Investment Opportunities Yearbook
44.	France Business and Investment Opportunities Yearbook
45.	Gabon Business and Investment Opportunities Yearbook
46.	Gambia Business and Investment Opportunities Yearbook
47.	Georgia Business and Investment Opportunities Yearbook
48.	Germany Business and Investment Opportunities Yearbook
49.	Germany Business and Investment Opportunities Yearbook
50.	Ghana Business and Investment Opportunities Yearbook
51.	Gibraltar Business and Investment Opportunities Yearbook
52.	Greece Business and Investment Opportunities Yearbook
53.	Greenland Business and Investment Opportunities Yearbook
54.	Grenada Business and Investment Opportunities Yearbook
55.	Guam Business and Investment Opportunities Yearbook
56.	Guatemala Business and Investment Opportunities Yearbook
57.	Guernsey Business and Investment Opportunities Yearbook
58.	Guinea Business and Investment Opportunities Yearbook
59.	Guinea-Bissau Business and Investment Opportunities Yearbook
60.	Guyana Business and Investment Opportunities Yearbook
61.	Haiti Business and Investment Opportunities Yearbook
62.	Honduras Business and Investment Opportunities Yearbook
63.	Hungary Business and Investment Opportunities Yearbook
64.	Hungary Business and Investment Opportunities Yearbook
65.	Iceland Business and Investment Opportunities Yearbook
66.	India Business and Investment Opportunities Yearbook
67.	India Business and Investment Opportunities Yearbook
68.	Indonesia Business and Investment Opportunities Yearbook
69.	Indonesia Business and Investment Opportunities Yearbook
70.	Iran Business and Investment Opportunities Yearbook
71.	Iraq Business and Investment Opportunities Yearbook
72.	Ireland Business and Investment Opportunities Yearbook
73.	Israel Business and Investment Opportunities Yearbook

74. Italy Business and Investment Opportunities Yearbook
75. Jamaica Business and Investment Opportunities Yearbook
76. Japan Business and Investment Opportunities Yearbook
77. Jersey Business and Investment Opportunities Yearbook
78. Jordan Business and Investment Opportunities Yearbook
79. Kazakhstan Business and Investment Opportunities Yearbook
80. Kenya Business and Investment Opportunities Yearbook
81. Kiribati Business and Investment Opportunities Yearbook
82. Korea, North Business and Investment Opportunities Yearbook
83. Korea, South Business and Investment Opportunities Yearbook
84. Kuwait Business and Investment Opportunities Yearbook
85. Kyrgyzstan Business and Investment Opportunities Yearbook
86. Laos Business and Investment Opportunities Yearbook
87. Latvia Business and Investment Opportunities Yearbook
88. Lebanon Business and Investment Opportunities Yearbook
89. Lesotho Business and Investment Opportunities Yearbook
90. Liberia Business and Investment Opportunities Yearbook
91. Libya Business and Investment Opportunities Yearbook
92. Liechtenstein Business and Investment Opportunities Yearbook
93. Lithuania Business and Investment Opportunities Yearbook
94. Luxembourg Business and Investment Opportunities Yearbook
95. Macau Business and Investment Opportunities Yearbook
96. Macedonia Republic Business and Investment Opportunities Yearbook
97. Madagascar Business and Investment Opportunities Yearbook
98. Malawi Business and Investment Opportunities Yearbook
99. Malaysia Business and Investment Opportunities Yearbook
100. Maldives Business and Investment Opportunities Yearbook
101. Mali Business and Investment Opportunities Yearbook
102. Malta Business and Investment Opportunities Yearbook
103. Man Business and Investment Opportunities Yearbook
104. Marshall Islands Business and Investment Opportunities Yearbook
105. Mauritania Business and Investment Opportunities Yearbook
106. Mauritius Business and Investment Opportunities Yearbook
107. Mayotte Business and Investment Opportunities Yearbook
108. Mexico Business and Investment Opportunities Yearbook
109. Micronesia Business and Investment Opportunities Yearbook
110. Moldova Business and Investment Opportunities Yearbook
111. Monaco Business and Investment Opportunities Yearbook
112. Mongolia Business and Investment Opportunities Yearbook
113. Monserrat Business and Investment Opportunities Yearbook

114. Morocco Business and Investment Opportunities Yearbook
115. Mozambique Business and Investment Opportunities Yearbook
116. Myanmar Business and Investment Opportunities Yearbook
117. Namibia Business and Investment Opportunities Yearbook
118. Nauru Business and Investment Opportunities Yearbook
119. Nepal Business and Investment Opportunities Yearbook
120. Netherlands Business and Investment Opportunities Yearbook
121. New Caledonia Business and Investment Opportunities Yearbook
122. New Zealand Business and Investment Opportunities Yearbook
123. Nicaragua Business and Investment Opportunities Yearbook
124. Niger Business and Investment Opportunities Yearbook
125. Nigeria Business and Investment Opportunities Yearbook
126. Niue Business and Investment Opportunities Yearbook
127. Northern Mariana Islands Business and Investment Opportunities Yearbook
128. Norway Business and Investment Opportunities Yearbook
129. Oman Business and Investment Opportunities Yearbook
130. Pakistan Business and Investment Opportunities Yearbook
131. Palau Business and Investment Opportunities Yearbook
132. Palestine Business and Investment Opportunities Yearbook
133. Panama Business and Investment Opportunities Yearbook
134. Papua New Guinea Business and Investment Opportunities Yearbook
135. Paraguay Business and Investment Opportunities Yearbook
136. Peru Business and Investment Opportunities Yearbook
137. Philippines Business and Investment Opportunities Yearbook
138. Pitcairn Islands Business and Investment Opportunities Yearbook
139. Poland Business and Investment Opportunities Yearbook
140. Polynesia French Business and Investment Opportunities Yearbook
141. Portugal Business and Investment Opportunities Yearbook
142. Romania Business and Investment Opportunities Yearbook
143. Russia Business and Investment Opportunities Yearbook
144. Rwanda Business and Investment Opportunities Yearbook
145. Saint Kitts and Nevis Business and Investment Opportunities Yearbook
146. Saint Lucia Business and Investment Opportunities Yearbook
147. Saint Vincent and The Grenadines Business and Investment Opportunities Yearbook
148. Samoa (American) A Business and Investment Opportunities Yearbook
149. Samoa (Western) Business and Investment Opportunities Yearbook
150. San Marino Business and Investment Opportunities Yearbook
151. Sao Tome and Principe Business and Investment Opportunities Yearbook
152. Saudi Arabia Business and Investment Opportunities Yearbook
153. Senegal Business and Investment Opportunities Yearbook
154. Serbia Business and Investment Opportunities Yearbook
155. Seychelles Business and Investment Opportunities Yearbook
156. Sierra Leone Business and Investment Opportunities Yearbook
157. Singapore Business and Investment Opportunities Yearbook
158. Slovakia Business and Investment Opportunities Yearbook
159. Slovenia Business and Investment Opportunities Yearbook
160. Solomon Islands Business and Investment Opportunities Yearbook
161. Somalia Business and Investment Opportunities Yearbook

162. South Africa Business and Investment Opportunities Yearbook
163. South Sudan Business and Investment Opportunities Yearbook
164. Spain Business and Investment Opportunities Yearbook
165. Sri Lanka Business and Investment Opportunities Yearbook
166. St. Helena Business and Investment Opportunities Yearbook
167. St. Pierre & Miquelon Business and Investment Opportunities Yearbook
168. Sudan Business and Investment Opportunities Yearbook
169. Suriname Business and Investment Opportunities Yearbook
170. Swaziland Business and Investment Opportunities Yearbook
171. Sweden Business and Investment Opportunities Yearbook
172. Switzerland Business and Investment Opportunities Yearbook
173. Syria Business and Investment Opportunities Yearbook
174. Taiwan Business and Investment Opportunities Yearbook
175. Tajikistan Business and Investment Opportunities Yearbook
176. Tanzania Business and Investment Opportunities Yearbook
177. Thailand Business and Investment Opportunities Yearbook
178. Timor Leste Ecological and Nature Protection Guide
179. Togo Business and Investment Opportunities Yearbook
180. Tonga Business and Investment Opportunities Yearbook
181. Trinidad and Tobago Business and Investment Opportunities Yearbook
182. Tunisia Business and Investment Opportunities Yearbook
183. Turkey Business and Investment Opportunities Yearbook
184. Turkmenistan Business and Investment Opportunities Yearbook
185. Tuvalu Business and Investment Opportunities Yearbook
186. Uganda Business and Investment Opportunities Yearbook
187. Ukraine Business and Investment Opportunities Yearbook
188. United Arab Emirates Business and Investment Opportunities Yearbook
189. United Kingdom Business and Investment Opportunities Yearbook
190. Uruguay Business and Investment Opportunities Yearbook
191. Uzbekistan Business and Investment Opportunities Yearbook
192. Vanuatu Business and Investment Opportunities Yearbook
193. Venezuela Business and Investment Opportunities Yearbook
194. Vietnam Business and Investment Opportunities Yearbook
195. Virgin Islands, British Business and Investment Opportunities Yearbook
196. Yemen Business and Investment Opportunities Yearbook
197. Zambia Business and Investment Opportunities Yearbook

WORLD CUSTOMS AND TRADE REGULATIONS LIBRARY
(PRICE $149.95)

0739757075	Afghanistan Customs, Trade Regulations and Procedures Handbook
0739757109	Albania Customs, Trade Regulations and Procedures Handbook
073975713X	Algeria Customs, Trade Regulations and Procedures Handbook
0739757148	Angola Customs, Trade Regulations and Procedures Handbook
0739757164	Antigua and Barbuda Customs, Trade Regulations and Procedures Handbook
0739757172	Antilles (Netherlands) Customs, Trade Regulations and Procedures Handbook
0739757199	Argentina Customs, Trade Regulations and Procedures Handbook
0739757210	Armenia Customs, Trade Regulations and Procedures Handbook
0739757229	Aruba Customs, Trade Regulations and Procedures Handbook
0739757245	Australia Customs, Trade Regulations and Procedures Handbook
0739757253	Austria Customs, Trade Regulations and Procedures Handbook
073975727X	Azerbaijan Customs, Trade Regulations and Procedures Handbook
0739757296	Bahamas Customs, Trade Regulations and Procedures Handbook
0739757318	Bahrain Customs, Trade Regulations and Procedures Handbook
0739757350	Bangladesh Customs, Trade Regulations and Procedures Handbook
0739757377	Barbados Customs, Trade Regulations and Procedures Handbook
0739757385	Belarus Customs, Trade Regulations and Procedures Handbook
0739757407	Belgium Customs, Trade Regulations and Procedures Handbook
0739757423	Belize Customs, Trade Regulations and Procedures Handbook
073975744X	Benin Customs, Trade Regulations and Procedures Handbook
0739757466	Bermuda Customs, Trade Regulations and Procedures Handbook
0739757490	Bhutan Customs, Trade Regulations and Procedures Handbook
0739757512	Bolivia Customs, Trade Regulations and Procedures Handbook
0739757539	Bosnia and Herzegovina Customs, Trade Regulations and Procedures Handbook
0739757555	Botswana Customs, Trade Regulations and Procedures Handbook
0739757598	Brazil Customs, Trade Regulations and Procedures Handbook
073975761X	Brunei Customs, Trade Regulations and Procedures Handbook
0739757636	Bulgaria Customs, Trade Regulations and Procedures Handbook
0739757652	Burkina Faso Customs, Trade Regulations and Procedures Handbook
0739757679	Cambodia Customs, Trade Regulations and Procedures Handbook
0739757725	Cameroon Customs, Trade Regulations and Procedures Handbook
0739757741	Canada Customs, Trade Regulations and Procedures Handbook
0739757849	Chile Customs, Trade Regulations and Procedures Handbook
0739757865	China Customs, Trade Regulations and Procedures Handbook

---

To order and for additional analytical and marketing information, please contacrt International Business Publications, USA at:
P.O. Box 15343, Washington, DC 20003, USA. Phone: (202) 546-2103. Fax: (202) 546-3275.
E-mail: rusric@erols.com

0739757881	Colombia Customs, Trade Regulations and Procedures Handbook
0739757911	Comoros Customs, Trade Regulations and Procedures Handbook
0739757942	Costa Rica Customs, Trade Regulations and Procedures Handbook
073975601X	Croatia Customs, Trade Regulations and Procedures Handbook
0739756044	Cuba Customs, Trade Regulations and Procedures Handbook
0739756079	Cyprus Customs, Trade Regulations and Procedures Handbook
0739756117	Czech Republic Customs, Trade Regulations and Procedures Handbook
0739756141	Denmark Customs, Trade Regulations and Procedures Handbook
0739756222	Ecuador Customs, Trade Regulations and Procedures Handbook
0739756249	Egypt Customs, Trade Regulations and Procedures Handbook
0739756265	El Salvador Customs, Trade Regulations and Procedures Handbook
073975632X	Estonia Customs, Trade Regulations and Procedures Handbook
0739756370	Fiji Customs, Trade Regulations and Procedures Handbook
0739756400	Finland Customs, Trade Regulations and Procedures Handbook
0739756435	France Customs, Trade Regulations and Procedures Handbook
0739756486	Georgia (Republic) Customs, Trade Regulations and Procedures Handbook
0739756516	Germany Customs, Trade Regulations and Procedures Handbook
0739756540	Ghana Customs, Trade Regulations and Procedures Handbook
0739756575	Gibraltar Offshore & Customs, Trade Regulations and Procedures Handbook
073975677X	Greece Customs, Trade Regulations and Procedures Handbook
0739756893	Haiti Customs, Trade Regulations and Procedures Handbook
0739756915	Honduras Customs, Trade Regulations and Procedures Handbook
073975694X	Hungary Customs, Trade Regulations and Procedures Handbook
0739756966	Iceland Customs, Trade Regulations and Procedures Handbook
0739756990	India Customs, Trade Regulations and Procedures Handbook
0739755013	Indonesia Customs, Trade Regulations and Procedures Handbook
0739755048	Iran Customs, Trade Regulations and Procedures Handbook
0739755072	Iraq Economic Sanctions, Customs, Trade Regulations and Procedures Handbook
0739755080	Ireland Customs, Trade Regulations and Procedures Handbook
0739755102	Israel Customs, Trade Regulations and Procedures Handbook
0739755137	Italy Customs, Trade Regulations and Procedures Handbook
0739755153	Jamaica Offshore Customs, Trade Regulations and Procedures Handbook
0739755188	Japan Customs, Trade Regulations and Procedures Handbook
073975520X	Jordan Customs, Trade Regulations and Procedures Handbook
0739755226	Kazakhstan Customs, Trade Regulations and Procedures Handbook
0739755242	Kenya Customs, Trade Regulations and Procedures Handbook
0739755269	Korea, North Customs, Trade Regulations and Procedures Handbook
0739755285	Korea, South Customs, Trade Regulations and Procedures Handbook
0739755331	Kuwait Customs, Trade Regulations and Procedures Handbook
0739755358	Kyrgyzstan Customs, Trade Regulations and Procedures Handbook
0739755374	Laos Customs, Trade Regulations and Procedures Handbook
07397554404	Latvia Customs, Trade Regulations and Procedures Handbook
0739755439	Lebanon Customs, Trade Regulations and Procedures Handbook
0739755471	Libya Customs, Trade Regulations and Procedures Handbook

To order and for additional analytical and marketing information, please contacrt
International Business Publications, USA at:
P.O. Box 15343, Washington, DC 20003, USA. Phone: (202) 546-2103. Fax: (202) 546-3275.
E-mail: rusric@erols.com

073975551X	Lithuania Customs, Trade Regulations and Procedures Handbook
0739755544	Macao Customs, Trade Regulations and Procedures Handbook
0739755587	Macedonia Customs, Trade Regulations and Procedures Handbook
0739755609	Madagascar Customs, Trade Regulations and Procedures Handbook
0739755633	Malaysia Customs, Trade Regulations and Procedures Handbook
0739755684	Malta Customs, Trade Regulations and Procedures Handbook
0739755730	Mauritius Customs, Trade Regulations and Procedures Handbook
0739755757	Mexico Customs, Trade Regulations and Procedures Handbook
0739755854	Moldova Customs, Trade Regulations and Procedures Handbook
0739755889	Mongolia Customs, Trade Regulations and Procedures Handbook
0739755900	Morocco Customs, Trade Regulations and Procedures Handbook
0739755943	Myanmar Customs, Trade Regulations and Procedures Handbook
0739755986	Nepal Customs, Trade Regulations and Procedures Handbook
0739754009	Netherlands Customs, Trade Regulations and Procedures Handbook
0739754025	New Zealand Customs, Trade Regulations and Procedures Handbook
0739754068	Nicaragua Customs, Trade Regulations and Procedures Handbook
0739754091	Nigeria Customs, Trade Regulations and Procedures Handbook
0739754130	Norway Customs, Trade Regulations and Procedures Handbook
0739754165	Oman Customs, Trade Regulations and Procedures Handbook
0739754211	Pakistan Customs, Trade Regulations and Procedures Handbook
0739754246	Panama Customs, Trade Regulations and Procedures Handbook
0739754289	Peru Customs, Trade Regulations and Procedures Handbook
0739754327	Philippines Customs, Trade Regulations and Procedures Handbook
0739754386	Philippines National Police Force Handbook
0739754408	Poland Customs, Trade Regulations and Procedures Handbook
0739754424	Portugal Customs, Trade Regulations and Procedures Handbook
0739754467	Qatar Customs, Trade Regulations and Procedures Handbook
0739754491	Romania Customs, Trade Regulations and Procedures Handbook
073975453X	Russia Customs, Trade Regulations and Procedures Handbook
0739754602	Saudi Arabia Customs, Trade Regulations and Procedures Handbook
0739754629	Scotland Customs, Trade Regulations and Procedures Handbook
0739754696	Singapore Customs, Trade Regulations and Procedures Handbook
0739754750	Slovak Republic Customs, Trade Regulations and Procedures Handbook
0739754726	Slovak Republic Customs, Trade Regulations and Procedures Handbook
0739754807	South Africa Customs, Trade Regulations and Procedures Handbook
0739754858	Spain Customs, Trade Regulations and Procedures Handbook
0739754874	Sri Lanka Customs, Trade Regulations and Procedures Handbook
0739754912	Sudan Customs, Trade Regulations and Procedures Handbook
0739754939	Suriname Customs, Trade Regulations and Procedures Handbook
0739754963	Sweden Customs, Trade Regulations and Procedures Handbook
0739754998	Switzerland Customs, Trade Regulations and Procedures Handbook
0739759019	Syria Customs, Trade Regulations and Procedures Handbook
0739759043	Taiwan Customs, Trade Regulations and Procedures Handbook
0739759086	Tajikistan Customs, Trade Regulations and Procedures Handbook

0739759116	Thailand Customs, Trade Regulations and Procedures Handbook
0739759167	Tunisia Customs, Trade Regulations and Procedures Handbook
0739759183	Turkey Customs, Trade Regulations and Procedures Handbook
0739759221	Turkmenistan Customs, Trade Regulations and Procedures Handbook
0739759264	Ukraine Customs, Trade Regulations and Procedures Handbook
0739755280	United Arab Emirates Customs, Trade Regulations and Procedures Handbook
0739759310	United Kingdom Customs, Trade Regulations and Procedures Handbook
0739759485	United States Customs, Trade Regulations and Procedures Handbook
0739759663	Uzbekistan Customs, Trade Regulations and Procedures Handbook
0739759779	Vietnam Financial and Trade Policy Handbook
0739759736	Serbia Customs, Trade Regulations and Procedures Handbook

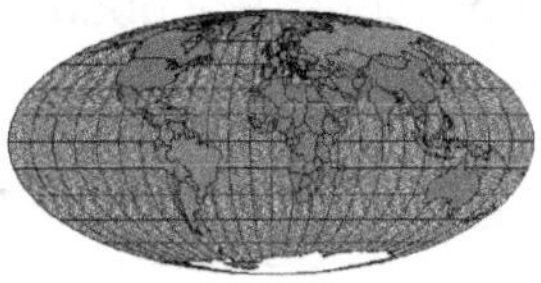

www.ingramcontent.com/pod-product-compliance
Lightning Source LLC
LaVergne TN
LVHW080036210926
848481LV00011B/3208